ABOUT THIS BOOK

'Patrick McCully's *Silenced Rivers* could not come at a better time. Now, with *Silenced Rivers*, we have strong medicine against the Promethean capitalism of the hydrologic engineers. It's all here. The power and the glory, the money and the lies, the fear, the broken dreams, the inescapable geological, financial and ecological realities. And, from California to India to Nepal to China, the grassroots resistance... You need a good book on dams. Here it is.'

TOM ATHANASIOU, author of *Divided Planet: The Ecology of Rich and Poor*

'A superlative account of the plethora of problems with dams. McCully provides enormously instructive information for those seeking to learn about the astonishing array of impacts caused by damming rivers and what is being done to look at alternatives and to resist the powerful dam-building lobby. McCully's book should be required reading for all politicians and a prime text for engineering schools.'

BRENT BLACKWELDER, President of Friends of the Earth USA

'This book has brilliantly consolidated all the scientific, environmental, social and economic evidence, backed by case studies from every continent, proving clearly the non-viability and non-sustainability of large dams. Those of us struggling against such dams in Third World countries desperately need this book.'

NALNI JAYAL, Secretary of the Himalaya Trust, Dehra Dun, India

'This is the most thorough and devastating critique of the global dam-building industry that I know. Impressively documented and argued with tough-minded passion, it shows convincingly how the conquest of nature is an outmoded and dangerous idea.'

DONALD WORSTER, Hall Distinguished Professor of American History, University of Kansas, and author of *Rivers of Empire*, *Dust Bowl*, *The Wealth of Nature* and *Under Western Skies*

'The best-researched, best-written account ever of what we have done to our rivers. McCully lays it all out – the tragedy, the waste, the vainglory, and the profits. And he provides hard-headed evidence that there are much more sensible ways of dealing with these bountiful and beautiful aspects of creation.'

CATHERINE CAUFIELD, author of *In the Rainforest*

'McCully's challenge to the dam industry is stark: unless dams become sustainable they will languish, thus delaying the urgent transition to renewable energy. McCully graphically enumerates what errors have been perpetrated; now it is up to dam proponents to learn from this warning and strive for sustainability.'

ROBERT GOODLAND, Environment Department of the World Bank

'A fantastic work. Provides the most comprehensive case against large dams. All the arguments used to justify large dams are analysed and demolished by the use of a wealth of empirical evidence from all over the world. A great scholarly work accessible to all. One wonders how the building of a large dam can ever be regarded as rational from now on.'

GAUTAM APPA, London School of Economics

'A wide-ranging definitive study that is long overdue. This book contains a powerful plea for the world to adopt a sane and restrained river policy for the next century.'

STEWART L. UDALL, US Secretary of the Interior, 1960–68;
author of *The myths of August: A Personal Exploration of Our Tragic Cold War Affair with the Atom*

'The best analysis yet of the political economy of dam building. McCully brings together a wealth of new information to lay bare the networks of power that have led to dams being built at the expense of people and the environment – and to document the rising tide of resistance to the dam-building industry.'

NICHOLAS HILDYARD and EDWARD GOLDSMITH, authors of
The Social and Environmental Effects of Large Dams

'Dams and diversions have forever altered the natural riverine landscapes of the world. Patrick McCully has captured the legacy of man's bad judgement on the control of rivers and the resulting loss of ecosystem diversity, environmental health and biodiversity. This book should be required reading for all those who think that control of rivers is the solution to man's problems.'

DAVE WEGNER, US Department of the Interior,
Glen Canyon Environmental Studies

'One hopes this painstaking and wide-sweeping *magnum opus* will go a long way to raise awareness of the enormous human and environmental costs of the engineering approach to development and help people see a way to a sustainable and just development. *Silenced Rivers* will provide strength and support to anti-dam people's movements the world over.'

MEDHA PAKTAR, Save the Narmada Movement, India

ABOUT THE AUTHOR

Patrick McCully is Campaigns Director of the California-based International Rivers Network. He is also an associate editor of *The Ecologist* and is a contributing writer for *Multinational Monitor*. Previous to that he was co-editor of *The Ecologist* and at one time also worked for an environment non-governmental organization in Uruguay. Since 1992 he has worked with activists in India opposing the Sardar Sarovar Dam on the Narmada River. He is co-author of two books: *Imperilled Planet* (1990) and *The Road to Rio: An NGO Action Guide to the Earth Summit* (1992).

SILENCED RIVERS

The Ecology and Politics of Large Dams

PATRICK McCULLY

ZED BOOKS
London & New Jersey

Silenced Rivers was first published in 1996 by
Zed Books Ltd, 7 Cynthia Street, London N1 9JF, UK, and
165 First Avenue, Atlantic Highlands, New Jersey 07716, USA,

in association with the International Rivers Network (IRN),
1847 Berkeley Way, Berkeley, California 94703, USA,
and with *The Ecologist*, Agriculture House, Bath Road,
Sturminster Newton, Dorset DT10 1DU.

Cover designed by Andrew Corbett
Typeset in Monotype Garamond by Lucy Morton, London SE12
Printed and bound in the United Kingdom
by Biddles Ltd, Guildford and King's Lynn

A catalogue record for this book is available from the British Library
US CIP data is available from the Library of Congress

ISBN 1 85649 435 7 Hb
ISBN 1 85649 436 5 Pb

Contents

List of Tables and Figures

Acknowledgements

This book would not have been written – or if written would have been far inferior – were it not for the help and encouragement of a multitude of people and organizations. Edward Goldsmith and Nicholas Hildyard introduced me to the problems with large dams, advocated that I update their book on dams, and then supported my decision to write my own book, which, although not an updated version of theirs, would not have been possible had theirs not been written first. The inspiration to write *Silenced Rivers* came from the unshakeable commitment and integrity of the Narmada Bachao Andolan and the deceitfulness of the backers and builders of the Sardar Sarovar Dam. Financial support came from the Goldsmith Foundation, the Foundation for Deep Ecology and International Rivers Network. Owen Lammers, Executive Director of IRN, and the rest of IRN's staff and board (in particular Juliette Majot, Petra Yee, Elizabeth Hennin, Glenn Switkes and Rani Derasary), also provided vital encouragement, support, faith and patience, as well as an office base and logistical support. Robert Molteno of Zed Books also supplied large quantities of support, faith and patience. Aleta Brown of IRN was an invaluable, good-humoured and diligent researcher, assistant and reviewer. Demon editor Lori Pottinger of IRN bullied and shamed me into making huge improvements to my first drafts.

Numerous people gave invaluable help by reviewing my draft chapters and giving me comments and corrections. Special mention must go to David Wegner of the Bureau of Reclamation's Glen Canyon Environmental Studies Program who sent me extensive and perceptive comments. Philip Williams, President of IRN and of Philip Williams & Associates, also reviewed my drafts and gave me invaluable advice on technical matters as well as moral support. Robert Goodland, Environmental Adviser at the World Bank, and Thayer Scudder, Professor of

Anthropology at the California Institute of Technology, were also critical and patient reviewers. Author Thomas Athanasiou, Michael Goldman and Leonard Sklar of the University of California at Berkeley, Janos Vargha of Hungary's Danube Circle, Brent Blackwelder of Friends of the Earth US, Gráinne Ryder of Probe International in Canada, Himanshu Thakker of the New Delhi-based Centre for Science and Environment, Shripad Dharmadhikary and Medha Patkar of the Narmada Bachao Andolan, and Maria Clara Soares of the Brazilian Institute for Social and Economic Analysis also gave comments on some of my draft chapters.

IRN interns Elizabeth Carpino, Colette Mercier and Davor Orsic gave me research help, as did Peter Worster of the Mono Lake Committee. Numerous others sent me comments and/or information, encouraged and supported me, answered my questions or helped me write this book in some other way. These include Gautam Appa (London School of Economics), Peter Bosshard (Berne Declaration, Switzerland), Margaret Bowman (Hydropower Reform Coalition, USA), Catherine Caufield, Michael Cernea (World Bank), Pratap Chatterjee (Inter-Press Service), Andrew N. Cohen, Philip Fearnside (National Institute for Amazonian Research, Manaus), Giancarlo Di Giambattista (Ontario Hydro), Youssef Halim (Department of Oceanography, Alexandria University), Erik Høines (FIVAS, Norway), Rita Kassai (Office of Edward Goldsmith), Adam, Simon and Rebecca McKee (Ballydoo Farm), Francesco Martone (Campagna per la Riforma della Banca Mondiale), Sarah Mason, Lyla Mehta (Institute of Development Studies, UK), Deborah Moore (Environmental Defense Fund, California), Wendy Rees (Quaker Peace and Service, London), David Rosenberg (Department of Fisheries and Oceans, Manitoba), Steve Rothert (Hydropower Reform Coalition, USA), Anthony Oliver-Smith (Department of Anthropology, University of Florida), Michael Rozengurt (Orange County Sanitation District, California), Heffa Schücking (Urgewald, Germany), Bina Srinivasan (Swashraya, Gujarat), Nantiya Tangwisutijit (*The Nation*, Bangkok), John Thibodeau (Probe International, Toronto), Lori Udall, Stewart L. Udall, and Ann Daniya Usher.

To all the others who helped me and who I have forgotten to mention, I thank you and apologize. None of the above bears any responsibility for any positions advocated or factual errors in this book.

Last but very decidedly not least, I must acknowledge and thank the support, patience, understanding, ideas, criticisms and edits of my wife Angela Gennino.

Glossary

ACRE-FOOT: amount of water it takes to cover one acre to a depth of one foot (325,900 gallons or 1,233 cubic metres).

ABUTMENT: part of valley side against which dam is constructed.

AGGRADATION: raising of riverbed due to SEDIMENT deposition.

AGROFORESTRY: farming system in which the growing of trees and shrubs is integrated with production of other crops and/or animal husbandry.

ALLUVIUM: sediments transported by a river and deposited on its bed and floodplain.

ANADROMOUS FISH: fish born in fresh water that spend most of their life in the ocean and then ascend rivers to spawn.

AQUIFER: geological formation of high porosity and high permeability that yields significant quantities of GROUNDWATER.

ARCH DAM: concrete or masonry dam which is curved upstream so as to transmit the major part of the weight of the water to the ABUTMENTS.

ARMOURED RIVERBED: riverbed from which easily removable sediment has been eroded, leaving a surface of cobbles or boulders.

BARRAGE: RUN-OF-RIVER DAM, usually built across the lower reaches of a river and used to divert water for irrigation.

BASIN IRRIGATION: technique where fields are irrigated by trapping floodwaters behind embankments or in depressions.

BENTHIC: pertaining to the bottom of a body of water.

BuRec: US Bureau of Reclamation – agency within the US Department of Interior responsible for managing federal irrigation schemes in the western US.

CANAL IRRIGATION: irrigation with water supplied via canal, usually having been diverted from regulated river or reservoir.

CATCHMENT: see WATERSHED.

COFFER-DAM: temporary dam built to keep riverbed dry to allow construction of permanent dam or other infrastructure.

CONSUMPTIVE USE: non-reusable withdrawal of water where the water is evaporated, transpired by plants, incorporated into products or crops, or consumed by humans or animals.

DEAD STORAGE: that part of a reservoir which lies beneath the elevation of the bottom of the dam's lowest outlet.

DECOMMISSIONING: when applied to dams in US can refer to anything from merely stopping electricity generation to removing a dam totally and attempting to restore the river to its pre-dam state.

DEGRADATION: lowering of riverbed due to erosion.

DELTA: flat area of ALLUVIUM formed at the mouth of some rivers where the main stream divides into several DISTRIBUTARIES before reaching a sea or lake.

DISTRIBUTARY: river branch flowing away from the main stream of a river.

DRAINAGE BASIN: see WATERSHED.

DRAWDOWN: the difference between two surface levels of a reservoir. Used as a verb, it is to lower the reservoir level.

DRIP IRRIGATION: efficient irrigation system that delivers water directly to the roots of plants, e.g. through perforated or porous pipes.

EARTH (OR EARTHFILL) DAM: EMBANKMENT DAM in which more than half of the total volume is formed of compacted earth.

EMBANKMENT DAM: dam constructed of excavated natural materials. Usually triangular in cross-section with a broad base that distributes weight over a wide area and can thus be constructed on a soft, unstable riverbed.

EPILIMNION: surface layer of a lake or reservoir.

ESTUARY: semi-enclosed coastal body of water with free connection to the open sea in which the salinity is diluted by freshwater from a river.

EUTROPHICATION: process of nutrient enrichment of a body of water. In advanced state causes severe deoxygenation of water body.

EVAPOTRANSPIRATION: water transmitted to the atmosphere by a combination of evaporation from the soil and transpiration from plants.

FLOOD CONTROL: reducing risk by building dams and/or embankments, and/or altering river channel.

FLOOD CROPPING: farming dependent on the moisture and nutrients from floods.

FLOOD MANAGEMENT: reducing flood risk by actions such as discouraging floodplain development, establishing flood warning systems, protecting urban areas and isolated buildings, and allowing the most flood-prone areas to remain as wetlands.

FLOOD RECESSION AGRICULTURE: FLOOD CROPPING technique where crops are planted on floodplains at the end of the wet season to exploit the moisture left behind by retreating floods.

FLOODPLAIN: area of valley floor inundated during a flood.

FLUSHING FLOW: large release of water from reservoir intended to wash away downstream accumulations of boulders and gravel.

GIGAWATT: unit of power equal to 1,000 MEGAWATTS.

GIGAWATT-HOUR: unit of energy equal to 1,000 MEGAWATT-HOURS.

GRAVITY DAM: dam built of concrete and/or masonry which relies on its own weight and internal strength for stability.

GROUNDWATER: subsurface water contained in saturated soils and rocks.

HEAD POND: reservoir behind RUN-OF-RIVER DAM.

HEAD: for a hydrodam, equals the vertical distance between the elevation of the surface of a reservoir and the surface of the river where turbined water re-enters downstream.

HYDROLOGICAL CYCLE: the continuous interchange of water between land, sea or other water surface, and the atmosphere.

HYPOLIMNION: bottom layer of a lake or reservoir.

ICOLD: International Commission on Large Dams – a Paris-based dam industry association.

INSTREAM FLOW: water which is allowed to remain in a river for fisheries, water quality, navigation or recreation purposes.

INUNDATION MAP: map delineating areas that would be flooded by particular flood events.

IRRIGATION EFFICIENCY: proportion of water used for crop growth relative to the total amount of water withdrawn by the irrigation system.

KILOWATT: unit of power equal to 1,000 WATTS.

KILOWATT-HOUR: unit of energy equal to 1,000 WATT-HOURS.

LARGE DAM: usually defined by ICOLD as a dam measuring 15 metres or more from foundation to crest. Dams of 10–15 metres may be defined as large dams by ICOLD if they meet the following requirements: crest length 500 metres or more; reservoir capacity at least 1 million cubic metres; maximum flood discharge at least 2,000 cubic metres per second; 'specially difficult foundation problems'; or 'unusual design'.

LEVEE: US term for flood control embankment.

LIFT IRRIGATION: usually refers to irrigation using groundwater but can include irrigation using water pumped from canals and reservoirs.

LIVE STORAGE: that part of a reservoir which lies above the elevation of the bottom of the dam's lowest outlet.

MAJOR DAM: defined by ICOLD as a dam meeting at least one of the following requirements: at least 150 metres high; having a volume of at least 15 million cubic metres; reservoir storage capacity of at least 25 cubic kilometres; or generation capacity of at least one GIGAWATT.

MAXIMUM CREDIBLE EARTHQUAKE (MCE): the most severe earthquake that can be expected to occur at a given site on the basis of geological and seismological evidence.

MEAN-ANNUAL FLOOD: arithmetic mean of the highest peak discharge during each year of record.

MEGAWATT: unit of power equal to 1,000 KILOWATTS.

MEGAWATT-HOUR: unit of energy equal to 1,000 KILOWATT-HOURS.

MICROCATCHMENTS: small basins constructed to collect rainwater.

MICRO-HYDRO: usually defined as a hydroplant with an installed capacity of up to 100 KILOWATTS.

MICRO-IRRIGATION: (1) irrigation system using super-efficient sprinklers or DRIP IRRIGATION; (2) the use of irrigation on a small scale by gardeners growing for their own families or local markets.

MINI-HYDRO: usually defined as a hydroplant with an installed capacity of up to 1 MEGAWATT.

OUSTEES: people displaced by development projects. Originally used in India, the term is increasingly used by social scientists internationally.

PEAKING (PEAK) POWER: electricity supplied at times when demand is highest.

PENSTOCK: pipe or shaft which delivers water to turbines.

PICO-HYDRO: usually defined as a hydroplant with an installed capacity of up to 20 KILOWATTS.

PIPING: internal erosion through a dam caused by seepage.

PLANT FACTOR: relationship between a powerplant's capacity to generate electricity and the actual amount of electricity it generates. Plant factor for a specific year is calculated according to the formula PF = (IGC × 24 × 365)/AG, where IGC = installed generating capacity (MW) and AG = annual generation (MWh).

PLUNGE POOL: a natural or artificially created pool that dissipates the energy of water at the bottom of a SPILLWAY.

POWERHOUSE: building or cavern housing turbines and generators.

PROBABLE MAXIMUM FLOOD (PMF): largest flood considered reasonably possible at a site as a result of meteorological and hydrological conditions.

PUMPED-STORAGE PLANT: plant used to generate PEAKING POWER which has two reservoirs at different elevations (or one reservoir above and a river below). During hours of peak electricity demand, water from the upper reservoir is released through turbines into the lower one. The water is later pumped back uphill using cheap off-peak electricity.

RAINWATER HARVESTING: farming technique which conserves water by collecting rainwater run-off behind earth or rock bunds or in small basins.

REGULATED RIVER: river of which the natural flow pattern is altered by a dam or dams.

RIPARIAN: of or relating to or located on the bank of a river.

RIVERINE ECOSYSTEM: zone of biological and environmental influence of a river and its floodplain.

ROCKFILL DAM: EMBANKMENT DAM in which more than half of the total volume is formed of compacted or dumped cobbles, boulders or rock fragments.

RUN-OF-RIVER DAM: dam which raises upstream water level but creates only a small reservoir and cannot effectively regulate downstream flows.

RUN-OFF: precipitation which drains into a watercourse rather than being absorbed by soil.

RUN-OFF FARMING: dryland farming which maximizes available moisture by directing water running off slopes onto fields below.

SALINIZATION: the accumulation of salt in soil or water to a harmful level.

SEDIMENT: mineral and organic matter transported or deposited by water or air.

SEDIMENT LOAD: amount of SEDIMENT carried by a river.

SEDIMENT FLUSHING: method of reservoir operation in which the reservoir is temporarily lowered so that fast-flowing water can erode accumulated SEDIMENTS on the reservoir bed.

SEDIMENT SLUICING: method of reservoir operation in which the reservoir is lowered at the start of the flood season, speeding the movement of water through the reservoir and hence reducing its capacity to trap SEDIMENT.

SELECTIVE WITHDRAWALS: water withdrawn from intakes at different reservoir elevations to influence thermal, physical and/or chemical properties of downstream water.

SILT: sediment composed of particles between 0.004 mm and 0.06 mm in diameter.

SLUICE: structure with a gate for stopping or regulating flow of water.

SMALL DAM: defined by ICOLD as dam measuring less than 15 metres from foundation to crest.

SMALL HYDRO: usually defined as a hydroplant with an installed capacity of up to 10 MEGAWATTS.

SMOLT: juvenile salmon.

SPILLWAY: structure which discharges water from a reservoir.

TAILRACE: pipe or channel through which turbined water is discharged into a river.

TAILWATER: water in river immediately downstream from dam or TAILRACE.

TRAP EFFICIENCY: the proportion of a river's total SEDIMENT load which is trapped in a reservoir.

TUBEWELL: deep, mechanically drilled well.

TVA: Tennessee Valley Authority.

WATER TABLE: surface of GROUNDWATER.

WATERLOGGING: saturation of soil with water.

WATERSHED: used here in its US sense of the entire area drained by a river (synonymous with catchment, catchment area, basin and drainage basin). A single large watershed includes many smaller tributary watersheds.

WATT: unit of power equal to a rate of working of one joule per second.

WATT-HOUR: unit of energy equal to one WATT supplied for one hour.

WEIR: RUN-OF-RIVER DAM, usually a low wall of stone, concrete or wicker.

WETLAND: area of land which is seasonally, intermittently or permanently WATERLOGGED.

1

The Power and the Water

I came, I saw, and I was conquered.

President Franklin D. Roosevelt at Hoover Dam inauguration ceremony, 30 September 1935

Hoover Dam, an astonishingly graceful curve of concrete pushing back the Colorado River to fill its deep canyon on the Arizona–Nevada border, unleashed the big dam era. Wallace Stegner, the great novelist and essayist of the US West, was overawed when he visited the 221-metre-high dam in 1946, a decade after its completion:

> It is certainly one of the world's wonders, that sweeping cliff of concrete, those impetuous elevators, the labyrinth of tunnels, the huge power stations. Everything about the dam is marked by the immense smooth efficient beauty that seems peculiarly American.[1]

To many other writers, leaders, engineers, bureaucrats, nationalists and revolutionaries of the subsequent six decades, big dams have been potent symbols of both patriotic pride and the conquest of nature by human ingenuity. Providers of electric power, water and food; tamers of floods; greeners of the desert; guarantors of national independence – for most of our century, dams, the largest single structures built by humanity, have symbolized progress, whether that amorphous concept be the creation of capitalist wealth, the spreading of the fruits of socialism, or the great march of communism.

At the opening of the Nangal Canal in the Punjab in 1954, Pandit Jawaharlal Nehru, the first Prime Minister of India, described his 'strange exhilaration and excitement' at seeing the canal and the construction site of the Bhakra Dam. Nehru expressed his awe through nationalism mixed with religious reverence:

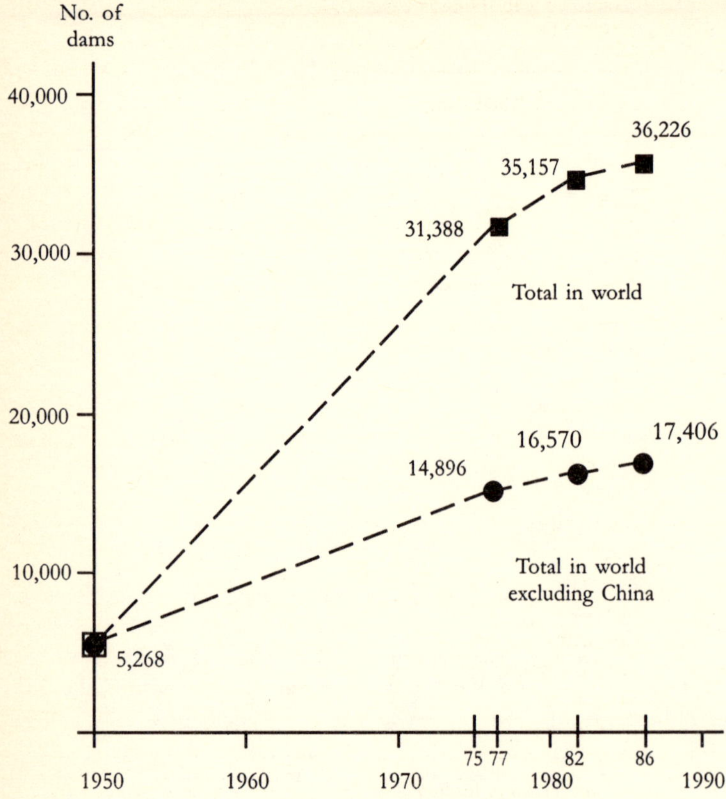

Figure 1.1 Rate of large-dam building, 1950–86
Source: ICOLD, *World Register of Dams*, Paris 1988.

> What a stupendous, magnificent work – a work which only that nation can take up which has faith and boldness! … it has become the symbol of a nation's will to march forward with strength, determination and courage…. As I walked around the [dam] site I thought that these days the biggest temple and mosque and *gurdwara* is the place where man works for the good of mankind. Which place can be greater than this, this Bhakra-Nangal, where thousands and *lakhs* [hundreds of thousands] of men have worked, have shed their blood and sweat and laid down their lives as well? Where can be a greater and holier place than this, which we can regard as higher?[2]

Massive dams are much more than simply machines to generate electricity and store water. They are concrete, rock and earth expressions of the dominant ideology of the technological age: icons of economic

Table 1.1 Countries with the most large and major dams (as defined by ICOLD)

	Large dams (1986 data)		Major dams (1994 data)	
1	China	18,820	USA	50
2	USA	5,459	CIS	34
3	CIS	c. 3,000*	Canada	26
4	Japan	2,228	Brazil	19
5	India	1,137	Japan	19
6	Spain	737	Turkey	11
7	South Korea	690	China	10
8	Canada	608	Germany	9
9	Great Britain	535	Italy	9
10	Brazil	516	Switzerland	9
11	Mexico	503	Argentina	8
12	France	468	India	7
13	South Africa	452	France	5
14	Italy	440	Mexico	5
15	Australia	409	Austria	4
16	Norway	245	Colombia	4
17	Germany	191	Iran	4
18	Czechoslovakia	146	Spain	4
19	Switzerland	144	Australia	3
20	Sweden	141	Pakistan	3

* The former USSR declared to ICOLD only the 132 large hydroelectric dams under the control of the Ministry of Energy and Electrification. If the dams built by the Ministry of Agriculture and local authorities were included, according to ICOLD, the number of large dams in the USSR (now CIS) should be 2,000–3,000. See text for explanation of ICOLD definitions.

Sources: ICOLD, *World Register of Dams*, Paris 1988; *International Water Power & Dam Construction Handbook 1995*, IWPDC, Sutton, UK 1995.

development and scientific progress to match nuclear bombs and motor cars. The builders of Hoover were advised by an architect to strip the dam of planned ornamentation in order to accentuate the visual power of its colossal concrete face. Theodore Steinberg, a historian at the University of Michigan, says that Hoover Dam 'was supposed to signify greatness, power and domination. It was planned that way.'[3]

According to the estimates of the International Commission on Large Dams (ICOLD), the leading dam-industry association, the world's rivers are now obstructed by more than 40,000 large dams, all but 5,000 of them built since 1950. A 'large dam' is usually defined by ICOLD as

Table 1.2 The world's highest dams

	Dam	Country	Completed	Dam type	Height (m)
1	Nurek	Tadjikistan	1980	E	300
2	Grande Dixence	Switzerland	1961	G	285
3	Inguri	Georgia	1980	A	272
4	Vaiont	Italy	1961	A	262
	Tehri	India	U/C	E/R	261
5	Chicoasén	Mexico	1980	E/R	261
6	Mauvoisin	Switzerland	1957	A	250
7	Guavio	Colombia	1989	E/R	246
8	Sayano-Shushensk	Russia	1989	A/G	245
9	Mica	Canada	1973	E/R	242
	Ertan	China	U/C	A	240
10	Chivor	Colombia	1957	E/R	237
	Kishau	India	U/C	G	236
11	El Cajón	Honduras	1985	A	234
12	Chirkey	Russia	1978	A	233
13	Oroville	USA	1968	E	230
14	Bhakra	India	1963	G	226
15	Hoover	USA	1936	A/G	221
16	Contra	Switzerland	1965	A	220
16	Mrantinje	Yugoslavia	1976	A	220
18	Dworshak	USA	1973	G	219
19	Glen Canyon	USA	1966	A	216
20	Toktogul	Kirghizstan	1978	G	215

Dam types: A = arch; E = earthfill; G = gravity; R = rockfill; U/C = under construction.

Source: *International Water Power & Dam Construction Handbook 1995*, IWPDC, Sutton, UK 1995.

one measuring 15 metres or more from foundation to crest – taller than a four-storey building. China has taken on damming with the most fervour: the country had eight large dams at the time of its revolution in 1949; 40 years later it had around 19,000. The US is the second most dammed country with some 5,500 large dams, followed by the ex-USSR, Japan and India (see Table 1.1 and Figure 1.1). (The US is estimated to have around 96,000 small dams. If the proportion of small to large dams is similar in other countries, then at a rough estimate there are around 800,000 small dams in the world.[4])

As the number of dams increased, so did their size and geographical distribution. Hoover remained the world's highest dam for more than

Table 1.3 Dams with largest capacity reservoirs

	Dam	Country	Completed	Reservoir volume ($m^3 \times 10^6$)
1	Owen Falls*	Uganda	1954	2,700,000
2	Kakhovskaya	Ukraine	1955	182,000
3	Kariba	Zimbabwe/Zambia	1959	180,600
4	Bratsk	Russia	1964	169,270
5	Aswan High	Egypt	1970	168,900
6	Akosombo	Ghana	1965	153,000
7	Daniel Johnson	Canada	1968	141,852
8	Guri	Venezuela	1986	138,000
9	Krasnoyarsk	Russia	1967	733,000
10	W.A.C. Bennett	Canada	1967	70,309
11	Zeya	Russia	1978	68,400
12	Cabora Bassa	Mozambique	1974	63,000
13	La Grande 2	Canada	1978	61,715
14	La Grande 3	Canada	1981	60,020
15	Ust-Ilim	Russia	1977	59,300
16	Boguchany	Russia	1989	58,200
17	Kuibyishev	Russia	1955	58,000
18	Serra da Mesa (São Felix)	Brazil	1993	54,000
19	Caniapiscau	Canada	1981	53,800
20	Bukhtarma	Kazakhstan	1960	49,800

* The major part of the lake volume (Lake Victoria) is natural. The 31-metre-high dam added 270 cubic km of storage to the existing capacity of the lake.

Source: *International Water Power & Dam Construction Handbook 1995*, IWPDC, Sutton, UK 1995.

two decades until 1957 when it was overtaken by Mauvoisin in Switzerland. Four years later two more giants exceeded Hoover's height, Grande Dixence (also in Switzerland) and Italy's Vaiont Dam. In 1968 Hoover lost its position as the highest dam in the US to California's Oroville Dam. Seven more dams in Canada, Colombia, the USSR, Mexico and Honduras overtook Hoover in the 1970s and 1980s. The dam which is currently the world's highest, Nurek, completed in Tadjikistan in 1980, is an artificial mountain of earth and rock 300 metres high, as tall as the Eiffel Tower (see Tables 1.2–1.4).

The industry defines a 'major dam' on the basis of either its height (at least 150 metres), volume (at least 15 million cubic metres – six

Table 1.4 Dams with largest capacity hydroplants

	Dam	Country	Initial operation	Installed capacity in 1995 (MW)
1	Itaipú	Brazil/Paraguay	1983	12,600
2	Guri (Raul Leoni)	Venezuela	1986	10,300
3	Sayano-Shushensk	Russia	1989	6,400
4	Grand Coulee	USA	1942	6,180
5	Krasnoyarsk	Russia	1968	6,000
6	Churchill Falls	Canada	1971	5,428
7	La Grande 2	Canada	1979	5,328
8	Bratsk	Russia	1961	4,500
9	Ust-Ilim	Russia	1977	4,320
10	Tucuruí	Brazil	1984	3,960
11	Ilha Solteira	Brazil	1973	3,200
12	Tarbela	Pakistan	1977	3,046
13	Gezhouba	China	1981	2,715
14	Nurek	Tadjikistan	1976	2,700
15	Mica	Canada	1976	2,660
16	La Grande 4	Canada	1984	2,650
17	Volgograd 22nd Congress	Russia	1958	2,563
18	Paulo Afonso IV	Brazil	1979	2,460
19	Cabora Bassa	Mozambique	1975	2,425
20	W.A.C. Bennet	Canada	1968	2,416

Source: *International Water Power & Dam Construction Handbook 1995*, IWPDC, Sutton, UK 1995.

times the volume of the Great Pyramid of Cheops), reservoir storage (at least 25 cubic kilometres – enough water to flood the country of Luxembourg to a depth of 1 metre) or electrical generation capacity (at least 1,000 megawatts – sufficient to power a European city with a million inhabitants). In 1950, 10 behemoths met these criteria; by 1995 the number had soared to some 305. The leading builder of major dams is the US, followed by the ex-USSR, Canada, Brazil and Japan.[5]

Most of the world's major river basins are now girdled with dams; many great rivers are now little more than staircases of reservoirs. A meagre 70 kilometres of the 2,000 kilometres of the Columbia River flows unimpeded by the slackwater of the 19 dams which cut across it. In the continental US, only the Yellowstone River remains undammed out of rivers longer than 1,000 kilometres. In France, the only remaining free-flowing stretch of the Rhône was impounded by a dam in 1986. Elsewhere in Europe, neither the Volga, the Weser, the Ebro nor the Tagus has a stretch more than a quarter its length which has escaped being turned into reservoir.[6]

Worldwide, reservoirs are estimated to have a combined storage capacity of as much as 10,000 cubic kilometres, equivalent to five times the volume of water in all the rivers in the world.[7] The weight of large reservoirs is so great that they can trigger earthquakes – scores of examples of so-called reservoir-induced seismicity have been recorded. Geophysicists even estimate that the redistribution of the weight of the earth's crust due to reservoirs may be having a very slight but measurable impact on the speed at which the earth rotates, the tilt of its axis and the shape of its gravitational field.[8]

More than 400,000 square kilometres – the area of California – have been inundated by reservoirs worldwide.[9] The world's largest impoundment, the 8,500 square kilometre Volta Reservoir behind Akosombo Dam, flooded around 4 per cent of the land area of Ghana. In the US, reservoirs have submerged an area equivalent to New Hampshire and Vermont combined.[10] The 0.3 per cent of the global land surface which has been submerged represents a much greater loss than the raw statistic implies – the floodplain soils which reservoirs inundate provide the world's most fertile farmlands; their marshes and forests the most diverse wildlife habitats.

Freshwaters, because of a host of human assaults, but especially because of dams, are the most degraded of major ecosystems. A dam tears at all the interconnected webs of river valley life. Swedish ecologists concluded in 1994 that nearly four-fifths of the total discharge of the largest rivers in the US, Canada, Europe and the former USSR is 'strongly or moderately affected' by flow regulation, diversions and the fragmentation of river channels by dams.[11] The most extreme illustration of the downstream impacts of water diversions is the Aral Sea in Central Asia. Once the world's largest body of freshwater outside North America, the sea has shrunk to less than half its previous area and separated into three hypersaline lakes.

Dams are the main reason why fully one-fifth of the world's freshwater fish are now either endangered or extinct. The percentage rises even higher in the countries which have been most heavily dammed – to nearly two-fifths in the US and three-quarters in Germany. Amphibians, molluscs, insects, waterfowl and other riverine and wetland lifeforms are similarly imperilled.[12]

The human consequences of the damming of the world have been as dramatic as the ecological ones. Although the dam builders have not bothered to keep count, the number of people flooded off their lands by dams is certainly in the tens of millions – 30 million would be a conservative estimate, 60 million more likely. The available evidence suggests that very few of these people ever recovered from the ordeal, either economically or psychologically. Many more have suffered the loss of fisheries, the irrigation provided by seasonal floods and the wood, game and other benefits of now-submerged forests. Just as the valley bottoms flooded by dams are those most favourable to human settlement in the present, so they were in the past, and thus reservoirs have inundated countless important archaeological and cultural sites, many known, doubtless many more yet to be discovered at the time of their loss.

Diseases spread by vectors such as mosquitoes which thrive in irrigation canals and along the edges of reservoirs have taken an inestimable human toll. Dams can be lethal too because they break. More than 13,500 people have been swept to their deaths by the roughly 200 dams outside China which have collapsed or been overtopped during the twentieth century. A calamitous series of dam bursts in the Chinese province of Henan in August 1975 left perhaps 230,000 dead. Hundreds have also died because they resisted eviction to make way for dams. In Guatemala in 1982, 378 Mayan Indians, mainly women and children, were tortured, shot, stabbed, garrotted and bludgeoned to death in punishment for their community demanding they be properly compensated for the loss of their homes to the Chixoy Dam.

A Short History of Rivers

> To write history without putting any water in it is to leave out a large part of the story. Human experience has not been so dry as that.
>
> Donald Worster, *Rivers of Empire*, 1985

All land is part of a watershed or river basin and all is shaped by the water which flows over it and through it. Indeed, rivers are such an integral part of the land that in many places it would be as appropriate to talk of riverscapes as it would be of landscapes. Rivers are much more than merely water flowing to the sea. Rivers carry downhill not just water, but just as importantly sediments, dissolved minerals and the nutrient-rich detritus of plants and animals, both dead and alive. Their ever-shifting beds and banks and the groundwaters below are all integral parts of rivers. Even the meadows, forests, marshes and backwaters of floodplains can be seen as part of rivers – and rivers as part of them.

Watersheds start at mountain peaks and hilltops.[13] Snowmelt and rainfall wash over and through the high ground into rivulets which drain into fast-flowing mountain streams. As the streams descend, tributaries and groundwaters add to their volume and they become rivers. As they leave the mountains, rivers slow and start to meander and braid, seeking the path of least resistance across widening valleys with alluvial floors laid down by millennia of sediment-laden floods.

Eventually rivers will flow into a lake or ocean. Where the river is muddy and the land flat, the alluvial sediments may form a delta, splitting the river into a bird-foot of distributaries which discharge into the sea. Estuaries, the places where the sweetwaters of rivers mix with the ocean's salt, are among the most biologically productive parts of rivers – and of seas. Most of the world's fish catch comes from species which are dependent for at least part of their lifecycle on a nutrient-rich estuarine habitat.

The diversity of a river lies not only in the various types of country it flows through but also in the changing seasons and the differences between wet and dry years. Seasonal and annual variations in the amount of water, sediment and nutrients drained by a watershed can be massive, especially in dry areas where most of a year's rain may fall in just a few individual storms. On average 85 per cent of the annual discharge of the Limpopo in southern Africa flows from January through March; only 1 per cent from August through October. Rivers in the far north are also highly seasonal, with minimum flows during the frozen winter followed by huge floods during the summer melt.

The great milestones of human history took place by the banks of rivers. Fossilized remains of our earliest known hominid ancestor were found by Ethiopia's Awash River. Evidence of the momentous change from mostly nomadic hunting and gathering to sedentary farming first appears in the narrow river valleys of the mountains of the Near East at archaeological sites between nine and ten thousand years old. The first civilizations emerged in the third millennium BC along the Euphrates, Tigris, Nile and Indus, and a little later along the Yellow. Much later another momentous turning point in human history occurred along the rivers and streams of northern England which powered the early industrial factories.

Rivers, and the rich variety of plants and animals which they sustain, provide hunter-gatherer societies with water for drinking and washing, and with food, drugs and medicines, dyes, fibres and wood. Farmers reap the same benefits as well as, where needed, irrigation for their crops. For pastoral societies, who graze their herds over wide areas of often parched plains and mountains, perennial vegetation along the banks of rivers provides life-sustaining food and fodder during dry seasons and droughts. Towns and cities use (and misuse) rivers to carry away their wastes. Rivers also serve as roadways for commerce, exploration and conquest. With the exception of a few maritime societies, 'all the great historic cultures', writes technology historian Lewis Mumford, 'have thriven through the movement of men and institutions and inventions and goods along the natural highway of a great river.'[14]

The role of rivers as the sustainers of life and fertility is reflected in the myths and beliefs of a multitude of cultures. In many parts of the world rivers are referred to as 'mothers': *Narmadai*, 'Mother Narmada'; the Volga is *Mat' Rodnaya*, 'Mother of the Land'. The Thai word for river, *mae nan*, translates literally as 'water mother'. Rivers have often been linked with divinities, especially female ones. In Ancient Egypt, the floods of the Nile were considered the tears of the goddess Isis. Ireland's River Boyne, which is overlooked by the island's most impressive prehistoric burial sites, was worshipped as a goddess by Celtic tribes.

The rivers of India are perhaps wrapped in more myths, epic tales and religious significance than those of any other nation. Environmentalist Vijay Paranjpye describes a sacred text which holds that 'all sins are washed away by bathing thrice in the Saraswati, seven times in the Yamuna, once in the Ganges, but the mere sight of the Narmada is enough to absolve one of all sins!' Another ancient text describes the Narmada River as 'giver of merriment', 'flavourful', 'of graceful attitude' and 'one who radiates happiness'.[15]

Of the life sustained by rivers, salmon have perhaps been imbued with the most mythological significance. The 'Salmon of Knowledge', legend had it, swam in a pool near the source of the Boyne. Anyone who tasted the fish would acquire understanding of everything in the world, past, present and future. Native Americans in the Pacific Northwest believed salmon to be superior beings who ascended rivers for the benefit of people, died, and then returned to life in a great house under the ocean where they danced and feasted in human form. Some tribes welcomed the first salmon of the season with the ceremony due to a visiting chief.

While rivers provided life, they also brought death. Settlement on the plains, which enabled people to take advantage of the rich alluvial soils, also exposed crops and villages to the risk of catastrophic floods. Gilgamesh, the earliest surviving epic tale, tells of a great flood unleashed by God to scourge the sinful in Mesopotamia. Myths and legends of huge floods are common to many cultures around the world, from the Old Testament Jews to the pagan Norse and the indigenous people of the Americas.

The damming of the world has brought a profound change to watersheds. Nothing alters a river as totally as a dam. A reservoir is the antithesis of a river – the essence of a river is that it flows, the essence of a reservoir that it is still. A wild river is dynamic, forever changing – eroding its bed, depositing silt, seeking a new course, bursting its banks, drying up. A dam is monumentally static; it tries to bring a river under control, to regulate its seasonal pattern of floods and low flows. A dam traps sediments and nutrients, alters the river's temperature and chemistry, and upsets the geological processes of erosion and deposition through which the river sculpts the surrounding land.

Dams: What They Are and What They Do

> A reservoir is a man's triumph over nature and the sight of a vast sheet of water brings an inner satisfaction to those who behold.
>
> S.H.C. de Silva, Consultant to the Irrigation Department of Sri Lanka, 1991

Dams have two main functions. The first is to store water to compensate for fluctuations in river flow or in demand for water and energy. The second is to raise the level of the water upstream to enable water to be diverted into a canal or to increase 'hydraulic head' – the difference in height between the surface of a reservoir and the river downstream. The creation of storage and head allows dams to generate electricity (hydropower provides nearly a fifth of the world's electricity); to supply water for agriculture, industries and households; to control flooding; and to assist river navigation by providing regular flows and drowning rapids. Other reasons for building dams include reservoir fisheries and leisure activities such as boating.

Hydropower generation capacity is a function of the amount of flow and hydraulic head. Although the head is usually related to the height of the dam, a low dam can have a high head if the powerhouse with its turbines and generators is located some distance downstream of the dam. Pipes known as 'penstocks' direct water to the turbines. Once the water has spun a turbine it flows into the 'tailwater' below the dam through a 'tailrace' pipe.

One advantage of hydro over other ways of generating electricity is that reservoirs can store water during times of low demand and then quickly start generating during the peak hours of electricity use. Nuclear, coal and oil power plants take much longer to start up from cold than hydro plants. Hydro's suitability for generating valuable 'peaking' power has in recent years encouraged a boom in what are known as pumped-storage plants. These involve two, normally relatively small, reservoirs, one above the other. During peak hours, the water from the upper reservoir falls through turbines into the lower one, generating electricity. The water is then pumped back uphill using cheap off-peak electricity.

Weirs and barrages are different types of 'run-of-river' dams; this means that while they raise the water level upstream they create only a small reservoir ('head pond') and cannot effectively regulate downstream flows. A weir is normally a low wall of stone, concrete or wicker. A barrage can be a huge structure 10 or 20 metres high extending for hundreds of metres across the bottom reaches of a wide river. The electricity generation of a 'run-of-river' hydropower dam is proportional to the flow of the river at any one time.

While they tend to have less damaging consequences than storage dams, run-of-river dams are far from environmentally benign, and the distinction between a 'run-of-river' and a 'storage' dam is not always clear. Dam proponents have in some cases sought to downplay the impact of planned dams by claiming that they will be run-of-river. Thailand's Pak Mun Dam, for example, is repeatedly described by officials as a run-of-river project; yet for much of the time the dam's gates remain closed and it operates as a storage dam. Despite years of protestations from its builders and funders that it would have minimal impacts on the river, Pak Mun managed within a couple of years to destroy one of the country's richest freshwater fisheries.[16]

Just as every river and watershed is unique, so is every dam site and every dam. There are, however, three main types of dam design – embankment, gravity and arch – selected mainly according to dam-site topography and geology. Earth and rock embankments, which are usually the cheapest to build, make up more than 80 per cent of all large dams. Embankments are generally built across broad valleys near sites where the large amounts of construction material they need can be quarried. Large embankment dams are the most massive structures humanity has ever erected. The most voluminous dam in the world, Tarbela in Pakistan, contains 106 million cubic metres of earth and rock, more than 40 times the volume of the Great Pyramid.

Gravity dams are basically thick, straight walls of concrete built across relatively narrow valleys with firm bedrock. Arch structures, also made from concrete, are limited to narrow canyons with strong rock walls and make up only around 4 per cent of large dams. An arch dam is in form like a normal architectural arch pushed onto its back, with its curved head facing upstream and its feet braced against the sides of its canyon. The inherent strength of the arch form enables the thin wall of an arch dam to hold back a reservoir with only a fraction of the concrete needed for a gravity dam of similar height.

A dam contains a number of structural features other than the main wall itself. Spillways are used to discharge water when the reservoir threatens to become dangerously high. Dams built across broad plains may include long lengths of ancillary dams and dikes. The five reservoirs of Phase 1 of the La Grande hydropower scheme in northern Quebec, for example, are impounded by 11 dams and more than 200 accompanying dikes stretching for a total length of 124 kilometres.

A Short History of Damming

> Then nothing will remain of the iron age
> And all these people but a thigh-bone or so, a poem
> Stuck in the world's thought, splinters of glass
> In the rubbish dumps, a concrete dam far off in the mountain...
>
> Robinson Jeffers, 'Summer Holiday', 1925

Farmers in the foothills of the Zagros mountains on the eastern edge of Mesopotamia may have been the first dam builders. Eight-thousand-year-old irrigation canals have been found in the area and it is not unlikely that small weirs of brushwood and earth were used to divert water from streams into the canals. By 6,500 years ago the Sumerians were criss-crossing the plains along the lower Tigris and Euphrates with networks of irrigation canals. Again no physical evidence of dams has been found from this period but it is likely that they were used to control flows of irrigation water.

The earliest dams for which remains have been found were built around 3,000 BC as part of an elaborate water supply system for the town of Jawa in modern-day Jordan. The system included a 200-metre-wide weir which diverted water via a canal into 10 small reservoirs impounded by rock and earth dams. The largest of the dams was more than 4 metres high and 80 metres long. Some 400 years later, around the time of the first pyramids, Egyptian masons constructed the Sadd el-Kafra, or 'Dam of the Pagans', across a seasonal stream near Cairo. This squat mass of sand, gravel and rock was 14 metres high and 113 metres long, and retained by some 17,000 cut stone blocks. After perhaps a decade of construction, but before it could be completed, the dam was partly washed away and was never repaired. The failed dam may have been intended to supply water to local quarries. Because the Nile's floods inundated their fields before the planting season each year, the farmers of ancient Egypt did not need dams for irrigation.

By the late first millennium BC, stone and earth dams had been built around the Mediterranean, in the Middle East, China and Central America. The ingenuity of Roman engineers is perhaps most visible in their dams and aqueducts. The most impressive surviving Roman dams are in Spain, which continued to be pre-eminent in hydraulic engineering through the Moorish period and into modern times. A 46-metre-high stone dam near Alicante begun in 1580 and completed 14 years later was the highest in the world for the better part of three centuries.

South Asia, too, has a long history of dam building. Long earthen embankments were built to store water for Sri Lankan cities from the fourth century BC. One of these early embankments was raised in AD 460 to a height of 34 metres and was the world's highest dam for more than a millennium. King Parakrama Babu, a twelfth-century Sinhalese ruler notorious as a tyrant and megalomaniac, boasted to have built and restored more than 4,000 dams. One old embankment he enlarged to a height of 15 metres and an incredible length of nearly 14 kilometres. No dam equalled it in volume until the early twentieth century.[17] Parakrama Babu's large dams, believes anthropologist Edmund Leach, were of little use to most Sri Lankan villagers, who relied for irrigation on small artificial ponds known as 'tanks'. The large dams, says Leach, 'are monuments, not utilitarian structures'.

Technologies to convert the energy of flowing water into mechanical energy have a history almost as long as that of irrigation. A type of waterwheel known as the Noria which has buckets around its rim to scoop up water from a river or canal was used in ancient Egypt and Sumeria. By the first century BC, watermills were used to grind corn in Rome. The Domesday Book of 1086 records 5,624 watermills in England – roughly one to every 250 people.

Watermills were not only built for raising water and grinding corn. During the later Middle Ages they performed numerous tasks in the great industrial centres of Germany and northern Italy, including pulping rags for paper, hammering iron, beating hides in tanneries, spinning silk, crushing ores and pumping water from mines. Ores from the famous 'silver mountain' at Potosí in Bolivia were ground in well over a hundred watermills. In the early seventeenth century, the dam holding back one of the largest of the 32 reservoirs supplying water to the mills collapsed, washing away 4,000 people along with almost all the mills. By the beginning of the industrial revolution some half a million watermills were powering Europe's factories and mines.

Almost 200 dams higher than 15 metres were built in fast-industrializing nineteenth-century Britain, mainly to store water for its expanding cities. In 1900, Britain had nearly as many large dams as the rest of the world put together. Nineteenth-century dams were mainly earth embankments designed largely on the basis of trial and error – until the 1930s there was little scientific understanding of how soil and rock behaved under pressure. Dam builders in the nineteenth century (and even today in some parts of the world) also had little streamflow or rainfall data, and few statistical tools to analyse what hydrological data had been gathered. As a consequence, their structures collapsed with alarming frequency. Two hundred and fifty people were killed when a water supply dam in Yorkshire burst in 1864. The US had a particularly bad safety record: nearly one in ten embankments built in the US before 1930 failed. More than 2,200 people were swept to their deaths when a dam above the town of Johnstown, Pennsylvania, collapsed in 1889. The earthen embankment had held back the largest reservoir in the US.

French engineer Benoit Fourneyron perfected the first water turbine in 1832, hugely boosting the efficiency of watermills (a turbine, which converts the potential energy of falling water into mechanical energy, is far more efficient than a waterwheel, which is powered by the kinetic energy of flowing water). The full significance of the turbine became clear in the latter part of the nineteenth century with advances in electrical engineering which led to the building of power stations and transmission lines. The world's first hydro plant, a run-of-river dam in

Appleton, Wisconsin, began producing power in 1882. The following year hydro dams were built in both Italy and Norway.

Over the next few decades small hydro dams proliferated on the swift-flowing rivers and streams of Europe, most notably in Scandinavia and the Alps. After the turn of the century, the size of the dams and power stations being built began rapidly to increase. Progress in turbine design increased the head at which turbines could operate from 30 metres in 1900 to more than 200 metres by the 1930s, and improvements in dam engineering allowed the high dams to be built to create this head.[17]

Throwing water across the land: big dams in the US

> Now what we need is a great big dam,
> To throw a lot o' water out across that land,
> People could work and stuff would grow,
> And you could wave goodbye to the old skid row.
>
> Woody Guthrie, 'Washington Talkin' Blues', 1941

The conquest and settlement of the dry US West in the late nineteenth century owes more to dams than cowboys. Early settlers saw the damming and redirecting of desert streams onto their fields as both an economic necessity and a spiritual duty, furthering God's work by turning the wilderness into a garden. By the end of the nineteenth century, most of the best sites for the small dam and irrigation schemes which groups of farmers or private companies could afford had been exploited. The increasingly unfavourable economics of new irrigation schemes at this time meant that many irrigation companies were going to the wall.

In 1902, Congress passed the National Reclamation or 'Newlands' Act, described by environmental historian Donald Worster as 'the most important single piece of legislation in the history of the [US] West'. The Act set up the Reclamation Service – later to become the Department of Interior Bureau of Reclamation or BuRec – to build irrigation projects to be financed by selling government land and later by selling water and electricity ('reclamation' is a semantically curious term which in the US usually means bringing irrigation to arid land).

The Newlands Act passed amidst a spate of rhetoric on how irrigation in the West would attract the homeless and landless in the East, serving as a safety valve for the discontented and a bolster to democracy. Irrigation would also allow the US to settle the sparsely populated Western half of their country. Within a few years of the Act passing, however, it became clear that there were no legions of impoverished Easterners eager to become farmers in the desert and that federal irrigation was no more economically viable than its private counterpart. In the words of Donald Worster, the federal reclamation programme was 'hopelessly unrealistic, expensive, unworkable, and naive'. By 1930, says

Worster, 'it was so manifest a failure that, had there not been powerful groups and strong cultural imperatives supporting it, federal reclamation would have died an ignominious death.'[18]

To limit the concentration of ownership of federally irrigated land, no farmer was to own more than 160 acres in a reclamation project. This requirement, however, was studiously ignored or reinterpreted so that speculators and large landowners – together with construction companies – were the greatest beneficiaries of Western water development. The greatest losers were the federal taxpayers who had to subsidize the schemes and the Native Americans who lost untold numbers of sacred sites and reservation land under the reservoirs, water to which they had treaty rights, and most of the prodigious salmon fishery of the Pacific Northwest.

The glory years of the Bureau of Reclamation began with the first blasting at the site of Hoover Dam in 1931. The Bureau had already engineered 50 concrete dams, but Hoover was something else – the 60 million tonnes of concrete it contained outweighed all their previous dams put together. Hoover stood an incredible 85 metres higher than any other dam in the world. Yet before Hoover was even finished the Bureau was overseeing the construction of Shasta Dam on California's Sacramento River with a volume of concrete twice that of Hoover and the even more massive Grand Coulee Dam in Washington state, a 1,500-metre-long, 168-metre-high monster described by one hyperbolic western Senator as 'the biggest thing on earth'.[19]

Electricity from the big western dams helped to win the Second World War. By June 1942, almost all the power from Grand Coulee and Bonneville Dam, built by the Army Corps of Engineers on the Lower Columbia, was going to war production, most of it to producing aluminium for aeroplanes. Later the hydropower of the Northwest was turned to another use: the highly energy-intensive production of plutonium for nuclear bombs. In 1945 the first and second biggest sources of electricity on the planet were Grand Coulee and Hoover, with respective generating capacities of 2,138 and 1,250 megawatts.

While the activities of BuRec are confined to the western US, the hundreds of dams of the US Army Corps of Engineers have been built all over the country. In the nineteenth century, the Corps' mission was to engineer rivers to accommodate river traffic and control floods. Like BuRec, however, it expanded its role, taking on hydropower production, 'reservoir recreation' and irrigation. The four huge dams the Corps constructed on the Missouri – Garrison, Oahe, Fort Peck and Fort Randall – form respectively the third, fourth, fifth and seventh largest capacity reservoirs in the US (the other top seven places are occupied by the reservoirs behind BuRec's Hoover, Glen Canyon and Grand Coulee dams).

Although it has built dams in only one river basin, the Tennessee Valley Authority may have had the most influence worldwide of any of the US dam-building bureaucracies. Established by the federal government in 1933 as a largely autonomous agency with wide powers over the lives of the valley residents, including the right to expropriate land, the TVA has inspired numerous river basin development authorities around the world. While the TVA is still regarded as synonymous with dam building, the authority built most of its 38 large dams before 1945, after which it turned to coal and nuclear plants. Despite the tens of billions of dollars spent by the TVA, the population of the Tennessee Basin is in many ways poorer than those living in nearby areas who did not 'benefit' from TVA development.[20]

Making mad rivers sane in the USSR

> There is far more important information about the history of hydroelectric construction in the USSR in Alexander Solzhenitsyn's *Gulag Archipelago* than in all the textbooks on hydraulic engineering.
>
> Zeyev Volfson, *The Destruction of Nature in the Soviet Union*, 1970s

The history of large dam building in the Soviet Union, like that in the US, is one of powerful bureaucracies staffed by thousands of engineers eager to build prestige projects and sustained by an ideological vision of human progress through the total control of nature. Soviet dam builders sought to make 'mad rivers sane', in the words of writer Maxim Gorky. The big dam era in the USSR was launched with long embankments across wide valleys, flooding huge areas of rich agricultural land and thousands of villages. By the 1970s, the country's reservoirs covered some 120,000 square kilometres – two-and-a-half times the area submerged in the US.

Until its transfer to the Ministry of Energy in 1960, the main Soviet dam-building bureaucracy, the Hydroproject Institute, was a subdivision of the KGB. Secret police and dams were bonded as only the gulags could provide the huge labour force needed to build the massive Soviet dams. The first major dam in the USSR, Dneprostroi, a 60-metre-high embankment stretching for three-quarters of a kilometre across the Dnieper River, was the most powerful hydroplant in the world when completed in 1932. It flooded so much prime Ukrainian farmland that Soviet hydrologists have claimed that burning hay harvested from the area submerged could have yielded as much annual energy as has been generated by the power plant.[21]

After the Second World War, a series of hydrodams were built in western Russia and the Ukraine as part of the 'Great Stalin Plan for the Transformation of Nature'. One hundred thousand prisoners are said to have worked on Kuibyishev Dam on the Volga.[22] The Volga's six major dams have transformed Europe's longest river into a string of shallow, stagnant, polluted reservoirs. The other great rivers of the region, the Don and the Dnieper, have suffered a similar fate. As a direct result, the previously lucrative commercial fisheries in these rivers and their estuaries have been all but wiped out. Once all the main rivers in the European USSR had been shackled with chains of dams, the Hydroproject Institute turned its attention east and south, repeating the process of destruction in Siberia, Central Asia and the Caucasus, as well as in developing countries.

The southward spread of large dams

> One day, every last drop of water which drains into the whole valley of the Nile ... shall be equally and amicably divided among the river people, and the Nile itself ... shall perish gloriously and never reach the sea.
>
> Winston Churchill, 1908

British colonialists were the most ardent dam builders outside Europe and North America in the late nineteenth and early twentieth centuries, leaving their mark most firmly on the basins of the Indus, Ganges and Nile. The British sought to encourage the conversion of land in their colonies from peasant farms growing crops for local consumption into irrigated tracts on which farmers with the capital to invest in dams and canals would grow high-value crops such as cotton, sugar cane and opium. Much of the crops were destined for export to Britain or elsewhere in the Empire.

In 1902, the British constructed the Low Aswan Dam to regulate the Nile in order to irrigate cotton for the mills of Lancashire. The dam, which had a crest nearly 2 kilometres long, was raised twice, reaching a height of 36 metres in 1933. Unlike the later High Aswan Dam, which stores the annual flood and traps almost all the Nile's sediment load, the Low Dam was lined with sluice gates which were opened to let pass most of the flood season water and sediment. Britain also dammed the Nile further upstream at Sennar in the Sudan. Sennar Dam, completed in 1925, holds back water for the Gezira Scheme, one of the world's largest cotton plantations.

When the winds of change swept the colonial world to independence in the decades following the Second World War, politicians and technocrats in the new countries continued the work of colonial dam builders. The new leaders looked on the huge dams of the US and USSR and saw shining monuments to progress and prosperity. Up to 1980, about 15 per cent of independent India's total national expenditure had been spent on the construction of more than a thousand large dams and their associated infrastructure.[23]

Foreign financiers, 'water resources experts' and industrialists have promoted dams in developing nations as fervently as their countries' own political, military and corporate elites. John L. Savage, the chief designer of Hoover and the other big BuRec dams, helped conceive the first plan for China's Three Gorges Project as well as major multi-dam schemes for the Indus and Mekong. Bureau of Reclamation Commissioner Michael Straus claimed in 1955 that 'the American concept of comprehensive river basin development ... has seized the world imagination.'[24]

The bland nomenclature of 'comprehensive' or 'integrated' 'river basin development' or 'river basin planning' masks the true meaning of the terms. River basin planning has long been a euphemism for the establishment of powerful and largely autonomous agencies filled with dam and irrigation engineers who have strewn watersheds with dams and then hoped that the associated energy-intensive industries and irrigation schemes would successfully follow in their wake.

In countries where Cold War politics made the US and its allies unwelcome, the Soviet Union provided technical and financial assistance for dams, the most notable Soviet-aided project being the High Aswan Dam. After China's 1949 revolution, engineers from the Hydrological Planning Agency replaced BuRec's dam advisors in the country. The Soviet dam designers were then themselves kicked out after the Sino-Soviet split of the 1960s.

China was dammed at a breakneck pace – an average of more than 600 large dams were built every year in China in the three decades following the revolution. Probably the most intense burst of dam building was sparked by the Great Leap Forward of the late 1950s. Officials took Mao Zedong's command to aim for 'higher and higher' economic targets to mean the building of more and bigger dams. Economic planners discarded advice from hydrologists and built thousands of dams to contain floodwaters at the expense of maintaining traditional flood control measures like levees and diversion channels. The result was the 1975 Henan catastrophe and several thousand other dam-burst floods. Another example of hydropolitical lunacy was the rush to start work on Gezhouba Dam on the Yangtze in time for Mao's 77th birthday in 1970. The planning was so hasty that shortly after construction began on the huge dam it had to be stopped and the whole project redesigned. Projected to take 5 years to build, Gezhouba took 18.[25]

The World Bank is today the biggest foreign financier of large dams in China – as historically it has been worldwide. The Bank's first loan to a developing country helped pay for three dams. Since then it has lent some $58 billion (in 1993 dollars) for more than 600 dams in 93 countries, including many of the world's largest and most controversial projects. The other multilateral development banks – especially the Inter-American and Asian development banks – and the specialized agencies of the United Nations – especially the Food and Agriculture Organization (FAO) and UN Development Programme (UNDP) – have also played a major role in promoting large dams and irrigation schemes in developing countries. Bilateral 'aid' agencies like the US Agency for International Development (USAID) and the British Overseas Development Administration (ODA) are other important funders and planners of dams, often in partnership with the World Bank and the UN agencies.

Since the 1970s, aid has provided a huge subsidy to sustain dam-building engineering and construction companies in Northern countries which have faced dwindling orders at home. Major dams are among the most expensive of infrastructure projects. Itaipú on the Brazilian–Paraguayan border, currently the world's most powerful hydrodam with a generating capacity of 12,600 megawatts, cost some $20 billion. As of August 1996, the latest official projections for China's 18,200 megawatt Three Gorges Dam run to between $30 and $50 billion.[26] Worldwide some $20 billion is spent every year on building and refurbishing dams.

The corporate beneficiaries of dam building – including environmental consultancies and electricity-intensive industries like aluminium – are not just passive recipients of government largesse but actively persuade politicians and bureaucrats to build more dams. Such 'lobbying' routinely involves bribery: the massive costs of large dams means that they are an almost uniquely effective channel for kick-backs, greatly increasing their attractiveness for business executives, aid bureaucrats and politicians. In recent years dams have been at the centre of major corruption scandals in Britain, Malaysia, Kenya, Japan, Italy, Brazil, Paraguay and Argentina.

The disease of giganticism

Dam building and other attempts to gain control of rivers have probably always provoked conflict. Indeed, the word 'rival' comes from the Latin *rivalis*, 'one using the same brook as another'. Dam historian Norman Smith describes disputes in medieval England which echo problems besetting the operators of modern-day multipurpose dams. When dams were used both for turning a waterwheel (which required a high head of water) and for navigation (which required keeping gates open to allow boats to pass) 'the dams always became the centre of argument and litigation, and not infrequently spontaneous fights broke out.' Smith also writes of an attempt by a group of Scottish fishermen to destroy a newly completed weir in the seventeenth century.[27]

Prime Minister Jawaharlal Nehru, often thought of as the father of India's programme of giant multipurpose dams, seems to have had second thoughts about these modern 'temples' later in his political career. 'I have been beginning to think that we are suffering from what we may call "disease of giganticism",' Nehru told the 1958 annual meeting of the Central Board of Irrigation and Power. 'We want to show that we can build big dams and do big things ... but the idea of having big undertakings and doing big tasks for the sake of showing that we can do big things is not a good outlook at all.'[28]

In the same year, First Secretary Nikita Krushchev spoke out against the huge dams in the USSR at a banquet dedicated to the opening of the Kuibyishev Dam. Krushchev 'cited the high price of hydroelectric power stations, the irretrievable losses of the best floodplains and fields on the middle Volga, and the economic advantages of thermoelectric power plants'. According to Igor A. Nikulin, an engineer who worked on the Kuibyishev project, the speech 'reflected the then current discussions about hydroelectric power'. Krushchev's arguments against dams, like those of Nehru, went largely ignored and, Nikulin says, the 'powerful, consolidated administrative forces brought up on the hydrotechnological constructions of the gulag era prevailed.'[29]

Over the last decade, citizen protests against dams have grown and become better organized and able to fight projects on the local, national and international levels. During the 1980s, the anti-dam movement has stood up in the face of denigration and intimidation and forced the indefinite postponement or cancellation of numerous large, prestige projects: the Franklin Dam in Australia, Nam Choan in Thailand, Nagymaros in Hungary, Silent Valley in India, Babaquara in Brazil, Katun in Russia and Serre de la Fare in France are some of the most important examples. In the late 1980s and 1990s, the epic struggle of the Save the Narmada Movement, or Narmada Bachao Andolan, against the powerful backers of India's giant Sardar Sarovar Dam has inspired environmentalists around the world and humbled the mighty World Bank, forcing it to quit the project in 1993. Two years later the World Bank was pressured into pulling out of the controversial Arun III Dam in Nepal and accepting the main arguments of its opponents. The World Bank now appears willing only to fund huge dams in countries with repressive regimes which can ensure that popular resistance is crushed.

Although the World Bank is currently supporting a number of huge dams in China, the country's gargantuan Three Gorges project – which, if it is ever finished, will displace some 1.3 million people – is too controversial for the Bank and most other foreign lenders. In September 1993, BuRec pulled out of its contract to provide technical support for Three Gorges, with its Commissioner, Daniel Beard, saying that the dam was 'outdated and overly expensive' and that the Bureau's 'current priorities are water resource management and environmental restoration, not large dam projects'.[30]

It is, however, far too early to write the epitaph of the large dam. Although the rate of building has declined sharply from the nearly 1,000 large dams which came into operation every year from the 1950s to the mid-1970s, there were still some 260 large dams being completed every year during the early 1990s. According to ICOLD, nearly 1,200 dams with a height of at least 15 metres were under construction at the beginning of 1994. Furthermore, there is a trend for the dams which are being built to be higher than before.[31] China, Brazil, Laos, Vietnam, Turkey, Spain, India, Mexico, Burma, Argentina and Malaysia are all building or planning numerous dam projects which would have massive impacts on riverine ecosystems and people.

If economic and political circumstances change and become more propitious for dam building, the industry is ready with schemes which would make Stalin's 'Great Plan for the Transformation of Nature' look environmentally sensitive. A plan to dam the Amazon was dreamt up in the 1960s. The 190,000 square kilometre reservoir – larger than the nation of Uruguay – would be impounded by a 64-kilometre-long dam with a generating capacity of up to 80,000 megawatts.[32]

Dams planned by the Russian Hydroproject Institute include a 20,000 megawatt giant at Turukhansk on an eastern tributary of the great Yenisei River in Siberia. The Hydroproject Institute was praised in a 1994 *Hydro Review Worldwide* editorial for the 'bold thinking' behind a paper entitled 'Bering Strait Transcontinental Railway Road and the Future of Hydropower Development'. Under the scheme, hydropower would supply tens of thousands of megawatts for a railway linking Siberia with Alaska and for the timber, mining and other industries set up along the route.[33]

The hydropower industry is also gazing longingly at the Zaire River – second only to the Amazon in terms of the volume of its discharge. Near the centre of the western coast of Africa is Inga Falls, one of the world's most powerful single concentrations of hydroelectric potential. So far two large hydro schemes have been built at the site. Neither involves a dam across the river, instead diverting a small proportion of the massive flow around the falls and through turbines. The developers' dream is to dam the Zaire at Inga, exploiting the site's full potential of some 40,000 megawatts – an amount twice that of the installed hydro capacity in the whole of Africa in the mid-1990s. Power from Inga would be transmitted the length of the continent and even into the Middle East, Turkey and Europe. In 1995, energy officials from South Africa and Egypt began discussing building a high-voltage link between Cape Town and Cairo with its keystone the 'Grand Inga' project.[34]

Prolonged droughts in arid areas, growing demand for water and hikes in food prices would all act to increase the attractiveness of new irrigation and inter-basin diversion schemes. Russian water minister Nikolai Mikheev announced in 1995 that his government was considering once more a mammoth scheme to reverse several of the major Siberian rivers so that they would flow south to Central Asia and the Aral Sea.[35] In India, water technocrats advocate building strings of reservoirs and canals linking the

Brahmaputra, Ganges, Mahanadi, Godavari, Krishna, Pennar, Cauvery, Tapi, Narmada, Ken and Yamuna rivers, with the aim of moving 'surplus' water from the east and north to the west and south.[36]

'A boondoggle visible from Mars' was author Wallace Stegner's description of NAWAPA – the North American Water and Power Alliance.[37] NAWAPA, conceived in the 1950s, would use dams up to 520 metres high (twice the height of Chicoasén in Mexico, currently the highest dam in the Americas) to decant the flow of at least 19 rivers in Alaska and British Colombia into an 800-kilometre-long mega-reservoir in the Canadian Rockies. Some of the water would be channelled east into the Great Lakes and eventually into the St Lawrence, Illinois and Mississippi. The main reason for the scheme, however, would be the diversion of water south through a Brobdingnagian plumber's fantasy of pumps, tunnels, reservoirs and rivers turned into huge canals. California, Arizona and Texas would receive massive new infusions of irrigation water. Mexico would get enough to triple its irrigated area. Even after pumping the water, there would still be a surplus power capacity of 50,000 to 80,000 megawatts.

'NAWAPA is the kind of thing you think about when you're smoking pot,' a US hydrologist told author Marc Reisner. 'People who say it will be built are crazy.' Others, however, believe that while the full plan may never happen, some kind of British Colombia to Southwest US water diversion scheme may well be built.[38]

Not wanting to lose out on water diversion megalomania, eastern Canada has its own version of NAWAPA – the Grand Replenishment and Northern Development Canal Concept, or GRAND Canal. According to this plan, 160 kilometres of dikes would be built across the northern end of James Bay, cutting it off from Hudson Bay and the ocean. The rivers flowing into James Bay would then turn it into a freshwater reservoir the size of Lake Superior. Aqueducts would carry the water south into the Great Lakes and then on to the Canadian prairies and the US midwest and southwest. The estimated cost: some $100 billion.[39] Even more hallucinogenic than GRAND and NAWAPA is the suggested Atlantropa Project. This mind-boggler would involve damming the Straits of Gibraltar and converting the floor of the Mediterranean into polders irrigated with freshwater brought all the way from the Zaire River.[40]

The End of the Big Dam Era?

> I hope future generations will not look back upon their ancestors with scornful contempt, as they ask, 'Why in the name of all the fishes that swim the seas, did they permit the engineers to utterly destroy our streams?'
>
> Ed Averill, President of the Oregon Wild Life Federation, 1937

The massive momentum provided by bureaucratic structures, careers, ideology and profit has kept the big-dam machine rolling over the past six decades with few insiders ever questioning the damage done or evaluating whether the promises of water, power, food and prosperity for all have actually been realized. The industry has never carried out a credible and comprehensive retrospective assessment of the ecological, economic and social effects of a representative sample of large dams – or even of a single project.

A growing number of academic and activist researchers, however, have been building up an impressive corpus of data showing the extensive damage which dams and their associated irrigation schemes cause to watersheds, cultures and national economies. Furthermore, the evidence is steadily mounting to show how dams have not fulfilled the promises made for them. Dams invariably cost much more than claimed, diverting investments from more beneficial uses. Reservoirs tend to fill with silt long before predicted and hydroplants to supply much less electricity than promised. Irrigation schemes are badly managed, destroy soils, bankrupt small farmers and turn lands used to feed local people over to the production of crops for export. Dams assist the powerful and wealthy to enclose the common land, water and forests of the politically weak. By misleading people into thinking that they can control huge floods, dams encourage settlement on floodplains, turning damaging floods into devastating ones.

The credibility of dam opponents is strengthened by the increasing realization that the genuine needs supposed to be satisfied by dams can be met in other ways. Water can be provided for drought-prone areas much more quickly, cheaply and equitably with the use of small-scale schemes, some using traditional techniques, some using new methods and some a combination of both. Increasing the efficiency of water supply and use can hugely expand the availability of water without the need for more dams. Similarly, all countries have a massive potential to reduce their energy use through conservation and efficiency – to generate 'negawatts' rather than megawatts. The costs of renewable generating sources, especially wind and solar power, are now falling rapidly and are already cheaper than hydropower for many areas and uses.

Opponents of large dam projects sometimes cite small dams as alternatives. The issue of small versus large dams, however, is fraught with problems. One is the question of what is 'small' and what is 'large': the distinction is usually made on height, but it can also be made on area of reservoir, generating capacity or area irrigated, and the definitions can vary widely between countries and agencies. Tallness is often not a reliable guide to the impact of a dam – a 100 metre giant in a deep mountain valley could flood less land, displace fewer people and have fewer impacts on river ecology than a 15 metre barrage on a densely populated floodplain. Along with siting, the function and operating regime of a dam can also be more significant than its height. India's Farakka Barrage, for example, which by diverting the flow of the Ganges has had a catastrophic impact upon the economy and ecology of downstream Bangladesh, is less than 15 metres high. In general, however, once a dam site and operating pattern is chosen, the higher the dam is built (or, more correctly, the higher the operating level of its reservoir), the more severe will be its impacts.

The main argument used against those who advocate small dams as alternatives to large projects is that if the small dams are to create the same amount of storage and generation capacity as a large dam, so many small dams would have to be built that their effects would be even worse than that of the single dam they would replace. Small reservoirs do usually flood much more land per unit of water stored than larger ones. Yet no realistic advocate of small dams believes that they can achieve the same level of output as megadams: clogging South America's Paraná River with 15,700 one-megawatt dams is not an alternative to the combined 15,700 megawatt capacity of Itaipú and Yacyretá dams; similarly no number of small dams on the Colorado could have matched the 68 billion cubic metre water storage capacity of Hoover and Glen Canyon.

The sensible alternatives to building the behemoths on the Paraná would not have been small dams, but measures to reduce the growth of demand for electricity in Brazil and Argentina, and non-hydro generation methods. The alternatives to the water stored and supplied from the Colorado to desert cities and farms in southern California, Arizona and Nevada would have been urban and agricultural development policies which respected the limits of an arid land by discouraging lawns, fountains and golf courses in the desert, and by not subsidizing water for crops more wisely grown in areas with higher rainfall.

Small dams do, however, have advantages over their bigger siblings. Small dams are cheaper and less risky for investors, whether public or private, and will not bankrupt a nation if they experience construction problems or do not work as planned. The smaller the dam, the more likely that the benefits of its construction and operation can be captured by local communities rather than outsiders. Small dams can provide electricity to remote villages which the national grid may never reach. They can provide water to local farmers, rather than diverting it to cities and farmers elsewhere. It is easier to compensate displaced people, find them replacement land and maintain their social ties when only a small part of a community is affected, and a small percentage of the local land submerged. The silt in small reservoirs can be dug out and spread over nearby land, maintaining reservoir capacity and the fertility of the fields. Furthermore, while small dams are no less likely to break than larger ones, fewer people are at risk when they fail.

A World Bank consultant wrote in 1987 that 'most scenarios of future developments in water resources agree that ultimately, say by the mid-21st century', all of the runoff in all of the world's rivers 'must be stored by reservoirs or other methods'.[41] Today, only the most fundamentalist hydrocrats would support this claim. In a number of countries, opposition – together with the lousy economics of dam building and the lack of good sites which remain undammed – appears to be bringing the dam industry to a shuddering halt. Almost all the remaining free-flowing rivers in Sweden and Norway are now legally protected against dam building. Around 16,000 kilometres of 'outstanding' sections of rivers and streams in the US are now 'preserved in free-flowing condition' under the 1968 federal National Wild and Scenic Rivers Act. Many more tens of thousands of kilometres are protected under state river conservation laws.[42] In the US, the rate at which large dams are being built is now lower than at any other time in the twentieth century.

The big dam era was born in the United States. Hopefully, the long-term future of dams and of international dam fighting will also follow the lead of the US. Having made it all but impossible for dam builders to construct large new projects, US river advocates are now turning their attention to mitigating the impacts of existing dams, in particular to forcing dam operators to release water in a pattern mimicking natural flows and so try to re-create the original downstream habitats.

Dam operators, however, while they can reduce the extent of damage that dams cause, cannot replicate a wild river. Advocates of river restoration are thus now going beyond mitigation to campaigning for dams to be pulled down and letting rivers flow unhindered again. Few dams of any size have yet been removed and no one knows how it will be done for large projects or how much it will cost. Nevertheless, the growing movement to tear down dams in the US offers long-term hope that the world's rivers can be brought back from the brink.

Notes

1. Quoted in R. Martin, *A Story That Stands Like a Dam*, Henry Holt, New York 1989, p. 42. Although the inauguration ceremony for Hoover was held in 1935 the dam was not completed until 1936.

2. J. Nehru, *Speeches, Vol. III. March 1953–August 1957*, Publications Division, Government of India, Calcutta, 1958, pp. 2–3.

3. T. Steinberg, '"That World's Fair Feeling": Control of Water in Twentieth-Century America', *Technology and Culture*, Vol. 34, No. 2, April 1993, p. 402.

4. ICOLD's 1988 register gives 36,200 large dams in 1986. This figure excludes 2,000–3,000 large dams in the USSR. According to ICOLD instructions, national dam commissions can report dams of 10–15m to ICOLD as large dams if they meet the following requirements: crest length ≥ 500m; reservoir capacity ≥ 1 million m^3; max. flood discharge ≥ 2,000 m^3/s; 'specially difficult foundation

problems'; or 'unusual design' (ICOLD, *World Register of Dams*, Paris 1988, pp. 9, 21, 62, 109). Since 1986 large dams have been built at a rate of around 260 a year. Figure of dams in US from USCOLD, 'US and World Dam, Hydropower and Reservoir Statistics', Denver, CO, 1995.

5. T.W. Mermel, 'The World's Major Dams and Hydro Plants', in *International Water Power & Dam Construction Handbook 1995*, IWPDC, Surrey, UK, 1995. Mermel's 1995 list includes more than 350 major dams, but at least 40 do not appear to meet his 'major dam' criteria.

6. S.F. Bates et al., *Searching out the Headwaters*, Island Press, Washington, DC, 1993, p. 19; J.A. Gore and G.E. Petts, 'Preface', in J.A. Gore and G.E. Petts (eds.), *Alternatives in Regulated River Management*, CRC Press, Boca Raton, FL, 1989; M. Dynesius and C. Nilsson, 'Fragmentation and Flow Regulation of River Systems in the Northern Third of the World', *Science*, Vol. 266, 4 November 1994.

7. B.F. Chao, 'Anthropological Impact on Global Geodymanics Due to Reservoir Water Impoundment', *Geophysical Research Letters*, Vol. 22, No. 24, 1995.

8. Ibid.

9. I.A. Shiklomanov, 'World Fresh Water Resources', in P.H. Gleick (ed.), *Water in Crisis: A Guide to the World's Fresh Water Resources*, Oxford University Press, Oxford 1993, p. 14.

10. R.S. Devine, 'The Trouble With Dams', *Atlantic Monthly*, August 1995.

11. Dynesius and Nilsson, 'Fragmentation and Flow Regulation'.

12. World Resources Institute, *World Resources 1994–95*, Oxford University Press, Oxford 1994, p. 184.

13. In UK English, 'watershed' means the line separating two river basins, known as a 'divide' in the US. In US English and in most hydrological literature, 'watershed' connotes the entire area of a river basin. It is used in this book in its latter sense.

14. L. Mumford, *Technics and Civilization*, Harcourt, Brace and World, New York 1963 (orig. 1934), p. 61.

15. V. Paranjpye, *High Dams on the Narmada*, INTACH, New Delhi 1990, p. 3; C. Deegan, 'The Narmada in Myth and History', in W.F. Fisher (ed.), *Towards Sustainable Development? Struggling Over India's Narmada River*, M.E. Sharpe, Armonk, NY, 1995, p. 65.

16. See, e.g., T.R. Roberts, 'Just Another Dammed River? Negative Impacts of Pak Mun Dam on Fishes of the Mekong Basin', *Natural History Bulletin of the Siam Society*, Vol. 41, 1993.

17. J. Guilaine (ed.), *La Préhistoire, d'un continent à l'autre*, Larousse, Paris 1986, pp. 96–7; N. Smith, *A History of Dams*, Peter Davies, London 1971, pp. 1, 8, 48, 123–5, 138, 164, 213–17; N.J. Schnitter, *A History of Dams: The Useful Pyramids*, Balkema, Rotterdam 1994, pp. 96–7, 1–4; Edmund A. Leach, 'Hydraulic Society in Ceylon', *Past and Present*, No. 15, April 1959, p. 21, quoted in E. Goldsmith and N. Hildyard, *The Social and Environmental Impacts of Large Dams. Vol.1*, Wadebridge Ecological Centre, Cornwall 1984, p. 293; J.-C. Debeir et al., *In the Servitude of Power: Energy and Civilization through the Ages*, Zed Books, London 1991, pp. 75, 91; Mumford, *Technics and Civilization*, p. 112; J.R. Moreira and A.D. Poole, 'Hydropower and its Constraints', in T.B. Johansson et al. (eds.), *Renewable Energy: Sources for Fuels and Electricity*, Island Press, Washington, DC, 1993, pp. 78–9.

18. D. Worster, *Rivers of Empire: Water, Aridity and the Growth of the American West*, Oxford University Press, Oxford 1985, p. 130.

19. Ibid., p. 270.

20. W. Chandler, *The Myth of TVA: Conservation and Development in the Tennessee Valley 1933–1983*, Ballinger, Cambridge, MA, 1984.

21. B. Komarov, *The Destruction of Nature in the Soviet Union*, Pluto Press, London 1980, p. 57. Boris Komarov is a pseudonym for Zeyev Volfson. The Hydroproject Institute was originally named the Hydrological Planning Agency.

22. I.A. Nikulin, 'The Virus of Giganticism', *Novy Mir* 5, 1991, translated by Michelle Kellman, Baikal Watch.

23. E.G. Thukral, 'Introduction', in E.G. Thukral (ed.), *Big Dams, Displaced People: Rivers of Sorrow, Rivers of Change*, Sage Publications, New Delhi 1992, p. 9.

24. Quoted in D. Worster, 'The Hoover Dam: A Study in Domination', in E. Goldsmith and N. Hildyard (eds.), *The Social and Environmental Impacts of Large Dams. Vol. 2: Case Studies*, Wadebridge Ecological Centre, Cornwall 1986, p. 21.

25. Human Rights Watch/Asia, 'The Three Gorges Dam in China: Forced Resettlement, Suppression of Dissent and Labor Rights Concerns', Human Rights Watch, New York 1995, p. 41; Dai Qing, 'An Interview with Li Rui', in Dai Qing, (edited by P. Adams and J. Thibodeau), *Yangtze! Yangtze!*, Probe International, Toronto and Earthscan, London 1994, p. 126.

26. T. Walker, 'Building China: Big Promise but Tough Terms', *Financial Times*, 19 March 1996.

27. Smith, *A History of Dams*, p. 165.

28. *Irrigation and Power*, Vol. XVI, No. 1, January 1959, p. 172.

29. Nikulin, 'The Virus of Giganticism'.

30. 'Statement of Bureau of Reclamation Commissioner Dan Beard Regarding Bureau Involvement in Three Gorges Dam Project', Department of the Interior Press Release, 16 September 1993.

31. ICOLD, *World Register of Dams*, p. 11; ICOLD, 'Annual Report', Paris 1994.

32. J.G. Mitchell, *The Man Who Would Dam the Amazon & Other Accounts from Afield*, University of Nebraska, Lincoln 1990, p. 12.

33. C. Vansant, 'Consider the Possibilities!', *Hydro Review Worldwide*, Winter 1994.

34. F. Pearce, 'The International Grid', *New Scientist*, 8 July 1995; M.M. Abaza, 'Africa–Europe Electrical Interconnection and Prospects of Worldwide Interconnections', *Global Energy Network International*, First Quarter, 1995; 'High Voltage Link from Cape to Cairo', *Africa Analysis*, 7 April 1995.

35. 'River Diversion Project Resurrected?', *OMRI*, 28 September 1995.

36. Y.K. Murthy, 'Urgent Need for National Plan for Inter-Basin Transfer of Water in India', undated.

37. Quoted in Worster, *Rivers of Empire*, p. 316.

38. M. Reisner, *Cadillac Desert: The American West and its Disappearing Water*, Secker & Warburg, London 1986, pp. 505–13.

39. Ibid., p. 513; S. McCutcheon, *Electric Rivers: The Story of the James Bay Project*, Black Rose Books, Montreal 1991, p. 136.

40. R.B. Cathcart, 'Mediterranean Basin – Sahara Reclamation', *Speculations in Science and Technology*, Vol. 6, No. 2, 1983.

41. K. Mahmood, *Reservoir Sedimentation: Impact, Extent and Mitigation*, World Bank Technical Paper 71, 1987, p. 6.

42. Gleick (ed.), *Water in Crisis*, Table F.21; T. Palmer, *Endangered Rivers and the Conservation Movement*, University of California Press, Berkeley 1986; L. Lövgren, 'The Dams Debate in Sweden', in A.D. Usher (ed.), *Nordic Dam-building in the South: Proceedings of an International Conference in Stockholm 3–4 August, 1994*, SSNC, Stockholm 1994.

2

Rivers No More: The Environmental Effects of Dams

Despues de años mil, vuelve el río a su cubil.
(After a thousand years, the river returns to its original bed.)

Spanish proverb

Conservationist-philosopher Aldo Leopold had a 'shining adventure' canoeing through the 'milk and honey wilderness' of the Colorado River Delta in 1922. Leopold lyrically described the delta as a 'hundred miles of lovely desolation', a huge oasis of green lagoons, mesquite and willow amidst the thorny desert of northwest Mexico. He delighted in the quail, the snowstorms of egrets, fleets of cormorants, skittering mullets, avocets, yellow-legs, widgeon, teal, bobcats, coyotes, burro deer and, hidden among the trees and long grass, the jaguar, 'Despot of the Delta'.

Leopold never returned to the delta, fearing that he would find it despoiled. But it is unlikely that even in his most gloomy moments he foresaw just how complete the destruction would eventually be. Since Leopold's canoe trip the Colorado has been dammed and diverted so many times that the delta is a delta no more.

Since 1960, the Colorado has only reached the sea during rare flood years. More usually it ends somewhere just south of the US border in a few stagnant pools of pesticide- and salt-laced agricultural run-off. Besides decimating the waterfowl and mammals of the delta, the loss of the freshwater and nutrients flushing into the Colorado estuary has contributed to the near collapse of a once highly productive fishery and the virtual extinction of the vaquita, the world's smallest porpoise.

The human communities of the delta are as blighted as the eco-system that once supported them. Fishing villages are suffering deep economic recession. The indigenous Cucapá, or 'people of the river', who once fished, farmed and hunted the delta, have been reduced from

The Main Environmental Impacts of Dams

A. Impacts due to existence of dam and reservoir

1. Upstream change from river valley to reservoir.
2. Changes in downstream morphology of riverbed and banks, delta, estuary and coastline due to altered sediment load.
3. Changes in downstream water quality: effects on river temperature, nutrient load, turbidity, dissolved gases, concentration of heavy metals and minerals.
4. Reduction of biodiversity due to the blocking of the movement of organisms and because of changes 1, 2 and 3 above.

Superimposed upon the above impacts may be:

B. Impacts due to pattern of dam operation

1. Changes in downstream hydrology:
    (a) change in total flows;
    (b) change in seasonal timing of flows;
    (c) short-term fluctuations in flows;
    (d) change in extreme high and low flows.
2. Changes in downstream morphology caused by altered flow pattern.
3. Changes in downstream water quality caused by altered flow pattern.
4. Reduction in riverine/riparian/floodplain habitat diversity, especially because of elimination of floods.

a population of 1,200 a century ago to just 40 or 50 families barely subsisting on a diet of beans and junk food.[1]

Environmental experiments

While the death of the Colorado Delta was completely foreseeable – impound and divert all of a river's flow and it is quite obvious that the river will run dry – most of the impacts of river engineering are extremely difficult, and in many cases impossible, to predict with certainty. Theories on the ecological dynamics of rivers are mainly based on short-term studies of small temperate watersheds, so there is a limited understanding of the functioning of large rivers in temperate regions – or of rivers of any size in the tropics. Most of the major rivers in Europe and the US were diked, straightened, dredged and dammed long before their ecology or hydrology had been seriously studied. In the tropics, where research funds are few, often the only scientific study of a river system has been done to find where best to dam it.[2]

As every river is unique in terms of its flow patterns, the landscapes it flows through and the species it supports, so the design and operating pattern of every dam is unique, as are the effects the dam has on the river and its associated ecosystems. While the great majority of the world's large dams and all of the major dams have been completed within the last six decades, some of the environmental effects of a dam may not be realized for hundreds of years after construction.[3] A dam can thus be regarded as a huge, long-term and largely irreversible environmental experiment without a control.

The two main categories of environmental impacts of dams, those which are inherent to dam construction and those which are due to the specific mode of operation of each dam, are outlined in the box on p. 30. The most significant consequence of this myriad of complex and interconnected environmental disruptions is that they tend to fragment the riverine ecosystem, isolating populations of species living up and downstream of the dam and cutting off migrations and other species' movements. Because almost all dams reduce normal flooding, they also fragment ecosystems by isolating the river from its floodplain, turning what fish biologists term a 'floodplain river' into a 'reservoir river'.[4] The elimination of the benefits provided by natural flooding may be the single most ecologically damaging impact of a dam. This fragmentation of river ecosystems has undoubtedly resulted in a massive reduction in the number of species in the world's watersheds.

Some of the environmental effects of dams can benefit certain species. For example, impounding a reservoir will create habitat for lake fish, and warm water released from a reservoir can increase the abundance of species which failed to thrive in the cool river. But because dams alter the conditions to which local ecosystems have adapted, the overall impact of a dam will almost without exception be to reduce species diversity.

No one has yet managed to assess with any accuracy the global extent of the fragmentation of river ecosystems by dams and water diversions. Two Swedish ecologists, however, have estimated the degree of damage to river systems in the US, Canada, Europe and the former USSR. Mats Dynesius and Christer Nilsson of the University of Umeå found that fully 77 per cent of the total water discharge of the 139 largest river systems in these countries is 'strongly or moderately affected by fragmentation of the river channels by dams and by water regulation resulting from reservoir operation, interbasin diversion and irrigation'. 'As a result of habitat destruction and obstruction to organism dispersal,' Dynesius and Nilsson conclude, 'many riverine species may have become extinct over vast areas, whereas populations of others have become fragmented and run the risk of future extinction.'[5]

Flooding for Posterity

> We're going to save all this for posterity. We're going to cover it up with water so that no one can disturb it.
>
> Comment by Brazilian dam engineer viewing scenic stretch of river to be flooded by Cachoeira Porteira Dam, 1984

The permanent inundation of forests, wetlands and wildlife is perhaps the most obvious ecological effect of a dam. Reservoirs have flooded vast areas – at least 400,000 square kilometres have been lost worldwide. Yet it is not only the amount of land lost which is important, but also its quality: river and floodplain habitats are some of the world's most diverse ecosystems. Plants and animals which are closely adapted to valley bottom habitats can often not survive along the edge of a reservoir. Dams also tend to be built in remote areas which are the last refuge for species that have been displaced by development in other regions. No one has any idea how many species of plants and animals are now extinct because their last habitat was flooded by a dam, but the number is likely far from negligible. As well as destroying habitat, reservoirs can also cut off migratory routes across the valley and along the river. Because it isolates populations, this ecosystem fragmentation also leads to the risks of inbreeding from a smaller genetic pool.

The five-dam Mahaweli megascheme in Sri Lanka, the main purpose of which is to expand irrigation in previously forested areas, has submerged and turned into agricultural land the habitat of at least seven endangered and two threatened animal species, the purple-faced langur and the toque macaque, both of which only occur on the island. One of the endangered species is the elephant, 800 of which lived in the project area. An important migratory route for the elephants has been cut off by reservoirs and canals, and the animals have now become a dangerous pest for the farmers who have been brought into the area, reducing the survival chances of the remaining animals.[6]

It is often not just the forests within the reservoir area, around the dam site and transmission lines and in the areas slated to be converted to agriculture which are lost when a dam is built in a forested area. In many cases farmers displaced by a reservoir have had to clear forests further up the sides of the valley to grow their crops and build new homes. The access to previously remote areas allowed by new roads and reservoirs can also accelerate deforestation: every large dam which has been built in a forest area in Thailand has attracted loggers as well as developers who have built golf courses and resorts along the edges of reservoirs.[7]

The number of fish species which thrive in the relatively uniform habitats created by reservoirs is only a tiny fraction of the number which have evolved in the diverse niches provided by rivers. Because few areas have economically valuable fish adapted to the still waters of an artificial lake, fishery departments across the world have introduced into reservoirs a handful of species – mainly types of tilapia and carp in the tropics, and trout, bass and catfish in temperate regions – which can be reared in hatcheries and can support reservoir fisheries. These introductions, which compete with those native species that persist in the reservoir, and also spread far upstream and downstream of the dam, have greatly magnified the effects of dams and diversions in hastening the decline and extinction of fish species around the world.[8]

As well as flooding and fragmenting some of the world's best wildlife habitats, reservoirs have also inundated some of the world most beautiful and spectacular river scenery. Probably the greatest loss of the planet's scenic heritage to a reservoir was the inundation of the Sete Quedas waterfall at Guáira on the Brazilian–Paraguayan border, now just a rock formation at the bottom of Itaipú Reservoir. At Guáira the mighty Paraná suddenly narrowed to a width of just 60 metres – less than a tenth as wide as the Horseshoe Falls at Niagara – and then thundered over 18 separate cataracts each more than 30 metres high. More water surged and boiled through the rocks and whirlpools of Sete Quedas than any other waterfall in the world – about half as much again as over both falls at Niagara combined. 'A more imposing spectacle can scarcely be conceived,' a nineteenth-century French traveller wrote of Sete Quedas.[9]

Dams and Geology: Morphological Effects

> I find that the water, that falls at the foot of dams of rivers … carries away from the foot of the dam all the material on which it strikes as it falls.
>
> Leonardo da Vinci, *Notebooks*, *c.* 1510

All rivers carry sediments eroded from the soils and rocks over which the river, and the water flowing into it, pass. All dams and reservoirs trap some of this sediment, especially the heavy gravels and cobbles, and thus starve the river downstream of its normal sediment load. Large reservoirs and dams without low-level outlets will typically trap more than 90 per cent, and sometimes almost 100 per cent, of incoming sediment. Clear water below a dam is said to be 'hungry': it will seek to recapture its sediment load by eroding the bed and banks of the river. The sediment picked up by the hungry river may be deposited further downstream, and erosion (degradation) of the riverbed below the dam will then be replaced by its raising (aggradation) further downstream.

Over time all the easily erodible material on the riverbed below the dam will eventually be removed, and the bed will become 'armoured' with rocks. An armoured riverbed below a dam does not have the gravels needed for spawning of fish such as salmon and as habitat for benthic (river-bottom) invertebrae such as insects, molluscs and crustaceans. These benthic creatures are an important food source for fish and waterfowl. Meanwhile aggradation of the channel may also reduce the area of gravels by smothering them in silt.[10]

Riverbeds are typically eroded by several metres within a decade of first closing a dam. Within nine years of the closure of Hoover Dam, hungry water had washed away more than 110 million cubic metres of material from the first 145 kilometres of riverbed below the dam, lowering it in places by more than 4 metres. The deepening of the Colorado has undermined bridge foundations and rendered useless numerous intakes for the supply of municipal and irrigation water. Riverbed deepening will also lower the groundwater table along a river, causing a drop in the level of water in wells on the floodplain and threatening to dry out local vegetation. The related erosion of riverbanks – the banks of the Colorado below Hoover have in places been scoured back as much as 15 metres in a year – can undermine riverside property and structures such as road embankments and flood control levees.[11]

In the long run, the major impact on the downstream river channel will often be to make it deeper and narrower, turning wide-braided, meandering rivers with gravel bars and beaches and multiple channels into relatively straight single channels. The regulation by dams of the Platte River in Nebraska, for example, has shrunk one stretch of its channel by three-quarters, from a width of one kilometre late in the last century to just 265 metres in the 1960s. Reduced channel capacity is especially likely where undammed tributaries wash their sediments into a regulated river which no longer has the regular flood flows that would previously have dislodged them.[12] Reducing a braided river to a single channel will greatly diminish the diversity of plants and animals it can support.

Hungry plains

> ...especially in the part called the Delta, it seems to me that if ... the Nile no longer floods it, then, for all time to come, the Egyptians will suffer.
>
> Herodotus, *History*, *c.* 442 BC

Before the High Aswan Dam the Nile carried an average of some 124 million tonnes of sediment to the sea each year and deposited another 9.5 million tonnes or so on the narrow floodplain and delta which are home to almost all of Egypt's people. In ancient times the Nile's silt was regarded with awe: soil scientist Daniel J. Hillel writes that it 'was considered the prototype and mother lode of all material substances'.[13] Today more than 98 per cent of the Nile's sediment drops to the bottom of the vast Nasser Reservoir. The loss of the silt – which is low in nitrogen but rich in silica, aluminium, iron and other vital trace elements – is believed by many to have had a serious effect on Egyptian agriculture, resulting in the need for ever larger amounts of artificial fertilizers and a long-term decline in trace element levels in soils. The silt also used to add around one millimetre to the depth of the soil every year.[14]

The loss of sediment is particularly significant in the delta, an area the size of Northern Ireland which constitutes two-thirds of Egypt's cropland. Deltas are formed by the accumulation of tens of thousands of years of deposits of river sediments, partly counteracted by their settling and compaction and by erosion from the sea. Remove the incoming sediment, and the land will subside and be eaten away. The slow accretion of the Nile Delta was reversed with the construction of the Delta Barrage in 1868. Other dams built on the Nile throughout the twentieth century further reduced the sediment reaching the delta, but it was only with the building of the High Dam that the Nile all but ceased to wash sediments into the Mediterranean. Today the Nile no longer has a true delta.

Over the last millennium the Nile has reached the Mediterranean through two distributaries – the Rosetta and Damietta Promontories – which have built their own 'sub-deltas'. The most severe erosion has been on the western side of Rosetta Promontory, which retreated by nearly 6 kilometres between 1900 and 1991, washing out to sea a lighthouse and a resort and flooding coastal villages. A replacement lighthouse built 1 kilometre inland in 1970 is now 'offshore a long distance away from land'. Before the closure of the High Dam in 1966 the rate of retreat was around 20 metres per year; by 1991 the annual rate had accelerated to 240 metres.

Most of the rest of the delta coastline is being eaten away at an annual rate of around 5 to 8 metres. Increasing soil exhaustion and salinity (both related to the loss of silt and the expansion of perrenial irrigation after the Nile was regulated by the High Aswan Dam), the long-term rise in the level of the Mediterranean due to global warming, and the subsidence of the Egyptian coast because of geological factors compound the crisis facing the delta.[15]

The sediment discharged through the Mississippi Delta has fallen by more than half since 1953 mainly because of the huge dams built on the Missouri (the Mississippi's main tributary and sediment supplier). A massive programme of stabilizing the channel of the Mississippi with rip-rap (boulders) and concrete for navigation and flood control purposes has also deprived the river of the sediments that it would previously have torn away from its banks. The result of sediment deprivation, together with land subsidence due to oil and gas extraction, is that 10,000 hectares of Louisiana disappear into the sea each year.

Author John McPhee describes one of the Mississippi Delta parishes as 'coming to pieces like an old rotted cloth'.[16]

Hungry coast

The consequences of robbing rivers of sediment extends out from their mouths to affect long stretches of coastline which now have to face erosion from the waves without the sediments from the land which once replenished them. Sediments move along shorelines, washing on and off beaches with waves and tides, within geographic units known as 'littoral cells'. These include the sediment sources (mainly rivers and cliff erosion), the shoreline along which the sediments migrate, and their final sinks (mainly currents to deep water and submarine canyons).

Since the 1920s dams have reduced by four-fifths the sediment reaching the coast of Southern California. This has had dramatic effects on the region's beaches, which are now partly maintained at great expense with sand dredged from offshore. The beaches in a 90-kilometre-long littoral cell north of San Diego were more than 300 metres wide in 1922. Today some have entirely disappeared. The beaches once protected cliffs from wave erosion; their disappearance has led to cliff collapses which caused millions of dollars of damage to property and roads during the 1980s.[17]

One of the most dramatic examples of dam-caused coastal erosion is along the Bight of Benin east of the mouth of the Volta River in Ghana. Akosombo Dam has virtually halted the supply of sediment to the Volta estuary and so to the eastward-flowing coastal current. The shoreline of neighbouring Togo and Benin is now being eaten away at a rate of 10 to 15 metres per year. The sea advanced by 20 metres in places during a single storm in 1984, taking with it a large chunk of the main Ghana–Togo–Benin highway. A project to strengthen the Togolese coast with groynes and boulders has cost $3.5 million for each kilometre protected, yet even the project's supervisors admitted that by stopping sediments being washed off one stretch of shore it would reduce the beach-building material available further along the coast and so accelerate coastal erosion in Benin.[18]

Dirty Dams: Effects on Water Quality

> In an imperfect world, hydroelectric power is a form of energy which has the fewest imperfections of all. It is virtually non-polluting.
>
> Robert Bourassa, *Power from the North*, 1983

The chemical, thermal and physical changes which flowing water undergoes when it is stilled can seriously contaminate a reservoir and the river downstream. The extent of deterioration in water quality is in general related to the retention time of the reservoir – its storage capacity in relation to the amount of water flowing into it. Water in a small headpond behind a run-of-river dam will undergo very little or no deterioration; that stored for many months or even years behind a major dam may be lethal to most life in the reservoir and in the river for tens of kilometres or more below the dam.

Water released from deep in a reservoir behind a high dam is usually cooler in summer and warmer in winter than river water, while water from outlets near the top of a reservoir will tend to be warmer than river water all year round. Warming or cooling the natural river affects the amount of dissolved oxygen and suspended solids it contains and influences the chemical reactions which take place in it.[19] Altering natural seasonal changes in temperature can also disrupt the lifecycles of aquatic creatures – breeding, hatching and the metamorphosing of larvae, for example, often depend on thermal cues.[20]

The pre-dam temperatures of the Colorado in Glen Canyon varied seasonally from highs of around 27 degrees centigrade to lows of near freezing. However, the temperature of water flowing through the intakes at Glen Canyon Dam, 70 metres below the full reservoir level, varies only a couple of degrees around the year with an average of less than 8 degrees centigrade. The Colorado is now too cold for the successful reproduction of native fish as far as 400 kilometres below the dam – although introduced trout thrive in the cold water.[21]

Relatively warm winter releases from reservoirs in cold climates will inhibit the formation of ice downstream. Reduced ice cover makes hazardous or impossible the use of frozen rivers as winter roads: in northern Scandinavia, for example, dams mean that the Sami people can no longer use many of their traditional winter reindeer herding routes which follow frozen rivers.[22] Cold winter air passing over the relative warmth of some of the huge Russian and Canadian reservoirs can cause long spells of freezing fog.[23]

In the same way that reservoirs trap river sediments, they also trap most of the nutrients carried by rivers. During warm weather, algae are likely to proliferate near the surface of a highly nutrient-enriched, or eutrophic, reservoir. Through photosynthesis the algae consume the reservoir nutrients and produce large amounts of oxygen. Summer releases from the surface layer, or epilimnion, of a reservoir will thus tend to be warm, nutrient-depleted, high in dissolved oxygen, and may be thick with algae. High levels of algae can provide food for fish but also give water an unpleasant smell and taste, clog water supply intakes, coat gravel beds and restrict recreation.[24] Massive algal blooms in the shallow, stagnant reservoirs of the ex-USSR have rendered their water unfit for either household or industrial use.[25]

When algae in a reservoir die they sink to its bottom layer, or hypolimnion, where they decay and in doing so consume the already limited hypolimnion oxygen (there is usually not enough light for photosynthesis at the bottom of a reservoir). The acidity of this oxygen-depleted water often renders it capable of dissolving minerals, such as iron and manganese, from the lake bed. Warm weather releases from a dam with low-level outlets will thus be cold, oxygen-poor, nutrient-rich and acidic, and may contain damagingly high mineral concentrations. The presence of an adequate level of dissolved oxygen in a river is one of the main indicators of good water quality. Water poor in dissolved oxygen can 'suffocate' aquatic organisms and make water unfit to drink. Dissolved oxygen, furthermore, is vital to enable bacteria to break down organic detritus and pollution.

Young reservoirs

During the first years after a reservoir is filled the decomposition of submerged vegetation and soils can drastically deplete the level of oxygen in the water. Rotting organic matter can also lead to releases of huge amounts of the greenhouse gases methane and carbon dioxide (for more on this see Chapter 5, pp. 141–5). Reservoirs often 'mature' within a decade or so, although in the tropics it may take many decades or even centuries for most of the organic matter to decompose.[26] Thorough clearing of vegetation in the submergence zone before the reservoir is filled can reduce this problem, but because it is difficult and prohibitively expensive, especially for large reservoirs, this is usually only partially done.

The most notorious examples of the large-scale flooding of forest have occurred in South America. Brokopondo Dam in Surinam submerged 1,500 square kilometres of rainforest – 1 per cent of the country. The decomposition of the organic matter in its shallow reservoir severely deoxygenated the water and caused massive emissions of hydrogen sulphide, a corrosive and foul-smelling gas. Workers at the dam had to wear masks for two years after the reservoir started to fill in 1964. The cost of repairing damage done to Brokopondo's turbines by the acidic, deoxygenated water was estimated in 1977 to have totalled $4 million, more than 7 per cent of the total project cost.[27] Studies carried out in 1967 showed that oxygen levels in the river only began to recover around 110 kilometres downstream of the dam, depriving many riverside communities of drinking water and fish.[28]

Despite a legal requirement to clear vegetation from all areas to be submerged, the Brazilian electricity utility Eletronorte cleared less than a fifth of the 2,250 square kilometres of rainforest inundated by Tucuruí and only a token 2 per cent of the 3,150 square kilometres of forest inundated by Balbina Dam.[29] Clearing all of the Tucuruí reservoir would have increased the project's cost by an estimated $440 million, or 9 per cent.[30] Because Balbina's turbine intakes are at the very bottom of the 50-metre-high dam, the Uatumã River, a north-bank tributary of the Amazon, is receiving almost totally deoxygenated water from the reservoir.[31] The consumption of oxygen by decomposing vegetation in the newly filled reservoir behind Yacyretá Dam on the border between Argentina and Paraguay is believed to have killed the more than 120,000 dead fish found downstream after the first test of the dam's turbines in August 1994.[32]

Nutrient-enriched tropical reservoirs are particularly prone to colonization by aquatic plants. Mats of floating plants can impede fishing boats and nets, block out light for other organisms, clog turbines and provide an excellent habitat for disease vectors such as mosquitoes and the snails which host the schistosomiasis parasite. Through transpiration, aquatic plants can also lower reservoir levels: losses of water from evaporation and transpiration in weed-covered reservoirs can be up to six times higher than those from evaporation in open waters.[33]

Reservoir operators' most dreaded weed is the water hyacinth (*Eichhornia crassipes*), a native of Amazonia which is now found throughout the tropics. Water hyacinths can proliferate at an extraordinary rate in eutrophic reservoirs, largely stymieing efforts to eradicate them by physically removing the plants or by spraying them with herbicides (the latter bringing in its wake its own inevitable problems). Two years after Brokopondo began to fill, over half its reservoir was covered with water hyacinth. The plant was partially brought under control by a long-term programme of aerial spraying with the carcinogenic herbicide 2,4-D, which also poisoned many other plants and animals.[34] African reservoirs have also suffered serious infestations of water hyacinths and other plants. At one point a fifth of the surface of Kariba Reservoir – more than 1,000 square kilometres – was smothered by aquatic plants.[35]

Scientists have only relatively recently become aware of what now appears to be a pervasive reservoir contamination problem, the accumulation of high levels of mercury in fish. Mercury is naturally present in a harmless inorganic form in many soils. Bacteria feeding on the decomposing matter under a new reservoir, however, transform this inorganic mercury into methylmercury, a central nervous system toxin. The methylmercury is absorbed by plankton and other creatures at the bottom of the aquatic food chain. As the methylmercury passes up the food chain it becomes increasingly concentrated in the bodies of the animals eating contaminated prey. Through this process of bioaccumulation, levels of methylmercury in the tissues of large fish-eating fish at the top of the reservoir food chain can be several times higher than in the small organisms at the bottom of the chain.

Elevated mercury levels in reservoir fish were first noticed in South Carolina in the late 1970s. Since then they have been recorded in Illinois, northern Canada, Finland and Thailand. The problem is in fact probably much more widespread than the few studies done suggest: scientists from Canada's Department of Fisheries and Oceans say that fish mercury concentrations 'have increased in all reservoirs for which pre- and post-impoundment data have been collected'.[36]

The best researched case of reservoir methylmercury is at the La Grande hydrocomplex in Quebec, part of the huge James Bay Project. Ten years after the La Grande 2 Reservoir was first impounded, mercury levels in pike and another predatory fish called walleye had risen to six times their pre-reservoir level and showed no signs of levelling off. As fish are a major part of the traditional diet of the local Cree native people, mercury levels in their bodies have risen dangerously. By 1984, six years after La Grande 2 Dam was completed, 64 per cent of the Cree living on the La Grande estuary had blood mercury levels far exceeding the World Health Organization tolerance limit.[37]

Turning sweet water to salt

Because they greatly multiply the surface area of water exposed to the rays of the sun, dams in hot climates can lead to the evaporation of huge amounts of water. In the region of 170 cubic kilometres of water evaporates from the world's reservoirs every year, more than 7 per cent of the total amount of freshwater consumed by all human activities. The annual average of 11.2 cubic kilometres of water evaporated from Nasser Reservoir behind the High Aswan Dam is around 10 per cent of the water stored in the reservoir and is roughly equal to the total withdrawals of water for residential and commercial use throughout Africa.[38]

The massive amount of water evaporated from the reservoirs behind Hoover and the other dams on the Colorado – one-third of the river's flow is evaporated from reservoirs – is one of the reasons why the salinity of the river has risen to damaging and costly levels.[39] High salt concentrations are poisonous to aquatic organisms and they corrode pipes and machinery: the increased Colorado River salinity costs Southern California's water users millions of dollars each year.[40]

Soils are often naturally saline in arid areas like the US West and are made even saltier when irrigated. Irrigation water percolates through the soils, picking up salts, then returns to the river. On the Colorado the same water may be used for irrigation 18 times over. The salinity of the Colorado at Imperial Dam, just north of the Mexican border, increased from an average of 785 parts per million (ppm) between 1941 and 1969, to over 900 ppm in 1990. It is predicted to exceed 1,200 ppm after the year 2000.[41] The US standard for drinking water is 500 ppm.

In the early 1960s, a surge in salt levels caused a dramatic decline in yields on fields irrigated with Colorado water in Mexicali, one of Mexico's most productive agricultural regions. Mexico City made a formal protest to Washington, DC, and finally in 1974 the two countries signed an agreement under which the salinity of the Colorado River at the Mexican border must not exceed 1,024 ppm. The Bureau of Reclamation's 'salinity control program', initiated after the treaty with Mexico, had cost taxpayers $660 million by 1993. The centrepiece of the programme is a money-sucking, technological non-fix – one of the world's largest and most expensive desalination plants. The plant, built at Yuma, Arizona, cost $256 million. It began operation in May 1992, but was closed again in January 1993 after floods destroyed some of the drains bringing it saline water. Federal budget cuts mean that the plant may never start up again. 'In a region covered with water-reclamation projects of fabulous expense and questionable usefulness,' wrote Martin Van Der Werf in the *Arizona Republic*, 'the Yuma plant may be the biggest laughing stock of all.'[42]

They Shall Not Pass: Dams and Migratory Fish

> You fish people are very skilful in getting these fish into cans. Cannot you be just as skilful in getting these fish to be raised up over a dam?
>
> Comment at public hearing on a proposal for the first dam on the mainstream of the Columbia River, 1924

The annual run of adult salmon and steelhead trout in the huge Columbia River basin – which covers an area larger than France – is estimated to have averaged between 10 and 16 million fish before non-native settlers first arrived in the nineteenth century. Today, after decades of decline due overwhelmingly to the 130 or so dams in the basin, only some 1.5 million salmon and steelhead enter the Columbia each year, and around three-quarters of these are hatchery-reared, rather than wild, river-spawned fish. The National Marine Fisheries Service have estimated the cost of salmon fishery losses due to dams in the Columbia Basin for the period between 1960 and 1980 alone at $6.5 billion.[43]

Salmon and steelhead are anadromous fish, meaning that they are born in freshwater, migrate to the ocean to mature and then return to rivers to spawn, and, in the case of most salmon, die. Salmon always return to the same stretch of river or shallow lake bed where they hatched. Fish which return to different rivers at different times of the year are known as 'stocks'; different stocks are genetically distinct and generally only breed with other fish from the same stock. Out of the original 400 or so salmon and steelhead stocks of the US Pacific coast only 214 remain, out of which 169 are at high or moderate risk of extinction.[44]

The simplest way to wipe out large numbers of salmon stocks is to build a dam without fish ladders or other means of allowing salmon to surmount it and reach spawning sites upstream. The massive Grand Coulee Dam was built without any fish passage facilities and cut off from the sea nearly 2,000 kilometres of salmon spawning grounds on the upper Columbia, eliminating a fishery worth a quarter of a million dollars a year. An estimated 30 to 50 per cent of the original anadromous spawning habitat on the Columbia Basin is now either submerged under reservoirs or blocked by dams without adequate bypass facilities.[45]

While most adult salmon swimming upstream can negotiate their way up fish ladders, the slackwater of reservoirs provides a much more formidable barrier to their offspring. The downstream migration of the juvenile salmon, or smolts, can be fatally delayed by the time needed to drift and swim through multiple reservoirs – if the smolts do not reach the sea within around 15 days after spawning they may lose their downstream swimming behaviour and their ability to change from a freshwater to saltwater environment. During years of relatively low flows, smolts from the upper Snake River, the Columbia's main tributary, can now take up to 39 days to swim to the sea, compared with less than three days before the dams were built.[46]

Besides the effects of a delayed journey to the sea, the smolts also face the threat of being eaten by the many predator fish in reservoirs or by birds which find rich pickings where the often stunned fish emerge at the foot of dams.[47] The surface layer of a reservoir can become so warm that it is lethal to young salmon, while the cooler, deep water can be fatal due to oxygen depletion. The concentration of pollutants in reservoirs can also add to the stress suffered by migrating smolts and increase their susceptibility to disease. Yet another lethal obstacle to both adults and smolts is 'gas-bubble disease', the piscine version of the 'bends' suffered by scuba divers. Gas-bubble disease is caused by the supersaturation of water with atmospheric gases at the bottom of spillways during high-flow years. The cumulative impact of these threats is that more than 95 per cent of upper Snake River smolts may die before reaching the ocean.[48]

The pattern of destruction on the Columbia and the other rivers of the US Pacific seaboard has been repeated elsewhere. The Atlantic salmon population in the US declined from half a million in the early eighteenth century to a few thousand, mainly hatchery-reared, fish in the 1990s.[49] By the end of the nineteenth century, dams had eliminated Atlantic salmon from France's Dordogne, Meuse and Moselle. During the twentieth century salmon have disappeared from the Garonne and the Seine. The Loire and its tributary the Allier are now the only long French rivers which can sustain wild salmon.[50]

Other anadromous species such as lamprey eels and sturgeon have also suffered calamitous declines due to the loss of habitat behind dams. The number of lampreys in the Columbia has fallen to less than 1 per cent of the 400,000 recorded when dams were first built in the lower basin. Dams and pollution have reduced the numbers of the pallid sturgeon of the Mississippi–Missouri to such low levels that it is no longer certain they are reproducing in the wild.[51]

The impacts of dams on migratory fish other than salmon and a handful of other species are largely unknown but have probably been just as severe as those on salmonids. The hilsa, a migratory fish of great commercial importance in South Asia, was deprived of 60 per cent of its previous spawning areas on the Indus by Pakistan's Gulam Mohammed Dam; while the Stanley Dam wiped out the hilsa from the Cauvery River in south India.[52] The Sardar Sarovar Dam is likely to eradicate the Narmada hilsa fishery, probably the most productive left in India. Although the hilsa is not thought to migrate as far upstream as the dam, the drastic reduction in the flow of the Narmada due to diversions for irrigation would make its spawning migration impossible. The giant freshwater prawn, another commercially important migratory species found in the Narmada, would likely suffer a similar fate. The other important hilsa fishery in western India, in the estuary of the Tapi River, just south of the Narmada, has already been affected by the Ukai Dam.[53]

The long-term survival of river dolphins, found in South America and Asia, is seriously threatened by dams which form impassable barriers and fragment the already small populations of dolphins into genetically isolated groups. The drowning of river habitat, downstream changes in river water quality, and the reduction in the numbers of their fish prey are also killing dolphins. The population of the Indus dolphin, the bhulan, is now split up by dams and barrages into five or less isolated groups of which only two may be genetically viable. The Three Gorges Dam could deal the final blow to the Yangtze river dolphin, the baiji, one of the world's most endangered species, with only 150 to 300 animals left. Other aquatic mammals such as the manatee also suffer habitat fragmentation and other harmful impacts when dams are built.[54]

Foil'd Wanderers: Hydrological Effects

> But the majestic River floated on,
> Out of the mist and hum of that low land...
> Oxus, forgetting the bright speed he had
> In his high mountain cradle in Pamere,
> A foil'd circuitous wanderer...
>
> Matthew Arnold, 'Sohrab and Rustum', 1853

Riverine ecosystems and human societies have evolved with, and often become dependent upon, seasonal changes in river flows. All storage dams alter to some extent these seasonal patterns, in most cases ironing out hydrological extremes by storing floods and increasing dry period flows. The exact nature of the impacts, however, will depend on the design, purpose and operating regime of the dam and the size of the reservoir.

Dams and barrages used to divert water, especially for irrigation, reduce, sometimes calamitously, the downstream flow. Undoubtedly the worst ecological disaster caused by river diversion is the shrinking of the Aral Sea in Central Asia. Evaporation from the sea used to be matched by inflows of water from the Amu Darya and Syr Darya rivers (the Oxus and Jaxartes of classical times). Since the 1960s, however, the building of an extensive network of dams and canals for cotton irrigation has virtually eliminated the flow of water into the sea. In 1995, the area of the Aral Sea was only 30,000 square kilometres, compared to some 64,500 square kilometres in 1960. Its volume has dropped by more than three-quarters. A commercial fishing industry which once supported 60,000 workers ground to a halt in 1982 with what was left of the once freshwater lake now more saline than the oceans. By the early 1990s, 20 of the 24 fish species once caught in the sea had disappeared; the number of bird species found in the Amu Darya Delta had declined from 319 to 168, the delta forests had died, and only 30 out of 70 species of mammals remained.[55]

The salt-encrusted, dried-up bed of the lake is now known as the Akum Desert. Wind-blown dust from the new desert, laden with heavy metals and other toxins from fertilizers and pesticides used upstream, has been detected as far away as Alaska, and together with the heavily contaminated water supply has had a catastrophic effect on the health of millions of people living around the sea. The republic of Karakalpakia which surrounds the southern end of the sea has the highest rates of infant and maternal mortality in the former Soviet Union. The incidence of typhoid fever, hepatitis, kidney disease and chronic gastritis in the republic has rocketed as much as sixtyfold. In the town of Muynak, nearly 70 per cent of the remaining population of 2,000 had 'pre-cancerous conditions' in 1994, according to the town's medical research centre. Life expectancy in Muynak tumbled from 64 years in 1987 to 57 in 1991. More than 80 per cent of women in the area suffer from anaemia and 12 kinds of pesticides have been found in their breast milk.[56]

The USSR Ministry of Water Management wanted to increase the area of cotton growing in Central Asia so that they could justify building more canals and thus secure their share of government spending: the inevitable decline in the Aral Sea was not only predicted but justified by the planners. A map issued by the USSR Academy of Sciences in 1981 showed the estimated area of dried up Aral Sea bed in the year 2000 being used to grow rice. In 1987, government water planners proclaimed in a magazine article: 'May the Aral Sea die in a beautiful manner. It is useless.'[57]

Estuarine impacts

Some 80 per cent of the world's fish catch comes from continental shelves.[58] Many of these fisheries are dependent on the volume and timing of the nutrients and freshwater discharged by rivers as well as on estuary habitats. Almost all the fish and shellfish caught along the US coast of the Gulf of Mexico, for example, live in estuaries for at least part of their lifecycle.[59] The productivity of the Grand Banks of Newfoundland, one of the world's greatest fishing grounds, is directly related to the amount and seasonality of freshwater and nutrients flowing out the mouth of the St Lawrence.[60] The alteration of estuarine flows by dams and diversions is therefore, together with overfishing, a major cause of the precipitous decline in many sea fisheries.

Dams and diversions have done to the commercial fisheries of the saltwater Black, Azov and Caspian seas almost as much damage as they did to those of the freshwater Aral Sea. The discharge of the Volga into the Caspian Sea has been reduced by almost 70 per cent; that of the Dniester, Dnieper and Don into the Black and Azov seas by around half. The salinity in the estuaries of these rivers has increased by up to four-fold and that in their deltas up to ten-fold. The most valuable commercial fisheries in the seas have now been reduced by 90 to 98 per cent. Sturgeon catches in the Caspian Sea are only 1 to 2 per cent of historical levels and have been totally eradicated in the northwestern Black Sea and Sea of Azov (a northeastern appendage of the Black Sea). Michael Rozengurt, a Russian oceanographer now living in the US, estimates the combined economic losses to the fishing industries of the Black, Azov and Caspian in the decade between 1977 and 1987 at $35 billion.[61]

Nutrients carried to sea during the flood season once caused a huge bloom of plankton at the mouth of the Nile. This plankton was grazed by great shoals of sardines which accounted for 30–40 per cent of the annual Egyptian sea catch. After the closure of the Aswan High Dam and the elimination of the annual flood, however, the sardine catch fell from 18,000 tonnes to less than a thousand tonnes in the late 1960s. The catch has since risen to a few thousand tonnes but this is attributed to improvements in fishing technology and greater numbers of boats. Shrimp catches at the mouth of the Nile decreased by two-thirds after the nutrient supplies were cut off. Landings of other fish in 1970 were 77 per cent below pre-dam levels.[62]

Estuarine mangrove forests are valuable nurseries for fish and shrimps as they provide cover and also food when they shed leaves, flowers, fruit and twigs. Nearshore fish catches in some tropical areas are proportional to the mangrove cover of the adjacent coast. Mangroves are also directly used by people for fuel, animal fodder and fibre. The 80 per cent reduction in the discharge through the Indus Delta because of dams and barrages in Pakistan and India has killed off almost all the delta's mangrove forests which once covered a quarter of a million hectares (although mangroves can tolerate salinity much better than other plant species, they still require freshwater to thrive).[63]

River plumbing

> The unregulated Colorado was a son of a bitch. It wasn't any good. It was either in flood or in trickle.
>
> Floyd Dominy, US Bureau of Reclamation Commissioner, 1969

The major hydrological impact of hydro dams is to impose on the river an unnatural pattern of flow variations. As Wallace Stegner puts it, 'a dammed river is not only stoppered like a bathtub, but it is turned on and off like a tap.'[64] In Quebec, peak electricity consumption occurs during winter when river flows are naturally at their lowest because water is locked up in snow and ice. To meet the demand for electricity during cold weather, dams and diversions have increased the winter flow on the La Grande River by eight times (from 500 to 4,000 cubic metres per second) and in order to store water for the following winter have eradicated the spring flood (flow reduced from 5,000 to 1,500 cubic metres per second). Interbasin diversions compound the effects of dam operation on rivers: redirecting water from the Eastmain River into the La Grande to increase generation has doubled the La Grande's total average annual discharge into James Bay, while reducing by 90 per cent flows to the Eastmain estuary.[65]

Superimposed upon the seasonal post-dam pattern of downstream flows are short-term daily or even hourly fluctuations in river levels, sometimes of as much as several metres, due to releases to meet peak demands for power. The link between water releases and power demand means that river levels downstream of Glen Canyon now change not according to rainfall in the Colorado Basin but because of factors like the drop in electricity use on Sundays and public holidays. Releases from Glen Canyon Dam cause daily river level fluctuations of 1.5 metres compared to natural daily changes of a few tens of centimetres. Increases in demand for power from Kariba Dam on the Zambezi River can cause the downstream water level to rise by 5 metres in just half an hour.[66]

Flow alterations on this scale have numerous ecological consequences. Rapid water-level fluctuations speed up erosion downstream and can wash away river-bank trees, shrubs and grasses. Without the riparian vegetation to hold it in place, the bank then erodes even faster. Riparian vegetation provides food and shelter for riverside creatures and branches on which birds such as kingfishers can wait for their prey to swim by. It also prevents the river becoming dangerously hot during the summer by providing shade. Furthermore, leaves and twigs falling into the river are an important source of food for insects and other aquatic fauna.

Rapid fluctuations in reservoir levels can prevent fish spawning by alternately exposing and submerging the favoured nesting areas in shallow waters. Nests of waterfowl may be similarly affected. The fluctuations also prevent riparian and marsh vegetation from growing along the reservoir shore and so render lifeless the nearshore shallows – usually the most biologically prolific areas of natural lakes and ponds.[67] The six hydro-reservoirs on the La Grande river have submerged some 83,000 kilometres of natural shorelines with their fringing woods and shrubs; the shores of the reservoirs, meanwhile, are broad, lifeless banks of mud, rock and dead trees.[68]

Cutting off the floodplain

> In my view, nature is awful and what we do is cure it.
>
> Camille Dagenais, former head of Canadian dam engineering firm SNC, 1985

Even if flood control is not an intended consequence of a project, a storage dam will almost always delay floods downstream and reduce the size of average flood peaks, commonly by more than a quarter (even a flood control dam, however, may have little effect upon extremely large and infrequent floods – making the 'flood control' offered by dams often dangerously deceptive for people who move onto the downstream floodplain). The Warragamba Dam in Australia, for example, reduced the 'mean annual flood' (a flood likely to recur on average every 2.3 years) by more than half, while the size of the flood likely to recur every 50 years barely changed.[69]

River and floodplain ecosystems are closely adapted to the annual cycle of flooding and drying. Many species depend on seasonal droughts or pulses of nutrients or water to give the signals to start reproduction, hatching, migration or other important lifecycle stages. Annual floods replenish wetlands not only with water but also with nutrients, while flooded manure from both domestic and wild animals on the floodplain enriches the river. Floods sweep fish eggs and fry into floodplain backwaters and lakes where they hatch and grow before joining the river again after the next annual floods. Adult fish and other aquatic animals such as turtles also follow the flood to take advantage of the new food sources offered in the submerged shrubs and woods.

For large floodplain rivers the floodplain is just as much a part of the river as the main channel itself. Most fish in the Amazon basin, for example, spend much of their lifecycle in the *várzea*, the tens of thousands of square kilometres of seasonally flooded forests and grasslands along Amazonian rivers. Some of the *várzea* forests are flooded for 10 months or more each year and some fish and other aquatic species may never make direct use of the main channel. Many Amazonian fish eat the fruits of flooded plants and play an important role in dispersing plant seeds. The renowned biodiversity of the Amazon rainforest is mainly in the *várzea* – the much greater area of dry forest is relatively unproductive and poor in species.[70]

What ecologist Peter Bayley terms the 'flood pulse advantage' is the main reason for the astonishing diversity and productivity of rivers and floodplains – on a per unit area basis the diversity of fauna in rivers is 65 times greater than in the seas. Annual floods on tropical rivers are estimated to produce fish yields a hundred times higher than in rivers without floodplains, and, on a per hectare basis, around four times more than in tropical lakes or reservoirs. Most freshwater fish species are found in rivers and floodplains: few are adapted only to life in lakes.[71]

It is generally recognized by biologists that dams and other flood control schemes are the most destructive of the many abuses which are causing the rapid disappearance of riverine and riparian species. At least 20 per cent of the world's 9,000 recognized freshwater fish species have become extinct, threatened or endangered in recent times.[72] Out of the 170 fish species endemic to the heavily dammed western US, 105 are officially listed as threatened or endangered or are being considered for such a listing. A further 17 Western fish species have been exterminated during this century.[73] The situation of some non-fish freshwater species is even worse: around two-thirds of the several hundred crayfish and freshwater mussel species in North America are on the danger list.[74] In the little-studied rivers of the tropics many species unknown to science have almost certainly been extinguished, or are about to be extinguished, by the building of dams (there are three times more known species in the Mekong than in the Mississippi, yet there have been *10,000 times* more scientific articles published on Mississippi fauna).[75]

The plants and animals of the river bank and floodplain also suffer when the plain no longer floods – or when the river is in spate at the wrong time. Unseasonably high discharges from dams on the Savannah River in Georgia, for example, killed almost all the bald cypress seedlings along the river banks. Studies on the floodplains of the Missouri and the Pongolo River in South Africa have both shown a reduction in the diversity of forest species after dam construction upstream. The forest on the floodplain of Kenya's Tana River appears to be slowly dying out as it loses its ability to regenerate because of the reduction in high floods due to a series of dams upstream.[76]

The 6,000-square-kilometre floodplain of the Kafue River in Zambia, known as the Kafue Flats, was once one of the richest wildlife habitats in the world. The Kafue, a main tributary of the Zambezi, was impounded in the 1970s by the Gorge Dam, which permanently flooded much of the Flats, and then by the Itezhitezhi Dam upstream, which eradicated the seasonal floods over the remaining part of the plain. Biologist Walter A. Sheppe visited the Flats before and after the dams. On his first visit in May 1967, 'the extensive annual floods were largely hidden by a dense growth of emergent grasses reaching to the horizon.' Large herds of antelope grazed the edges of the flooded area and zebra and wildebeest fed on the higher ground. The water and shore were dense with birds. Sixteen years later Sheppe returned to the same spot. This time the lowest part of the plain was covered by Gorge Reservoir and the rest was dry. The productive grasses that had depended on the seasonal floods had been replaced by aquatic plants on the open water, and on the dry former floodplain by a sparse cover of low grasses and scrub. There were few birds, relatively few antelope, and no zebra or wildebeest.[77]

The Mitigation Game

Dam builders and operators have been forced over the years to take a number of steps to mitigate the impact of their projects. Some mitigation measures can reduce some of the harmful impacts of dams, others may be worse than useless. Mitigation is especially dangerous when it misleads the public into believing that dam builders can re-create the characteristics of wild rivers and fisheries and so allows more dams to be built.

The most common mitigation measure taken in the US is to release more water from the reservoir than would be the case if the dam were operated only to maximize power or water storage. These 'instream flows' are usually spilled for the benefit of fish downstream but can sometimes be released in large 'flushing flows' intended to wash away harmful accumulations of boulders and gravel. The US Federal Energy Regulatory Commission now requires the operators of many privately owned hydrodams in the US to release instream flows as a condition of renewing their federal dam licences. The average loss in power generation for relicensed dams having to guarantee instream flows is around 8 per cent and in one case was almost a third. The drop in revenues due to lowered power production have forced some dam operators to close down their hydroplants and to give up plans for new projects.[78]

While instream flows can generally be assumed to be beneficial, they can also be little more than a palliative. In most countries instream flows are defined according to arbitrary criteria with little, if any, ecological basis. In Spain, for example, dams are supposed to release an 'ecological flow' which is 10 per cent of the average annual flow – an amount which would in most cases be totally insufficient to retain the ecological characteristics of the regulated rivers.[79] Instream flow requirements usually give little consideration to the importance of natural seasonal flow variations: releases which raise levels during normally dry spells can even do more harm than good. Instream flow requirements also rarely allow for the releases of the occasional exceptionally large flood flows which are an essential part of most fluvial ecosystems. In general, instream flows can mitigate the effects of dams but cannot re-create the essential variability and dynamism of a wild river.

One of the advantages of spilling extra water is that it will tend to increase downstream dissolved oxygen levels. Other measures can also be taken which increase oxygenation such as artificially aerating the water passing through turbines. Increasing dissolved oxygen is one of the cheapest forms of mitigation and appears generally to be effective, although as with instream flows there are problems in deciding exactly what dissolved oxygen level is the most beneficial and how to trade off its costs and benefits.[80]

Another form of mitigating the effects of a dam on downstream water quality is to regulate the temperature of releases by fitting the dam with intakes which can withdraw water from different levels of the reservoir. Around a hundred federal dams in the US are able to make so-called 'selective withdrawals'. In 1995, BuRec began work on a 35-storey-high steel selective withdrawal tower in the reservoir behind California's huge Shasta Dam at a projected cost of $80 million. Shasta was built in the 1940s with just one outlet which when the reservoir is low releases water so warm that it is lethal to the few wild salmon remaining downstream. While selective withdrawals can improve thermal conditions below a dam, they can rarely replicate the original seasonal variations in river temperatures as at times the reservoir will not have sufficient water at the right temperature.[81]

The hatchery debacle

Probably the most controversial form of environmental 'mitigation' is the use of hatcheries for artificially rearing fish whose natural habitat has been destroyed by dams. Since the late 1940s the US government has spent hundreds of millions of dollars on hatcheries to mitigate the impacts of dams on Pacific salmon. The Bonneville Power Authority, which operates most of the big dams on the Columbia, now spends some $350 million annually on 'fish and wildlife investments' – mainly hatcheries. Yet not only has the number of adult salmon plummeted, but hatchery fish are degrading the genetic diversity of the remaining wild salmon and helping push them toward extinction.

The hatchery programme has failed because dams are continuing to destroy salmon habitat, and also because of the inherent limitations of hatcheries. The genetically homogenous hatchery fish mate with their wild relatives and thereby reduce their genetic fitness: the effects on the natural stock include 'decreased survival and stock size, poor stamina and disease resistance, inappropriate territorial and hiding behavior and other poor performance'.[82] The overcrowding in fish farms, furthermore, means they are highly prone to diseases, which are then spread to wild populations. A 1995 report by the US National Research Council warned that current hatchery policies in the Pacific Northwest were 'based on deep ignorance'. 'It isn't enough to focus only on the abundance of salmon,' the NRC concluded. 'The long-term survival of salmon depends crucially on a diverse and rich store of genetic variation.'[83] Some fish biologists in the Northwest now believe that all the hatcheries should be shut down.[84]

Despite the expensive failure of hatcheries in the Pacific Northwest and elsewhere in North America, hatcheries are regularly promoted by government fisheries departments and environmental consultants as a means of mitigating the destruction of natural fisheries by dams in other parts of the world. Part of the 'mitigation' for the Pak Mun Dam in Thailand, for example, is the hatchery rearing of some two dozen species of local fish – only around 10 per cent of the number of species found in the undammed river. Mekong fisheries specialist Walter Rainboth of the University of California believes that the hatcheries at Pak Mun are merely 'public relations gimmicks'.[85]

The backers of the Sardar Sarovar Dam claim they will 'mitigate' the loss of the hilsa fishery by stocking the reservoir and ponds in the estuary with hatchery-bred fish. But fisheries scientists have not yet been able to breed hilsa artificially. In fact the rearing of hilsa currently depends on obtaining spawn from wild adults, which would in all probability be eliminated by the desiccation of the river.[86]

Down the river...

Aiding smolts on their danger-filled voyage toward the sea is a cornerstone of the authorities' costly but so far largely fruitless plan to restore the Columbia River salmon. One part of this plan is the installation and improvement of screens and bypass systems which prevent young fish from being sucked down turbine intakes. The Army Corps of Engineers is spending $345 million on upgrading fish facilities at its eight dams on the Columbia and lower Snake.[87] The bypass systems, however, do not help the smolts negotiate the warm, predator-infested reservoirs. The preferred technofix for this is 'barging' – in a striking illustration of how far the Columbia has been transformed from a wild into a managed river, smolts are trapped, crammed into barges and motored through reservoirs and dams. While the survival rate of barged smolts is higher than for those left to negotiate the reservoir on their own, mortality due to stress and exposure to diseases in the barges is still high.

Salmon advocates on the Columbia claim that drawing down the reservoirs during the spring and summer migration is the key to helping the fish stocks to recover. The hydropower and navigation interests on the river, however, are strongly resisting pressure to make the dam operators spill water. The drawdowns would certainly not come cheap: the Corps of Engineers estimates that the necessary structural modifications to the eight relevant dams on the Columbia and Snake would cost up to $4.9 billion – and this sum does not include the huge cost to the dam operators of lost revenues from foregone power production and barge fees.[88]

...and back up again

While salmon are by far the best known of migratory fish there are many hundreds of other species with very different migration patterns, especially on large floodplain rivers in the tropics. 'Catadromous' fish live most of their lives in rivers but spawn in estuaries or in the sea, the opposite to salmon; 'amphidromous' species spawn and mature in both salt and fresh water; 'potamodromous' fish migrate entirely within freshwaters. Because these fish do not follow the classic anadromous migratory pattern and have mostly been very little studied, they are sometimes not even regarded as migratory and so dam builders have often assumed that they do not need to bother building fishpass facilities in rivers without salmon.[89]

Yet even where fishways have been built they are invariably based on the salmon fishpass model and have been impassable for many native species. In southeastern Australia, where many dams were fitted with fishways modelled on those on European and North American rivers, native potamodromous silver perch have declined by more than 90 per cent since the 1940s and are now listed as a threatened species. Dams have totally eradicated migratory grayling and bass from some coastal rivers in the region.[90]

In the tropics there are only a small number of examples of fish ladders being successfully used by native species.[91] 'Experiences with such structures as fish ladders in Africa', says UN Food and Agriculture Organization fishery biologist G.M. Bernacsek, 'have been few and unsatisfactory.'[92] In South America, Yacyretá Dam on the Paraná River has been fitted with fish elevators costing $30 million which, according to the World Bank, were designed 'based upon the consultants' knowledge and experience with fish migrations on the Columbia River'. While only a few of the more than 250 species in the Paraná are well studied, it is known that at least some of its species migrate up and down the river several times during their lives. 'This aspect', an internal World Bank evaluation of its loans for Yacyretá dryly notes, 'was not considered'. And so the Yacyretá elevators, based on salmon migrations, only transport fish upriver.[93]

World Bank and Thai government officials for years refuted the claims of independent Mekong fisheries experts and local fishing communities that the fish ladder planned for the highly controversial Pak Mun Dam would be largely useless and that the dam would have a devastating impact on the Mun River's highly diverse and productive fishery. Thai electricity utility EGAT even produced a video for national television promoting the experimental ladder as 'helping to conserve biodiversity'. Well before the dam was completed in 1994, however, fish catches in the Mun, the largest tributary of the Mekong, had dropped disastrously. In 1995, the Thai Department of Fisheries admitted that the experimental fish ladder was not working and EGAT agreed that local fisherpeople should be compensated for the loss of their fishery (although the World Bank still claimed that 'there has been no evidence to suggest that the dam will adversely affect fish stocks'). When a journalist from the *Wall Street Journal* visited Pak Mun in March 1996, 'two, small, dead fish [were] the only signs of life' in the ladder.[94]

Furthermore, there are no bypass facilities at the dam, which is just upstream from the mouth of the Mun, to allow the scores of migratory fish species in the river to descend the river without a potentially lethal trip through the dam's turbines. Plodprasop Suraswadi, director of Thailand's Department of Fisheries, admitted to the Bangkok *Nation* newspaper in 1995 that there was a problem for fish migrating down the Mun, but claimed that this would in fact be a good thing. 'This will pose no severe consequences,' Plodprasop said, 'as it would be beneficial for Thailand not to lose this group of fish to other downstream countries.'[95]

Mitigating for the cameras

To alleviate public concern over the massive numbers of animals drowned when a large reservoir is filled, dam authorities often plan highly publicized rescue operations. Despite decades of experience that these rescues are of extremely little benefit and repeated criticism from wildlife conservationists, dam builders still insist on mounting them, mostly because, as William Partridge, a senior World Bank environmental employee, has cynically remarked about the Yacyretá rescue effort, 'the rescue of individual animals makes good television'.[96]

Wildlife rescue plans fail to capture all but a tiny proportion of the affected animals, most of which drown or starve to death after being stranded on small islands or at the tops of partly flooded trees. The rescue operation at Thailand's Chiew Larn Dam, for example, captured only an estimated 5 per cent of the animals in the submergence zone.[97] Furthermore, once the animals which have been captured are released they are often lethally stressed, frequently injured, and usually have no replacement habitat in which to live – if a suitable habitat is available it will already be inhabited by competitor animals. Rogério Gribel of the Amazonian research institute INPA says that 'saved' or not, 'all the animals from the flooded area should be considered dead.'[98]

The EIA Industry

> Our experience with environmental impact assessment is that when you predict major environmental impacts, the likelihood is that you will get major environmental impacts. The only problem is that you don't ever get quite the impacts you expect...
>
> Professor Frank Grad, Columbia University Law School, 1992

Since the end of the 1960s a growing number of countries and international development agencies have followed the lead of the US in insisting that an environmental impact assessment (EIA) be written before any major infrastructure project is built. A thorough assessment of a proposed dam's possible environmental impacts should indeed be required before any project goes ahead. Unfortunately, governments and dam builders have invariably turned the EIA process into a bureaucratic formality, merely another regulatory hurdle which developers must jump before they can get their project approved. Governments and funders rarely treat EIAs as objective studies to be used to inform an open debate on whether or not a project is desirable, but instead employ them as rubber stamps for projects they have already decided to build.

International environmental consulting is now a big and very profitable business. According to the British Consultants Bureau, UK consultants earned $2.5 billion on overseas contracts in 1994 – and the second biggest sector of the market after project management was writing EIAs.[99] The environmental assessments for large internationally funded dam projects are invariably written by consultants from a relatively small number of companies, some of which, such as German consultants Lahmeyer International, are also directly involved in dam building. Others, such as Norwegian firm Norconsult, are subsidiaries of dam builders. There is an obvious conflict of interest when the company assessing the environmental viability of a project is also likely to get the contract to build it.[100]

Even apparently independent environmental consultancies with no direct link to dam builders have a strong self-interest in underplaying the environmental impacts of projects and exaggerating their benefits. If their conclusions are not favourable to the dam funders or builders, then the consultants will be less likely to get contracts from those agencies or companies in future (the World Bank's guidelines on environmental assessment specify that consultants must be 'acceptable to both the World Bank and the local contracting agencies'). Consultancies, funders and builders often have warm and mutually rewarding relationships. British consultancy Environmental Resources Limited, for example, was awarded at least eleven contracts on World Bank development projects and eight on projects funded by the UK government's Overseas Development Administration between 1985 and 1992 in South Asia alone.[101]

Furthermore, there is no quality control on the consultants' reports – they are usually not peer reviewed as they would be were they to be published in an academic journal, and much worse they are often treated as state or commercial secrets and hidden from public scrutiny. This inbuilt bias for consultants writing EIAs to conclude what their clients want to hear means that the conclusions of an EIA for a large dam can often be guessed before reading the report: the dam's environmental impacts can be accurately predicted, will be relatively minor, and can be relatively cheaply and easily mitigated. In one form or another these seem to be the conclusions of almost every EIA for an international dam project.[102]

Even when individual sections of an EIA are critical or raise concerns that some effects cannot be predicted, these points are invariably toned down in the report's overall conclusions (and criticisms in drafts frequently disappear when they appear in final form). The Executive Summary of a 1994 feasibility study for a cascade of dams on the Mekong written by Canadian engineering and environmental consultants Acres International and French dam agency Compagnie International de Rhône, for example, states that the 'environmental impacts of the proposed projects are expected to be... not severe'.[103] Yet the fisheries volume of the study, written separately by US consultants, warns that the proposed dams 'may cause a wholesale decline in the fishery throughout the lower Mekong River'.

One of the clearest examples of a corrupting relationship between a dam-building agency and an environmental consultancy is that between Thai utility EGAT and TEAM Consulting Engineering Company. In 1978, EGAT commissioned TEAM Consulting to write the EIA for the Nam Choan Dam. Their final report was never publicly released but was used by EGAT to claim that the project would not have serious impacts on the two wildlife sanctuaries that it would partially flood. The Wildlife Ecology section of the EIA, however, was obtained by Belinda Stewart Cox, a British biologist doing research on the birdlife in the sanctuaries.

The TEAM consultants were unable to enter the submergence zone because it was held by communist insurgents, so they surveyed an area downstream which they presumed had similar habitats and then extrapolated this to the reservoir. Although the study contained no maps or location description, Stewart Cox concluded from the species listed and omitted that TEAM had probably not studied riverine forest at all. TEAM's report failed to mention the ecologically valuable nature of the sanctuary areas which would be flooded; the effect of the reservoir on fragmenting animal populations; and the effect on aquatic species of converting a river to a reservoir. TEAM claimed that only six of the mammals it listed were classified as rare; Stewart Cox says that 35 listed mammals were protected under Thai law.

TEAM also said that the reservoir would 'create favourable conditions for most bird species' because 'water birds find it easier to catch fish'. Yet, according to Stewart Cox, only two out of 113 listed bird species would be likely to catch fish in the reservoir. Similarly TEAM stated that otters – which favour shallow, shady rivers – would benefit from the reservoir. Stewart Cox concluded that overall the TEAM report was 'inadequate, inaccurate, sloppy, misleading and, in some instances, apparently fraudulent. It is, in every respect, an inadmissible and unprofessional document.'[104]

The storm of protest which Nam Choan provoked among environmentalists and local people forced EGAT to suspend the project. But EGAT did not blame TEAM for misleading them as to Nam Choan's possible impact. Instead they rewarded them with another EIA contract, this time for the World Bank-funded Chiew Larn Dam. Here TEAM's 'experts' found 122 wildlife species in the reservoir area – while the Thai Royal Forestry Department's largely futile animal rescue operation found 338 species.[105] Undaunted by TEAM's incompetence, EGAT then contracted them to do an environmental assessment for Pak Mun. TEAM claimed there were 80 fish species in the Mun – later surveys found more than 230 species.[106] Mekong fisheries specialist Walter Rainboth reviewed a leaked copy of the Pak Mun EIA. 'Based on the importance of the project and the capacity for irreversible damage,'

Rainboth concluded, 'the report is *criminal.* If something like this were submitted to Congress in order to solicit funds, its fraudulent nature would deserve criminal indictment.'[107]

The extent to which the original purposes of environmental assessments have been subverted can clearly be seen at the Sardar Sarovar Project. In this case the World Bank and Indian authorities agreed that environmental studies for the world's biggest dam and irrigation project should be done parallel with, rather than before, work on the dam. Repeated criticisms of this approach were defended with the assertion that any environmental impacts would necessarily be less than the project benefits (although the authorities did not know what the environmental conditions prior to construction were, what the scale of the impacts would be, nor how much project benefits might be curtailed by environmental factors such as unsuitable soils in the areas slated for irrigation). The independent commission set up by the World Bank to review Sardar Sarovar concluded that this approach 'subverts any acceptable notion of ecological planning'.[108]

Sardar Sarovar's backers have also claimed that continued monitoring will enable any serious environmental problems to be identified and mitigated. But this attitude fails totally to allow for the fact that many environmental impacts cannot be mitigated once the project is built (and that many others can only be by substantially redesigning the project). It is in fact depressingly common to find the assumption in EIAs that 'monitoring' is the same as mitigation, and that recording environmental damage will somehow stop it.

Consultants invariably write EIAs as if the projects were being built in a world without pressure to maximize profits and cut costs on environmental mitigation. EIAs very rarely discuss whether the mitigation measures they recommend have been implemented – and, if implemented, whether they are effective – for past projects. Nor do they tend to mention what the environmental impacts of other projects have been and whether they were accurately predicted. Even if consultants did wish to discuss the success or otherwise of environmental mitigation, however, their ability to do so would be restrained by the fact that environmental studies usually end before construction is finished. More than 60 per cent of 31 national dam agencies surveyed by the industry journal *Water Power & Dam Construction* in 1991 stated that they had no formal system for monitoring the impacts of dams in operation – despite the claim in almost every EIA that environmental monitoring will be a key part of mitigation.[109]

The secrecy which frequently surrounds EIAs is the most indefensible part of the EIA industry. The environmental impacts of dams are extremely complex and difficult to predict. Putting a price tag on possible environmental costs and then comparing these with supposed economic benefits is a process fraught with difficulty, assumptions and personal bias. Coming to a decision on whether or not the environmental damage done by a dam will outweigh its benefits is ultimately a subjective and political decision which should be made after an informed debate by the affected people and the general public. Weighing up the cost of the extinction of a species or the desiccation of an estuary against the benefit provided by increased electricity generation should not be the sole remit of a firm of consultants with a vested interest in ensuring that more dams are planned and built.

An argument often used by dam builders and backers in developing countries to defend incomplete and biased environmental surveys is that concern for the environment is a 'first world luxury' which they cannot afford. In fact the opposite is the case. The majority of people in developing countries depend directly on their environment to provide them with subsistence. The environmental destruction caused by dams in developing countries (and to a lesser extent elsewhere) thus carries a major human cost, which falls most heavily on the poorest sections of society. People in developing countries, in fact, can *least* afford the environmental impacts of large dams.

Notes

1. A. Leopold, *A Sand County Almanac with Essays on Conservation from Round River*, Ballantine Books, New York 1989, pp. 150–58. Leopold's Colorado Delta essay was first published in 1953. J. Carrier, 'The Colorado: A River Drained Dry', *National Geographic*, June 1991; S Postel, 'Where Have All the Rivers Gone?', *World Watch*, May/June 1995; P.L. Fradkin, 'The River Revisited', *Los Angeles Times*, 29 October 1995.

2. See, e.g., A.P. Covich, 'Water and Ecosystems', in P.H. Gleick (ed.), *Water in Crisis: A Guide to the World's Fresh Water Resources*, Oxford University Press, Oxford 1993, p. 41; B.L. Johnson et al., 'Past, Present and Future Concepts in Large River Ecology', *BioScience*, Vol. 45, No. 3, March 1995, p. 134.

3. See, e.g., G.E. Petts, *Impounded Rivers: Perspectives for Ecological Management*, John Wiley, Chichester 1984, p. 119.

4. See, e.g., R.L. Wellcome, *Fisheries Ecology of Floodplain Rivers*, Longman, London 1979.

5. M. Dynesius and C. Nilsson, 'Fragmentation and Flow Regulation of River Systems in the Northern Third of the World', *Science*, Vol. 266, 4 November 1994, p. 759.

6. L. Alexis, 'Sri Lanka's Mahaweli Ganga Project: The Damnation of Paradise', in E. Goldsmith and N. Hildyard (eds.), *The Social and Environmental Impacts of Large Dams. Vol. 2: Case Studies,* Wadebridge Ecological Centre, Cornwall 1986 (hereafter *SEELD 2*). 'Endangered species' are in immediate danger of extinction if some active conservation measures are not taken; 'threatened species' are likely to become endangered in the near future.

7. V. Thiraprasart 'Why the Nam Theun 2 Dam Won't Save Wildlife...', *Watershed*, Bangkok, Vol. 1, No. 3, March–June 1996.

8. See, e.g., P.B. Bayley and H.W. Li, 'Riverine Fishes', in P. Calow and G.E. Petts (eds.), *The Rivers Handbook: Hydrological and Ecological Principles*, Blackwell, Oxford 1992, p. 251.

9. C. Bradley et al., *Rand McNally Encyclopedia of World Rivers*, Rand McNally, New York 1980, p. 342; R.B. Cunninghame Graham, *A Vanished Arcadia*, Century, London 1988, pp. 74–7.

10. D.W. Reiser et al., 'Flushing Flows', in J.A. Gore and G.E. Petts (eds.), *Alternatives in Regulated River Management*, CRC Press, Boca Raton, FL, 1989.

11. Petts, *Impounded Rivers*, p. 141; T. Dunne, 'Geomorphic Contributions to Flood Control Planning', in V.R. Baker et al. (eds.), *Flood Geomorphology*, Wiley, New York 1988, p. 426; G. Stamm and E.A. Lundberg, 'Colorado River Front Work and Levee System Arizona–California', Bureau of Reclamation, December 1993, p. 9.

12. Reiser et al., 'Flushing Flows', p. 101.

13. D.J. Hillel, *Out of the Earth: Civilization and the Life of the Soil*, Free Press, New York 1991, p. 89.

14. See, e.g., M. Lavergne, 'The Seven Deadly Sins of Egypt's Aswan High Dam', in *SEELD 2*; and Y. Halim, 'Manipulations of Hydrological Cycles', in *UNEP Regional Seas Reports and Studies*, No. 114/1, Annex VI, 1991, p. 251. Some scientists claim that the loss of nutrients from Nile sediments is 'insignificant' (see, e.g., M. Abu Zeid, 'Environmental Impacts of the High Aswan Dam: A Case Study', in N.C. Thanh and A.K. Biswas (eds.), *Environmentally-Sound Water Management*, Oxford University Press, Delhi 1990).

15. A.A. Khafagy and A.M. Fanos, 'Impacts of Irrigation Control Works on the Nile Delta Coast', and A. Abdel Megeed and E. Aly Makky, 'Shore Protection of the Nile Delta after the Construction of High Aswan Dam', both in Egyptian National Committee on Large Dams (ed.), *High Aswan Dam Vital Achievement Fully Controlled*, ENCOLD, Cairo 1993, pp. 303, 314, 320; D.J. Stanley and G.A. Warne, 'Nile Delta: Recent Geological Evolution and Human Impact', *Science*, Vol. 260, 30 April 1993.

16. R.H. Meade et al., 'Movement and Storage of Sediment in Rivers of the US and Canada', in M.G. Wolman and H.C. Riggs (eds.), *Surface Water Hydrology*, Geological Society of America, Boulder, CO, 1990, p. 367; J. McPhee, *The Control of Nature*, Pimlico, London 1991, p. 150.

17. S.A. Jenkins et al., 'The Impact of Dam Building on the California Coastal Zone', *California Waterfront Age*, September 1988.

18. G. Bourke, 'Subduing the Sea's Onslaught', *South*, July 1988.

19. D.E. Walling and B.W. Webb, 'Water Quality: I. Physical Characteristics', in Calow and Petts (eds.), *The Rivers Handbook*, p. 58.

20. Petts, *Impounded Rivers*, pp. 175–7, 197, 220, 223.

21. Bureau of Reclamation, *Operation of Glen Canyon Dam: Draft EIS. Summary*, Bureau of Reclamation, Salt Lake City, UT, 1994, pp. 12, 36; G.E. Petts, 'Perspectives for Ecological Management of Regulated Rivers', in Gore and Petts (eds.), *Alternatives in Regulated River Management*, p. 7.

22. L. Lövgren, 'Moratorium in Sweden: A History of the Dams Debate', in A.D. Usher (ed.), *Dams as Aid: A Political Anatomy of Nordic Development Thinking*, Routledge, London forthcoming.

23. I.A. Nikulin, 'The Virus of Giganticism', *Novy Mir* 5, 1991, translated by Michelle Kellman, Baikal Watch; ICOLD, 'Dams and Environment: Water Quality and Climate', *Bulletin 96*, Paris 1994, p. 75.

24. Petts, *Impounded Rivers*, pp. 54, 79, 159.

25. M. Lemeshev, *Bureaucrats in Power: Ecological Collapse*, Progress Publishers, Moscow 1990, p. 61.

26. G.R. Ploskey, *Impacts of Terrestrial Vegetation and Preimpoundment Clearing on Reservoir Ecology and Fisheries in the US and Canada*, FAO, Rome 1985, p. 2; Petts, *Impounded Rivers*, p. 63; P.M. Fearnside, 'Hydroelectric Dams in the Brazilian Amazon as Sources of "Greenhouse" Gases', *Environmental Conservation*, Vol. 22, No. 1, 1995.

27. C. Caufield, 'Brazil, Energy and the Amazon', *New Scientist*, 28 October 1982.

28. S. Van der Heide, *Hydrobiology of the Man-Made Brokopondo Lake*, Brokopondo Research Report, Suriname, Part II, Natuurwetenschappelijke Studiekring Voor Suriname en de Nederlandse Antillen (NSVSNA), Utrecht 1976.

29. P.M. Fearnside, 'Brazil's Balbina Dam: Environment versus the Legacy of the Pharaohs in Amazonia', *Environmental Management*, Vol. 13, No. 4, p. 408; Fearnside, 'Hydroelectric Dams'.

30. J.R. Moreira and A.D. Poole, 'Hydropower and its Constraints', in T.B. Johansson et al. (eds.), *Renewable Energy: Sources for Fuels and Electricity*, Island Press, Washington, DC, 1993, p. 100.

31. Fearnside, 'Brazil's Balbina Dam'.

32. 'Yacyretá Killing Fish', *World Rivers Review*, Second/Third Quarter, 1994.

33. M. Kassas, 'Environmental Aspects of Water Resource Development', in A.K. Biswas et al. (eds.), *Water Management for Arid Lands in Developing Countries*, Pergamon, Oxford 1980.

34. J. Van Donselaar, *The Vegetation in the Brokopondo Lake Basin (Surinam) Before, During, and After the Inundation, 1964–1972*, Brokopondo Research Report, Suriname, Part III, NSVSNA, Utrecht 1989, p. 26; A. Gregoire and C. Sissakian, 'The Environmental Impact of the Petit Saut Reservoir in French Guiana', *Water Power & Dam Construction*, September/October 1993.

35. G.M. Bernacsek, *Dam Design and Operation to Optimize Fish Production in Impounded River Basins*, FAO, Rome 1984, p. 35.

36. D.M. Rosenberg et al., 'Environmental and Social Impacts of Large Scale Hydroelectric Development: Who is Listening?', *Global Environmental Change*, Vol. 5, No. 2, 1995.

37. P.H. Harper, 'La Grand Rivière: A Subarctic River and a Hydroelectric Megaproject', in Calow and Petts (eds.), *The Rivers Handbook*, p. 442.

38. I.A. Shiklomanov, 'World Fresh Water Resources', in Gleick (ed.), *Water in Crisis*, pp. 19, 20. A.K. Afifi and H. Osman, 'Water Losses from Aswan High Dam', and M.N. Ezzat, 'Nile Water Flow, Demand and Water Development', both in ENCOLD (ed.), *Aswan High Dam*. Afifi and Osman estimate the annual average evaporation up to 1990 as 9.6km^3, but this is calculated from 1964 when the reservoir began to fill. My figure is calculated from their annual figures between 1970, when the reservoir filled, and 1991.

39. Dynesius and Nilsson, 'Fragmentation and Flow Regulation'.

40. See, e.g., M. Reisner and S. Bates, *Overtapped Oasis: Reform or Revolution for Western Water*, Island Press, Washington, DC, 1990, p. 128.

41. M. Reisner, *Cadillac Desert: The American West and its Disappearing Water*, Secker & Warburg, London 1986, p. 477.

42. Ibid., pp. 481–2; M. Van der Werf, 'Desalting Plant: White Elephant of Desert', *Arizona Republic*, 14 November 1993.

43. S.F. Bates et al., *Searching out the Headwaters*, Island Press, Washington, DC, 1993, p. 98; A. Netboy, 'The Damming of the Columbia River: The Failure of Bio-Engineering', in *SEELD 2*, p. 46. Average of 1.5m fish from 1975–94, calculated from 'Status Report: Columbia River Fish Runs and Fisheries 1938–94', Oregon and Washington Departments of Fish and Wildlife, August 1995.

44. W. Nehlsen et al., 'Pacific Salmon at the Crossroads: Stocks at Risk from California, Oregon, Idaho and Washington', *Fisheries*, Vol. 16, No. 2, 1991.

45. W.A. Dick, 'Dammed Salmon: Economy, Equity, Ecology, and Columbia River Dams in the 1930s', conference paper presented at 'Power and Place in the North American West', Seattle, WA, 3–5 November 1994.

46. R.I. White, 'Why Wild Fish Matter: Balancing Ecological and Aquacultural Fishery Management', *Trout*, Autumn 1992.

47. A number of predator fish, including walleye, bass, catfish and crappies, have been introduced into reservoirs in the Columbia basin for sports fishing.

48. White, 'Why Wild Fish Matter'.

49. D.N. Carle, 'Restore the Endangered Wild Atlantic Salmon', *RESTORE: The North Woods*, January 1994.

50. G. Billen et al., 'Atlantic River Systems of Europe', in C.E. Cushing et al. (eds.), *River and Stream Ecosytems,* Elsevier, Amsterdam 1995, p. 409.

51. H. Harrison, 'The Forgotten Fish', *Northwest Energy News*, Summer 1995; R.H. Boyle, 'The Cost of Caviar', *Amicus Journal*, Spring 1994, p. 23.

52. Wellcome, *Fisheries Ecology*, p. 249.

53. B. Morse et al, *Sardar Sarovar: The Report of the Independent Review*, RFI, Ottawa 1992, pp. 280, 289; 'Environmental Changes Downstream of Sardar Sarovar Dam', HR Wallingford and World Bank, March 1993, p. 49.

54. E.A. Carpino, 'River Dolphins: Can They Be Saved?', International Rivers Network, Working Paper 4, Berkeley, CA, May 1994; E. Afum, 'Renewed Hope to Conserve Manatee', IPS Feature Service, 16 May 1994.

55. V.M Kotlyakov, 'The Aral Sea Basin: A Critical Environmental Zone', *Environment*, January/February 1991; W.T. Davoren, 'How the Silk Road Turned into a Cotton Highway', *Surviving Together*, Fall/Winter 1992; D. Hinrichsen, 'Requiem for a Dying Sea', *People & the Planet*, Vol. 4, No. 2, 1995.

56. F. Wilkie, 'Disaster-Struck Sea Has a Chance of Returning', *Financial Times*, 28 October 1993; Hinrichsen, 'Requiem for a Dying Sea'.

57. M.I. Zelikin and A.S. Demidov, 'The Aral Crisis and Departmental Interests', mimeo (undated).

58. M.A. Rozengurt, 'Alteration of Freshwater Inflows', in R.H. Stroud (ed.), *Stemming the Tide of Coastal Fish Habitat Loss*, Proceedings of a Symposium on Conservation of Coastal Fish Habitat, Baltimore, MD, 7–9 March 1991, National Coalition for Marine Conservation, Savannah 1992, p. 73.

59. R. Fritchey, 'Healthy Estuaries Need a Delicate Balance of Fresh and Salt Water', *National Fisherman*, August 1993.

60. H.J.A. Neu, 'Man-Made Storage of Water Resources – A Liability to the Ocean Environment? Part I', *Marine Pollution Bulletin*, Vol. 13, No. 1, 1982, p. 7.

61. Rozengurt, 'Alteration of Freshwater Inflows'; M.A. Rozengurt, 'Strategy and Ecological and Societal Results of Extensive Resources Development in the South of the USSR', in *Soviet Union in the Year 2000*, Proceedings of a symposium at Georgetown University, 26–27 June 1990, US Army Intelligence Agency 1991, p. 132.

62. G. White, 'The Environmental Effects of the High Dam at Aswan',

Environment, Vol. 30, No. 7, 1988, p. 34; Halim, 'Manipulations of Hydrological Cycles'.

63. S.C. Snedaker, 'Mangroves: A Summary of Knowledge with Emphasis on Pakistan', and J.T. Wells and J.M. Coleman, 'Deltaic Morphology and Sedimentology, with Special Reference to the Indus River Delta', both in B.U Haq and J.D. Milliman (eds.), *Marine Geology and Oceanography of Arabian Sea and Coastal Pakistan*, Van Nostrand Reinhold, New York 1984, p. 99.

64. W. Stegner, *Where the Bluebird Sings to the Lemonade Springs: Living and Writing in the West*, Penguin, New York 1992, p. 90.

65. Harper, 'La Grand Rivière', p. 420.

66. Petts, *Impounded Rivers*, p. 51.

67. See, e.g., P.B. Moyle and J.J. Cech Jr., *Fishes: An Introduction to Ichthyology*, second edition, Prentice Hall, Englewood Cliffs, NJ, 1988, p. 377.

68. S. McCutcheon, *Electric Rivers: The Story of the James Bay Project*, Black Rose Books, Montréal 1991, p. 98.

69. Petts, *Impounded Rivers*, p. 37.

70. M. Goulding, *Forest Fishes of the Amazon*, Pergamon, Oxford 1985, p. 270; H. O'Reilly Sternberg, 'Waters and Wetlands of Brazilian Amazonia: An Uncertain Future', in T. Nishizawa and J.I. Uitto (eds.), *The Fragile Tropics of Latin America: Sustainable Management of Changing Environments*, UN University Press, Tokyo 1995; W.M. Lewis et al., 'Rivers and Streams of Northern South America', in Cushing et al., *River and Stream Ecosystems*, p. 249.

71. P.B. Bayley, 'The Flood Pulse Advantage and the Restoration of River–Floodplain Systems', *Regulated Rivers: Research and Management*, Vol. 6, 1991; Bernacsek, *Dam Design and Operation*, p. 57; Covich, 'Water and Ecosystems', p. 41; Moyle and Cech, *Fishes*, p. 374.

72. J.N. Abramovitz, 'Aquatic Species Disappearing', in L. Starke (ed.), *Vital Signs 1996: The Trends that are Shaping Our Future*, W.W. Norton, New York 1996, p. 124.

73. W.L. Minckley and M.E. Douglas 'Discovery and Extinction of Western Fishes', in W.L. Minckley and J.E. Deacon (eds.), *Battle Against Extinction: Native Fish Management in the American West*, University of Arizona Press, Tucson 1991, pp. 12–15.

74. Abramovitz, 'Aquatic Species Disappearing'.

75. W. Rainboth, 'Information About the Mekong Fish Fauna', Appendix I to 'Comments on IBRD Pak Mun Dam Mid-Term Review Fisheries Section', presentation to World Bank, 19 November 1993.

76. F.M.R. Hughes, 'The Influence of Flooding Regimes on Forest Distribution and Composition in the Tana River Floodplain, Kenya', *Journal of Applied Ecology*, Vol. 27, 1990.

77. W.A. Sheppe, 'Effects of Human Activities on Zambia's Kafue Flats Ecosystems', *Environmental Conservation*, Vol. 12, No. 1, Spring 1985. The scarcity of wildlife in 1983 would likely have been exacerbated by the severe drought afflicting southern Africa at that time.

78. R.H. Hunt, 'How Does Hydropower Compare?', *Independent Energy*, November 1993; 'Tacoma Pulls Out of Elkhorn Hydro Project', *International Water Power & Dam Construction*, June 1995.

79. Petts, 'Perspectives for Ecological Management', p. 14.

80. M.J. Sale et al., *Environmental Mitigation at Hydroelectric Projects. Vol. 1: Current Practices for Instream Flow Needs, Dissolved Oxygen, and Fish Passage*, Idaho Field

Office, US Department of Energy 1991.

81. R.A. Cassidy, 'Water Temperature, Dissolved Oxygen, and Turbidity Control in Reservoir Releases', in Petts and Gore (eds.), *Alternatives in Regulated River Management*, pp. 30–38; P. McHugh, 'Plumbing the Depths', *San Francisco Chronicle*, 4 June 1995.

82. White, 'Why Wild Fish Matter', p. 22.

83. A. Barnum, 'Hatcheries Catch Blame on Salmon', *San Francisco Chronicle*, 9 November 1995.

84. A.M. Gillis, 'What's at Stake in the Pacific Northwest Salmon Debate?', *BioScience*, Vol. 45, No. 3, March 1995, p. 127.

85. T.R. Roberts, 'Just Another Dammed River? Negative Impacts of Pak Mun Dam on Fishes of the Mekong Basin', *Natural History Bulletin of the Siam Society*, Vol. 41, 1993, p. 123; Rainboth, 'Information About the Mekong Fish Fauna'.

86. Morse et al., *Sardar Sarovar*, p. 280; HR Wallingford and World Bank, 'Environmental Changes Downstream of Sardar Sarovar Dam', p. 48.

87. *Northwest Energy News*, November/December 1993.

88. 'Fish Pose a Costly Problem', *Engineering News Record*, 21 December 1992.

89. See, e.g., Roberts, 'Just Another Dammed River?', p. 126.

90. M. Mallen-Cooper, 'How High Can a Fish Jump?', *New Scientist*, 16 April 1994.

91. Wellcome, *Fisheries Ecology*, p. 250.

92. Bernacsek, *Dam Design and Operation*, p. 62.

93. K. Treakle, 'Briefing Paper No. 1: Yacyretá Hydroelectric Project II', Bank Information Center, Washington, DC, August 1992; World Bank, 'Project Completion Report: Argentina Yacyretá Hydroelectric Project and Electric Power Sector Project', 14 March 1995, pp. 25, 35.

94. G. Ryder, 'Case Study: Pak Mun Dam in Thailand', paper presented at symposium 'Both Sides of the Dam', Delft University of Technology, Netherlands, 22 February 1995; P.M. Sherer, 'Thai Villagers Wish This Dam Was Never Built', *Wall Street Journal*, 12 March 1996.

95. M. Traisawasdichai, 'Dam Poses Uphill Battle for Fish Species', *The Nation*, Bangkok, 27 January 1995.

96. Comment made during interview for *The Dammed*, a Canadian Broadcasting Corporation television documentary, broadcast 17 February 1995.

97. M. Traisawasdichai, 'Lessons of Chiew Larn Dam Go Unheeded in Laos', *The Nation*, Bangkok, 15 August 1995.

98. R. Gribel, 'The Balbina Disaster: The Need to Ask Why?', *The Ecologist*, Vol. 20, No. 4, July/August 1990.

99. A. Taylor, 'Consultants Win More Income Overseas', *Financial Times*, 9 November 1995.

100. For a critique of an EIA in which Lahmeyer was involved, see 'Reappraisal of the Adquacy of the EIA Report for the Nam Leuk Hydropower Development Project, Conclusions of a Consultancy Report to the Protected Areas and Watershed Management Division of the Ministry of Forestry, Lao PDR', mimeo, Vientiane, 16 November 1994. For a critique of a Norconsult EIA, see A.D. Usher and G. Ryder, 'Vattenfall Abroad: Damming the Theun River', in Usher (ed.), *Dams as Aid.*

101. See 'ERL Statement of Experience: Sri Lanka and South Asia', ERL, London, undated. Some contracts were on joint ODA/World Bank projects.

ERL was also awarded an ODA/World Bank contract on Sardar Sarovar not included in this list.

102. See, e.g., 1993 reports on Sardar Sarovar by ERL and HR Wallingford; 'Privatisation of the Bakun Hydroelectric Project: EIA. Interim Report', Ekran Berhad, 7 November 1994; B. Williams et al., 'A Review of the EIA (Interim Report) of the Bakun Hydroelectric Project', IRN, Berkeley 1995; M. Barber and G. Ryder, *Damming the Three Gorges: What Dam Builders Don't Want You to Know*, Earthscan, London 1993.

103. 'Mekong Mainstream Run-of-River Hydropower: Main Report', CNR, Lyon/Acres International, Calgary/Mekong Secretariat, Bangkok, December 1994, p. 18.

104. B. Stewart Cox, 'Thailand's Nam Choan Dam: A Disaster in the Making', *The Ecologist*, Vol. 17, No. 6, 1987, p. 215.

105. Traisawasdichai, 'Lessons of Chiew Larn Dam'.

106. Traisawasdichai, 'Dam Poses Uphill Battle'.

107. Quoted in B. Rich, *Mortgaging the Earth: The World Bank, Environmental Impoverishment, and the Crisis of Development*, Beacon Press, Boston 1994, pp. 11–12. The emphasis is Rainboth's.

108. Morse et al., *Sardar Sarovar*, p. 230.

109. 'World Survey on Environmental Management Practice', *Water Power & Dam Construction*, May 1991.

3

Temples of Doom: The Human Consequences of Dams

The government wanted our land to build Sardar Sarovar Dam and some of our men agreed to move to Parveta village in Gujarat. Since then, we have known only grief and the strain of trying to build our lives in an alien place.

This village, Parveta, is different from Manibeli. There we lived by the river, and the forest was close by. Our children would take cattle to graze and made them drink from the river. We could go to the forest and get wood. We could catch fish in the river. We got so much else from the forest – bamboo with which to build, fibre to make rope with, food to eat, all kinds of herbs, and animals to hunt. Now all that is gone and we are poor....

We now have to pump water for all our cattle and goats. And the pump itself – how can it replace our wide, freely flowing river where we could bathe and wash and drink?...

The soil in Parveta is different from Manibeli. The land here calls for water, fertilizer and pesticides, which we haven't used before. We need money for this, but since we do not have titles to the land, it is hard to get loans.... Forty households moved from Manibeli to Parveta. In our first year here, we watched 38 of our children die.... Now we live far away and, though Parveta is by the road, we cannot go home, because it means spending money for the bus. So only men travel; we cannot. We have to stay in Parveta, where our presence is resented by the people who live here from before. We lived in the mountains. Parveta is on the plain and flat so you see everything around. In Manibeli we could defecate when we wanted to; the hills would hide us. This is one of the many freedoms we have left behind. Here we have to wait until dark or rise before dawn.

We have to live here now in this land where we and our children go hungry, even though we get no rest from work. The promise of new wealth lured our men, but we now wish we had stayed behind in Manibeli, among the people and on the land we call our own.

From the translation of a letter written to the 'Independent Review' of the Sardar Sarovar Project, 1992

Over the last six decades, the builders of dams have evicted from their homes and lands many tens of millions of people, almost all of them poor and politically powerless, a large proportion of them from indigenous and other ethnic minorities. These legions of dam 'oustees', as they are called in India, have, in the great majority of cases, been economically, culturally and emotionally devastated. In many cases the people have been flooded out with only minimal compensation – often none at all – and many once self-sufficient farming families have thus been reduced to eking out a living as migrant labourers or slum dwellers.

Those displaced by reservoirs are only the most visible victims of the designers, funders and builders of large dams. Millions more have lost land and homes to the canals, irrigation schemes, roads, power lines and industrial development which follow dams into valleys. Many more have not physically been displaced from their homes but have lost their access to clean water, fish, game, grazing land, timber, fuelwood and wild fruits and vegetables in the dammed river and valley. Others downstream have been deprived of the annual flood which once irrigated and fertilized their fields and recharged their wells. Millions, too, have suffered from the diseases which dams and large irrigation projects in the tropics almost inevitably bring in their wake.

Dammed Lies and Statistics

The number of people who are forced out of their homes by dams is staggering. It is, however, difficult to give even a reasonably accurate estimate of the total who have been evicted as the industry and their government sponsors have rarely bothered to collect reliable oustee statistics. Not surprisingly, given their size, population densities and number of dams, India and China have displaced and are displacing more people than any other nation. Researchers from the Indian Social Institute in New Delhi estimate 'conservatively' that more than 14 million people have been displaced by reservoirs and associated irrigation projects in post-Independence India.[1]

The World Bank uses Chinese government figures to estimate that 10.2 million people were displaced by reservoirs in China between 1950 and 1989.[2] This figure includes the four largest single dam oustee totals on record: Sanmenxia with 410,000; Danjiangkou with 383,000 (plans exist to raise the dam height and displace a further 225,000 people, many of them oustees from the original reservoir); Xinanjiang with 306,000; and Dongpinghu with 278,000.[3] It is very difficult to verify the Chinese government's resettlement statistics. Given China's high population density and the huge number of dams it has built, however, the actual number of oustees is likely to be much greater than the official estimate. Chinese dam critic Dai Qing believes that the true figure of Chinese dam oustees is between 40 and 60 million.[4]

Data gathered for this book give a total of 2.2 million displaced by 134 completed dams in countries for which information is available, excluding China and India (see Appendix 3). This is less than 1 per cent of the large dams built outside China and India but includes most of those with the largest numbers of evictions. A conservative estimate of worldwide dam evictees (taking the Chinese government figure at face value) would therefore be around 30 million. A more realistic estimate (using a number for China from the bottom end of Dai Qing's range) would be around 60 million – more than the entire population of the United Kingdom.[5]

Most displacement statistics include only reservoir oustees – yet these are often surpassed by those deprived of land and livelihood by the other parts of dam projects or by their long-term ecological effects. These people are rarely defined as 'project affected' and as a result are rarely eligible for compensation (and also fail to show up in resettlement statistics). Similarly, families which lose part or all of their land but not their house are often not labelled as 'displaced', even though the loss of even a small part of a poor household's land can make the difference between subsistence and starvation. People who farm or graze their livestock in river valleys without formal legal rights, as is the case with indigenous people and pastoralists in many parts of the world, seldom receive compensation for the loss of land. Those who traditionally use the valley for hunting game or collecting wild fruits and vegetables, timber, fodder or firewood are even less likely to be recognized as affected. Families may also end up stranded on newly formed islands or peninsulas, their normal routes to neighbours, schools and markets flooded by the reservoir.

The many, often unrecognized, ways in which people can lose their livelihood to a huge dam project are well illustrated by India's Sardar Sarovar Project (SSP):

- Eight hundred families lost their land to the new town built for the SSP construction workers. Although land acquisition began in 1961, the families were still fighting for adequate compensation 35 years later.
- Tens of thousands of *adivasis* (India's indigenous people) could be thrown off their traditional land to make way for a wildlife sanctuary supposed to 'mitigate' the loss of wildlife to the SSP reservoir.
- Thousands are being deprived of access to cropland which the government is turning into tree plantations to 'mitigate' for submerged forests.

- Tens of thousands who grow crops, gather fuelwood and fodder, or are employed on the forest and farmland being taken over to resettle the reservoir oustees are suffering what is known as 'secondary displacement'.
- An estimated 140,000 landholders would lose at least some of their land to SSP's network of irrigation canals, with 25,000 ending up with less than two hectares, regarded as the minimum viable holding.
- A large area of farmland, many villages and even whole towns could eventually be flooded by the so-called 'backwater' effect, caused by the gradual rise in water levels due to sedimentation in the upper reaches of the reservoir.
- Downstream, SSP is planned to eradicate the flow of the Narmada between the dam and the sea for most of the year, destroying the livelihood of thousands of fishing families and boatmen and affecting the water supply of up to a million people.

When the World Bank agreed to lend the Indian government $450 million for SSP in 1985 the official estimate for the total number of families who would need to be compensated was 6,603. In 1996 the latest government estimate of 'affected' families was 41,500 to be displaced by the reservoir alone. Add in the families affected by other aspects of the project and the number rises well into the hundreds of thousands.[6]

Down the river

> Those who remain in their villages, in spite of their work, harvest very little, sometimes nothing. The fish have disappeared. Our livestock die. The trees die. The land is becoming exhausted.... The development of the river is condemning us to live without hope.
>
> Declaration of the Peasant Associations of the Senegal River Valley, April 1992

Some of the most serious long-term social effects of dams are suffered by the people who live downstream. In Africa, the loss of the annual flood below dams has devastated traditional floodplain farming, fishing and grazing. Kainji Dam in Nigeria, for example, directly displaced 44,000 people, but adversely affected hundreds of thousands more who had formerly grazed their livestock and grown crops on land irrigated by the annual flood. Floodplain yam production reportedly fell by 100,000 tonnes after the dam was completed in 1968 and downstream fish catches plummeted by 60–70 per cent.[7] Incredibly, one of the original aims of Kainji Dam, according to Salah El-Din El-Zarka of the UNDP/FAO Kainji Lake Research Project, was 'control of floods of the River Niger to lessen ... seasonal inundation ... and to allow thereby the expansion of agriculture'.[8]

Another Nigerian dam, Bakolori, on the Sokoto, a tributary of the Niger, reduced the area of rice grown downstream by 7,000 hectares and that of dry season crops by 5,000 hectares. William Adams, who worked as a consultant on irrigation projects in Nigeria in the 1970s, says that as the dam altered both the timing and the extent of flooding the farmers 'no longer knew what to expect from the flood, and their ability to match expected flooding, soil and crop type broke down'. During the dry season, the falling water table meant that farmers had to dig their wells ever deeper, greatly increasing the time and money spent on watering their crops. A survey in the 1980s found that three-quarters of the dry-season irrigators in affected villages had given up farming. In general, only the richer farmers survived.[9]

The designers of Brazil's World Bank-funded Sobradinho Dam, which directly flooded out some 72,000 people in the mid-1970s, were taken by surprise when the high dry-season river levels caused by the dam threatened to flood thousands of hectares of rice fields some 800 kilometres down the São Francisco river. The authorities launched an emergency operation to protect the floodplain by building a series of dikes and pumping stations, converting 25,000 hectares of seasonally flooded land to year-round irrigation. The projects, 'executed under considerable time pressure and social tension', according to the World Bank's Operation Evaluation Department, displaced over 50,000 share-croppers and other rural poor people. While many of these families were presumably among the 20,000 people given land on the newly irrigated polders, no attempt was made to resettle those who did not find land on the scheme and it is not known what has become of them. Farmers resettled on the newly irrigated lands have had to cope with poor drainage, increasing soil salinity and a lack of advice on irrigated farming techniques. The resulting poor yields, falling incomes and indebtedness have forced many families to abandon the new lands.[10]

Six years after Sobradinho was completed the gates were closed at another major Brazilian dam, Tucuruí on the Tocantins, a major tributary of the Amazon. While just under 24,000 people were flooded out by Tucuruí, approximately 40,000 living on hundreds of islands below the dam have had to endure filthy water discharged from the reservoir and the loss of the regular floods. After the dam began operation, the normally clear Tocantins was covered with a thick algal scum. Many people experienced severe stomach problems after drinking the water and several children died. All the island inhabitants suffered skin rashes and women were plagued with vaginal infections so severe that many thought they had contracted a venereal disease. The fish and shrimp which had formerly provided most of the people's protein and income virtually disappeared. Crop production also plummeted.[11]

The Final Blow: Dams and Indigenous People

> Dams are not planned to submerge highly developed areas. Often the quality of life of the displaced indigenous population was low, and therefore there could be an opportunity to improve living standards; the construction of large dams can sometimes offer such an opportunity. If the people prefer, however, to continue living as they have in the past, they can do so by moving upstream in the river valley.
>
> Ernest Razvan, Associate Professor, International Institute for Hydraulic and Environmental Engineering, The Netherlands, 1992

Indigenous and tribal peoples and other marginalized ethnic minorities make up a disproportionately large percentage of those who lose their livelihoods to dams. Areas with people who are well off and well connected do not make good reservoir sites. In India, according to government estimates, 40 per cent of all those who have been displaced by dams are *adivasis*, who represent less than 6 per cent of the Indian population. Almost all the larger dam schemes built and proposed in the Philippines are in the land of the country's 4.7 million indigenous people.[12] The majority of the 58,000 people evicted to make way for Vietnam's largest dam, Hoa Binh, came from ethnic minority groups, as would most of the 112,000 to be displaced by the even bigger Ta Bu Dam planned further downstream.[13]

The impact of dams upon indigenous people is especially harmful as most of their communities have already suffered centuries of exploitation and displacement, and their remote mountain valley, forest or desert reservations are often their last refuge from cultural obliteration. The trauma of resettlement is also exacerbated for indigenous communities because of their strong spiritual ties to their land, and because many of the communal bonds and cultural practices which help define their societies are destroyed by displacement and by the loss of the common resources on which their economy is based.

In Brazil, the social disruption caused by dams and the influx of workers and settlers which follows in their wake has been among the most devastating of the recent blows suffered by those of its indigenous people who have managed to survive European colonization. The depressing story of the Waimiri-Atroari tribe on the Uatumã tributary of the Amazon is similar to that of other dam-affected Indians in Brazil. In 1905, it was estimated that the tribe numbered 6,000. Eighty years later, massacres and disease left only 374 Waimiri-Atroari alive. In 1987, the gates of Balbina Dam were closed, flooding two villages in which lived 107 of the remaining members of the tribe and blocking the annual upstream migration of the turtles whose eggs are a staple of their diet.

The Waimiri-Atroari are now further threatened by a plan to divert the river Alalaú to increase the flow into Balbina Reservoir. 'If this happens,' says Rogério Gribel of the Amazonian research institute INPA, 'it will have a catastrophic effect upon the Indians, who depend upon the Alalaú both physically and culturally (especially since the Uatumã was dammed). The final blow will come with the invasion of their land by thousands of workmen, dozens of heavy machines and the alcohol, prostitutes and violence which always accompany such operations.'[14]

Although indigenous areas may seem remote and sparsely populated to planners in the cities, the strips of riverside farmland and forest which are flooded by dams are usually the best lands in their region and so much more economically and culturally important than their size suggests. The US-funded Kaptai hydropower dam in the Chittagong Hill Tracts in south-east Bangladesh displaced more than 100,000 people from the Chakma ethnic minority – one-sixth of the total Chakma population – and flooded around two-fifths of their cultivable land. The resulting land shortage and resentment of the government helped spark off the bloody conflict between the Buddhist Chakma and Muslim Bengali settlers which has ravaged the region since Kaptai was completed in 1962.[15]

One of the least-known consequences of water development in the US is its impact on Native Americans. A quarter of the North Dakota reservation of the Three Affiliated Tribes (the Mandans, Hidatsas and Arikas) and almost all of their productive land was flooded by Garrison Dam. Eighty per cent of the reservation's population were displaced. The Three Tribes pressed the government for compensation, including permission to graze their cattle along the margins of the reservoir and first rights to harvest the timber in the submergence zone. Yet even these modest demands were refused. Marc Reisner describes the scene in the Washington, DC, office of Interior Secretary Cap Krug at the signing of the bill authorizing the seizure of the Three Tribes' land in May 1948:

> Standing behind Krug ... was handsome George Gillette, the leader of the tribal business council, in a pinstripe suit. 'The members of the tribal council sign this contract with heavy hearts,' Gillette managed to say. 'Right now the future does not look good to us.' Then, as Krug reached for a bundle of commemorative pens to sign the bill, and as the assembled politicians and bureaucrats looked on embarrassed or stony-faced, George Gillette cradled his face in one hand and began to cry.[16]

C. Patrick Morris of the Center for Native American Studies at Montana State University believes that Garrison and the other reservoirs on the Missouri are 'a major contributor to the 70–90 per cent unemployment rates on the region's Indian reservations today'.[17]

In the Columbia Basin, the dam builders' greatest crime against Native Americans has not been the theft of their land or water, but the destruction of the salmon fisheries on which their economy and much of their culture were based. On 17 June 1940, several tribes gathered at their fishing site of Kettle Falls, soon to be flooded by Grand Coulee Dam, to hold a 'ceremony of tears' in place of their traditional celebration of the spring salmon run as the representation of the renewal of life. Not for more than half a century did the federal government agree to pay reparations to the Colville Confederated Tribes who lost villages, land, salmon runs and burial sites to Grand Coulee. None of the tribal council members who filed the compensation claim in 1951 lived to hear of Congress's approval in 1994 of one of the largest payments ever made to a Native American tribe: a lump sum payment of $54 million, then annual payments of $15.25 million to continue for as long as Grand Coulee produces power.[18]

Waiting for the Dam

> We will request you to move from your houses after the dam comes up. If you move, it will be good, otherwise we shall release the waters and drown you all.
>
> Indian Finance Minister Moraji Desai speaking at a public meeting in the submergence zone of the Pong Dam, 1961

The pain of displacement is usually the culmination of years, sometimes decades, of waiting, hearing rumours, receiving threats. As soon as a dam is proposed, people in the reservoir area begin to suffer the withdrawal of government and private investment. Property prices fall, banks refuse to give loans, no new schools or health centres are built. Existing facilities may be closed long before people move out of the area. By the time resettlement starts, the oustees are often already much worse off than people in neighbouring areas. This problem is worse for dams than other types of projects as their gestation period is so long, the larger projects taking many decades from their first conception to completion. The Three Gorges Project was first envisaged in 1919; the first draft plan drawn up in 1944; detailed designs made in 1955; preliminary construction began in 1993; and resettlement is not expected to be completed until the year 2008.[19]

Coupled with the progressive withdrawal of services and investment is the uncertainty of not knowing whether or not the dam will actually be built, how many houses, farms and workplaces will be submerged if it is, who will be eligible for compensation, and how much compensation they will receive. Even after construction starts, these uncertainties may not be resolved: compensation rules may change several times over the period of project construction and the affected area may increase or decrease according to design or operating changes made for technical, economic or political reasons. Sometimes inadequate surveying means that the authorities do not even know how much land will be flooded until the reservoir fills.

Once a dam is nearing completion, the process of moving people from the area to be flooded is frequently rushed and accompanied by violence and intimidation. This is partly because people refuse to leave their homes and partly because of poor planning which fails to ensure that construction and resettlement proceed at a similar pace. The police of what was then the British colony of Northern Rhodesia shot dead eight villagers and wounded over thirty in a confrontation during the 'poorly conceived and trauma ridden crash programme' to clear the lands that were to become Kariba Reservoir.[20] Anthropologist Elizabeth Colson describes the 1958 evacuation to a resettlement area of some of the 57,000 Gwembe Tonga people displaced by Kariba:

> They rode the swaying, open lorries for a hundred miles, over rough roads, in the blazing sun of the hottest period of the year … to reach an unknown land they dreaded.… The misery of the trip was increased by nausea.… They emerged exhausted and sick to find themselves in what they regarded as a wilderness….[21]

Before reservoirs were filled in the Soviet Union, evictees were often forced to take part in the burning and destruction of their own houses, orchards and churches and the exhumation of relatives' coffins.[22] When some of the 21,000 Mazatec Indians displaced by Mexico's Miguel Aleman Dam in the late 1950s refused to move, employees from the Papaloapan River Commission set fire to their homes. The army had to called in several times to quell the resulting unrest in Indian communities.[23]

Harrowing stories have recently appeared in English of the evictions of hundreds of thousands of people to make way for China's Xinanjiang Dam. Although the relocation programme was supposed to have been done in steps over several years, the policy was suddenly changed at the height of the Great Leap Forward in 1958 and the peasants forced out *en masse*. Local Party officials ordered resettlement to be carried out 'like a battle action' and instructed people to 'take more good ideology with them and less old furniture'. The officials sent in labourers to tear down houses and ordered the gates of the dam to be shut prematurely to flood out those at lower elevations. 'At this,' Chinese sources relate, 'widespread protests erupted. Some people smashed up their own property and refused to move; others, overwhelmed by shock … went mad; others still burned down their houses, and old people clung to the ground and refused to budge. But all were finally forced out.' The traumatized evictees were forced to walk for several days to reach the resettlement sites. On the way, cold and hunger killed several; pregnant women gave birth by the roadside. The marching peasants were said to have resembled columns of wartime refugees.[24]

A dam built with blood: the Chixoy massacres

> The Chixoy Dam was built with the blood of the inhabitants of Río Negro.
>
> Guatemalan human rights activist, 1993

Almost certainly the most awful human rights atrocity associated with dam evictions was the murder of 378 Maya Achí Indians from the tiny village of Río Negro in the submergence zone of Guatemala's Chixoy Dam. Río Negro's nightmare started in 1976 when a helicopter filled with officials from Guatemalan power utility INDE descended on the village to tell its inhabitants they would soon be flooded out by a huge dam. Over the next four years, INDE and a committee of villagers negotiated resettlement terms. When the people from Río Negro were shown the cramped houses and poor land slated to become their new home, however, they felt that they had been tricked and refused to move.

At this point, the authorities began a campaign of terror against the recalcitrant villagers. In March 1980, three military policemen based at the dam site came to Río Negro purportedly to arrest some villagers accused of stealing from the project stores. When the community refused to hand over the alleged thieves the police opened fire, killing seven people. The villagers then chased the police away and one, according to the people of Río Negro, drowned in the river. INDE and the army, however, accused the villagers of murdering the policeman and of keeping his rifle – and, ominously, of being supporters of the country's guerrilla movement. In July 1980 two representatives from Río Negro acceded to a request from INDE to come to the dam site to present the resettlement documents that they had signed with the utility. The mutilated bodies of the two men were found a week later. The documents were never found.

Nearly two years later, in February 1982, 74 men and women from Río Negro were ordered by the local military commander to report to Xococ, a village upstream from the reservoir zone which had a history of land conflicts and hostility with Río Negro. Only one woman out of the 74 villagers ever returned to Río Negro – the rest were raped, tortured and then murdered by Xococ's Civil Defence Patrol, or PAC, one of the notorious paramilitary units used by the state as death squads. After the woman who escaped told the rest of the people of Río Negro about the killings, the men in the village took to the mountains to hide. The woman stayed behind, believing that the patrollers would only come to look for the men.

On 13 March 1982, 10 soldiers and 25 patrollers arrived in Río Negro to look for 'guerrillas'. Infuriated not to find any men, they rounded up the remaining women and children and marched them to a hill above the village. There the soldiers and patrollers began to rape the women, and then to kill them. Some were garrotted, some beaten to death with clubs and rifle butts, others had their throats slit or were decapitated. Children were murdered by tying ropes around their ankles and smashing their heads against rocks and trees. Seventy women and 107 children were massacred. Only two women managed to escape. Eighteen children were taken back to Xococ as slaves for the patrollers.

Two months later a further 82 people from Río Negro were massacred. In September, 35 orphaned children from Río Negro were among 92 people machine-gunned and burned to death in another village near the dam. Filling of the Chixoy reservoir began soon after this final massacre.

The Río Negro massacres must be seen in the context of the brutal government counterinsurgency campaign which nationwide left 72,000 Guatemalans dead or missing between 1980 and 1984 alone. Local church workers and journalists, foreign human rights groups and the survivors themselves, however, all directly link the massacres to INDE's attempts to clear the reservoir area. All also deny that there was ever any organized guerrilla activity in Río Negro. US human rights group Witness for Peace, which is working with the survivors of the massacres, says that 'the Río Negro victims died because they blocked the "progress" of the Chixoy Project.' Many believe that INDE encouraged the violence so that their officials could pocket the compensation payments due to the villagers. 'I'll tell you the real reason for the violence,' one survivor said to Witness for Peace; 'They wanted our land for their cursed reservoir and dam, and we were in the way.'

Culpability for the massacres must also lie with the foreign companies and donors who were happy to design, build and fund a high dam in a country ruled by a military dictatorship with a record of brutality against its own indigenous population. The dam was planned by LAMI Consortium, a group of engineering consultants comprising Lahmeyer International of Germany, Motor Columbus of Switzerland and International Engineering Company of the US.[25] LAMI's feasibility study callously dismissed the 3,400 indigenous people who would be displaced: 'In the tract of the study ... there is almost no population', the consultants wrote.

Loans for Chixoy came from a number of sources, including the World Bank, Inter-American Development Bank (IDB) and Italian government. All appear to have turned a blind eye to the massacres and to have refused to acknowledge them in project documents: no references to the massacres are made in any of the funders' internal reports on Chixoy to which outside researchers have been able to gain access. World Bank personnel spent some thirty staff weeks on supervision missions to Guatemala between 1979 and 1989. According to local people, everyone at the dam site and virtually everyone in the region knew about the massacres, so it is hard to believe that the World Bank and other funders did not also know. Yet despite the bloodshed the World Bank agreed to give a follow-up loan to INDE in 1985 to help meet the massive cost overruns on the dam.

The World Bank's confidential 1991 'Project Completion Report' on Chixoy nowhere mentions that more than one in ten of the 1,500 people to be resettled had been massacred before the reservoir was filled. The closest the report comes to mentioning the mass murders is a reference to the resettlement plans as 'conceptually ... seriously flawed' and a mention of 'delays in implementing the program due to intensive insurgency activity in the project area during the years 1980–1983 – two resettlement officers were killed while performing their duties – and to difficulties with respect to [land] purchasing.' Witness for Peace in their 1996 report on Chixoy conclude that:

> If the [World] Bank knew about the massacres, then giving an additional loan to the project was at best a calculated cover up, and at worst an act of complicity in the violence. If the Bank did not know about the slaughter, then it was guilty of gross negligence. Either way, the Bank is implicated in the horrors perpetrated against the village of Río Negro in 1982.[26]

After the Deluge

> ...every person who will be uprooted from the soil ... will exchange his shovel for a decent cottage, darkness for light and fanaticism for faith...
>
> N.V. Gadgil, Minister in charge of India's multi-dam Damodar Valley Corporation Project, 1948

The great majority of those displaced by dams have statistically disappeared, swallowed up by the slums and the camps of migrant labourers. In India, perhaps three-quarters of the millions of dam oustees were given no replacement land or housing; at best they received a small sum of cash compensation, often they got nothing at all.[27] And numerous studies show that even those Indian oustees who were 're-settled' invariably also ended up impoverished, demoralized and bitter. 'Submerged destitutes' is the sadly apt name given to the people displaced by Rengali Dam in the state of Orissa by their new neighbours at their resettlement sites.[28] In China, according to official statistics, only one-third of reservoir oustees have been able to 'reestablish their lives at satisfactory standards'. Another third reportedly 'settled into subsistence livelihoods' and the remainder 'were mired in poverty'.[29]

In the rest of the world, many more 'submerged destitutes' have been created by dam builders. In almost all of the resettlement operations for which reliable information is available, the majority of the oustees have ended with lower incomes; less land than before; less work opportunities; inferior housing; less access to the resources of the commons such as fuelwood and fodder; and worse nutrition and physical and mental health.

Where displaced farmers receive cash compensation for lost land, it is invariably far lower than the cost of replacement land. Sometimes this is because the value of land is estimated according to out-of-date tax assessments; other times it is because of inflation in the years between surveys of land to be submerged and the actual payments – hyperinflation in Vietnam during the 1980s reduced the value of compensation given to farmers displaced by the Hoa Binh Dam to as little as five cents.[30] This latter problem is exacerbated by the almost inevitable boom in land prices near a new reservoir due to the greater demand for the remaining farmland. Land compensation paid may also be insufficient simply because the authorities do not have the money or desire to pay an adequate amount.[31]

Land compensation received may also be inadequate because corrupt officials or other middlemen skim off a cut for themselves. When the Colombian authorities announced the compensation package for farmers affected by the Guavio Dam in 1981, 'sharp lawyers and other middlemen familiar with Colombia's land acquisition system' arrived in the area and offered the farmers immediate cash payments worth about half of the market rate of the land being acquired. Around 60 per cent of the mostly illiterate peasants, who had little experience of dealing with official paperwork, handed over their land titles to the conmen, who then claimed from the authorities the market value of the land.[32]

As most oustees are farmers, a large drop in the size of landholdings can lead to a disastrous drop in income. In 1981, 100,000 people living in the submergence zone of the Srisailam Dam in the Indian state of Andhra Pradesh were cruelly driven out of their homes in what the authorities called 'Operation Demolition'. Three years later a team from New Delhi-based social research NGO Lokayan surveyed 258 Srisailam oustee households. They concluded that since eviction the families' incomes had declined by more than 80 per cent, mainly because of the loss of farmland. Compensation for submerged land had amounted to only one-fifth of its market value. Ownership of livestock and agricultural equipment had fallen drastically, and average family debts had risen by more than 150 per cent.[33]

Researchers working on resettlement are unanimous that giving land-for-land is far more successful than cash compensation. But even when replacement land has been given it is often inadequate for similar reasons to why people do not get decent cash compensation – a lack of legal title to all the lands they farm, for example, or a lack of government commitment or resources to buy them land of sufficient size and quality. The issue of quality is key as oustees are invariably losing fertile valley land and therefore should receive a larger area of the normally much poorer replacement land.

The *adivasi* families displaced by Bargi Dam in Madhya Pradesh, the first dam to be built across the Narmada, were promised 2 hectares of replacement land each when their fields were submerged in the late 1980s, even though many of their previous holdings had been much larger than this. The promise, such as it was, was not fulfilled, and most of the 114,000 oustees were given only house plots and pitifully low amounts of cash compensation. Because of incompetent surveying, many of the resettlement areas were in fact still in the submergence zone, so the oustees were, without warning, flooded out a second time when the reservoir finally filled in 1990 (the Madhya Pradesh government had estimated that Bargi would submerge 26,729 hectares; the actual area submerged is more than three times this).

Some of the families displaced by the second round of submergence – who had spent most of their compensation money on building new houses only to see them washed away – were moved to what the government termed the 'ideal village' of Gorakhpur. Houses, a school and drug dispensary had been built at the new site. Yet there were no teachers or medical personnel at Gorakhpur; nor was there any available land, nor any source of fodder for the villagers' livestock. Deprived of almost any means of subsistence, five people died of starvation in the 'ideal village' between 1990 and 1992.[34] By 1993, many of the Bargi oustees had gone to nearby towns to find work. Indian journalist Shailendra Yashwant describes the villagers' plight:

> In Jabalpur there is a slum settlement around the weed infested Ranital lake into which the sewerage is discharged ... the residents are ... once-prosperous peasants from Gumti, Bargi and Meli villages in the Bargi dam submergence zone. The men are either rickshawpullers or construction labourers and the women manage to get road building work or domestic employment. 'It has killed our pride, living like animals here. Our children will never believe we were once thriving farmers. All they have seen is this filthy living', says a distraught Omkarnath, whose father owned 12 acres in Gumti.[35]

For people who are not landholders the loss of their jobs or businesses because of displacement means that they lose their source of livelihood. New jobs may be available at the dam site but unskilled oustees will invariably get the worst paid and most dangerous work. In any case almost all these jobs are lost once the project is complete. Furthermore, pressure on the local job market is increased because so many formerly self-sufficient farmers are made landless by the dam. The sudden influx of oustees into a resettlement area may also have the effect of lowering wages and reducing job opportunities for the people already living there.

The loss of the commons

> Our firewood comes from the forest, our fodder comes from there, our herbs and medicines come from there, the mahua flowers we collect [for mahua wine] come from there, our fish come from the river down here – which rehabilitation scheme of theirs will even look at all these as our earnings, as items to be compensated?
>
> Luaria, an *adivasi* to be displaced by Sardar Sarovar, 1994

For many rural people, and especially the poorest among them, the submergence of the commons is one of the worst losses to a reservoir. In semi-arid areas of India, for example, poor villagers collect almost all their firewood, and meet up to four-fifths of their grazing needs, from common lands. Yet these losses are rarely compensated. A 1994 World Bank internal review of 192 projects it had funded involving resettlement could find only one in which explicit provisions had been made for compensating common property losses.[36]

While the planners of the resettlement programme for the Manantali Dam on the Bafing River in Mali realized the need to compensate the 10,000 oustees for lost cropland, they failed to recognize that the sustainability of the Malian villagers' agriculture requires a reserve of fallow land at least equal to that on which crops are grown in any given year. The importance of common land to provide grazing for livestock was also ignored as the local people were defined by the planners as 'farmers' rather than 'herders', and farm animals were therefore assumed to be peripheral to the local economy. The importance of women's kitchen gardens and the wild foods that the women gather were similarly overlooked.[37]

Slashing the size of landholdings and people's access to the commons brings a large risk that hunger will follow in the wake of eviction – an ironic fact given that most dams are built with the rationale of increasing food production through irrigation. The Bombay-based Tata Institute of Social Sciences reports that fish and meat have vanished from the diets of the thousands of Sardar Sarovar oustees who moved to resettlement sites between 1986 and 1993, and that 'a general shortage of pulses and vegetables has been noted in some resettlement colonies.' In general, says the Tata Institute, resettlement 'has meant a decline in the variety, quantity and quality of food consumed' by the oustees.[38]

A 1992 study of a village in which some of the people evicted to make way for Hoa Binh Dam were resettled found that while prior to displacement most farmers could grow enough rice to last their families all year round, after the dam few had enough for more than three months. The families could grow some maize and cassava on the small patches of infertile hillside land onto which they had been forced but for several months of the year had to eat nutritionally poor and bitter wild yams. Children in the village displayed the distended bellies and spindly arms and legs of malnourishment.[39]

Resettled to death

Evidence from numerous dam projects shows that resettlement kills: sickness and death rates usually increase markedly after displacement, especially among the very young and very old. The main causes of illness are malnutrition, poor hygiene and sanitation at resettlement sites, and the parasitic water-borne diseases which invariably follow large water development projects in the tropics (see below). In addition, oustees displaced to ecologically different areas are often confronted with new types and strains of diseases to which they have little immunity, or do not know how best to prevent or cure. The psychological stress of displacement also increases their susceptibility to disease.

During a two-month period shortly after resettlement, outbreaks of sleeping sickness, dysentery, measles and chicken pox killed more than 121 of the Kariba oustees, most of them children. Nearly a year later, in September 1959, an unexplained disease broke out which over the following year claimed the lives of 56 women and children.[40] The Tata Institute found unusually high mortality rates among the 60 families at the resettlement site of Parveta in the first few years after oustees began to move there in 1984, with 17 deaths, 11 of them in children less than 4 years old.[41]

Drowning is another cause of death among dam-affected people, often because their small river boats are unsafe on the exposed waters of a reservoir. Another reason is that people living on the edge of a reservoir usually have little or no warning of fluctuations in the water level due to dam operation. In Indonesia, 106 people drowned in Saguling reservoir within 14 months of the completion of the dam in 1984; three years later, 10 people drowned in the 10 months following the impoundment of Cirata reservoir; and in the six months after the closure of Kedung Ombo dam in January 1989, six people drowned.[42]

An end to gaiety

The hardships of eviction and resettlement are not shared equally. Women are often left worse off than men, as the World Bank's 1994 resettlement review explains, because 'compensation payments are usually paid only to the [male] heads of households, converting the collective assets of the family to cash in male hands, and leaving women and children at higher risk of deprivation.'[43] Women may also be affected disproportionately because of their greater dependence on common property: in many cultures women have the responsibility for getting water and collecting fuelwood, fodder, wild vegetables and other produce of the commons. In Africa, women frequently tend gardens on unregistered land for which they are very unlikely to be compensated. Enakshi Ganguly Thukral says that,

> Because women in India are much less mobile than men, the breakdown of village and social units [because of displacement] affects them much more severely. The fact that she might be leaving relatives and friends behind, or may never again meet her daughter who is married into a village which will not be displaced, is a great cause of concern for the woman...[44]

Traditional community elders and leaders are often marginalized by displacement as it shows them as impotent to protect their community from eviction. They may also be usurped by younger community members with more formal education better able to negotiate with government officials. Religious leaders and protectors of sacred sites may also lose their social status when religious ceremonies based on flooded sites cannot be continued.

One of the most severe long-term problems faced by oustees is indebtedness. Resettlement, by replacing dependence on subsistence economies and the commons by dependence on cash and the market, increases people's vulnerability to debt and reduces their ability to make it through lean years. While indebtedness was virtually unknown in their riverside village of Manibeli, four-fifths of the households in the SSP resettlement site of Parveta were forced to take out loans in the eight years after displacement began.[45] Families who are unable to pay back their loans will eventually have no choice but to sell what little assets they have and, ultimately, their most important asset, their land.

Although it may seem obvious that displacement and the impoverishment it invariably entails would have severe consequences for a community's cultural and social well-being, this aspect of resettlement is rarely recognized in resettlement literature or resettlement plans, which normally deal only with the strictly economic consequences of displacement. One common result of resettlement is that villages, hamlets and even families are physically broken up: the 19 villages displaced by Sardar Sarovar in Gujarat state have been resettled in no less than 175 different locations.[46]

In their study of a village displaced by Rengali Dam in Orissa, anthropologists N.K. Behura and P.K. Nayak note a wide range of symptoms of social and cultural breakdown. The oustees' impoverishment meant that they could not fulfil their traditional obligations to help members of their extended families and castes, while their obligations increased as they depended on their non-oustee kin to help them cope with the ordeal of displacement. Disputes over the sharing of family compensation money 'have bred distrust and bitterness in family life'. Because the social prestige of the oustee families slumped, after displacement they could find marriage partners only among other oustee families. Traditional large multi-family households were broken up into nuclear families because compensation was paid on a nuclear-family basis. At the village level, say Behura and Nayak, 'the groups that provided political, economic, and ritual coordination have started to dissolve.' The enthusiasm, lavishness and pomp of festive occasions declined: the village festivals were now 'marked more by melancholy than by gaiety'.[47]

The Failure of Resettlement Policies

> Resistance and such stubbornness
> Thwart the most glorious success,
> Till in the end, to one's disgust,
> One soon grows tired of being just.
>
> Johann Wolfgang von Goethe, *Faust*, 1833

The World Bank's 1980 policy on 'involuntary resettlement' was the first issued by a major development agency. The policy has since been updated and improved and has been used as a model by numerous other international agencies. In its own words, the 'fundamental goal of the Bank's policy is to restore the living standards and earning capacities of displaced people – and when possible to improve them.'[48] However, for the vast majority of dams it has funded the Bank has no data on the 'living standards and earning capacities of displaced people', before or after resettlement. Moreover, an internal *Bankwide Review of Projects Involving Involuntary Resettlement 1986–1993* concedes that what evidence is available

> ...points to unsatisfactory income restoration more frequently than to satisfactory outcomes.... Declining income among affected populations is significant, reaching in some cases as much as 40 percent among populations that were poor even before displacement...[49]

Of the 192 World Bank-funded projects examined for the 1994 *Bankwide Review*, half had no resettlement plans when they were approved by the Bank's board of executive directors, a direct violation of the institution's own policy. Also in violation of the Bank's policy, 70 per cent of the resettlement plans which had been prepared provided only for cash compensation, and not for the replacement of land and other productive assets.[50] Only 15 per cent, therefore, were in compliance with two of the resettlement policy's most basic provisions.

A recurrent finding of reviews of resettlement operations is that the numbers of people to be displaced are almost always underestimated (see Table 3.1). Planning documents for the projects examined by the *Bankwide Review* indicated a total of 1.34 million people to be displaced by all 192 projects combined. When the *Bankwide Review* assessed current progress on these projects they found that in fact at least 1.965 million people were being evicted (63 per cent of them by dams). World Bank staff and borrower country bureaucrats had failed to note the evictions of 625,000 people.[51]

The main reason for the consistent underestimates is almost certainly that it suits project authorities and lending agencies to distort the figures to make projects look more viable. A 1986 internal review written by the Bank's senior sociologist Michael Cernea (co-author of the 1994 review) noted that 'borrowing agencies sometimes deliberately under-represent the scale of resettlement to Bank missions.'[52] Yet, although underestimates are the norm rather than the exception, Bank missions rarely question the figures they are given.

The World Bank's 1984 pre-project appraisal of the Ruzizi II hydro-plant on the Rwanda–Zaire border, which it co-funded with the European Development Fund, claimed that 'the dam and generating station would have little effect on the daily lives of the inhabitants of the proposed site', and that only 135 people would need to be evicted. The 1994 *Bankwide Review*, however, found that 15,000 people had been displaced – more than 111 times the Bank's original estimate. A 1989 World Bank memo recounts the fiasco of resettlement at another Bank-funded hydro project in East Africa, Kiambere on Kenya's Tana River. According to the leaked document, the original project appraisal 'guessed a figure of 1,000 people living on both sides of the riverbank, of which an unspecified number might have to be resettled'. Later surveys found that seven times this number had been displaced.[53] Consistent underestimates of eviction numbers are of much more than purely statistical interest. Even if written with the best of intentions, a plan which is budgeted on the premiss that 135 people have to be compensated and found alternative land will fall to pieces when 15,000 need to be moved.

The 1994 *Bankwide Review* could find only one Bank-funded dam – Khao Laem in Thailand – where the 'fundamental goal' of the Bank's policy had been met and 'incomes for all households rose after re-settlement.'[54] However, a close read of the study of resettlement at Khao Laem by the World Bank's Operations Evaluation Department (OED) – the study on which the *Bankwide Review*'s conclusion is based – reveals a rather less rosy picture. The OED study claims only that

Table 3.1 The underestimation of oustee numbers

Dam (project)	Country	Original estimate (year)	Revised estimate (year)	Ref.
Itá	Brazil	13,800 (1987)	19,200 (1993)	2
Guavio	Colombia	1,000 (1981)	5,500 (1994)	1
Akosombo	Ghana	62,500 (1956)	84,000 (1965)	5,8
(Andhra Pradesh Irrigation II)	India	63,000 (1986)	150,000 (1994)	1
(Gujarat Medium Irrigation II)	India	63,600 (19??)	140,370 (1994)	3
(Karnataka Irrigation /Upper Krishna)	India	20,000 (1978)	240,000 (1994)	1,5
(Madhya Pradesh Medium Irrigation)	India	8,000 (1981)	19,000 (1994)	1
Sardar Sarovar	India	33,000 (1985)	320,000 (1993)	4
Upper Indravati	India	8,531 (19??)	16,080 (1994)	3
Kiambere	Kenya	1,000 (1983)	7,000 (1995)	5
Bakun	Malaysia	4,300 (1988)	9,430 (1995)	7
Funtua	Nigeria	100 (19??)	4,000 (1994)	5
Tarbela	Pakistan	85,000 (19??)	96,000 (19??)	6
Ruzizi II	Zaire/ Rwanda/ Burundi	135 (1984)	15,000 (1994)	1

Sources:

1. World Bank, *Resettlement and Development: The Bankwide Review of Projects Involving Resettlement 1986–1993*, 8 April 1994.
2. M.M. Cernea and S.E. Guggenheim (eds.), *Anthropological Approaches To Resettlement: Policy, Practice and Theory*, Westview Press, Boulder, CO, 1993.
3. World Bank, 'Resettlement and Rehabilitation in India: A Status Update of Projects Involving Involuntary Resettlement', 1994.
4. Narmada Bachao Andolan, 'Supreme Court of India Writ Petition', 1994.
5. C.C. Cook (ed.), *Involuntary Resettlement in Africa: Selected Papers from a Conference on Environment and Settlement Issues in Africa*, World Bank Technical Paper 227, 1994.
6. Peter Ames, Harza Engineering, personal communication.
7. 'Bakun Hydroelectric Project: Energy Security Via Hydropower', GTZ, Eschborn 1988; 'Bakun: Green Energy for the Future', Prime Minister's Department, Kuala Lumpur 1996.
8. National Electric Power Authority, 'Lokoja Hydroelectric Project: Feasibility Study, Appendix C2. International Resettlement Experience', Lagos, March 1979.

the *average* incomes of a sample of 200 families *living at resettlement sites* had risen. Yet as many as one in five of the displaced families, most of them from the Karen ethnic minority, did not possess legal residence papers and were not eligible for land or house plots at the resettlement sites.[55] The World Bank has ignored the fate of these families, at least some of whom have been forced into farming illegally in an internationally important wildlife sanctuary nearby.[56] Of the 1,949 families who did move to the resettlement villages, more than 20 per cent had left the area by 1989, four years after the dam was completed, the time of the survey used by the OED. The fate of these families is also unrecorded.[57]

Average inflation-adjusted incomes of the 200 families surveyed, says the OED, rose from $118–235 per capita in 1979, to $260 per capita in 1989. Yet the pre-dam income figures are likely to be spurious. The people displaced were largely subsistence rice farmers, and the estimate of their previous incomes is based on what the OED admits was inconsistent and unreliable information on the value of the rice they grew.[58] Basing the families' income on the value of their agricultural production, furthermore, fails to take into account the very significant contribution which common property resources made to their livelihoods.

The conclusion that the OED's finding of improved incomes is largely a convenient statistical artefact is reinforced by the oustees' own perceptions. Figures buried in the appendices of the OED report show that four out of five of the resettlers surveyed in 1989 considered themselves economically worse off than before resettlement. Only 14 per cent thought that their incomes were higher than before the dam was built. The OED admits that settlers complained it was more expensive to live in the resettlement areas than in their original villages, and that five years after displacement the oustees continued to hold demonstrations and protests to demand better compensation. Despite the Khao Laem oustees' obvious unhappiness, the OED concludes that as their 'incomes have increased', therefore their 'living standards have improved', and that 'the resettlement outcome was satisfactory'.[59]

Holding up Khao Laem as its only dam resettlement success story indicates how desperate the situation is at the rest of the World Bank's resettlement operations. The World Bank consistently claims in its own defence that while its resettlement record is poor, that of the projects in which it is not involved is even worse. While there is no statistical evidence to back up this claim, it is certainly unlikely that the record of restoring living standards and self-respect is on average any better in non-World Bank projects.

Dams and Disease

> Should there be rivers in the land which drain off from the ground the stagnant water and the rain water, then [the people] will be healthy and bright. But if there be no rivers, and the water that the people drink be marshy, stagnant, and fenny, the physique of the people must show protruding bellies and enlarged spleens.
>
> Hippocrates, Treatise on *Airs, Waters and Places*, *c.* 400 BC

It is not only oustees who get sick and die because of dams. As they radically alter ecological conditions and trigger large population movements, dams are a powerful agent in the spread of disease, especially in tropical and subtropical areas, and in particular when they are accompanied by irrigation schemes. While properly funded and implemented public health measures can reduce – although not eradicate – dam-related disease, such measures are very much the exception rather than the rule.

The first health risk from a dam project begins with the arrival into a remote area of large numbers of construction workers, most of them poor, unskilled labourers who, especially in tropical countries, commonly carry a wide range of infectious diseases, such as tuberculosis, measles, influenza, leishmaniasis, syphilis and AIDS. Some of the diseases, or strains of diseases, carried by the construction workers are likely to be new to the dam region and local people may have little immunity to them.

At its maximum, 38,000 workers were employed on the construction of Itaipú Dam on the border of Brazil and Paraguay, with, at the end of 1978, 2,000 people leaving or joining the workforce each day. According to the World Health Organization:

> The incoming workers and their families increased the population of nearby villages 3–7 fold. Living mostly in overcrowded slums with neither sanitation nor adequate health care, they were exposed to the common infectious diseases, particularly respiratory and diarrhoeal infections, malnutrition and polyparasitism, leading to impaired development of children. The living conditions were also conducive to prostitution and promiscuity, with a high frequency of sexually transmitted disease.[60]

The HIV virus is believed to have been introduced into the southern African kingdom of Lesotho by construction workers on the $8 billion dam-and-diversion Lesotho Highlands Water Project. HIV is now making inroads into local communities. In 1992, random tests found that more than 1 in 20 dam construction workers were infected, as were around 1 in 120 people from the same age group in nearby villages. 'Grave concern is now warranted as the country is destined to experience a rapid rise in HIV', warned an article in a 1995 American Medical Association journal. 'Increased surveillance, health education opportunities and aggressive prevention activities at the Katse Dam construction site are imperative to arrest the spread of HIV from construction workers to nearby villagers.'[61]

Workers on dam sites also face the risk of death and injury due to the dangerous working conditions inherent in most dam projects. The World Bank's Industry and Energy Department admits that 'worker deaths are unfortunately common in all tunnelling, dam-building and earth-moving activities.'[62] More than 100 workers were killed at Kariba; at least 154 died building India's Nagarjunasagar Dam; and in Colombia in 1983 more than 200 lives were lost in a landslide during construction of the Guavio Dam.[63] François L. Lempérière, a senior member of the French Committee on Large Dams, calculates that altogether some 100,000 workers have died building dams and many hundreds of thousands have been seriously injured.[64]

Schistosomiasis: dams and snails

The main reason why dams and irrigation systems spread disease is that they create habitats in which insects, snails and other animals that serve as vectors for water-borne disease parasites can thrive. The magnitude of the global incidence of the debilitating disease schistosomiasis (bilharzia) is directly connected with the construction of dam and irrigation projects. These have both allowed the disease to flourish in areas where it was previously unknown, and increased its severity where it was already a problem. A 1977 UN-sponsored conference on the environmental problems of irrigation concluded that: 'Invasion by schistosomiasis of irrigation schemes in arid lands is so common that there is no need to give examples. The non-invasion of schemes in a region where the disease exists is exceptional.'[65]

In 1947, an estimated 114 million people worldwide were infected with schistosomiasis. Since then the number has grown to around 200 million, despite the development, in the 1980s, of a 'wonder drug' cure, praziquantel (the effectiveness of which now appears to be waning), and numerous efforts to try to control the disease. Schistosomiasis is endemic in more than 70 countries. It is especially severe in Africa, and is also a problem in parts of the Middle East, the Philippines, China, the Caribbean and, increasingly, Brazil.[66]

The two most common species of the flatworms known as schistomes which infect people are *Schistosoma haematobium* (found in Africa and the Middle East) and *S. mansoni* (found in Africa and South America). The eggs of the worms enter water courses in human excreta and are then taken up by snails of the species *Bulinus* and *Biomphalaria*. Inside the snails, the schistome eggs hatch and the snails then excrete the larvae back into the water, where they come to rest on the stems and leaves of aquatic plants. When people brush against the plants the larvae rapidly penetrate their skin and enter their bloodstream.

Once in their human host, the larvae mature into adult worms. *S. haematobium* worms move to the bladder to reproduce, a single pair producing up to 3,000 eggs a day for around eight weeks. The eggs provoke allergic reactions in the urinary system. The *S. mansoni* worms, which can live for up to 35 years, reproduce in the intestine. Some of the eggs are excreted in faeces or urine for the cycle to begin again. Those that remain spread around the body, causing irritation to various organs. Intestinal schistosomiasis is the most serious of the two forms of the disease.

The worms and their eggs produce an enormous range of illnesses. The most common effect is a general mild fatigue and listlessness. Other symptoms range from minor local skin infections, to life-threatening heart-disease, epilepsy, kidney failure and cancer. In all cases the infected person is made more susceptible to other diseases. In areas where schistosomiasis is endemic, infection rates can reach 100 per cent of the local population.

The waters along the edges of tropical reservoirs and irrigation canals tend to be still, shallow, warm, weedy and well lit, excellent habitat for *Bulinus* and *Biomphalaria* snails. Reservoirs and irrigation schemes also greatly increase human contact with snail- and plant-infested water bodies: farmers and fishers work in and around the canals and reservoirs, their families wash themselves and their clothes in them, and their children play in them. The large amount of time which children in hot areas spend playing near water means that they are particularly prone to becoming – and staying – infected. The development of perennial irrigation schemes means that people are exposed to schistosomiasis infection all year round, whereas previously when their agriculture depended on seasonal rainfall or the annual flood, the only period of contact between humans and snails was during the short rainy season.[67]

Schistosomiasis has infected Egyptians since Pharaonic times, but only this century has it become a serious problem. The building and subsequent heightenings of the Low Aswan Dam in the early twentieth century, and the associated conversion of fields from traditional flood irrigation to year-round irrigation with canals and ditches, increased the incidence of urinary schistosomiasis in four villages surveyed in Upper Egypt from a maximum of 11 per cent in 1934 to up to 75 per cent three years later. Since the 1930s, however, improved public sanitation and health care has slowly reduced urinary schistosomiasis rates.

Since the construction of the High Aswan Dam, however, infections of the much more dangerous intestinal schistosomiasis have risen markedly, especially in the Nile Delta, possibly because the increased salinity of water in the delta favours the *Biomphalaria* snails, which carry

S. mansoni, over the *Bulinus* species, which carry *S. haematobium*. The loss of the flood which once swept the snails out to sea, and the explosion of freshwater vegetation in the new irrigation canals, also helped the *Biomphalaria* snails.[68]

In Ghana, all reservoirs – large and small – have become infested with *Bulinus* snails. Around the vast Volta Reservoir, urinary schistosomiasis rates rocketed from less than 10 per cent in riverside villages in 1966 to around 90 per cent in children living near the new reservoir in 1969. In some villages adjacent to the reservoir, every person was infected. Intestinal schistosomiasis has not occurred around the reservoir, although in villages downstream from Akosombo, near the smaller dam at Kpong, more than one-third of villagers are infected with *S. mansoni*.[69]

A consultant's study funded by the US Agency for International Development concluded in 1982 that the planned Diama Dam on the estuary of the Senegal River and the associated expansion of irrigated rice might cause little increase in local schistosomiasis rates (at that time only the urinary form was present in the lower Senegal Basin).[70] As dam building and the expansion of irrigation almost everywhere else in West Africa had dramatically increased the spread of schistosomiasis, it is hard to see how this conclusion was reached. In early 1988, 18 months after Diama was completed, the first cases of an unusually severe and difficult-to-treat form of intestinal schistosomiasis were found. By 1994, rates of infection with this type of schistosomiasis in communities near the lower Senegal irrigation schemes ranged from 25 to 82 per cent.[71]

In Asia, the dominant form of schistosomiasis is intestinal and is caused by *S. japonicum*, which is similar in its habits to *S. mansoni*, although its health effects are often more severe. In the Philippines, where *S. japonicum* is the major public health problem on irrigation schemes, people with schistosomiasis are estimated to be unable to work for up to 42 days out of every year.[72] Conditions in India do not appear favourable for the spread of schistosomiasis, its transmission only having been verified in one small village in Maharashtra state. However, there are fears that the infection could be brought to India by the large number of Indian nationals working in endemic areas, especially the Middle East.[73] If the disease were to take hold in India, with its large area under canal irrigation, dense population and poor health care infrastructure, the result would be a public health disaster.[74]

Attempts around the world to control schistosomiasis have met with limited success, often managing to contain, but not eradicate, the disease. A programme on Volta Reservoir, supported by the WHO and UNDP, which involved spraying molluscicides and treating infected people, halved the incidence of schistosomiasis between 1975 and the end of the programme in 1981, but it still left almost two-fifths of the people in the project area infected – and it only covered a 60 kilometre stretch of the reservoir's 5,000 kilometre shoreline. Egypt spends a huge amount on its schistosomiasis control programme – 8 per cent of the country's total health budget in 1984 – yet is still suffering an epidemic of the disease.[75] In the 1970s, China was thought to have reduced schistosomiasis, chiefly through improved sanitation and the destruction of snail habitats, to the point where 'it is no longer of public health importance.'[76] In 1994, however, the Beijing *Economic Daily* reported that

> ...since the 1970s, more and more cases of the disease have been discovered ... and so far 1.5 million people ... along the Yangtze River have been found to be affected ... the country is facing a serious situation in preventing the recurrence of schistosomiasis.[77]

Malaria: an ecological disaster

In spite of a strenuous worldwide eradication effort, malaria is one of the world's most widespread and lethal diseases, and is becoming ever more dangerous. In 1990, malaria parasites infected over 300 million people, and probably killed well over 1 million. The great majority of malaria infections and deaths occur among children in Africa. The director-general of the WHO, Dr Hiroshi Nakajima, warned in 1992 that 'globally, the malaria situation is serious and getting worse.'[78]

Malaria in humans is caused by four species of protozoa, of which *Plasmodium vivax* and *Plasmodium falciparum* are the most common. The *Plasmodium* parasites must spend part of their lifecycle within females of many different species of mosquitoes of the *Anopheles* genus, and the rest within a warm-blooded host such as a human. The main factors determining the incidence of malaria in a given area are climate and humidity (warm summers are needed for the *Plasmodium* parasites to survive; humid summers are necessary for the mosquitoes to live long enough for the parasites to reach their infective stage); the presence and density of *Anopheles* mosquitoes; the extent of the mosquitoes' interaction with people; and the presence of infected humans to spread the parasites to the mosquitoes. The ecological changes caused by dams and perennial irrigation schemes in arid and semi-arid areas tend to boost *Anopheles* populations by increasing the area of stagnant water in which they breed, and by extending the period during which standing water is present.[79]

A study of mosquito species found on irrigated and non-irrigated areas on the Kano Plains of southwest Kenya in the 1970s showed that not only did irrigation lead to a fourfold increase in mosquito populations, but also that it greatly favoured the proliferation of *Anopheles* at the expense of other species of mosquitoes. *A. gambiae*, the main vector of malaria in semi-arid Africa, was found to thrive in the shallow waters of rice fields in the Kano Plains; *A. funestus*, the second most common African vector, bred largely in the irrigation canals and drains. In 1988, nearly one in five of the inhabitants of the plains were infected with malaria. In two other irrigated areas in Kenya, the incidence of malaria in 1990 was 26 and 54 per cent higher than in surrounding non-irrigated areas.[80]

The *A. gambiae* mosquito is one of the most dangerous malaria vectors. It breeds prolifically in warm, shallow pools of water as small as rain-filled hoofprints, and has a high rate of infection with the *Plasmodium falciparum* parasite which can cause cerebral malaria – the most lethal form of the disease. *A. gambiae* is attracted to sunlight and its population density tends to increase with environmental degradation, especially deforestation and the flooding of forest or savannah areas. A devastating malaria epidemic which struck Upper Egypt in 1942–43, killing 130,000 people, followed an invasion of *A. gambiae* from the Sudan. According to the WHO, the epidemic 'must be seen as a consequence of water development'.[81]

Large water projects also encourage people to work and live near *Anopheles* breeding areas, and, as land use shifts from livestock herding to crop growing, or from forest to village, so the mosquitoes switch from biting animals to biting humans. On the rangelands of Kenya's Kano Plains, 70 per cent of *A. gambiae* feed on cattle, the rest on humans; on irrigated fields nearby the reverse is true.[82] In the area of Sri Lanka's five-dam Mahaweli project, deforestation greatly reduced the animal population on which the main vector of malaria in South Asia, *Anopheles culicifacies*, used to feed, so the mosquitoes turned for their source of blood sustenance to the settlers who were flooding into the area. Low water flow downstream of the five major Mahaweli dams, leaving pools of stagnant water in the river bed, increased the breeding habitat for *A. culicifacies*. In 1986–87 outbreaks of malaria due to *P. falciparum* occurred for the first time ever in the Mahaweli area.[83]

In some places anopheline mosquitoes are present, but not the *Plasmodium* parasites. Malaria may be introduced to these areas by migrants from infected areas who come to work on dam sites or settle on irrigation schemes. An epidemic of malaria in the region around Itaipú Dam in 1989 was caused by a combination of an increase in the local density of *A. darlingi*, the most important malaria vector in Brazil, and the huge influx of labourers from the Amazon region infected with *Plasmodium* parasites. Before 1986, malaria had been considered eradicated in southern Brazil, and had been reduced to very low levels across the Paraná River in Paraguay.[84]

Dam planners frequently play down the risk of their projects increasing malaria, claiming that the spraying of pesticides to kill mosquitoes and the establishment of proper health care facilities in affected areas can control the disease. Both of these assertions, however, are fast becoming untenable in the face of the widespread resistance of mosquitoes to pesticides and the equally widespread resistance of the parasites to chemical treatment. Indeed, it now appears that the conventional modern methods of controlling malaria have only created the ecological conditions to make the disease even more deadly.

The global campaign to eradicate malaria began in 1958 under the aegis of the WHO. The weapons chosen were chiefly DDT and the anti-malarial drug chloroquine. At first the campaign appeared to be reaching its goal. Sri Lanka, which had one million malaria cases in 1955, had just 18 in 1963 when the eradication campaign was at its zenith. The apparent success and huge cost of the eradication programme meant that when malaria infections dropped dramatically in a region, funds were allocated elsewhere and the control effort was wound down. Unfortunately, along with the drop in infections came a rise in the vulnerability to malaria of people living in *Anopheles* endemic areas (immunity to malaria rapidly disappears without regular exposure to the parasites). Therefore when the spraying stopped and the mosquitoes returned the disease came back with a vengeance. By 1975, the number of malaria cases in Sri Lanka had soared back up to more than 400,000; worldwide, the number of cases was about two-and-a-half times what it had been in 1961.[85]

While malaria rates surged around the world in the 1960s, two disasters struck hopes of ever defeating the disease: mosquitoes began to develop genetic resistance to DDT; and *Plasmodium* parasites began to develop resistance to chloroquine. The mosquito resistance to DDT meant that spraying programmes had to switch to much more expensive alternatives, to which, over time, mosquitoes also gained resistance.

Even worse, *Plasmodium* strains resistant to chloroquine which first appeared in isolated pockets in Asia in the 1950s had spread throughout Asia and Latin America during the 1960s and 1970s. By 1990, chloroquine resistance was widespread in Africa, and the new resistant strains of *P. falciparum* seemed to be more virulent than older types. In Asia, the evolution of multiple resistance to the increasingly expensive anti-malarials developed to replace chloroquine has accelerated through the decades. Although multiple resistance is not yet common in Africa, a strain of *falciparum* was found in Mali in 1993 that was resistant to *all* anti-malarials.

Today, far more people die from malaria than three decades ago. In Brazil in 1960, malaria was virtually extinct; in 1990, 560,000 cases were recorded. Deaths due to malaria in Africa were at a historic all-time high in 1993.[86]

Dams and other mosquito-borne diseases

In 1977, a mysterious haemorrhagic disease broke out near Aswan in Egypt. About 18,000 cases were recorded and some 600 people died. The illness was later identified as Rift Valley fever, a viral disease with symptoms similar to yellow fever. Rift Valley fever had previously been a disease of livestock in eastern sub-Saharan Africa: animal losses during the Aswan epidemic were so great that Egypt suffered serious meat shortages.

Scientists believe that the Aswan epidemic began as an outbreak among livestock in northern Sudan and then spread to Egypt for the first time via either human migration or wind-blown mosquitoes. Once the virus arrived in Egypt it was rapidly spread by the mosquitoes which thrived around the margins of Nasser Reservoir. Another severe outbreak of the disease hit the Aswan area in the early 1990s.[87] In October 1987, Rift Valley fever appeared for the first time in West Africa, killing almost 300 people in Rosso, Mauritania. The outbreak happened at a time when mosquitoes were unusually abundant due to the recent filling of Diama Dam and the subsequent increase in irrigated rice fields.[88]

Seventy-five million people around the world are believed to be infected with lymphatic filariasis, caused by a parasitic worm spread by several species of mosquitoes. The most notorious form of lymphatic filariasis is elephantiasis, which occurs after years of repeated infection, and can cause the victim's arms, legs, genitals and breasts to swell to monstrous proportions. Forty per cent of the population of irrigated areas in southwest Burkina Faso were found to be infected with lymphatic filariasis in the mid-1970s. Mosquitoes which spread lymphatic filariasis proliferate in weed-infested reservoirs in Asia.[89]

Another serious disease associated with water development projects in Asia is Japanese encephalitis, spread by the *Culex tritaeniorhyncus* mosquito. The virus is currently subsiding in China, Japan and South Korea, but spreading in Bangladesh, India, Burma, Nepal, Thailand and Vietnam, primarily, it is believed, because of the switch from rainfed to perennially irrigated rice farming.[90]

Mosquitoes transmit many other diseases, including yellow fever and dengue fever. The insects can also make life extremely uncomfortable even if they do not carry infections. The stagnant water and rotting vegetation in Brazil's Tucuruí Reservoir caused an infestation of flies and of a particularly aggressive strain of mosquito with a painful bite. The insects made life misery for the 8,000 people living around the reservoir, some claiming to have been bitten as many as 700 times in an hour. A wave of diseases, including malaria and leishmaniasis, struck the area, and many people were forced to abandon their homes and farms. Leishmaniasis, also called kala-azar and Dumdum fever, can cause localized skin infection, fever, anaemia, dysentery and pneumonia, and is fatal in extreme cases. It is caused by a protozoon spread by sandfly bites.[91]

Flies and worms

> The worms crawl out and the worms crawl in,
> The ones that go in, are lean and thin,
> The ones that crawl out, are fat and stout,
> Be merry, my friends, be merry.
>
> Traditional English rhyme

Onchocerciasis, or river blindness, is caused by a worm transmitted by the bite of a blackfly which breeds in fast-flowing water. River blindness infects 25 million people in 26 African countries and in Yemen and small areas of Central America and northern South America. The eyesight of at least 1 million people is impaired by the disease, and more than 350,000 victims have become blind. Large dams are a mixed blessing in the case of river blindness: Akosombo in Ghana and Kossou in Côte d'Ivoire both flooded huge areas of blackfly breeding sites under their reservoirs, but worsened the disease downstream because of the breeding grounds created by spillways and altered river flow patterns.[92] Manantali Dam, however, has both eradicated the disease from the area around its reservoir and helped reduce its incidence downstream.[93]

Small dams are more likely to increase river blindness infections overall: their spillways provide excellent habitat for the blackfly larvae in the wet season, but they may not flood any breeding sites. A rice irrigation scheme in the Tiao valley of Burkina Faso led to the infection of virtually everyone in the area by 1972, seven years after irrigation started. Fully half of the people aged over 40 became blind. River blindness had previously been rare in the valley.[94]

The West African Onchocerciasis Control Programme, started in 1975 by the World Bank and several UN agencies, is, according to its sponsors, a 'stunning success' and has 'virtually eliminated river blindness as a public health problem' in seven of the worst affected countries. Thirty million people formerly at risk are now claimed to be safe from the disease. The control programme has relied on the aerial spraying of blackfly larva breeding areas with insecticides, and the pharmaceutical treatment of victims of the early stages of the disease.[95]

Dam builders argue that while there are many health risks created by their projects in developing countries, these risks can be brought down to 'acceptable' levels by proper 'monitoring' and health care measures. Improved primary health care, especially the provision of proper sanitation, can certainly render illnesses less common and less lethal than would otherwise be the case, but they will rarely prevent increases in water-borne diseases when the ecological conditions are created for them to spread. The story of malaria eradication provides a clear illustration that it can be fatally foolish to trust in human ability to outwit microbe ecology. Furthermore, while provisions for health care may be made in project plans, there is no guarantee that these measures will actually be funded over the long term. 'Monitoring' – the almost inevitable development consultants' answer to any problem – by itself will not stop a single case of illness.

Another argument of dam proponents is that the projects provide improved water supplies, and therefore will reduce overall rates of illness. However, the larger dams are rarely built for domestic water supply, and when this is their aim, it is normally a minor part of the project – and a part which could be easily met with a smaller dam or other alternatives. Furthermore, water supply projects in the absence of other health measures usually do little to reduce the incidence of diseases.[96]

Dams and irrigation schemes can also decrease the availability of clean water: when water for domestic use comes from irrigation canals, it may be polluted with pesticide run-off and other agricultural wastes, heavily saline and contaminated with human sewage. Michael Goldman of the University of California reports that most of the households he visited during a research project on the huge Indira Gandhi Canal in the Rajasthan desert 'expressed concern for their children's stomach ailments' due to their contaminated water supply.[97] The World Bank and other proponents of Sardar Sarovar claim that the project will reduce the incidence of skin diseases as it will improve water supplies, yet Goldman notes that one of the consequences of the Indira Gandhi Canal (a project with many parallels to SSP) has been an epidemic of skin diseases.[98]

In general, when dam builders are faced with the negative social consequences of their projects these are claimed to be regrettable side-effects to projects which are in their entirety overwhelmingly beneficial. This argument assumes that dams fulfil the many promises which their backers make for them. As is described in the following chapters, this assumption is frequently wrong.

Notes

1. P. Panjiar, 'Refugees of Progress', *India Today*, 30 September 1993.
2. World Bank, *China: Involuntary Resettlement*, 8 June 1993, p. 72.
3. Ibid.; X. Cheung, 'Unleashing Hydroelectric Potential in a Challenging Environment', *Hydro Review Worldwide*, Winter 1993; P.E. Tyler, 'China Proposes Huge Aqueduct to Beijing Area', *New York Times*, 19 July 1994.
4. Dai Qing, personal communication, 24 October 1994.
5. World Bank researchers calculated in 1994 that 4–4.5 million are evicted by dams *every year*, an average of 14,000 people per dam. Multiplying this average by 40,000 (the number of large dams) gives a total of 560 million! This annual

estimate is therefore probably far too high. One of the Bank's repeated responses to critics of their resettlement record is that their projects are responsible for only a very small proportion of the total number being displaced by dams. The World Bank therefore has an interest in exaggerating the total number of people being displaced (World Bank, *Resettlement and Development: The Bankwide Review of Projects Involving Involuntary Resettlement 1986–1993*, 8 April 1994, p. 1/3).

6. B. Morse et al., *Sardar Sarovar: The Report of the Independent Review*, RFI, Ottawa 1992, pp. 89–94, 204, 274, 339–45, 340; 'Supreme Court of India Writ Petition', NBA, Baroda 1994, pp. 8–10; 'Forest Preservation: Which Way to Go? Sanctuary or Forest-Based Tribal Development', ARCH-VAHINI, Rajpipla, Gujarat, January 1994; HR Wallingford, 'Sediment and Backwater Aspects of Sardar Sarovar Project', HR Wallingford, UK and World Bank, March 1993, pp. 12–15.

7. T. Scudder, 'Social Impacts', in A.K. Biswas (ed.), *Handbook of Water Resources and Environment*, McGraw-Hill, New York forthcoming.

8. S. El-Din El-Zarka, 'Kainji Lake, Nigeria', in W.C. Ackermann et al. (eds.), *Man-Made Lakes: Their Problems and Environmental Effects*, American Geophysical Union, Washington, DC, 1973, p. 197.

9. W.M. Adams, *Wasting the Rain: Rivers, People and Planning in Africa*, Earthscan, London 1992, p. 145.

10. J. Redwood III, *World Bank Approaches to the Environment in Brazil: A Review of Selected Projects*, World Bank OED 1993, pp. 48–50.

11. P. Magee, 'Peasant Political Identity and the Tucuruí Dam: A Case Study of the Island Dwellers of Pará, Brazil', *Latinamericanist*, Vol. 24, No. 1, December 1989.

12. Government of India, *Report of the Committee on Rehabilitation of Displaced Tribals due to Development Projects*, Ministry of Home Affairs, New Delhi 1985, cited in E.G. Thukral, 'Introduction', in E.G. Thukral (ed.), *Big Dams, Displaced People: Rivers of Sorrow, Rivers of Change*, Sage Publications, New Delhi 1992, p. 8. The indigenous people of India are usually known as 'tribals' by English-speaking Indians. They are also often called, and refer to themselves as, *adivasis*, the Hindi word meaning literally 'original dwellers' (Anti-Slavery Society, *The Philippines: Authoritarian Government, Multinationals and Ancestral Land*, Anti-Slavery Society, London 1983).

13. P. Hirsch, 'Social and Environmental Implications of Resource Development in Vietnam: The Case of Hoa Binh Reservoir', RIAP Occasional Paper, University of Sydney 1992.

14. P.M. Fearnside, 'Brazil's Balbina Dam: Environment versus the Legacy of the Pharaohs in Amazonia', *Environmental Management*, Vol. 13, No. 4, 1989, p. 403; R. Gribel, 'The Balbina Disaster: The Need to Ask Why?', *The Ecologist*, Vol. 20, No. 4, 1990, p. 135.

15. A. Oliver-Smith, 'Involuntary Resettlement, Resistance and Political Empowerment', *Journal of Refugee Studies*, Vol. 4, No. 2, 1991, p. 143. Kaptai is also known as Karnafuli (the name of the river it impounds).

16. M. Reisner, *Cadillac Desert: The American West and its Disappearing Water*, Secker & Warburg, London 1986, pp. 191, 198.

17. C.P. Morris, 'Hydroelectric Development and the Human Rights of Indigenous People', in P.A. Olson (ed.), *The Struggle for the Land: Indigenous Insight and Industrial Empire in the Semiarid World*, University of Nebraska Press, Lincoln 1990, pp. 195, 197.

18. 'After 43 Years, Colvilles Settle Grand Coulee Dam Claims', *Seattle Post-Intelligencer*, 11 October 1994.

19. K. Chen, 'The Limited Benefits of Flood Control: An Interview With Lu Qinkan', and Y. Sun et al., 'Views and Suggestions on the Assessment Report of the Three Gorges Project', both in Dai Qing (edited by P. Adams and J. Thibodeau), *Yangtze! Yangtze!*, Probe International, Toronto and Earthscan, London 1994, pp. 182 and 57.

20. T. Scudder, 'Development-Induced Relocation and Refugee Studies: 37 Years of Change and Continuity Among Zambia's Gwembe Tonga', *Journal of Refugee Studies*, Vol. 6, No. 2, 1993, p. 141.

21. Quoted in ibid.

22. R.A. Mnatsakanian, *Environmental Legacy of the Former Soviet Republics*, Centre for Human Ecology, University of Edinburgh 1992, p. 179.

23. Morris, 'Hydroelectric Development', p. 203; S.E. Guggenheim, 'Peasants, Planners, and Participation: Resettlement in Mexico', in M.M. Cernea and S.E. Guggenheim (eds.), *Anthropological Approaches To Resettlement: Policy, Practice and Theory*, Westview Press, Boulder, CO, 1993, p. 205.

24. 'The Three Gorges Dam in China: Forced Resettlement, Suppression of Dissent and Labor Rights Concerns', *Human Rights Watch/Asia*, Vol. 7, No. 2, 1995, pp. 11–12.

25. International Engineering Company has since been taken over by Morrison-Knudsen Corporation of San Francisco.

26. Witness for Peace, *A People Dammed: The Impact of the World Bank Chixoy Hydroelectric Project in Guatemala*, Washington, DC, 1996, pp. 15–20; R. Alecio, 'Uncovering the Truth: Political Violence and Indigenous Organizations', in M. Sinclair (ed.), *The New Politics of Survival: Grassroots Movements in Central America*, Monthly Review Press, New York 1995, pp. 25–45; World Bank, 'Project Completion Report on Guatemala Chixoy Power Project', 31 December 1991, pp. 30, 40.

27. C. Maloney, 'Environmental and Project Displacement of Population in India. Part 1: Development and Deracination', *UFSI Field Staff Reports*, No. 14, 1990.

28. N.K Behura and P.K. Nayak, 'Involuntary Displacement and Changing Frontiers of Kinship: A Study of Resettlement in Orissa', in Cernea and Guggenheim (eds.), *Anthropological Approaches to Resettlement*, p. 303.

29. World Bank, *China*, p. 6.

30. C.P. Wallace, 'Is Asia Robbing Rural Poor to Power the Rich?', *Los Angeles Times*, 18 February 1992.

31. See, e.g., M.M. Cernea, 'Involuntary Resettlement in Bank-Assisted Projects: A Review of the Applications of Bank Policies and Procedures in FY79–85 Projects', World Bank 1986, p. 33.

32. S. Guggenheim, 'Resettlement in Colombia: The Case of El Guavio', *Practising Anthropology*, Vol. 12, No. 3, 1990.

33. Lokayan, 'Srisailam: The Shadow Grows Longer. Lokayan's Second Report', *Lokayan Bulletin*, 1985; The Fact-Finding Committee on the Srisailam Project, 'The Srisailam Resettlement Experience: The Untold Story', in E. Goldsmith and N. Hildyard (eds.), *The Social and Environmental Impacts of Large Dams. Vol. 2: Case Studies*, Wadebridge Ecological Centre, Cornwall 1986 (hereafter *SEELD 2*), p. 259.

34. Justice S.M. Daud, *The Indian People's Tribunal on Environment and Human Rights. First Report*, Bombay 1993; S. Yashwant, 'Bijasen, and Beyond: Driven Away by Dams', *Frontline*, 30 July 1993.

35. Yashwant, 'Bijasen and Beyond'.

36. World Bank, *Resettlement and Development*, p. 2/9; see also The Ecologist, *Whose Common Future?*, Earthscan, London 1992.

37. M.M. Horowitz et al., 'Resettlement at Manantali, Mali: Short-Term Success, Long-Term Problems', in Cernea and Guggenheim (eds.), *Anthropological Approaches to Resettlement.*

38. S. Parasuram, 'SSP: Summary of the Findings on the Status of R&R of Reservoir Displaced People in Maharashtra', Tata Institute of Social Sciences, Bombay, July 1994, mimeo, p. 17.

39. Hirsch, 'Social and Environmental Implications', p. 16.

40. Scudder, 'Development-Induced Relocation', p. 140.

41. Morse et al., *Sardar Sarovar*, p. 156.

42. World Bank, *Resettlement and Development*, p. 4/13; 'Kedung Ombo', *Down to Earth*, Jakarta, August 1989.

43. World Bank, *Resettlement and Development*, p. 2/9.

44. Thukral, 'Introduction', p. 23.

45. Tata Institute of Social Sciences, 'SSP: Summary of the Findings', p. 19; see also Justice S.M. Daud, 'The Fate of the Gujarat Oustees, Narmada Valley: Dispossessed, Hunted, Humiliated and Cast into Oblivion!', *The Indian People's Tribunal on Environment and Human Rights. Sixth Report*, Bombay 1994.

46. Tata Institute of Social Sciences, 'SSP: Summary of the Findings', p. 19.

47. Behura and Nayak, 'Involuntary Displacement', pp. 297–304.

48. M.M. Cernea, 'Anthropological and Sociological Research for Policy Development on Population Resettlement', in Cernea and Guggenheim (eds.), *Anthropological Approaches to Resettlement*, p. 297; World Bank, *Resettlement and Development*, p. 1/7.

49. World Bank, *Resettlement and Development*, pp. 4/1, 4/2.

50. Ibid., pp. 5/13, 5/16.

51. Ibid., p. 2/2.

52. Cernea, 'Involuntary Resettlement'.

53. World Bank, 'Resettlement in the Kiambere Project', Office Memorandum, 14 April 1989.

54. World Bank, *Resettlement and Development*, p. 4/3.

55. World Bank, 'Early Experience with Involuntary Resettlement: Impact Evaluation on Thailand Khao Laem Hydroelectric', Operations Evaluation Department, 29 June 1993, pp. 8, 15.

56. D. Hubbel, Project for Ecological Recovery, Bangkok, personal communication, 31 May 1994.

57. See A. Pongsapich et al., 'Social-Environmental Impact Assessment and Ethnic Minorities: State vs. Local Interest in the Construction of Khao Laem Dam', *Journal of Social Research*, Vol. 15, No. 1, 1992, Chulalongkorn University. Pongsapich et al. are the researchers commissioned by the OED to do the post-dam evaluation of Khao Laem resettlement. Pongsapich et al.'s conclusions differ markedly from the OED's claim of 'successful' resettlement, which it based on the Thai researchers' work.

58. World Bank, 'Early Experience', p. v.

59. Ibid., pp. iii, iv.

60. J.M. Hunter et al., *Parasitic Diseases in Water Resources Development: The Need for Intersectoral Negotiation*, WHO, Geneva 1993, p. 10.

61. J.D. Kravitz et al., 'Human Immunodifficiency Virus Seroprevalence in an Occupational Cohort in a South African Community', *Archives of Internal Medicine*, Vol. 155, No. 15, 7 August 1995.

62. E.W. Morrow and R.F. Shangraw, Jr., *Understanding the Costs and Schedules of*

World Bank Supported Hydroelectric Projects, World Bank Industry and Energy Department, Washington, DC, July 1990, p. 35.

63. D. Morrell, *Indictment: Power and Politics in the Construction Industry*, Faber & Faber, London 1987, p. 157; World Bank, 'Colombia: The Power Sector and the World Bank, 1970–1987. Volume II: Technical Report', Operations Evaluation Department, 28 June 1990, p. 21.

64. F. Lempérière, 'Cost Effective Improvements in Fill Dam Safety', *The International Journal of Hydropower & Dams*, January 1995.

65. G. White (ed.), 'The Main Effects and Problems of Irrigation', in E.B. Worthington (ed.), *Arid Land Irrigation in Developing Countries: Environmental Problems and Effects*, Pergamon, Oxford 1977, p. 48.

66. See E.J. Pearce, 'Schistosomiasis: Proselytizing with Immunity', *Nature*, Vol. 363, 6 May 1993; Hunter et al., *Parasitic Diseases*, p. 200; WHO, *The Work of WHO in the Western Pacific Region 1 July 1986–30 June 1987*, WHO, Manila, June 1987.

67. A.K. Biswas, 'Health, Environment and Water Development: An Understanding of the Interrelationships', *The Environmental Professional*, Vol. 7, 1985.

68. G. White, 'The Environmental Effects of the High Dam at Aswan', *Environment*, Vol. 30, No. 7, 1988, p. 37; Hunter et al., *Parasitic Diseases*, pp. 29, 43; 'Egypt's High Aswan Dam: A Bad Reputation Reexamined', *Hydropower and Dams*, January 1994; M. Sobhy, 'Effect of the High Dam on Malaria', in Egyptian National Committee on Large Dams (ed.), *High Aswan Dam Vital Achievement Fully Controlled*, ENCOLD, Cairo 1993, pp. 221–2.

69. Hunter et al., *Parasitic Diseases*, p. 35; R. Graham, 'Ghana's Volta Resettlement Scheme', in *SEELD 2*, 1986, p. 137.

70. Hunter et al., *Parasitic Diseases*, p. 40.

71. Environmental Health Project, 'Senegal River Basin Health Master Plan Study', Arlington, VA, December 1994, p. 38.

72. Hunter et al., *Parasitic Diseases*, pp. 50–116.

73. HR Wallingford, 'Sardar Sarovar Projects: Command Area Environmental Impact Assessment. Progress Report', HR Wallingford, UK and World Bank, March 1993, pp. 11, E5.

74. A consultant's report prepared for the World Bank in 1988 stated that the potential for schistosomiasis to develop in the SSP area 'must be viewed very seriously' and that if it did develop, then the millions of people at risk 'would either have to avoid exposure to the reservoirs and irrigation water for all time, which is practically impossible to accomplish, or most of the people in the areas would be subject to schistosomiasis from childhood onward' (Morse et al., *Sardar Sarovar*, p. 325).

75. Hunter et al., *Parasitic Diseases*, pp. 69–70, 73.

76. L. Obeng, 'Schistosomiasis – The Environmental Approach', in Worthington (ed.), *Arid Land Irrigation*, p. 405.

77. H. Xue, 'Effort Must Be Made to Prevent Schistosomiasis in Three Gorges Project', *Economic Daily*, Beijing, 13 March 1994.

78. Global statistics on malaria infections and mortality must be treated with caution as data for many countries are reported to the WHO only infrequently or not at all (see P. Gleick (ed.), *Water in Crisis: A Guide to the World's Fresh Water Resources*, Oxford University Press, Oxford 1993, Table C.20). Most cited estimates are of 'around one million deaths', but mortality estimates range up to 3.5 million (L. Garrett, *The Coming Plague: Newly Emerging Diseases in a World Out of Balance*, Farrar, Straus & Giroux, New York 1994, pp. 441, 447); WHO, 'Malaria Threat

Growing Around the World', *WHO Features*, 1992.

79. See, e.g., M.A. Farid, 'Irrigation and Malaria in Arid Lands', in Worthington (ed.), *Arid Land Irrigation*, pp. 416–17.

80. M.N. Hill, et al., 'A Comparison of Mosquito Populations in Irrigated and Non-Irrigated Areas of the Kano Plains, Nyanza Province, Kenya', in Worthington (ed.), *Arid Land Irrigation*, p. 314; Hunter et al., *Parasitic Diseases*, pp. 36, 37.

81. Hunter et al., *Parasitic Diseases*, pp. 29, 43.

82. M. Kassas (compiler), 'Discussion and Conclusions', in Worthington (ed.), *Arid Land Irrigation*, p. 338.

83. Hunter et al., *Parasitic Diseases*, pp. 30, 50.

84. Ibid., p. 47.

85. Garrett, *The Coming Plague*, p. 47; Gleick (ed.), *Water in Crisis*, Table C.20. Globally, $1.9 billion, in 1991 dollars, were spent on malaria eradication between 1958 and 1963 alone.

86. Garrett, *The Coming Plague*, pp. 441–3, 451–5. One consequence of *falciparum* drug resistance is that the ratio of *P. falciparum* to its less dangerous relative *P. vivax* is changing, increasing the incidence of fatal cerebral malaria. In India, 'where over 90% of all malaria was the milder *P. vivax* form in 1976, by 1989 only 65% were *vivax*, the remainder *falciparum*. In Sri Lanka, where *falciparum* had been virtually non-existent, by 1990 close to half of all disease was due to the more dangerous parasite' (Garrett, *The Coming Plague*, p. 450).

87. Ibid., pp. 204–5.

88. W.R. Jobin, 'Rift Valley Fever: A Problem for Dam Builders in Africa', *Water Power & Dam Construction*, August 1984; Environmental Health Project, 'Senegal River Basin', pp. 87–92.

89. Hunter et al., *Parasitic Diseases*, pp. 26, 30, 31.

90. Ibid., pp. 4–5.

91. Hunter et al., *Parasitic Diseases*, p. 48; Comissão Pró-Indio de São Paulo, 'Tucuruí Hydroelectric Power Plant: The Disaster Continues', mimeo, 1991; 'Violência e Conflitos no Projeto de Assentamento Rio Gelado', *Informativo do MAB*, São Paulo, January 1995; Garrett, *The Coming Plague*, p. 254.

92. Hunter et al., *Parasitic Diseases*, pp. 26, 33–4; D. Wigg, *And Then Forgot to Tell Us Why…: A Look at the Campaign against River Blindness in West Africa*, World Bank, Washington, DC, 1993.

93. Environmental Health Project, 'Senegal River Basin', p. 91.

94. Hunter et al., *Parasitic Diseases*, p. 31.

95. Wigg, *And Then Forgot*, p. 7.

96. See, e.g., A. Churchill et al., 'Rural Water Supply and Sanitation: Time for a Change', World Bank Discussion Paper 18, 1987.

97. M. Goldman, '"There's a Snake on Our Chests": State and Development Crisis in India's Desert', Ph.D. thesis, University of California, Santa Cruz, December 1994, p. 131.

98. T.A. Blinkhorn and W.T. Smith, 'India's Narmada: River of Hope. A World Bank Perspective', in W.F. Fisher (ed.), *Towards Sustainable Development? Struggling Over India's Narmada River*, M.E. Sharpe, Armonk, NY, 1995; HR Wallingford 'Sardar Sarovar Projects', p. E1; Goldman, '"There's a Snake"', p. 131.

4

When Things Fall Apart: The Technical Failures of Large Dams

> ...the river...
> Keeping his seasons and rages, destroyer, reminder
> Of what men choose to forget. Unhonoured, unpropitiated
> By worshippers of the machine, but waiting, watching and waiting.
>
> T.S. Eliot, *Four Quartets*, 1941

Dams are beset with technical problems, some of them inherent to the technology, some of them due to the lack of independent oversight of the dam-building process. These problems can cause long construction delays and plague project performance, economics and safety. The failure of dams to perform as promised is generally because the promises were based on highly overoptimistic assumptions made during project planning. Engineers' and politicians' claims of project viability are often made despite a lack of basic data on the geology of the dam site or the amount of water or sediment carried by the river. At other times data are collected but unfavourable findings are either ignored or are interpreted in as optimistic a light as possible.

World Bank sociologist Michael Cernea, when discussing the lack of time and money put into resettling people displaced by dams, castigates the 'engineering bias' of dam builders.[1] A more accurate description of the impetus behind dam construction, however, would be 'building bias': the dam industry makes money by building dams (and usually pays none of the costs of their poor performance) and considerations of whether or not their projects make good technical or economic sense are inevitably secondary to the desire to build.

Not on Solid Ground: Dams and Geology

> It was such an obviously lousy site to a trained geologist it makes you wonder what happens to human judgement inside a bureaucracy.
>
> Robert Curry, University of Montana, on the Teton Dam, 1976

Every dam site has unique geological characteristics. Gaining a thorough understanding of these characteristics is expensive and time-consuming: millions of dollars may have been spent on a geological survey before it finds that a site is unsuitable for a dam. It is therefore normal for dams to be designed with only a partial knowledge of local site conditions – the builders just have to hope that they will not find any unstable formations which will fail to support their foundations or cause the roofs of their tunnels to come crashing down. More than three-quarters of 49 projects assessed in a 1990 World Bank study of hydropower construction costs were found to have experienced unexpected geological problems of some kind. The study concluded that for hydrodams 'the absence of geological problems should be treated as the exception rather than the norm.'[2]

The Bureau of Reclamation was aware that there could be problems with the dam they wanted to build in a canyon on the Teton River in southern Idaho. Test drillings in the north wall of the canyon in 1970 had revealed cracks which Bureau geologists predicted would cause water to leak around the side of the dam. This leakage could turn the dam abutment and even part of the earthfill dam itself, into a 'quagmire', the Bureau geologists warned. Nevertheless, the Bureau started building the dam.

Soon after contractors started excavating Teton's foundations in early 1974, they found the north abutment to be riddled with a series of gigantic fissures far worse than the test bores had revealed. But the Bureau's site engineers, already well behind schedule, essentially decided to ignore them.

The 90-metre-high Teton Dam was completed in October 1975. The following spring the Teton River started rapidly to swell with snowmelt. Supposed to fill at a rate of around 1 metre a day, the reservoir rose at almost 4 metres a day. At the start of June 1976, dam operators first noticed water pouring from the north wall of the canyon just downstream of the dam. On the early morning of 5 June, they saw a muddy stream gushing through the dam's north abutment. A few hours later a large wet spot appeared on the dam's downstream face; the wet spot turned to a spring, then a waterfall; then a 20-storey-high torrent burst through the northern third of the dam. The ensuing deluge damaged or destroyed 4,000 homes and 350 businesses in three small towns downstream and scoured the topsoil off several thousand hectares of farmland. It killed either 11 or 14 people depending on which estimate is to be believed and caused property damage costing up to $1 billion. The death toll would have been much higher were it not for the timely evacuation of 12,000 people in the morning before the dam dissolved.[3]

The German–Swiss–US LAMI Consortium knew that the cavity-filled limestone, heavily fissured volcanic rocks and active seismic faults along the middle Chixoy River provided a very unstable foundation for any large construction project. Nevertheless, their 1974 feasibility study recommended that the Guatemalan electricity utility INDE should build a 130-metre-high hydropower dam on the Chixoy at a place called Pueblo Viejo. In February 1976, with a $105 million loan secured from the Inter-American Development Bank, construction of the dam was about to begin when a devastating earthquake hit Guatemala. The quake prompted a more detailed review of the seismology of the site – which found several previously undetected faults – and of the seismic strength of the planned dam. A subsequent redesign to make the dam better able to withstand earthquakes delayed construction for 15 months and increased the estimated cost of the project by nearly 10 per cent. In May 1977, with further international loans secured, contractors from eight different countries finally started to build Chixoy Dam. LAMI, predictably, received the lucrative contract as consulting engineers to oversee the construction of the dam they had designed and recommended be built.

Almost as soon as construction began it became apparent that it was not only LAMI's seismological investigations which had been inadequate: while preparing the dam foundations, the underlying rocks were found to be so riddled with faults and cavities that another major redesign of the dam was needed. This resulted in the final expenditure on the dam wall being 350 per cent higher than expected in 1977. Next, another undiscovered fault required design changes that more than doubled the cost of the Chixoy powerhouse. Finally, the 26-kilometre-long pressure tunnel intended to carry water from the reservoir to the powerhouse caved in twice during its excavation by German contractor Hochtief, delaying project completion by some 14 months.

Chixoy Dam finally began to produce power in July 1983, but after only five months further severe damage to the pressure tunnel forced INDE to shut the plant down. The subsequent repairs took two years and cost some $57 million, most of the money coming from a second loan from the World Bank. Commercial operation of Chixoy's five 60 MW turbines did not resume until April 1986. In 1974, LAMI estimated that Chixoy would cost $270 million; by 1988 it had cost $944 million.[4]

The problems of the 90 MW Aguacapa hydropower project in the south of Guatemala, begun at almost the same time as Chixoy, parallel those of the larger dam. Adequate rock on which to anchor the dam's foundations was not found at the level indicated in the dam design, and the contractors had to dig the foundations much deeper than expected. The lining of the pressure tunnel cracked after it was filled and had to be replaced. The failure of the tunnel resulted in the dam's powerhouse being flooded once during construction, and again just after completion in 1981. The dam took more than twice as long to build as estimated and cost 83 per cent more than its predicted price tag of $100 million. The second powerhouse washout permanently destroyed one of Aguacapa's three turbines so that at best it has only been able to operate at two-thirds its planned capacity.[5]

Political Hydrology

> The dam is doing fine. The only constraint is the water.
>
> Paul Back, Chief Technical Director, Sir Alexander Gibb & Partners, discussing the poor power production performance of Victoria Dam, Sri Lanka, 1994

Just as dam builders often skimp on geological surveys, so they have shown themselves willing to build on the basis of seriously inadequate hydrological data. When there is not enough water to turn a dam's turbines or fill its canals, or so much water that the dam is threatened with breaching, an 'Act of God' – drought or flood – will invariably be blamed for the ensuing electricity shortages or inundation. However, an act of dam builder – construction without sufficient data to predict how much water is likely to be available or deliberate disregard of unfavourable data – is more likely to be where the blame should be laid.

Hydrologists cannot predict exactly how much water will flow into a planned reservoir. To make a 'best guess' of what river discharge will be like during the life of a dam, they project past streamflow data into the future. At least several decades of streamflow records are usually necessary to make reasonably reliable predictions taking into account annual cycles of variations in rainfall – and even then there is no guarantee that rainfall patterns over the next, say, 50 years will be the same as those of the last 50 years, especially considering the hydrological wild card of global warming. Furthermore, to be able to estimate the maximum flood which a dam might have to discharge and to plan its pattern of releases it is necessary to know not only annual flow variations but also seasonal, monthly and even daily peaks and troughs.

Collecting reliable streamflow data is relatively expensive and difficult, and for most of the world's rivers very little good data exist. If the data do not exist, then a dam builder might have to wait many years for a time series long enough to be meaningful. Because of the lack of discharge data, hydrologists often extrapolate streamflow from rainfall statistics, which are generally more common and of better quality. However, this introduces even more uncertainties into the hydrologists' equations as it requires a number of assumptions to be made on the relationship between rainfall and run-off, taking into account numerous factors including rainfall intensity, evaporation and ground cover.

Especially in semi-arid areas, rainfall and river discharge can vary so much over time that even 'averages' based on many decades of reliable data may have little relevance in predicting future flows. Geographer William Adams explains that:

> To someone judging semi-arid Africa by the standards of what is normal in a temperate environment, the variability of climate is both bizarre and incomprehensible. Ideas of 'normal' rainfall, based upon notions of 'average' rainfall conditions, might be appropriate to temperate environments, but have tended to prove a poor basis for planning in Africa.... The use of computer simulation and statistical analysis serves to give confidence to the modern development planning process, but it does not always succeed in comprehending the variability of the African environment...[6]

A lack of reliable hydrological data, however, frequently does not stop dam builders, who have shown themselves prepared to go ahead with as little as a couple of years of discharge data.[7] Dam builders often build and hope for the hydrological best: there is therefore a pattern of overestimating annual flows and underestimating peak floods.[8]

Overestimates of average flows mean that many dams fail to yield as much power and water as predicted. The huge Buendía–Entrepeñas reservoir in central Spain is formed by two dams built on the Guadiela and Tagus rivers in the late 1950s during General Franco's decade-and-a-half dam-building binge. It has never been able to supply more than half the capacity of the aqueduct built to take its water to the Mediterranean coast. In early 1994 the reservoir contained just 17 per cent of its capacity.[9]

Lower than expected rainfall and higher than expected leakage through its limestone bed have meant that Thailand's largest volume reservoir, Srinakharin, completed in 1977, has never filled. During 1991, Thailand's 25 largest dams contained a total of just under half of their combined usable capacity; the following year this figure fell to just over one-third. Bhumibhol and Sirikit, World Bank-funded dams which impound the second and third largest reservoirs in Thailand, together contained only 7 per cent of their total usable volume in March 1994.[10] In their authoritative 1973 history of the World Bank, Edward Mason and Robert Asher of the Brookings Institution state:

> The electricity-generating capabilities of the Ping River, on which the Bhumiphol Dam was built, were substantially overestimated.... Taking into account the shortfall in the generating capacities of the Bhumiphol Dam and

> the ... disappointments in the project's contribution to agricultural output, a current reassessment of this sizeable multipurpose development effort would probably call into question its economic justification.[11]

The 1922 Colorado River Compact divided up the rights to the Colorado's water between the upper and lower basin states and Mexico – and thus laid the legal groundwork for the development of Hoover and the many other dams on the river. The writers of the Compact assumed on the basis of 18 years of streamflow measurements that the annual flow of the river averaged 17.5 million acre-feet (one acre-foot equals the amount of water which would flood one acre to a depth of one foot – 21.6 cubic kilometres). By the 1950s, however, it was apparent that the first two decades of this century had been exceptionally wet in the US Southwest. From 1930 to 1952, the Colorado's flow averaged only 11.7 million acre-feet.

Acceptance of this low flow figure would have brought to a shuddering halt the grandiose plans of the Bureau of Reclamation. In early 1953 the Bureau was lobbying Congress for funds to build its multi-dam Colorado River Storage Project, which was predicated on the 17.5 million acre-feet figure being *conservative.* Rather than scale back its ambitions, however, BuRec simply ignored the new data. BuRec did not admit to the Colorado's 'deficit' until 1965, when it conceded that the flow was likely to be around 15 million acre-feet.[12]

BuRec's inability to accept inconvenient streamflow data is paralleled by the refusal of the authorities building Sardar Sarovar to accept the overwhelming evidence that much less water is likely to be available than was assumed when the project was planned. SSP was designed in the 1970s on the assumption that over 27 million acre-feet of water flowed down the Narmada in three out of every four years. Yet in 1990 the 42 years of flow data then available gave a three out of four years' discharge past the dam site of just 22.7 million acre-feet. More recent figures indicate the flow may be even lower.

The Indian Central Water Commission (CWC) admits that its measurements now show there is less water in the Narmada than was previously assumed. Yet it continues to support building SSP to a height which would displace many tens of thousands more people than a smaller dam designed to take account of the actual flow data.[13] The CWC's justification for its seemingly untenable position is that:

> Since water resource development activity cannot be delayed for want of data of adequate quality and quantity, best judgement assessment has to be resorted to. In the field of hydrology one has to devise methods to suit the data available and come out with solutions. Accepting a solution in turn needs judgement with due consideration to sociological, economic and political situations.[14]

In other words, political pressure to build the higher dam makes it necessary for the Indian authorities to pretend that more water flows down the Narmada than their measurements show.

Mud against Dams: Sedimentation

> We build storage reservoirs or power dams to store water, and mortgage our irrigated valleys and our industries to pay for them, but every year they store a little less water and a little more mud. Reclamation, which should be for all time, thus becomes in part the source of a merely temporary prosperity.
>
> Aldo Leopold, *The Virgin Southwest*, 1933

All rivers contain sediments: a river, in effect, can be considered a body of flowing sediments as much as one of flowing water. When a river is stilled behind a dam, the sediments it contains sink to the bottom of the reservoir. The proportion of a river's total sediment load captured by a dam – known as its 'trap efficiency' – approaches 100 per cent for many projects, especially those with large reservoirs. As the sediments accumulate in the reservoir, so the dam gradually loses its ability to store water for the purposes for which it was built. Every reservoir loses storage to sedimentation, although the rate at which this happens varies widely. Despite more than six decades of research, sedimentation is still probably the most serious technical problem faced by the dam industry.

Professor Khalid Mahmood of George Washington University in Washington, DC, 'roughly estimated' for a 1987 World Bank study that around 50 cubic kilometres of sediment – nearly 1 per cent of global reservoir storage capacity – is trapped behind the world's dams every year. In total, calculated Mahmood, by 1986 around 1,100 cubic kilometres of sediment had accumulated in the world's reservoirs, consuming almost one-fifth of global storage capacity.[15]

The rate of reservoir sedimentation depends mainly on the size of a reservoir relative to the amount of sediment flowing into it: a small reservoir on an extremely muddy river will rapidly lose capacity; a large reservoir on a very clear river may take centuries to lose an appreciable amount of storage. Large reservoirs in the US lose storage capacity at an average rate of around 0.2 per cent per year, with regional variations ranging from 0.5 per cent per year in the Pacific states to just 0.1 per cent annually in the northeast. Major reservoirs in China – where soil erosion is a massive problem – lose capacity at an annual rate of 2.3 per cent.[16]

Apart from rapidly filling their reservoirs, sediment-filled rivers also cause headaches for dam operators due to the abrasion of turbines and other dam components. The efficiency of a turbine is largely dependent upon the hydraulic properties of its blades, just as an aeroplane depends on the aerodynamic properties of its wings. The erosion and cracking of the tips of turbine blades by water-borne sand and silt considerably reduce their generating efficiency and can require expensive repairs.[17]

By far the world's muddiest river is the Yellow, which flows through the easily eroded, light 'loess' soil of north central China. The average concentration of sediment in the Yellow is nine times greater than for any other major river – soil scientist Daniel J. Hillel describes it as a 'rippling tide of liquefied mud, resembling thick lentil soup'.[18] The record of reservoirs built on the Yellow is, not surprisingly, atrocious.

Sanmenxia (Three Gates Gorge) Dam was built – chiefly for flood control – on the lower Yellow with technical assistance from the Soviet Union. Construction started in 1957. Chinese hydrologists who protested that the reservoir would soon fill with mud were accused of being 'rightists' and silenced. Within just three years of reservoir impoundment in 1960, the river had deposited more than 50 billion tonnes of sediment at its upper end, raising the riverbed by several metres and threatening upstream areas, including the ancient capital Xian, with serious flooding. When Mao Zedong was told of the threat to Xian, he reportedly exclaimed: 'If nothing can be done about it, bomb the dam!' The measures taken were not quite so drastic, but between 1962 and 1973 the dam had to be redesigned twice to increase its ability to flush through sediments.

Originally planned as a 1,200 MW storage dam, Sanmenxia finally began to produce power in 1973 as a 250 MW run-of-river project. The new operating regime dictates that as much water as possible is allowed to flow through retrofitted low-level outlets during the July to October flood season when the river is at its muddiest – thereby negating its original main function of flood control. The sediment build-up in the reservoir has reportedly stabilized with about 40 per cent of its capacity filled. For its 250 MW output, Sanmenxia flooded 66,000 hectares of some of the world's most fertile farmland, and displaced 410,000 people – more than any other reservoir in the world.[19]

The Sanmenxia fiasco was repeated at other reservoirs begun on the upper Yellow River in the late 1950s. The 57-metre-high Yangouxia Dam lost almost one-third of its storage capacity *before it was even commissioned.* By 1966, three-quarters of Yangouxia's reservoir had been filled with sediment. Since 1967, the sedimentation of the reservoir has stabilized, mainly because the sediments which would have built up in it are now filling two newer reservoirs upstream.[20]

Sedimental journey

To make a meaningful economic forecast for a planned dam, it is necessary to be able to predict its sedimentation rate with reasonable accuracy. However, it is extremely difficult to estimate how much sediment will be trapped by a reservoir. Collecting data on sediment discharge is even more expensive and difficult than gathering streamflow data, and so there is little reliable information available on the sediment carried by the world's rivers. Sediment flows vary widely both annually and seasonally over time – far more than water flows – and so calculating an annual average needs a long run of data. According to Mahmood, dam planners should ideally have sediment statistics going back over a period equal to at least half the projected life of the dam. Such records, however, are available only in exceptional cases. As with river flows, the variability of sediment yield is greatest in arid and semi-arid climates – where the data tend to be sparsest.[21]

The amount of sediment carried into a reservoir is at its highest during floods: in the US, for example, commonly half of a river's annual sediment load may be transported during only five to ten days' flow. During and after a particularly violent storm a river may carry as much sediment as it would in several 'normal' years. Mudslides caused by earthquakes and volcanoes can also have a dramatic and unpredictable effect on reservoir sedimentation. Global warming, which is predicted to cause more intense storms, will likely increase both the unpredictability and rate of reservoir sedimentation.[22]

The storage capacity of Nepal's Kulekhani hydrodam was cut by nearly one-tenth by the sediment scoured off upstream mountainsides during a single 30-hour stormburst in July 1993. Kulekhani's sedimentation rate was predicted to be also greatly increased for years to come as the storm deposited huge amounts of sediments at the bottom of slopes upstream to be washed toward the dam by future floods. Sediments could put the 114-metre-high dam out of operation around the turn of the century. Yet, when it was completed in 1981, Kulekhani was predicted to have a design life of 75–100 years.[23]

Despite all the uncertainties over reservoir sedimentation, it is extremely rare for a planned project to be stopped because of a lack of adequate sediment data. In fact, time and again dam planners have made hugely overoptimistic predictions that reservoirs will fill much more slowly than they actually do. Chixoy is one of a number of very expensive hydrodams built in Central America during the 1970s and 1980s with loans from the World Bank and Inter-American Development Bank despite the very high and accelerating rates of erosion in their watersheds. These dams are now rapidly filling with sediment, leaving small, impoverished countries like Guatemala, Honduras and Costa Rica with huge debts and in desperate need of building new power plants to reduce their dependence on their white-elephant dams. A team from the US Army Corps of Engineers concluded in 1993 that sedimentation could reduce the life of the 135 MW Cerron Grande

Dam in El Salvador to 30 years – compared to the pre-construction prediction of 350 years.[24]

In India, government statistics on 11 of the country's reservoirs with capacities greater than 1 cubic kilometre show that all are filling with sediment faster than expected, with increases over assumed rates ranging from 130 per cent (Bhakra) to 1,650 per cent (Nizamsagar in Andhra Pradesh).[25] A 1990 World Bank paper on watershed development concluded that in India, 'erosion and [reservoir] sedimentation are not only severe and costly, but accelerating. It is now obvious that the original project estimates of expected sedimentation rates were faulty, based on too few reliable data over too short a period.'[26]

Most modern dams are designed so that they can afford to lose some storage capacity without their performance being impaired – the part of a reservoir known as 'dead storage' which lies beneath the elevation of the dam's lowest outlet. However, sediments do not build up evenly along a horizontal plane, so that some 'live storage' is usually lost long before the dead storage is filled. At Tarbela Reservoir in Pakistan, for example, 12 per cent of the live storage had been lost by 1992 (after 18 years of operation) while 55 per cent of the dead storage was still empty of sediment.

The actual process of sediment deposition is unique to every reservoir and is impossible to predict accurately. In general, the coarser, heavier sediments, the gravel and sand, tend to settle out at the upper end of the reservoir, forming a 'backwater' delta which gradually advances toward the dam. The lighter sediments, the silt and clay, tend to be deposited nearer the dam. In 1983 the crest of Tarbela's backwater delta had advanced to 19 kilometres from the dam: according to pre-construction predictions the delta should have been 48 kilometres behind the dam at this time. By 1991 the delta crest was just 14 kilometres from the dam.[27]

Mitigating geology

Economically viable methods of preventing sedimentation and restoring reservoir capacity are the Holy Grails of the dam industry. There are three categories of methods to prolong the life of a reservoir: reduce the amount of sediment flowing into the it; flush through the dam the sediment that has already accumulated; or dredge the sediment. All have severe limitations, either because they simply do not work, they are prohibitively expensive, or because they conflict with the dam's ability to supply water and power.

'Watershed management' – including afforestation and the promotion of farming practices which reduce soil erosion – is frequently advocated as the best way of cutting sediment deposition in reservoirs.

While these schemes may be recommended in project plans, they are rarely implemented: dam-building agencies are usually more interested in putting their funds toward building dams than planting trees and digging field terraces. When attempts are made to implement soil conservation schemes in the large tropical and sub-tropical watersheds which are most prone to erosion they are usually underfunded and opposed by local farmers, who, after already losing valuable riverside land to a reservoir, resist having more of their land taken over for tree plantations.

It is difficult to find any examples of the successful implementation of watershed anti-erosion measures in the tropics and sub-tropics. Khalid Mahmood believes that in any case, for most large river basins,

> ...over periods of engineering or economic interest, the sediment yields are largely unaffected by watershed management. The sediment sources within the basin, including the hillslopes, valley floors and river channels will amply make up for whatever reduction of erosion can be affected by watershed control.[28]

Overall, building a dam in a valley is much more likely to increase erosion than reduce it: dams open up remote areas to road builders, developers, loggers, farmers and miners, accelerating deforestation and soil loss. When insufficient resettlement land is made available, oustee farming families may have no choice but to clear land further up the valley or hillside. In any case, deforestation and soil erosion are both increasing rapidly around the world, and it should be assumed when dams are built that soil erosion in their watershed will increase over the projected economic life of the reservoir.

To sluice, to vent, perchance to dredge

Sediment sluicing is the name given to a type of reservoir operation which draws the reservoir down at the start of the flood season and then allows as much sediment-heavy flood water as possible to pass through the dam before it has a chance to settle. This method can drastically slow down the rate of reservoir sedimentation but has only been successfully used in a few projects, most notably the Low Aswan Dam. It is also the method which stabilized the sediment build-up at Sanmenxia. Sluicing is only effective for reservoirs which are small and narrow relative to river flow and it seriously reduces or eliminates the dam's ability to generate electricity and supply water during the prolonged period when the reservoir is lowered. It also conflicts with the aim of many projects to store flood waters.[29]

Sediment flushing is a method of washing out deposits which have already accumulated in a reservoir. Again it depends on the reservoir being drawn down, with the aim that fast-flowing water will erode the sediments on the reservoir bed and flush them through the dam. Flushing a long reservoir will require several months of drawdown to a level where the flow of water through the reservoir is close to that of the original river. While flushing can be effective at removing fine, silty deposits near the outlets, it usually has little impact upon the coarser deposits further upstream or cohesive sediments such as compacted clays. In general, flushing has little impact on a seriously sedimented reservoir.[30]

An obvious way of restoring reservoir capacity is dredging. However, this is extremely expensive and is normally only viable for small, urban water supply reservoirs where water consumers can afford the cost, and landfill sites are available to take the dredged sediment. Mahmood cites the cost of dredging at $2–$3 per cubic metre in 1987, around 20 times more than the cost of providing additional storage in a new dam. Restoring the original capacity of a major reservoir would require the removal (and transport and dumping) of billions of cubic metres of sediment. Based on Mahmood's cost estimate, dredging the annual volume of sediments deposited in Tarbela Reservoir each year would cost some $400–$600 million; dredging the sediments accumulating in reservoirs worldwide every year would cost $100–$150 billion.[31]

Reservoir-Induced Seismicity: Dams that Cause the Earth to Move

It is well established (although little known by the general public) that large dams can trigger earthquakes. The first observation of possible reservoir-induced seismicity (RIS) was noted for Algeria's Quedd Fodda Dam in 1932; the first extensive study of the correlation between increased earthquake activity and variations in reservoir depth was made in the 1940s for Hoover Dam. Today there is evidence linking earth tremors and reservoir operation for more than 70 dams.[32] Reservoirs are believed to have induced five out of the nine earthquakes on the Indian peninsula in the 1980s which were strong enough to cause damage.[33]

As with most aspects of seismology, the actual mechanisms of RIS are not well understood, and it is impossible to predict accurately which dams will induce earthquakes or how strong the tremors are likely to be. Most of the strongest cases of RIS have been observed for dams over 100 metres high – but dams just half this height are also believed to have induced quakes (see Table 4.1). Reservoirs can both increase the frequency of earthquakes in areas of already high seismic activity and cause earthquakes to happen in areas previously thought to be seismically inactive. The latter effect is the most dangerous as structures

Table 4.1 Reported cases of reservoir-induced seismicity greater than magnitude 4.0 (Richter scale)

Dam	Country	Dam height (m)	Reservoir volume ($m^3 \times 10^6$)	Impounding began	Largest earth-quake	Size
Koyna	India	103	2,780	1962	1967	6.3
Kariba	Zambia/ Zimbabwe	128	175,000	1958	1963	6.2
Kremasta	Greece	160	4,750	1965	1966	6.2
Xinfengjiang	China	105	14,000	1959	1962	6.1
Srinakharin[1]	Thailand	140	17,745	1977	1983	5.9
Marathon	Greece	67	41	1929	1938	5.7
Oroville	USA	236	4,400	1967	1975	5.7
Aswan	Egypt	111	164,000	1964	1981	5.6
Benmore	New Zealand	110	2,040	1964	1966	5.0
Eucumbene	Australia	116	4,761	1957	1959	5.0
Hoover	USA	221	36,703	1935	1939	5.0
Bajina-Basta	Yugoslavia	90	340	1966	1967	4.5–5.0
Bhatsa	India	88	947	1981	1983	4.9
Kerr	USA	60	1,505	1958	1971	4.9
Kurobe	Japan	186	149	1960	1961	4.9
Monteynard	France	155	275	1962	1963	4.9
Shenwo	China	50	540	1972	1974	4.8
Akosombo[2]	Ghana	134	148,000	1964	1964	4.7
Canelles	Spain	150	678	1960	1962	4.7
Danjiangkou	China	97	16,000	1967	1973	4.7
Grandval[2]	France	88	292	1959	1963	4.7
Kastraki	Greece	96	1,000	1968	1969	4.6
Lake Pukaki	New Zealand	106	9,000	1976	1978	4.6
Nurek	Tadjikistan	317	10,500	1972	1972	4.6
Fuziling	China	74	470	1954	1973	4.5
Khao Laem[3]	Thailand	130	8,860	1984	1985	4.5
Piastra	Italy	93	13	1965	1966	4.4
Vouglans	France	130	605	1968	1971	4.4
Clark Hill	USA	60	3,517	1952	1974	4.3
P. Colombia/ Volta Grande*	Brazil	40/56	1,500/ 2,300	1973/4	1974	4.2
Camarillas	Spain	49	37	1960	1964	4.1
Manicouagan 3	Canada	108	10,423	1975	1975	4.1

* Epicentre near Porto Colombia and Volta Grande dams.

Sources:

1. S. Klaipongpan, 'Geological and Seismicity Evaluation of Srinagarind Dam', in S. Prakash (ed.), *Proceedings of Second International Conference on Recent Advances in Geotechnical Earthquake Engineering and Soil Dynamics*, University of Missouri-Rolla 1991.
2. T. Vladut, 'Environmental Aspects of Reservoir Induced Seismicity', *Water Power & Dam Construction*, May 1993.
3. N. Hetrakul, 'Post Evaluation on Reservoir Triggered Seismicity of Khao Laem Dam', in Prakash (ed.), *Proceedings*.

All others: H.K. Gupta, *Reservoir-Induced Earthquakes*, Elsevier, Amsterdam 1992.

in areas thought to be quiescent are not built to withstand even minor earthquakes. Complicating the picture further are five reservoirs, including Tarbela, where a reduction in local seismic activity was noted after impoundment.[34]

The most widely accepted explanation of how dams cause earthquakes is related to the extra water pressure created in the microcracks and fissures in the ground under and near a reservoir. When the pressure of the water in the rocks increases, it acts to lubricate faults which are already under tectonic strain, but are prevented from slipping by the friction of the rock surfaces.[35]

For most well-studied cases of RIS, the intensity of seismic activity increased within around 25 kilometres of the reservoir as it was filled. The strongest shocks normally occurred relatively soon – often within days but sometimes within several years – after the reservoir reached its greatest depth. After the initial filling of the reservoir, RIS events normally continued as the water level rose and fell but usually with less frequency and strength than before. The pattern of RIS is, however, unique for every reservoir.

The most powerful earthquake thought to have been induced by a reservoir is a magnitude 6.3 tremor which flattened the village of Koynanagar in Maharashtra, western India, on 11 December 1967, killing around 180 people, injuring 1,500 and rendering thousands homeless. The dam was seriously damaged and the powerhouse put out of action, cutting off the power supply to Bombay and causing panic among its populace, who were able to feel the quake although 230 kilometres from its epicentre. The epicentre of the tremor and numerous foreshocks and aftershocks were all either near the 103-metre-high Koyna Dam or under its reservoir.[36]

RIS is suspected to have contributed to one of the world's most deadly dam disasters, the overtopping of Vaiont Dam in the Italian Alps in 1963. The 261-metre Vaiont – the world's fourth highest dam – was completed in 1960 in a limestone gorge at the base of Mount Toc. As soon as the reservoir started to fill, seismic shocks were recorded and a mass of unstable rock debris on the side of the mountain started to slide toward the reservoir. After reaching a maximum depth of 130 metres in late 1960, the reservoir was partially drained, and the seismic activity and slope movement almost stopped. The reservoir was then filled again, reaching 155 metres in April 1962, provoking a new increase in tremors. Despite the tremors, engineers and geologists, according to a later engineering report, decided 'that the mass … would keep moving so slowly that no problems would occur.'[37]

The experts were tragically wrong. Heavy late summer rains in 1963 swelled the reservoir to a depth of over 180 metres. In the first half of September, 60 shocks were registered and the movement on Mount Toc started to accelerate. On the night of 9 October, 350 million cubic metres of rock broke off Mount Toc and plunged into the reservoir. The gargantuan wave resulting from the impact overtopped the dam by 110 metres – the height of a 28-storey building. About two minutes later the town of Longarone, just over a kilometre downstream, was levelled and almost all its inhabitants killed. Altogether 2,600 people died in Longarone and three other villages.

The actual relationship between the seismic activity and the landslide is not certain – part of Mount Toc was clearly unstable and could have sheared off without the tremors occurring – but it is likely that the numerous shocks, which were at their most frequent just before the calamity struck, at the very least hastened the collapse of the mountainside.[38]

Leonardo Seeber, a seismologist at the Lamont–Doherty Earth Observatory at Columbia University, New York, believes that official maps which show the areas most at risk of earthquakes should also indicate the increased risk near many reservoirs.[39] If this were to happen, communities near reservoirs could presumably demand compensation to 'earthquake-proof' buildings, greatly increasing the cost of dams. The dam industry would presumably oppose any such measures to raise awareness of RIS. Seismologist Harsh Gupta, Vice-Chancellor of Cochin University in India and a professor at the University of Texas, notes a 'general reluctance in parts of the engineering community, worldwide, to accept the significance or even the existence of the phenomenon of reservoir-induced seismicity'.[40] Action in the courts could force the dam industry to accept the importance of RIS: a 1994 article in the *Journal of Environmental Law and Litigation* concluded that people who suffer from induced quakes would have grounds under US law to sue the operators of a reservoir.[41]

Iron Dams and Corpses: Dam Safety

> With the exception of nuclear power plants, no man-made structure has a greater potential for killing a large number of people than a dam.
>
> Joseph Ellam, Pennsylvania State Director of Dam Safety, 1987

By far the world's worst dam disaster occurred in Henan province in central China in August 1975. As many as 230,000 people may have died in the catastrophe, yet for two decades it was successfully airbrushed from history by the Chinese authorities. If the Chinese had not prevented news of the calamity from reaching the outside world, Henan would presumably represent for the public image of the dam industry what Chernobyl and Bhopal represent for the nuclear and chemical industries.[42]

Detailed information on the Henan catastrophe was first published in English by the US-based group Human Rights Watch in February 1995 in a report on human rights violations at the Three Gorges Dam. Their account is based on a small number of articles by top Chinese water resources experts published in limited-circulation books and journals in the relatively open period of the late 1980s, and on an unpublished account written under a pseudonym by a well-known mainland Chinese journalist.

Banqiao and Shimantan dams were built on the basin of the Huai River, a tributary of the lower Yangtze, in the early 1950s. Banqiao, according to Human Rights Watch, was considered 'an "iron dam" that could never collapse'. The dams were built to be capable of withstanding up to a 1-in-1,000-year flood. The freak typhoon which struck Henan between 5 and 7 August 1975, however, was estimated to be a 1-in-2,000-year event.

On 5 August, Banqiao Reservoir filled to close to maximum capacity. Its sluice gates were opened, but were found to be partly blocked with sediment. The following day the reservoir rose to more than 2 metres above its designed safe capacity. On the evening of 7 August, Banqiao Dam burst, and 500 million cubic metres of reservoir water surged over the downstream valleys and plains at nearly 50 kilometres per hour. 'Entire villages and small towns', says Human Rights Watch, 'disappeared in an instant.' The smaller Shimantan Dam collapsed shortly afterwards. In total as many as 62 dams are thought to have collapsed during the typhoon.

The floodwaters from the reservoirs and rivers of the Huai Basin combined to form a lake covering thousands of square kilometres, partially or completely submerging countless villages and small towns. Faith in the ability of dams to hold back floods had meant that for decades dike maintenance, river dredging and flood diversionary systems within the basin had been neglected, and there were few outlets through which the newly created lake could drain. A week after the lake formed, several of the surviving dams in Henan – including some built especially for flood control – were dynamited because it was decided that this was the only way to let the water escape.

The vast lake ruptured transport and communications throughout the region, making many areas inaccessible to disaster relief teams and medical workers. The pseudonymous Chinese journalist describes the aftermath of the dam bursts:

> August 13: Two million people across the district are trapped by the water.... In Runan, 100,000 who were initially submerged but somehow survived are still floating in the water. In Shangcai, another 600,000 are surrounded by the flood; 4,000 members of Liudayu Brigade in Huabo Commune have stripped the trees bare and eaten all the leaves...

> August 17: There are still 1.1 million people trapped in the water ... the disease morbidity rate has soared. According to incomplete statistics, 1.13 million people have contracted illnesses...
>
> August 18: Altogether 880,000 people are surrounded by water in Shangcai and Xincai. Out of 500,000 people in Runan, 320,000 have now been stricken with disease, including 33,000 cases of dysentery...
>
> Some two weeks after the disaster, when the flood waters finally began to retreat in certain areas of Zhumadian Prefecture, mounds of corpses lay everywhere in sight, rotting and decaying under the hot sun.

Human Rights Watch believes that the most likely interpretation of the few and contradictory statistics available on the death toll from the disaster is that 85,000 were killed by the immediate flood waves from the failed dams, and a further 145,000 died in the epidemics and famine which struck the area in the ensuing weeks.[43]

Statistic soup

More than 12,000 people have been killed this century by dam-bursts outside China for which data are available (see Table 4.2), excluding incidents caused by enemy action during war. Statistics on dam failures worldwide, however, are confusing and riddled with inconsistencies. Dam safety expert Robert Jansen, of the Bureau of Reclamation, cites a rough estimate of 2,000 dam failures, including partial collapses, since the twelfth century AD and 'about 200 notable reservoir failures' between 1900 and 1980. Professor H. Blind of Munich Technical University cites 166 recorded failures of large dams (dams with a height of 15 metres or more). According to Blind's figures, the rate of failure of small and large dams combined was at its highest in the 1910s and 1920s, with around 30 recorded failures in each decade. Since then the rate has varied between 8 and 25 per decade. Data collected for this book indicate that at least 17 dams failed in the six years between 1990 and 1995.

According to ICOLD data, around 2.2 per cent of all dams built before 1950 have failed and 0.5 per cent of dams built since then. Most of the failures are of small dams – which also make up the great majority of dams. Blind gives an average failure rate between 1900 and 1969 of 2.4 per cent for small dams and 1.7 per cent for large dams. These data explicitly exclude China and are also likely to be incomplete for other countries. Inside China, some 3,200 dams have failed since 1950, 4 per cent of the 80,000 classified dams in the country. The average worldwide risk of any dam failing in a given year is calculated to be in the order of 1 in 10,000.[44]

A huge number of things can go wrong with a dam. The two main reasons for dam failures are 'overtopping' (responsible for around 40 per cent of failures) and foundation problems (around 30 per cent).

Table 4.2 Recorded dam failures since 1860 which have killed more than 10 people

Dam	Country	Type	Height (m)
Dale Dyke (Bradfield)	England	E	29
Iruhaike	Japan	E	28
Mill River	MA, USA	E	13
El Habra[†]	Algeria	R	36
Valparaíso	Chile	E	17
South Fork (Johnstown)	PA, USA	E	22
Walnut Grove	AZ, USA	R	34
Bouzey	France	G	15
Austin	PA, USA	G	15
Lower Otay	CA, USA	R	40
Bila Desna	Czechoslovakia	E	17
Tigra	India	G	24
Gleno	Italy	M	44
Eigiau/Coedty[§]	Wales	G/E	11
St Francis	CA, USA	A	62
Alla Sella Zerbino	Italy	G	12
Vega de Terra (Ribadelago)	Spain	B	34
Malpasset (Fréjus)	France	A	61
Orós	Brazil	E	54
Babii Yar	Ukraine	E	
Panshet/Khadakwasla[§]	India	E/R	54/42
Hyokiri	S. Korea		
Kuala Lumpur	Malaysia		
Vaiont	Italy	A	261
Quebrada la Chapa	Colombia		
Swift	MT, USA		
Zgorigrad (Vratza)	Bulgaria	Ta	12
Nanaksagar	India	E	16
Sempor	Indonesia	R	54
Frías	Argentina	R	15
Buffalo Creek	WV, USA	Ta	32
Canyon Lake	SD, USA	E	6
Banqiao, Shimantan, 60 others	China	E	
Teton	ID, USA	E	90
Laurel Run	PA, USA		
Kelly Barnes (Toccoa Falls)	GA, USA	E	13
Machhu II	India	E	26
Gopinatham	India		
Tous	Spain	R	77
Stava	Italy	Ta	
Kantalai	Sri Lanka	R	15
Sargazon	Tadjikistan		23
Belci	Romania	E	18
Gouhou	China	R	71
Tirlyan	Russia	E	10
Virginia No. 15	S. Africa	Ta	47
Lake Blackshear Project/Flint River Dam	GA, USA	E	<15
N/A	Philippines	N/A	N/A

Year completed	Year failed	Cause of failure	People killed	Cost of damage
1858	1864	SF	250[1]	£0.5m
1633	1868	OT	>1,000[2]	
1865	1874	SF	143	>$1m
	1881	OT	209	
	1888	SF	>100	
1853	1889	OT	2,209	
1888	1890	OT	150	
1881	1895	SF	150[1]	
1909	1911	SF	80	
1897	1916	OT	30	
1915	1916	SF	65	
1917	1917	OT	>1,000[2]	
1923	1923	SF	600	
1908/1924	1925	PI/OT	16	
1926	1928	SF	450	
1923	1935	OT	>100	
1957	1959	SF	145	
1954	1959	F	421	
U/C	1960	OT	*c.*1,000	
	1961	OT	145	
U/C,1879	1961	SF, OT/OT	>1,000[2]	
	1961		250	
	1961		600	
1960	1963	OT	2,600	
	1963		250	
	1964		19[3]	
	1966	OT	>96	
1962	1967	SF/OT	*c.*100	
U/C	1967	SF/OT	*c.*200	
1940	1970	OT	>42	
U/C	1972	OT	125	$30–50m[15]
1938	1972	OT	237*	$60m
late 1950s	1975	OT	≤230,000[4]	
1976	1976	SF	11–14	$0.4–1bn
	1977		39[3]	$20–45m[a]
1899	1977	SF	39[3]	
1972	1979	OT	>2,000	$15m crops
1980	1981	OT	47[5]	
1980	1982	OT	>20[6]	
1960s	1985		269[7]	
1952	1986	PI	≤82[8]	
1980	1987		>19[9]	
1962	1991	OT	c.48[10]	
1987	1993	PI	342[11]	$18m
<1917	1994	OT	19–37[12]	Rs40bn
	1994		39[13]	$15m
	1994	OT	15[14]	
N/A	1995	N/A	c.30[15]	

Embankment dams, which make up about four-fifths of the world's dams, are most vulnerable to being washed away when water flows over their crest. There are, however, usually a number of interrelated reasons why any particular dam collapses. A dam may be overtopped, for example, because of the inadequate capacity of its spillways to discharge floodwaters, because of a spillway blockage with flood-borne debris, or due to mechanical or electrical problems which prevent the spillway gates being opened in time. The spillway gates may also be opened late because of poor operator judgement or incorrect predictions of the size of flood entering the reservoir. Internal erosion (known as 'piping') caused by leaks through the core of a dam can also cause it to slump and be overtopped.

Notes and Sources for Table 4.2

Dam types: E = earthfill; R = rockfill; G = gravity; M = multi-arch; B = buttress; A = arch; Ta = tailings dam; U/C = under construction.

Cause of failure: OT = overtopping; PI = piping; SF = structural failure; F = geological/foundation weakness.

* Unable to distinguish dam break fatalities from those caused by 'natural' flood.

† El Habra first failed in 1872 without loss of life. It was then rebuilt, failed again in 1881, rebuilt again, then failed again in 1927 (without fatalities) and was then abandoned.

§ The flood from the collapse of the first dam breached the second dam downstream.

Sources:

1. N. Smith, *A History of Dams*, Peter Davies, London 1971.
2. F. Lempérière, 'Dams That Have Failed by Flooding: An Analysis of 70 Failures', *Water Power & Dam Construction*, October 1993.
3. J.E. Costa, 'Floods from Dam Failures', in V.R. Baker et al. (eds.), *Flood Geomorphology*, Wiley, New York 1988.
4. Human Rights Watch/Asia, *The Three Gorges Dam in China: Forced Resettlement, Suppression of Dissent and Labor Rights Concerns*, New York, February 1995.
5. Centre for Science and Environment, *The State of India's Environment – 1982: A Citizen's Report*, CSE, New Delhi 1982.
6. 'Overtopped Spanish Dam Collapses as Spillway Gates Stay Shut', *World Water*, November 1982.
7. 'South African Dam Breach Followed Warnings', *Construction Today*, March 1994.
8. 'Kantalai Failure Leaves 18,000 Homeless', *Water Power & Dam Construction*, May 1986.
9. 'Burst Raises Doubts about Soviet Hydroelectricity Dam', *Nature*, 26 March 1987.
10. 'Flooding and Landslides Cause Three Major Failures in Romania', *Water Power & Dam Construction*, October 1991.
11. 'China Disciplines 15 for Dam Break', *Tibetan Environment & Development News*, Issue 16, 1994.
12. 'The Tirlyan Breakthrough', *Moscow News*, 19 August 1944.
13. 'When the Bough Breaks...', *Higher Values* (Minewatch Bulletin), April 1994.
14. 'Georgia Flood Deaths', *International Water Power & Dam Construction*, August 1994.
15. R. Tangbawan, 'Angela's Toll in Philippines Nearing 500', *San Francisco Chronicle*, 5 November 1995.
16. B. Ellingwood et al., 'Assessing Costs of Dam Failure', *Journal of Water Resources Planning and Management*, Vol. 119, No. 1, January/February 1993.

All others: R.B. Jansen, *Dams and Public Safety*, US Department of the Interior, Washington, DC, 1980.

Building a totally safe dam is simply not possible. Robert Jansen says that dams 'require defensive engineering, which means listing every imaginable force that might be imposed, examination of every possible set of circumstances, and incorporation of protective elements to cope with each and every condition'. This is clearly an unattainable target. In the real world, the degree of 'defensive engineering' applied to the design of a dam will be decided by economics. The safer a dam – the greater the capacity of its spillways to cope with floods, the better the quality of its construction materials, the more extensive the exploration of the local geology – the more it will cost. ICOLD itself recognizes the conflict, stating in its 1987 guidelines on dam safety that: 'For every dam project, a balance has to be found between dam safety and economy.'[45]

There will always therefore be pressure for dam builders to cut corners on safety, just as they cut corners on hydrological or sedimentation studies. A confidential 1991 World Bank report notes that because of 'financial factors and local pressure to take shortcuts or ignore poor quality work', construction quality in India is 'deficient for a number of dams, posing serious potential risk to downstream populations'. The report explains how during construction 'large illicit profits can be made by using substandard materials.'[46]

Although several large dams have been seriously damaged by earthquakes, none are yet known to have collapsed because of seismic shaking. At least part of the reason for the apparent resilience of large dams to earthquake damage is, as the US Committee on Large Dams notes, that most have been built very recently in seismic terms, and few 'have been shaken by earthquakes of local duration and intensity sufficient to jeopardize their structural integrity'. USCOLD also points out that 'a few dams have experienced significant damage under shaking less demanding than what had or should have been considered in their design.' The good luck that not many dams have yet been seriously tested in a severe earthquake is compounded with at least one incident where only luck prevented earthquake damage to a dam being translated into a catastrophe.

The Upper and Lower Van Norman Dams in the San Fernando Valley in southern California, completed between 1918 and 1921, were two of the most important dams in the Los Angeles water supply system. On 9 February 1971, a magnitude 6.5 quake struck the San Fernando Valley, with its epicentre about 11 kilometres from the dams. The upstream face of the 43-metre-high Lower Van Norman Dam slumped and collapsed into its reservoir. Due to a preceding dry winter the reservoir was only half full, its surface nearly 11 metres beneath the crest of the earthfill dam. After the tremor struck, only 1.5 metres separated the reservoir surface from the ragged top of the surviving embankment.[47]

The smaller upper dam also slumped during the quake, though less severely than its downstream neighbour. Had this upper dam failed, the ensuing spill would undoubtedly have overtopped and washed away the remaining part of the lower dam. Fears that aftershocks could have caused either or both dams to be breached led to the evacuation of 70,000 valley residents until the lower dam could be safely drained. 'There is no question that, if conditions had been just fractionally more adverse,' says BuRec's Robert Jansen, 'this event would have been recorded as one of the worst disasters in history.'[48]

Despite the massive risk to human life and property posed by large dams, few countries have comprehensive safety legislation covering such areas as the safety criteria that new dams should have to meet; the regular inspection and repair of old dams; and the preparation of emergency evacuation plans for people living downstream. Many older dams were not built with sufficient spillway capacity to pass what hydrologists would now consider the largest flood likely in their basin (conventionally classified as the 'Probable Maximum Flood' or PMF), or sufficient strength to withstand the most powerful earthquake the dam might have to survive (conventionally classified as the 'Maximum Credible Earthquake' or MCE). Yet in most countries there is no requirement for dam owners to upgrade their structures, little data with which to calculate the PMF and MCE, and rarely even agreement among different dam-building agencies over whether or not the PMF and MCE are suitable safety criteria.[49]

Studies in the US have shown that where early warning systems and evacuation plans are in place, the fatalities caused by dam-bursts are on average reduced by a factor of more than 100. However, such plans have been made for only a handful of the world's dams, mostly in the US, Canada and Australia. The first step in an emergency plan should be to draw up and make public a detailed 'inundation map' of areas at risk if a dam should burst. Yet, according to David Ingle Smith of the Australian National University in Canberra, of the few countries that have produced adequate inundation maps some regard them as so confidential that they do not allow even the emergency services to see them. This obsessive secrecy is sometimes due to concerns over the maps being used by the enemy in times of war: in other cases, says Smith, the authorities simply do not want to admit that all dams are potential threats to people living below them.[50]

Disasters waiting to happen

> When a big project has troubles, they may well be big troubles.
>
> John Lowe III and Wilson V. Binger, partners of New York consulting engineers TAMS, discussing their involvement in Tarbela Dam, 1982

Advances in hydrology and dam-building technology, especially in the understanding of the behaviour of rock, earth and water under pressure, means that, in general, new dams are progressively becoming less likely to collapse. However, the risk of another serious dam disaster occurring is continually rising as more dams are built; as their average height increases; as the best locations are used up, forcing dam builders onto increasingly difficult sites; and as the world's largest dams, almost all of which have been built since the 1950s, steadily age and deteriorate. Of the world's 300 'major' dams, as defined by the industry, only Vaiont has caused a major disaster, but a couple of known near misses indicate that these dams, some of which have the potential to kill hundreds of thousands, even millions, of people, are no more unbreakable than the *Titanic* was unsinkable.

Tarbela in Pakistan, a massive embankment of earth and rock nearly 3 kilometres long and at its highest point rising 143 metres above its foundations, is perhaps the world's most problem-stricken major dam. Only a highly expensive programme of emergency repairs and continual monitoring and maintenance have prevented its reservoir from bursting through the embankment and devastating the densely populated Vale of Peshawar below. The full story of how close the mammoth dam came to being breached has never been fully revealed. The following description is mainly taken from a leaked report written for the World Bank by their consultants on the project, UK engineering firm Sir Alexander Gibb & Partners.[51]

The catalogue of mishaps at Tarbela began with the first reservoir impoundment during the 1974 flood season when two out of four tunnels being used to control the rate of filling had to be closed due to serious damage to their linings and outlets. A week after their closure, one of the tunnels still in operation collapsed, bringing down nearly half a million cubic metres of the dam structure and nearby bedrock with it. This threat to the dam required an 'immediate emergency drawdown' of the reservoir through the sole remaining undamaged tunnel as well as through the least-damaged gates of the two tunnels which had earlier been shut.

After the emergency drawdown, engineers found that the blanket of silt and gravel laid on the reservoir bed near the dam to prevent seepage under the embankment had cracked and subsided at around 70 'sinkholes' up to 1 metre deep and 5 metres across. The following year several hundred more sinkholes appeared in the blanket, and in 1976 large depressions appeared in the upstream face of the main embankment and one of two smaller auxiliary embankments. Between 1975 and 1978 the sinkholes were covered by dumping thousands of barge-loads of earth into the reservoir. A large sinkhole which appeared in the main embankment in 1984 was in 1991 still causing concern that it could at some time affect the permeability of the dam.[52]

The designers of Tarbela's spillways knew that the force of flood water plunging off the concrete chutes and into the river below would erode away the fractured, soft rock at the spillway bases, but it was wrongly presumed that this would happen gradually and safely. The main spillway began full operation in the 1976 flood season. Within three weeks, the spilled water had gouged out a hole in the 'plunge pool' at its bottom in places 50 metres deep and 300 metres wide, causing the original sides of the pool to collapse. The following flood season the rocks at the base of the spillway began to be eaten away, threatening the safety of the huge concrete spillway, which at one point actually began to move.[53]

Tarbela's auxiliary spillway, originally designed only to be used in the event of the most extreme floods, had to be operated regularly from 1975 onwards to relieve some of the pressure on the main spillway. In 1979 it was found that the erosion in the auxiliary plunge pool had also been much more serious than expected, endangering the two auxiliary embankments holding back the reservoir in the spillway section of the dam. A massively expensive operation to stabilize the rock around the plunge pools took three years to complete.

The stop-gap programme to prevent disaster at Tarbela almost doubled the cost of the project. Estimated to cost $800 million in 1968, Pakistan had spent around $1.5 billion on Tarbela by 1986 (estimates in constant 1989 prices).[54]

Another notable near miss occurred at the 216 metre Glen Canyon Dam on the Colorado during heavy floods in June 1983. One of the dam's two spillways (which are tunnels through rock at the side of the dam rather than uncovered chutes as at Tarbela) partially caved in. The threat this posed to the stability of the dam abutments meant that both spillways had to be shut. Powell Reservoir, however, kept rising, and would have overtopped the gates of the endangered spillways had not plywood boards obtained from a local lumberyard been fastened to the top of the gates, holding back the reservoir for a few more nerve-wracking days.

BuRec engineers, according to an internal memo, thought there would be an 'uncontrolled release' if the reservoir reached 3,708.40 feet above sea level. The reservoir finally peaked at 3,708.34 feet. Less than an inch – around two centimetres – saved the lower Colorado from probably the most massive flood in human history.[55] Banqiao and Shimantan combined released 600 million cubic metres of water: Powell Reservoir in June 1983 held more than 33 *billion* cubic metres.

Getting Old: Dam Ageing and Decommissioning

> We're going to get their stinking dam. We've got secret plans. We're going to set up a laser beam below the dam, drill a tiny hole through the base of it. We've got underground chemists working on a formula for a new type of acid that will dissolve concrete under water. We have suicide freaks from Stockholm and Tokyo who want to grow up to be human torpedoes.... We've employed a crack team of serious Christians who are praying around the clock for an Act of God.... Long before it fills with mud, that Glen Canyon Dam is going to go...
>
> Edward Abbey, *The Hidden Canyon*, 1977

Once a dam has proved itself well enough built to hold back a reservoir (many dam failures occur either during construction or during or shortly after reservoir filling), its structure and component parts will begin to age. The unique nature of each dam means that every structure will age at a different rate in a different way. Some dams may remain safe for a thousand years, others may start to crack and leak after less than a decade. Around the world, some 5,000 large dams are now more than 50 years old, and the number and size of the dams reaching their half century is rapidly increasing. The average age of dams in the US is now around 40 years. According to a panel on dam ageing at ICOLD's 1991 Congress, 'in the future attention and activity [will] be more and more shifted from the design and construction of new dams to the restoration of the structural and operational safety of existing dams.'[56]

The risks to human life caused by the crumbling dams of the ex-Soviet Union are equivalent to the better known risks from its decrepit nuclear power plants. When three engineers from Hydro-Québec inspected Inguri Dam in the republic of Georgia in 1994, they found the world's third highest dam 'in a rare state of dilapidation'. Only two out of five groups of turbines were in working order, the turbine galleries were flooded by water leaking through the concrete arch dam, and the spillway was found to be 'defective'. Not only does Georgia not have the money for the urgently needed repairs, but at the time of Hydro-Québec's visit the staff working at the dam had not been paid for six months. Inguri was completed only in the 1980s: the condition of many of the older Soviet dams is presumably even worse.

International Water Power & Dam Construction reported in February 1996 that water levels behind the Kakhovskaya Dam in the Ukraine had recently receded after reaching 'excessively high' levels. Kakhovskaya holds back the world's largest capacity reservoir. Engineers reportedly warned the Ukrainian government that the failure of the earth embankment would 'create a 20–30m high wall of water, moving at a speed of around 130 kilometres per hour' threatening the lives of half a million people living in several cities and hundreds of towns along the Dnieper River.[57]

Dangerous dams, however, are far from purely a problem of the ex-Soviet republics. Between 1977 and 1982 the Corps of Engineers inspected 8,800 non-federal dams in the US, most of them privately owned, which it classified as 'high-hazard' – where a failure could cause significant loss of life. Around one-third of these dams – 2,900 – were considered to be 'unsafe', primarily because of inadequate spillway capacity. A 1994 survey showed at least 1,800 non-federal dams were still unsafe. The situation is similar for federal dams: in 1987 one-fifth of BuRec's 275 dams were classified as unsafe, as were one-third of the 554 dams operated by the Corps of Engineers.[58]

An Ontario Hydro study of data from several hundred North American dams shows that, on average, hydrodam operating costs rise dramatically after around 25–35 years of operation due to the increasing need for repairs. When the cost of maintaining an old dam exceeds the receipts from power sales, its owners must decide either to invest in rehabilitating the dam, or, if the cost of repairs would be prohibitive, to disconnect the dam from the grid and cease producing power.[59]

Many old dams in the US have simply been abandoned by their owners. According to the Michigan Department of Natural Resources (MDNR), several abandoned small dams have been washed out during storms in recent years. 'These failures', says the MDNR, 'have caused extreme erosion, excessive sediment deposition and destruction of aquatic habitat accompanied by the loss of the fisheries.' Michigan taxpayers, through the MDNR, have had to pay for removing several 'retired' hydroelectric projects, while their ex-owners have suffered no financial liabilities.[60]

Dam decommissioning (defined as anything from merely stopping electricity generation to removing a dam totally and restoring the river to its pre-dam state) has recently been forced onto the agenda of an unwilling hydropower industry in the US. More than 500 of the 50-year licences given by the US Federal Energy Regulatory Commission (FERC) to private hydrodam operators expire between 1989 and 2004. A coalition of river conservation groups have used this spate of expiring licences to urge FERC to institute a comprehensive dam decommissioning policy. The Hydropower Reform Coalition believes that new licences should only be given on the condition that owners pay into special decommissioning funds during the lifetime of their projects, just as nuclear power plant operators in the US have to put money aside to pay their inevitable decommissioning costs. Despite strong opposition from the hydropower lobby, FERC announced at the end of 1994 that it has authority to order owners of the more than 1,800 dams under its jurisdiction to decommission dams which fail to win new licences, although it has not yet conceded the coalition's call for it to require payments into decommissioning funds.[61]

Although hundreds of dams have been intentionally breached or torn down in the US, the vast majority have been only a few metres high: the largest to be removed is probably the 19 metre Grangeville Dam on the Clearwater River in Idaho, which was dynamited in 1963 to restore salmon runs. How exactly to dismantle a very large dam, what to do with the sediment clogging the reservoir behind it, and how much such an operation would cost is largely unknown. The Hydropower Reform Coalition believes that removing a hydrodam could cost more than building one. Furthermore, the cost would skyrocket where reservoir sediments contain heavy metals and other toxic contaminants.[62]

The best-known dam decommissioning controversy surrounds a pair of dams on the Elwha River in Washington State: the 30 metre Elwha and 70 metre Glines Canyon dams. Built in the 1910s and 1920s with a combined installed capacity of 19 MW, the dams all but wiped out the once-rich steelhead trout and salmon fisheries of the Elwha, fisheries to which the Elwha S'Klallam Tribe had been guaranteed rights 'in perpetuity' in the remarkably aptly named 1855 Treaty of Point No Point. Since the Glines Canyon Dam FERC licence came up for renewal in the late 1970s, the Lower Elwha S'Klallam and environmentalists have been trying to get the dams removed. In 1992 their long campaign started to bear fruit when Congress directed the Interior Department to detail the best plan for 'full restoration of the Elwha River ecosystem and the native anadromous fisheries'. The Interior Department concluded that only removing the dams could fully restore the ecosystem.[63]

Removing both dams and dealing with the 11.5 million cubic metres of sediment which has built up behind them is estimated to cost between $67 million and $80 million, although the full cost of restoring the river, including compensating the dam owners and the paper mill which uses their power, would be between $148 and $203 million over a 20-year period. The dams would be taken down after the river had been diverted around them. Removing the sediment would be the biggest problem and is planned to be done with a combination of dredging, allowing the newly free-flowing river to wash the sediments downstream, and stabilizing with vegetation the sediments higher up the river banks.[64]

No one knows how the major dams built in the last half century will be removed or where the money to pay for this will come from. Feasibility studies rarely – if ever – mention what will happen when a reservoir is choked with sediment or when a company no longer finds it economic to maintain a dam. The international industry has largely steered clear of the issue. 'I have only once seen a paper on the decommissioning of dams', Wolfgang Pircher, then President of ICOLD, said in a lecture to the British Dam Society in 1992.[65] It is, however, an issue which sooner, rather than later, will have to be addressed.

Notes

1. See, e.g., M.M. Cernea, 'Poverty Risks from Population Displacement in Water Resources Development', Harvard Institute for International Development, August 1990, p. 10.

2. E.W. Morrow and R.F. Shangraw, Jr., *Understanding the Costs and Schedules of World Bank Supported Hydroelectric Projects*, World Bank Industry and Energy Department, Washington, DC, July 1990, pp. 35, 19.

3. M. Reisner, *Cadillac Desert: The American West and its Disappearing Water*, Secker & Warburg, London 1986, pp. 398–425.

4. M. Gysel and M. Lommatzsch, 'Guatemala's Chixoy Hydroelectricity Scheme', *Water Power & Dam Construction*, June 1986; World Bank, 'Project Completion Report on Guatemala Chixoy Power Project', 31 December 1991; World Bank, 'Project Performance Audit Report on Guatemala – Aguacapa Power Project and Chixoy Power Project', OED, June 1992, p. 2; Witness for Peace, *A People Dammed: The Impact of the World Bank Chixoy Hydroelectric Project in Guatemala*, Washington, DC, 1996. The Chixoy site was initially identified in a joint World Bank and UN Special Fund (later UNDP) survey.

5. See World Bank, 'Project Performance Audit Report'; M. Davidson, 'Hydro Frustration in Guatemala', unpublished summary of Guatemalan press accounts and interviews with Guatemalan officials, 1987; and R. Yearly, 'The Lights Go Out in Guatemala', *Report on Guatemala*, Oakland, CA, 1992.

6. W.M. Adams, *Wasting the Rain: Rivers, People and Planning in Africa*, Earthscan, London, 1992, p. 61.

7. Hydrodams were being planned in Laos in the mid-1990s on the basis of only two to three years of streamflow records ('Potential and Planning Priorities in the Lower Mekong Basin', *The International Journal of Hydropower & Dams*, March 1995). According to Guatemalan press reports, INDE had only a two-year hydrological record when work started on Chixoy (Davidson, 'Hydro Frustration').

8. A World Bank-funded review of dam safety in India estimated that 'over two-thirds of the dams in India had deficiencies in regard to their capabilities of handling the appropriate magnitude of flood' (World Bank Office Memorandum from William A. Price to Shawki Barghouti, 1 February 1995).

9. T. Burns, 'Water Gets Political in a Very Dry Spain', *Financial Times*, 27 July 1994; M. Alonso Franco and J. Yagüe Cordova, 'The Development of Dam Construction in Spain', *Water Power & Dam Construction*, September 1992.

10. N. Tuntawiroon and P. Samootsakorn, 'Thailand's Dam Building Programme: Past, Present and Future', in E. Goldsmith and N. Hildyard (eds.), *The Social and Environmental Effects of Large Dams. Vol. 2: Case Studies*, Wadebridge Ecological Centre, Cornwall 1986, p. 296; 'Major Dams in Thailand and the Capacity of Their Reservoirs', *Thai Development Newsletter* 25, 1994; 'Water Supplies to be Cut Again', *The Nation*, Bangkok, 14 March 1994.

11. E.S. Mason and R.E. Asher, *The World Bank Since Bretton Woods*, The Brookings Institution, Washington, DC, 1973, p. 687. The Thai authorities' answer to their dam crisis is to propose more dams, canals and tunnels to divert water from the Mekong and Salween Rivers on Thailand's northern borders into Bhumibhol and Sirikit (see, e.g., D. Hubbel, 'Dams and Drought', *World Rivers Review*, First Quarter, 1994).

12. Reisner, *Cadillac Desert*, p. 272.

13. J. Patil et al., 'Report of the Five Member Group Set Up by the Ministry

of Water Resources to Discuss Various Issues Relating to the Sardar Sarovar Project', New Delhi, 21 April 1994; see also R.N. Ram, 'Muddy Waters: A Critical Assessment of the Benefits of the Sardar Sarovar Project', *Kalpavriksh*, New Delhi, August 1993; H. Thakker, personal communication, 28 December 1994.

14. Quoted in Patil et al., 'Report of the Five Member Group', p. 21.

15. K. Mahmood, *Reservoir Sedimentation: Impact, Extent and Mitigation*, World Bank Technical Paper 71, 1987, pp. 8–9.

16. P.H. Gleick (ed.), *Water in Crisis: A Guide to the World's Fresh Water Resources*, Oxford University Press, Oxford 1993, p. 367, Table G.17; H. Chunhong, 'Controlling Reservoir Sedimentation in China', *The International Journal of Hydropower & Dams*, March 1995.

17. According to a team of Indian engineers, 'most of the turbines in the northern part of India are plagued with this problem, which forces frequent shutdown of the machines for repair work.... The annual costs of efficiency losses and repairs due to abrasion damage are immense' (A. Swaroop et al., 'A New Design Philosophy for the Turbine Blades at the Chilla Hydro Project', *Water Power & Dam Construction*, November 1993, p. 37).

18. D.J. Hillel, *Out of the Earth: Civilization and the Life of the Soil*, Free Press, New York 1991, p. 170.

19. X. Wu, 'Environmental Impact of the Sanmen Gorge Project', *Water Power & Dam Construction*, November 1986; World Bank, *China: Involuntary Resettlement*, 8 June 1993, p. 3; Dai Qing, 'An Interview With Li Rui', in Dai Qing (ed. P. Adams and J. Thibodeau), *Yangtze! Yangtze!*, Earthscan, London 1994, p. 119; X. Cheung, 'Unleashing Hydroelectric Potential in a Challenging Environment', *Hydro Review Worldwide*, Winter 1993; Dai Qing, *Yangtze! Yangtze! Vol. II*, forthcoming.

20. X. Cheung, 'Reservoir Sedimentation at Chinese Hydro Schemes', *Water Power & Dam Construction*, October 1992. It is important to note that the usefulness of a reservoir is severely reduced long before it is fully filled with sediment. J.D. Pitt and G. Thompson, 'The Impact of Sediment on Reservoir Life', *Challenges in African Hydrology and Water Resources*, Proceedings of Harare Symposium, IAHS Pub. No. 144, 1984, introduces the concept of the 'half-life' of a reservoir. According to Pitt and Thompson's classification system, a reservoir with a half-life of 20–100 years will be impacted by loss of storage; for a reservoir with a half-life less than 20 years 'sedimentation will be a major problem'.

21. Mahmood, *Reservoir Sedimentation*, pp. 36–7; D.C. Bondurant and R.H. Livesey, 'Reservoir Sedimentation Studies', in W.C Ackermann (ed.), *Man-Made Lakes: Their Problems and Environmental Effects*, American Geophysical Union, Washington, DC, 1973, p. 364.

22. Mahmood, *Reservoir Sedimentation*, pp. 32–7; P.B. Williams, 'Adapting Water Resources Management to Global Climate Change', Villach Conference on Developing Policies for Managing the Effects of Climate Change, special issue of *Climate Change*, 1989.

23. 'Flood Damage Repaired at Kulekhani, but Sedimentation Shortens its Life', *The International Journal of Hydropower & Dams*, September 1994; 'Disastrous Sedimentation', *Himal*, May/June 1994.

24. Mahmood, *Reservoir Sedimentation*, p. 36; 'Study Links Development, Reservoir Silting', *Hydro Review Worldwide*, Winter 1993; 'IDB & Central America: Deforestation Threatens Big Hydro', *World Rivers Review*, January–April 1988; J.D. Gollin, 'Trees Down, Lights Out in Honduras', *Christian Science Monitor*, 15 November 1994.

25. S. Singh et al., 'Evaluating Major Irrigation Projects in India', in E.G. Thukral (ed.), *Big Dams, Displaced People: Rivers of Sorrow, Rivers of Change*, Sage Publications, New Delhi 1992, p. 9.

26. Quoted in B. Morse et al., *Sardar Sarovar: The Report of the Independent Review*, RFI, Ottawa, 1992.

27. Mahmood, *Reservoir Sedimentation*, pp. 55, 73; J. Lowe and I. Fox, 'Sediment Management Schemes for Tarbela Reservoir', paper presented at USCOLD annual meeting, San Francisco, 16 May 1995.

28. Mahmood, *Reservoir Sedimentation*, p. 78.

29. Ibid., p. 105.

30. Another drawback to flushing is that the sediment-filled water passed can damage the dam outlets by its scouring action, and can also block these outlets. Downstream, the sudden surge of a slug of sediment-laden water can have a disastrous effect on water quality and can cause flooding by blocking the river channel (ibid., pp. 89–100).

31. Mahmood, *Reservoir Sedimentation*, p. 107; Lowe and Fox, 'Sediment Management Schemes'.

32. H.K. Gupta, *Reservoir-Induced Earthquakes*, Elsevier, Amsterdam 1992. USCOLD compiled a bibliography in 1986 of more than 2,000 technical papers related to RIS.

33. L. Seeber, Lamont–Doherty Earth Observatory, personal communication, 18 January 1995.

34. Gupta, *Reservoir-Induced Earthquakes.*

35. The geological conditions near reservoirs that favour RIS are those which facilitate the circulation of water under pressure, such as heavily fractured and fissured rocks, or where there are rocks of many different types and water can easily travel between the different strata (ibid.).

36. Ibid., p. 33; 'Memories of Koyna Disaster', *Indian Express* (UK edition), New Delhi, 2 October 1993.

37. C. Clark, *Flood*, Time-Life Books, Alexandria, VA, 1982, p. 135.

38. J.P. Rothé, 'Summary: Geophysics Report', in Ackermann et al. (eds.), *Man-Made Lakes*, p. 445. The magnitude 6.4 shock which hit Killari, Maharashtra, in September 1993, killing 10,000 people, may have been caused by the Tirna reservoir, which began to fill three years before. Although the dam is small – only 15m of water were in the reservoir at the time of the quake – and no local seismograph was operating to show the correlation between reservoir depth and earth tremors, a rupture downstream of the dam was found 'just where we would expect to find a thrust earthquake that had been triggered by the reservoir' (L. Seeber, 'Killari: The Quake that Shook the World', *New Scientist*, 2 April 1994). Conventional seismological opinion on Killari, however, is that the quake was a natural event.

39. L. Seeber, Lamont–Doherty Earth Observatory, personal communication, 18 January 1995.

40. Gupta, *Reservoir-Induced Earthquakes*, p. 4.

41. D.A. Cypser and S.D. Davis, 'Liability for Induced Earthquakes', *Journal of Environmental Law and Litigation*, Vol. 9, No. 2, 1994.

42. Banqiao Dam was occasionally briefly mentioned in dam industry publications before information on the catastrophe was available in English (see, e.g., F. Lempérière, 'Cost Effective Improvements in Fill Dam Safety', *The International Journal of Hydropower & Dams*, January 1995; Z. Ding, 'Forest Cover', *World Water*

and Environmental Engineer, October 1992). It is not known if any in the international dam industry knew of the scale of the catastrophe before February 1995, although it is hard to believe that foreign engineers working in China and having contact with Chinese colleagues would not have known that a major calamity had taken place. If any did know they did not publish the information.

43. 'The Three Gorges Dam in China: Forced Resettlement, Suppression of Dissent and Labor Rights Concerns', *Human Rights Watch/Asia*, Vol. 7, No. 2, 1995, p. 43.

44. R.B. Jansen, *Dams and Public Safety*, US Department of the Interior, Washington, DC, 1983, p. 94; H. Blind, 'The Safety of Dams', *Water Power & Dam Construction*, May 1983; 'ICOLD Reports on Dam Failures', *International Water Power & Dam Construction*, May 1995; Dai Qing, *Yangtze! Yangtze! Vol. II*; J.E. Costa, 'Floods from Dam Failures', in V.R. Baker et al. (eds.), *Flood Geomorphology*, Wiley, New York 1988. Dam failure data usually include tailings (or 'slimes') dams built to contain mining wastes, which are significantly different in design and function from river dams (tailings dams have an abysmal safety record, and often leak toxic heavy metal residues into nearby rivers).

45. Jansen, *Dams and Public Safety*, p. 91; 'Dam Safety Recommendations', *ICOLD Bulletin* 59, 1987, Paris, p. 17.

46. World Bank, 'India: Irrigation Sector Review. Volume 1 – Main Report', India Department 1991, p. 38.

47. 'Had the reservoir been at its normal (and five-foot higher) water level at the time of the earthquake the 70,000 people that lived immediately downstream ... would not have been evacuated in time' (US Committee on Large Dams, *Observed Performance of Dams during Earthquakes*, USCOLD, Denver, CO, 1992, p. 62).

48. Jansen, *Dams and Public Safety*, p. 222.

49. Dams are built to safely pass their 'design flood', which most regulatory agencies define as the Probable Maximum Flood or as a flood which is statistically likely to occur once in a certain number of years (normally between 1,000 and 10,000) (see, e.g., J.J. Cassidy, 'Choice and Computation of Design Floods and the Influence on Dam Safety', *The International Journal of Hydropower & Dams*, January 1994). The statistical methods used by hydrologists to calculate floods of low exceedence such as those over 1:1,000 years are subject to many controversial assumptions.

50. D.I. Smith, 'A Dam Disaster Waiting to Break', *New Scientist*, 11 November 1989; N.M. Nielson, 'BC Hydro's Approach to Dam Safety', *Water Power & Dam Construction*, March 1993. In Britain people living below dams are never alerted to the fact that they could be at risk, no inundation maps exist, no emergency plans have been drawn up in case of a dam failure, and there is no agreement over who should be responsible for warning or evacuating people if a break does occur (J. Connolly, 'Fears Over Britain's Dams', *Sunday Times*, London, 28 July 1985; 'The Case of One Hundred Disappearing Reservoirs', *New Scientist*, 31 July 1993).

51. Sir Alexander Gibb & Partners, *The Tarbela Experience. A Report to the World Bank*, Reading, UK, June 1980, pp. 26–7.

52. 'Report of the 17th ICOLD Congress: Q65: Ageing of Dams and Remedial Measures', *Water Power & Dam Construction*, October 1991.

53. G. La Villa and J. Golser, 'Slopes of the Tarbela Dam Project', *Rock Mechanics*, Suppl. 12, 1982; J. Lowe III et al., 'Tarbela Service Spillway Plunge

Pool Development', *Water Power & Dam Construction*, November 1979.

54. J.A. Dixon et al., *Dams and the Environment: Considerations in World Bank Projects*, World Bank Technical Paper 110, 1989, p. 35.

55. See R. Martin, *A Story that Stands Like a Dam*, Henry Holt, New York 1989, pp. 315–17; P.L. Fradkin, 'The Year the Dam (Almost) Broke', *Los Angeles Times*, 29 October 1995.

56. 'Report of the 17th ICOLD Congress', p. 65; J.R. Shuman, 'The Importance of Environmental Assessments for Proposed Dam Removals', *River Voices*, Winter 1995.

57. 'Alerte sur l'Ingouri', *L'actualité*, Montreal, August 1995; 'Threat of Ukrainian Dam Burst Recedes', *International Water Power & Dam Construction*, February 1996. Owen Falls Dam in Uganda technically has a greater reservoir capacity but the dam did not create a totally new body of water, instead increasing the volume of a natural lake (Lake Victoria).

58. R. Wiseman, 'Many US Dams "Still Unsafe"', *World Water*, September 1987; B. Ingersoll, 'Dams' Safety Worries Officials Who Believe Repairs are Lagging', *Wall Street Journal*, 19 March 1987; '1994 Update Report on Review of State Non-Federal Dam Safety Programs', Association of Dam Safety Officials, Washington, DC, 1995.

59. T. Wong, 'Determining O&M Costs Over the Life of a Hydro Station', in *Hydro in the '90s*, Hydro Review Worldwide, Kansas City 1994. For multipurpose or non-hydro dams, the loss of storage to sediment, and the cost of maintaining the dam compared to income from water supply, navigation or recreation, will be the factors which will determine the dam's economic life.

60. Quoted in Hydropower Reform Coalition, 'Comments by Hydropower Reform Coalition on Notice of Inquiry Regarding Project Decommissioning at Relicensing', Washington, DC, January 1994, p. 14.

61. R. Bowers and M. Bowman, 'Hydroelectric Relicensing: How Relicensing Can Affect Dam Removals', *River Voices*, Winter 1995.

62. See, e.g., Shuman, 'The Importance of Environmental Assessments'; D. Winter, 'A Brief Review of Dam Removal Efforts in Washington, Oregon, Idaho and California', NOAA Technical Memorandum NMFS F/NWR-28, Seattle, WA, 1990.

63. L. Sklar, 'The Dams Are Coming Down', *World Rivers Review*, First Quarter, 1993.

64. Department of the Interior, *The Elwha Report: Restoration of the Elwha River Ecosystem and the Native Anadromous Fisheries*, Department of the Interior, Washington, DC, January 1994, p. xviii. If all the sediments were to be removed the cost would reach $307m. Just allowing the sediment to be washed downstream once the dams are taken out would have a serious effect on downstream water quality and fish habitat.

65. W. Pircher, '36,000 Large Dams and Still More Needed', paper presented at Seventh Biennial Conference of the British Dam Society, University of Stirling, 25 June 1992.

5

Empty Promises: The Elusive Benefits of Large Dams

> For every claim to virtue made by the proponents of big dams there is a clear-cut, factual and demonstrable refutation.
>
> Elmer T. Peterson, *Big Dam Foolishness*, 1954

While the drawbacks of dam projects are consistently belittled by the dam-building lobby, the benefits they provide are regularly exaggerated. One consistent misrepresentation is to play down the inherent conflicts between the different uses of a dam. Maximizing power production, for example, means keeping a reservoir high; flood control requires keeping it low to provide space for absorbing flood waters. Minimizing the rate of reservoir sedimentation on a highly seasonal river requires discharging as much sediment-filled water as possible during the flood season; water storage for the dry season requires capturing flood season flows. Despite these trade-offs, claims of the benefits provided by each purpose of the dam sometimes appear to be made as if that particular purpose was the dam's only function.

Dam proponents also change their claims of the chief reason for building an individual dam according to perceived political advantage. When floods happen along the Yangtze, for example, Three Gorges is touted as a flood control project; when China's great need for electricity is being discussed, it is chiefly a hydropower dam.[1]

Regardless of promises made before the dam is complete, the priority given to its various functions will invariably be based on political and economic power. If the farming lobby is politically strong, diverting water for irrigation may be given priority over hydropower. More often, the easily collected income from electricity production and the political power of electricity consumers will tilt the dam operators toward maximizing the amount of water flowing through their turbines.

As a World Bank internal review states, 'dam and reservoir operation is not dictated by optimization rules but by the struggles of interest groups.'[2]

Generating Risk and Debt: Hydropower

> If God had said 'Let There Be Light!' in Colombia, He would have run out of money for the rest of creation.
>
> *Semana* magazine, Bogotá, 4 April 1989

Mammoth hydrodams such as Itaipú (installed capacity 12,600 MW), Guri in Venezuela (10,300 MW), Sayano-Shushensk in Siberia (6,400 MW) and Grand Coulee (6,180 MW) are the largest single sources of electricity on the planet. By comparison, a major coal-fired or nuclear plant typically has a capacity of less than 1,000 MW. Almost all the world's 300 'major dams', as defined by ICOLD, generate electricity, although only a small minority of all large dams have turbines installed.[3]

At the beginning of the 1990s, around 18 per cent of the world's electricity and 6 per cent of primary energy supply (which includes, for example, fuelwood, and fossil fuels used directly for heating or transport) was provided by hydropower. The proportion of each continent's electricity generated by hydro varies from a low of around 15 per cent in Asia, to almost 60 per cent in South and Central America. Twenty-four countries, including Ghana, Zambia, Brazil, Guatemala, Honduras, Nepal, Laos, Sri Lanka, Albania, Iceland and Norway, are dependent on hydropower for over 90 per cent of their electricity supply; Congo, Paraguay and Bhutan receive all their electricity from dams. Global hydro generation rose by a fifth during the 1980s, most of the increase coming from Latin America and Asia.[4]

Japan, the USA and Canada have each exploited around 70 per cent of their estimated 'economically feasible' hydro potential; Europe about half of its potential; while Africa, China and Latin America have developed only around one-tenth of theirs. Estimates of unexploited potential must, however, be interpreted with caution, not least because of the paucity of reliable hydrological data for most of the world's rivers. Hydro potential data also take no account of geological constraints or the social and environmental impacts of the dams needed to tap unexploited potential. Furthermore the criteria used to define 'economically feasible' are vague and vary between countries.[5]

A serious problem for the hydro industry's dreams of expansion is that many potential dam sites are far from the cities and industries which are demanding more electricity. According to John Besant-Jones of the World Bank, nearly three-fifths of 'economic' hydropower potential is in countries where hydro development is 'moderately to severely constrained' by insufficient demand for electricity.[6]

The inflexibility of hydropower in terms of its siting is paralleled by its inflexibility to cope with changes in the rate of growth of energy demand over the many years it takes to plan and construct large dams. Energy demand forecasts – usually drawn up without public input by the electricity supply industry – consistently overestimate future needs for electricity. In more than 100 national demand forecasts used by the World Bank, actual demand seven years after the forecasts were made was on average one-fifth lower than had been projected (a major dam takes at the very least seven years to plan and build). The deviation between projected and actual demand increased with the number of years from the date of the forecast.[7]

The economic justification of the 3,100 MW Yacyretá Dam used the assumption that Argentinean electricity demand would grow at a rate of 8–10 per cent a year during the 1980s. In fact demand grew by an annual average of just over 2 per cent so that when the first turbines of the $11.5 billion megaproject came on-line in 1994 (eight years behind schedule), the country already had a sizeable surplus of generating capacity.[8]

Between 1970 and the mid-1980s, the World Bank and Inter-American Development Bank together lent Colombia a total of $3.8 billion for 12 large hydrodams and their associated infrastructure. Yet by 1986, when these dams had mostly been completed (after incurring extensive time and cost overruns), electricity demand in Colombia was one-third lower than forecast when the dams were planned, and the excess generating capacity was estimated to have cost Colombia more than $400 million. In a confidential report, the World Bank's Operations Evaluation Department (OED) concluded that this high cost of overcapacity highlights 'the vital importance of having more flexible investment programs' with smaller projects 'so that better responses can be had to the vicissitudes of demand uncertainties'.[9]

Colombia's hydropower splurge had a serious impact on the country's economy. By the mid-1980s, one-third of Colombia's total public investment was being eaten up by the power sector, and 60 per cent of this money was leaving the country to pay for imported goods and services. In 1987, interest payments on the power sector's foreign debt represented nearly two-fifths of Colombia's total public foreign debt repayments. Colombia's hydropower investment programme, the OED concludes, combined with the power utilities' low revenues and large external borrowing, 'undoubtedly had a negative impact on Colombia's economic growth and macrofinancial situation in the 1980s'.[10]

The need for foreign expertise and equipment frequently reduces the benefits which developing countries gain from hydro projects (and increases the desire of rich countries to subsidize dams overseas with aid loans). Around $784 million out of the $800 million spent on the Diama and Manantali Dams in the Senegal River Basin went to expatriate firms. The loans to pay for the dams came mostly from the Arab Gulf states (because they wanted to extend their influence in African Muslim states), and France and Germany (because their firms got the construction contracts). 'It's a ploy by the French and West Germans to revitalize their construction industry by using Arab money', a US aid official told the *New York Times* in 1981. Manantali is supposed to have an installed capacity of 200 MW, yet although the dam itself was completed in 1988, eight years later it still had no turbines.[11]

Over-reliance on a limited number of huge hydrodams lays countries open not only to the risk of wasting massive sums on unnecessary projects but also to the risk of power shortages in the case of drought, unexpectedly rapid sedimentation, miscalculated river flows or dam failure. Two hydrodams on the Volta River – Akosombo and the smaller Kpong Dam downstream – account for all but 88 MW of Ghana's total generating capacity of 1,160 MW. When the dams were crippled by a serious drought in 1982–83, Ghanaian electricity supplies had to be rationed for the next three years. Because of this experience, Akosombo was redesigned with a minimum operating level several metres lower than originally planned. In mid-1994, however, after two more dry years, the level of Volta Reservoir fell below the new minimum operating level. Ghanaian electricity consumers (only one in four households in Ghana receives electricity) suffered blackouts lasting 20 hours a week. Other African countries which are heavily dependent on hydropower have also suffered serious power shortages during recent droughts.[12]

All the nations in Central America rely on hydropower for well over half of their electricity. Sixty-five per cent of Guatemala's energy is provided by Chixoy Dam. In 1990 the country suffered a series of blackouts because of a lack of water at Chixoy. Two years later, another power shortage because of Chixoy's low reservoir resulted in electricity being rationed for more than a month, costing the country $2 million a day in lost industrial production. The 300 MW turbines of El Cajón Dam represent 70 per cent of the installed capacity of Honduras. Low rainfall through the early 1990s has meant that the level of El Cajón Reservoir has steadily fallen. By mid-1994, the dam was able to generate at only half capacity at best and Honduran electricity consumers were suffering blackouts of up to 14 hours a day.[13]

Exaggerating energy

There is an important difference between a power plant's capacity to generate power (properly defined as the rate of flow of energy) and its actual energy production. The standard unit of power is the watt

Table 5.1 Plant factors for hydro projects (selected according to available data)

Dam	Country	Installed capacity (*MW*)	Average annual output (*GWh/yr*)	(*year*)	Plant factor (%)	Ref.
Balbina	Brazil	250	970	(1993)	44	1
Bayano	Panama	150	523.5	(1993)	40	2
Bhumibol	Thailand	535	950	(?)	20	3
Cirata	Indonesia	500	1,438	(1990)	33	4
Gezhouba	China	2,715	16,000	(1989–93)	67	5
Guri	Venezuela	9,588	42,403	(1993)	50	2
Kariba South	Zimbabwe	666	2,094	(1993)	36	2
Kompienga & Bagré	Burkina Faso	30	47	(1993)	18	2
Kotmale	Sri Lanka	200	404	(?)	23	2
Kulekhani I & II	Nepal	92	100	(1993)	12	2
La Fortuna	Panama	300	1,233.5	(1993)	47	2
Macagua I	Venezuela	360	2,599	(1993)	82	2
Nurek	Tadjikistan	3,000	11,195	(1990)	43	6
Saguling	Indonesia	700	2,156	(1986–89)	35	4
Samanalawewa	Sri Lanka	120	280§		27	2
Sardar Sarovar	India	1,450	3,600–400*		28–3*	7
Tucuruí	Brazil	4,000	18,030	(1991)	51	1
Victoria	Sri Lanka	210	588	(?)	32	2
Sirikit	Thailand	275	550	(?)	17	3
Srinakharin	Thailand	720	1,158	(?)	18	3
Khao Laem	Thailand	300	760	(?)	29	3
Typical coal plant					75–81	8
Typical nuclear plant					68	8

* Projected. Output will decline over time as irrigation diversions are increased.
§ 'max. long-term average'.

Sources:

1. P. Fearnside, 'Hydroelectric Dams in the Brazilian Amazon as Sources of "Greenhouse" Gases', *Environmental Conservation*, Vol. 22, No. 1, 1995.
2. 'World Atlas of Hydropower & Dams', *The International Journal of Hydropower & Dams*, January 1995.
3. Norconsult, 'Promoting Subregional Cooperation... Subregional Energy Sector Study for Asian Development Bank', November 1994.
4. O. Soemarwoto, 'Introduction', in B.A. Costa-Pierce and O. Soemarwoto (eds.), *Reservoir Fisheries and Aquaculture Development for Resettlement in Indonesia*, ICLARM, Manila 1990.
5. Y. Liu, 'The Gezhouba Project in Operation', *International Water Power & Dam Construction*, August 1994.
6. M. Burkhanova, 'Ecological–Economic Problems of Constructing Large Mountain Reservoirs', unpublished MS, 1991.
7. S. Paranjape and K.J. Joy, 'The Alternative Restructuring of the Sardar Sarovar Project: Not Destructive Development but Sustainable Prosperity. A Note for Discussion', mimeo, 1994.
8. C. Flavin and N. Lenssen, *Power Surge: Guide to the Coming Energy Revolution*, W.W. Norton, New York 1994, p. 126.

Table 5.2 Projected and actual plant factors for hydro projects (selected according to available data)

Dam	Country	Installed capacity (*MW*)	Projected output (*GWh/yr*)	Projected plant factor (%)	Actual output (av.) (*GWh/yr*)	Actual plant factor (%)
Aswan[1]	Egypt	2,100	10,000	54	7,161[a]	40
Itaipú[2]	Brazil/Paraguay	12,600	79,000	72	63,839[b]	58
Akosombo[3]	Ghana	882	5,400	70	3,597[c]	46

[a] 1980–89; [b] 1993–94; [c] 1968–84

Sources:

1. Projected figure from R. Rycroft and J. Szyliowicz, 'The Technological Dimension of Decision Making: The Case of the Aswan High Dam', *World Politics: A Quarterly Journal of International Relations*, Vol. 33, No. 1, October 1980. Actual figure calculated from M.T. El Safty and H.A. Younes, 'Hydro Power Generation in Egypt', in Egyptian National Committee on Large Dams (ed.), *High Aswan Dam Vital Achievement Fully Controlled*, ENCOLD, Cairo 1993, p. 126.
2. Projected figure from 'Itaipú Binacional: The Biggest Hydroelectricity Undertaking of the XXth Century' (advertisement) *New York Times*, 30 October 1992. Actual figure from *International Water Power and Dam Construction*, March 1995, p. 2.
3. Both figures from F.S. Tsikata (ed.), *Essays from the Ghana–Valco Renegotiations, 1982–85*, Ghana Publishing Corporation, Accra 1986.

(1 megawatt equals 1 million watts). The standard unit of electrical energy is the kilowatt-hour (kWh), which represents 1,000 watts of power supplied for one hour. One kilowatt-hour of electrical energy can run a 100 watt light bulb for 10 hours. The energy production of large dams is normally expressed in kilowatt-hours per year (kWh/yr) or gigawatt-hours per year (GWh/yr – 1 gigawatt equals 1,000 megawatts).

If a hydroplant were able to generate power continuously night and day, all year round, at the full capacity of its turbines, it would have a 'plant factor' of 100 per cent. Of course, no power plant can perform at this level – and dams built to provide power only at times of peak demand are not designed to operate all the time. Factors which affect the availability of a dam's power supply include shutdowns for repairs and maintenance, and, in particular, seasonal and annual variations in streamflow.

Annual average hydropower plant factor in the US is put by industry sources at 46 per cent. According to the World Bank, average plant factor in developing countries during the 1980s was around 49 per cent.

By comparison, fossil fuel power stations in the US have an average plant factor of around 65 per cent.[14]

It is difficult to tell how much of the low plant factor for dams is due to projects being deliberately operated for peaking power and how much to the inherent limitations of dams. Figures for the actual long-term power production of individual dams are very hard to find (most of those which could be located during research for this book are listed in Table 5.1). Finding comparisons between projected and actual production is harder still. What statistics are available, however, suggest that consultants and other dam promoters may regularly exaggerate power production from planned dams (a conclusion supported by the power cuts described above).

Egyptian authorities claimed that the 2,100 MW High Aswan Dam would generate 10,000 GWh/yr, a plant factor of 54 per cent; actual average output in the 1980s, according to government statistics, was just 7,161 GWh/yr, a plant factor of 40 per cent. Newspaper advertisements placed by the binational utility which built Itaipú claimed it would generate 79,000 GWh/yr, a plant factor of 72 per cent. Actual average plant factor for Itaipú in 1993 and 1994 was 58 per cent. Akosombo was supposed to have a plant factor of 70 per cent; actual plant factor between 1968 and 1984 was just 46 per cent (see Table 5.2).[15]

In a 1983 feasibility study, a consortium led by German engineering consultants Lahmeyer International claimed that the 2,400 MW Bakun Dam in the Malaysian state of Sarawak would have an 'annual average energy output' of 18,000 GWh/yr – giving a plant factor of 86 per cent. After the veracity of this claim was challenged by project critics, the consultants slimmed down their projection to 16,785 GWh/yr, a plant factor of 80 per cent – which still appears unrealistically high.[16] The projected economic return from the Nam Theun 2 Dam in Laos is based on the 681 MW dam generating on average 4,864 GWh/yr, a plant factor of 81 per cent. From leaked project documents it appears that this remarkably optimistic prediction is based on just seven years of rainfall data for most of the Nam Theun basin.[17] Even with a long series of good streamflow data, the credibility of such a high plant factor prediction would be in doubt.

Newspaper advertisements and public statements by the backers of Sardar Sarovar proudly proclaim the dam's installed capacity of 1,450 MW – yet fail to mention that the average generation during the initial phase of the project is planned to be only 439 MW due to low power production during the long dry season. As the project's 80,000 kilometres of irrigation canals are completed, more and more water will be diverted from the reservoir before reaching the main turbines. Eventually average power output would fall to only 50 MW. Taking into account the substantial amount of power needed to pump water through the canals, Sardar Sarovar – like other large-scale water-transfer projects – would eventually become a net *consumer* of energy.[18]

An unsustainable potentially renewable

> Hydropower is proven to be a safe, clean, efficient and renewable source of energy...
>
> Interim Environmental Impact Assessment for Bakun Dam, 1994

Dam advocates have repeatedly insisted over the years that hydropower is clean, renewable and cheap. Yet, all three of these claims at best bend the truth. Hydro cannot seriously be considered a 'clean' energy source: the pollution caused by dams may be less obvious than the dirty columns of smoke belching from coal-burning plants, but it is pollution none the less. Hydro can seriously contaminate river water and it emits greenhouse gases due to the rotting of submerged vegetation and soils. The fragmentation and eradication of riverine ecosystems is also a form of pollution – one of the definitions of 'pollute' in *Chambers 20th Century Dictionary* is 'to make (any feature of the environment) offensive or harmful to human, animal, or plant life'.

Jan A. Veltrop, ex-President of the International Commission on Large Dams, writes that: 'Hydropower is renewable because it is powered by the hydrological cycle.'[19] This is confusing a renewable resource – streamflow – with the invariably unrenewable technology used to exploit it. Because the number of suitable dam sites is finite, and because dams age and their reservoirs fill with sediments, hydro can only be considered renewable if the mammoth costs of tearing down obsolete dams, disposing of the sediments which have accreted behind them, and then building new dams in their place is taken into account. While decommissioning and rebuilding may be economically and technically feasible for smaller projects, there are as yet no indications that this will be the case for the very large dams built in the past 60 years.

Hydropower is certainly not 'sustainable' according to the definition of sustainable development as popularized by the 1987 World Commission on Environment and Development (WCED) chaired by Norwegian Prime Minister Gro Harlem Brundtland. Sustainable Development, in the words of the WCED, is development 'that meets the needs of the present without compromising the ability of future generations to meet their own needs'. By destroying rivers and estuaries and extinguishing species, dams do compromise the ability of future generations to meet their needs. An accurate description of large hydro would therefore be 'unsustainable potentially renewable'.[20]

Hydro has been promoted as 'cheap' mainly because, unlike coal- or oil-powered plants, dams get their fuel – water – for free. This illusion of cheapness begins to dissipate when the economic cost of dam construction is taken into account, and totally vanishes when dams' frequent poor operating performance and even a small proportion of their environmental and social costs are factored into their economic valuation. These formerly hidden costs of dams have increasingly been forced into the open in recent years, so the hydro lobby has been forced to change its rhetorical justification for hydropower. The once popular claims of 'cheap hydro' are now being replaced by claims of hydro as the answer to global warming – in the words of Ted Haws, head of ICOLD's Environment Committee, hydro as the 'great global environmental benefit'.[21]

Dams to the Rescue? Hydro and Global Warming

> Hydropower plants produce no carbon dioxide ... no air emissions at all.
>
> US Department of Energy brochure prepared with the technical assistance of the National Hydropower Association and others, 1994

Hydropower's supposed potential for mitigating global warming – because it does not involve fossil-fuel burning – is now seen by the industry as one of its greatest selling points. Five out of 14 speakers at a 1994 international conference on financing dam projects referred to the importance of hydropower as a non-greenhouse-gas-emitting technology (and none of the speakers referred to hydro as 'cheap'). Also in 1994, state-owned utility Hydro-Québec advertised in energy industry journals that Canadian and US energy utilities 'can help reduce the threat of global warming for all of us' by importing hydroelectricity from Quebec. Some hydro advocates propose that industrialized countries should meet their obligations to limit greenhouse gas emissions under the UN's framework climate convention by helping to pay for hydrodams in developing countries.[22]

Global warming is clearly a very real and massive threat to human society and the natural world, and technologies and modes of political and social organization which can minimize greenhouse gas emissions – while not exacerbating other environmental and social problems – need urgently to be brought into use. Hydropower, however, is not only socially and environmentally destructive but is also far from being as 'climate-friendly' as its proponents allege. While little research has yet been done on greenhouse gas emissions from reservoirs, what has been carried out suggests that hydropower reservoirs, especially those in tropical forest areas, can make a significant contribution to global warming, in some cases as much or even more than fossil-fuel-burning power plants producing an equivalent amount of electricity.

Through the processes of growth and decay, soils, forests and wetlands continuously consume and emit large amounts of carbon dioxide (CO_2) and methane (CH_4), the two most important non-synthetic greenhouse gases. For mature forests and grasslands, the consumption and emission of CO_2 is usually in balance, and the ecosystems act as huge carbon stores with – as long as they remain undisturbed – no net effect on the concentration of greenhouse gases in the atmosphere. Many soils, however, consume more methane than they emit and are therefore net methane sinks. Temperate peatlands are sinks of both CO_2 and CH_4; tropical wetlands, on the other hand, are major sources of methane. Natural lakes are usually sources of methane but often sinks for carbon dioxide. Just as the fluxes of these gases from different ecosystems to and from the atmosphere vary widely, so does the amount of the carbon stored in biomass and soils: natural forests, for example, can store 20 to 100 times as much carbon per unit area as farmlands. The biomass of tropical forests tends to contain far more carbon than temperate forests; temperate grassland soils, on the other hand, can contain more carbon than tropical forest vegetation and soils put together.[23]

When these ecosystems are flooded, the pattern of the fluxes of CO_2 and CH_4 with the atmosphere is totally altered. Peat, which as a living ecosystem consumed the gases, when flooded rots and is a net source of them. Plants and soils decompose when flooded and will eventually release almost all of their stored carbon. Permanently flooding tropical wetlands will tend to increase their methane emissions and make them a net source of CO_2. Gases produced by reservoirs can be emitted through continuous diffusion into the atmosphere from the surface of the water; in sudden pulses when deep water in the reservoir rises to the surface in cold weather (cooling the water at the surface makes it denser and so causes it to sink); and from deep water being discharged through turbines.

The most comprehensive study of reservoir greenhouse gas emissions has been done by Philip Fearnside of the Brazilian National Institute for Research in Amazonia (INPA). Fearnside calculated the impact on global warming of Balbina and Tucuruí dams over the first 50 years of their lives by assessing the amount of forest they flooded and the rate at which vegetation would decay at different depths of their reservoirs. He concluded that immediately after reservoir filling there was a huge pulse of CO_2 emissions, which would then steadily decline over the years. Around half of the total CO_2 emissions from Balbina happened within seven years of impoundment, almost all of the gas being released from the parts of decaying trees above the water line.

The warm, nutrient-rich and severely oxygen-depleted water at the bottom of these shallow reservoirs creates ideal conditions for the methane-producing bacteria which feed on decaying vegetation. The rate of decay in the deoxygenated bottom layer of a tropical reservoir

Table 5.3 Greenhouse gas emissions from reservoirs in Brazil and Canada compared with fossil fuel emissions

Project	Reservoir area at operating level (*km*²)	Average annual generation (*Gwh/yr*)	Annual CO_2 emissions per km² (*t/km²/yr*)	Annual methane emissions per km² (*t/km²/yr*)	Emissions per gigawatt-hour (*10⁶t CO_2-equivalent/GWh*)[a]
Balbina Dam (Brazil)	3,147	970	7,550	45	26,200*
Tucuruí Dam (Brazil)	2,247	18,030	4,210	40	580*
Churchill/Nelson hydroscheme (Canada)	1,400	16,000	190–200	4–8	40–60†
Grand Rapids Dam (Canada)	1,200	1,700	190–200	4–8	300–500†
Conventional coal-fired generation					1,000†
Combined-cycle natural gas generation					400†

[a] Contribution of carbon dioxide and methane combined in CO_2-equivalent units
* Global warming potential for methane = 11
† Global warming potential for methane = 60

Sources: P.M. Fearnside, 'Hydroelectric Dams in the Brazilian Amazon as Sources of 'Greenhouse Gases', *Environmental Conservation*, Vol. 22, No. 1, 1995; J.W.M. Rudd et al., 'Are Hydroelectric Reservoirs Significant Sources of Greenhouse Gases?', *Ambio*, Vol. 22, No. 4, June 1993.

is incredibly slow – even leaves can take centuries to decompose completely. Methane production is only partly related to the original amount of flooded biomass as it is also emitted by the decay of aquatic plants and of organic matter which the river carries into the reservoir. For these reasons, methane emissions are fairly constant over time and do not decline significantly as the reservoir matures.

Fearnside calculates that in 1990 (six years after Tucuruí started to fill and three years after the gates were closed at Balbina) Tucuruí Reservoir emitted 9,450,000 tonnes of carbon dioxide and 90,000 tonnes of methane; Balbina emitted 23,750,000 tonnes of carbon dioxide and 140,000 tonnes of methane. Combining the effects of the two gases, Fearnside estimated that Tucuruí had 60 per cent as much impact on global warming as a coal-fired plant generating the same amount of electricity – but 50 per cent more impact than a gas-fired power station. Balbina Reservoir, meanwhile, had *26 times more* impact on global warming than the emissions from an equivalent coal-fired power station (see Table 5.3). While the emissions from the reservoirs will slowly decline over the years as the flooded biomass decays, the global warming impact of Balbina will always be far higher than that from equivalent fossil fuel generation.[24]

Fearnside's paper follows a study by a team of researchers led by John Rudd of the Canadian government's Freshwater Institute which estimated that there are also substantial emissions of CO_2 and methane from reservoirs in northern Canada. Rudd and his co-workers measured per-hectare gas releases from flooded forests and bogs and then extrapolated these findings to estimate the average annual emissions over 50 years of two large hydroelectric reservoirs in northern Manitoba. The researchers concluded that the contribution to global warming for every kilowatt-hour generated at Grand Rapids Dam was around the same as that from a gas-fired plant, while a kilowatt-hour from the huge Churchill/Nelson hydro scheme contributed only around an eighth as much as a gas plant.[25]

There are many uncertainties in calculating the contributions of different human activities to global warming. One major problem is comparing the impact of methane releases with those of carbon dioxide – an important issue when assessing the relative contribution to global warming of reservoirs and fossil fuels because methane is a major component of reservoir emissions while fossil-fuel emissions are largely carbon dioxide. Methane is a more powerful greenhouse gas than CO_2 on a molecule-by-molecule basis, but it is shorter lived in the atmosphere. There is no universally agreed factor (called a Global Warming Potential, or GWP) with which to multiply a unit of methane in order to give CO_2 equivalent units. Rudd and his colleagues use a multiple of 60, which according to the UN's panel of experts on climate change is roughly how much more a molecule of CH_4 contributes to global warming than a molecule of CO_2 over a 20-year time-span. Fearnside, however, uses a GWP for methane of only 11, a conservative figure which includes only the direct effects of the gas over a 100-year span. Including the indirect effects of methane (its reactions with other gases in the atmosphere) gives a GWP of 21. Had Fearnside used a methane GWP of 21 in his calculations the estimated contribution of Amazonian reservoirs to global warming would be substantially increased; had Rudd et al. used 21 their estimate for the contribution of Canadian reservoirs would be greatly reduced.[26]

These findings cannot easily be extrapolated to other reservoirs as emissions of greenhouse gases per hydroelectric kilowatt-hour will depend not only on the ratio of the area flooded to the energy produced (which can vary by a factor of at least 80,000) but also on local climate and vegetation.[27] A comprehensive accounting of a dam's contribution to global warming should also include the emissions from the fossil fuels used during dam construction, those from the production of the cement, steel and other materials used in the dam, and, probably more significantly, the changes in greenhouse gas fluxes due to the land use and other changes which the dam encourages, such as deforestation, the conversion of floodplain wetlands to intensive agriculture, the adoption of irrigation on once rainfed lands, and the increased use of fossil-fuel-based artificial fertilizers.[28]

Static dams, changing climate

Dam designers work on the assumption that historic hydrological variables such as average annual river flow, annual variability of flow, and seasonal distribution of flow are a reliable guide to the future. As global warming takes hold, however, there are likely to be significant changes in seasonal and annual rainfall patterns and other factors affecting streamflow such as the rate and timing of snowpack melting, and the nature of watershed vegetation. Historical and geological evidence for floods in past millennia indicate that even small changes in climate can cause major changes in the size of floods. Reservoir sedimentation will also likely be significantly affected: in arid areas, an increase in average annual precipitation of only 10 per cent can double the volume of sediment washed into rivers.[29]

Calculations of the amounts of water available to turn turbines, the maximum flood which spillways will have to discharge, and the rate at which reservoirs fill with sediment will thus become increasingly unreliable as global warming takes hold and as, inexorably, year by year, decade by decade, the earth's climate changes. Insurers are increasingly convinced that global warming is to blame for the increased frequency and severity of violent and expensive storms, floods and droughts since the late 1980s, weather events which have already resulted in burst dams, increased sedimentation and reduced hydropower capacity. A 1991 report from the UN Intergovernmental Panel on Climate Change noted that: 'Increased run-off due to climate change could potentially pose a severe threat to the safety of existing dams with design deficiencies. Design criteria for dams may require re-evaluation to incorporate the effects of climate change.' Thus, not only is global warming not the godsend to save an ailing industry which many hydro backers hope, but it is going to render dams less safe and less likely to perform as their builders' claim.[30]

The Great Illusion: Flood Control

Says Tweed to Till –
'What gans ye rin sae still?'
Says Till to Tweed –
'Though ye rin with speed
And I rin slaw,
For ae man that ye droon
I droon twa.'

Anonymous, 'Two Rivers', Scots rhyme

The US Army Corps of Engineers has spent over $25 billion on 500 dams and 16,000 kilometres of embankments in its war against floods. BuRec, the TVA and other federal, state and local bodies have spent billions more. Yet the inflation-adjusted annual cost of flood damage in the US has more than doubled since 1937, when the first federal Flood Control Act was passed. The number of people killed in floods each year has remained roughly the same. Flood damage to property in the US in the first half of the 1990s averaged around $3 billion a year. This pattern of rising spending on flood controls being accompanied by rising flood damage is seen around the world. India spent nearly a billion dollars on embankments and river channelization between 1953 and 1980, and many billions more on dams, yet both the area of cropland affected and the cost of damage from flooding rose dramatically over this period.[31]

There are a variety of reasons why flood damages are increasing. The deforestation, degradation and urbanization of watersheds is increasing the speed at which water runs off the land and into rivers; climate change may be increasing the variability, intensity and frequency of rainstorms. Probably the main factor behind the spiralling costs of floods around the world, however, is that dams and embankments induce a false sense of security. Deliberately or not, people are encouraged to settle on the floodplains, making future floods much more serious than if no controls had been built and the plains left undeveloped. Furthermore, the progressive loss of storage capacity to sedimentation reduces the ability of dams to capture flood waters, with the result that year by year the risk to the new floodplain dwellers increases.

Structural controls such as dams and embankments, while they can eliminate 'normal' annual floods, can also worsen the severity of extreme floods. By confining the river and straightening its course, embankments increase both the volume and speed of the river, increasing its capacity to cause damage downstream. Containing the river's sediment load within its banks raises the bed of the river, which means that the embankments must in turn be raised further to compensate. Not only is this constant rebuilding of levees extremely costly, but eventually the river level will rise above the height of the surrounding plain, providing the potential for disastrous flash-floods should the huge embankments break.[32]

A reservoir with sufficient capacity can help alleviate floods downstream by storing some or all of the excess flow after heavy rains. However, the very large dams which have the capacity to affect a flood on a major river are usually multipurpose projects, and financial and political pressures mean that keeping the reservoir high to maximize electricity generation and water supply frequently takes precedence over keeping it low to make room for floodwaters. The risk to people living below dams is compounded by the ever-present possibility of dam failure: a dam-burst flood is almost certain to be the most destructive which ever hits a river valley.[33]

High releases from some major hydrodams due to their operating regime can both increase the damage caused during the normal flood season and cause unprecedented out-of-season inundation. According to a team from Argentina's National Council for Scientific and Technical Studies, releases from Itaipú have caused 'recurrent – sometimes catastrophic – floods'.[34] Salto Grande, a 1,890 MW dam on the Uruguay River between Argentina and Uruguay, was supposed to reduce floods, but since it was completed flooding has increased, with, among other consequences, the forced abandonment of some of the many inhabited islands in the lower Uruguay Basin.[35]

Numerous cases have been recorded of floods which have been made worse because dam operators held back water while the reservoir was filling, and then, when the rains kept on coming, had hastily to open their floodgates to prevent their dam from being overtopped. India's Hirakud Dam was first justified in the name of flood control, yet extreme floods in the Mahanadi Delta between 1960 and 1980 were three times more frequent than before Hirakud was built. In September 1980, hundreds of people were killed after releases from Hirakud breached downstream embankments. Orissa's Chief Minister admitted that panic releases of water from Hirakud were responsible for much of the devastation but argued that if the water had not been discharged as quickly as possible, the dam could have failed.[36]

Many other deadly floods have been blamed on emergency releases from Indian dams. In 1978 nearly 65,000 people in the Punjab were made homeless by floods exacerbated by forced discharges from Bhakra Dam. A member of a committee set up to investigate the floods admitted that Bhakra had been close to being overtopped and stated that 'If something had happened to the dam, then half of Punjab would have been inundated.' Eleven years later a similar flood occurred. This time an official from the agency in charge of managing Bhakra argued that if the water had not been discharged, 'one of the worst catastrophes in living memory' would have occurred.[37]

Half a million people living in Sacramento, the state capital of California, narrowly escaped disaster in 1986 when releases from the Folsom Dam almost overtopped the levees protecting the city from the American River. Discharge data from Folsom showed that the dam operators had disregarded their own operating procedures, allowing floodwaters to fill up the reservoir for 36 hours, and then suddenly increasing discharges to beyond their designed maximum when the safety of the dam was threatened.[38]

Flooding to stop floods

In many cases, claims that a dam will help reduce flooding appear to be merely tactics to try to skew cost–benefit analyses. A 1980 Congressional subcommittee report on the Tennessee Valley Authority's Columbia Dam, for example, found that 11,130 hectares above the dam, almost all prime farmland, would be inundated or otherwise affected by the project to provide flood protection for less than a third as many hectares downstream. While the original project documents discussed the benefit of flood control, no mention was made of the multi-million dollar loss of farm production and related businesses to permanent flooding by the reservoir. When the subcommittee tried to identify the 43 buildings TVA claimed would be protected by the dam, they found 'numerous shack-type, abandoned, commercial structures'. Of eleven businesses which the TVA said existed along one section of the river, only five were listed in the local telephone directory.[39]

Claims as to how much flood protection the massive Three Gorges Dam will provide vary, but the most common is that 10 million people will be saved from the threat of flooding. Only floods caused by rain in the upper catchment above the dam would be controlled, however, while many of the severe floods on the middle and lower Yangtze are caused by local storms.[40] To provide this supposed flood control, some 1.3 million people will be permanently flooded out of their homes in the reservoir zone, and a further half million who live in the zone planned to provide emergency water storage will be flooded out in the case of exceptionally high flows. Even if the full emergency storage capacity were utilized, however, the effect on a major flood would be only marginal, the dam being able to store less than a tenth of the water expected in a 1-in-200-year flood.[41]

Too Much to Drink: Dams and Public Water Supply

When drinking water think of the spring.

Chinese Proverb

Only a tiny fraction of the water impounded by large dams is supplied for use by households or businesses. Of the 3,602 dams (all over 30 metres high) listed by name and function in ICOLD's 1984 register for the four most dammed countries – China, the USA, Japan and India – only around a fifth list public water supply as a project purpose (see Table 5.4). If a very large dam has a water supply component it is generally a minor purpose of the project: if large dams were only to provide municipal water they would be far smaller than the giants built to provide electricity and irrigation.

Of global water withdrawals from all sources in 1990, only around 7 per cent went to households and other municipal users. About 24 per cent of withdrawals went to industries. Of the rest, 65 per cent went to farmers, and 4 per cent evaporated from reservoirs.[42] Although no global data are available which break down the different sources of municipal water, it is likely that most of the world's municipal water supplies come from groundwater: even in the heavily dammed US more than half of the population are supplied from groundwater; in Europe, 65 per cent of people are dependent on groundwater.[43] Of the proportion of municipal supplies from surface water much comes from unregulated lakes and rivers (water can be taken from pipes placed directly in the river, or from wells dug in the river bed), and reservoirs and ponds behind small dams and weirs.

Out of the 1 billion people estimated by the World Health Organization to have no access to a decent source of water, 855 million live in rural areas. The hugely expensive, sophisticated and energy-intensive networks of pipes, aqueducts, pumps and treatment facilities that would be needed to provide drinking water to dispersed rural populations from large reservoirs means that big dams are usually not even an option worth considering for rural water supply in developing countries. The only way to provide water at low cost to these people is with small, community-managed schemes relying on local wells, springs, streams and rivers, very small reservoirs and other cheap, small-scale and easily maintained technologies.[44]

Ironically, because of the dewatering of rivers below dams and the lowering of groundtables due to the desiccation of floodplains, large dams can often reduce water availability (or expropriate the water used by people living along rivers for use by those connected to municipal supply systems). Perhaps the worst example is India's Farakka Barrage – which diverts water from the Ganges to the port of Calcutta – which has reduced drinking water availability for 40 million people downstream in Bangladesh.[45]

The deterioration of water quality and algal blooms in reservoirs can seriously contaminate water supplies. The stew of algae and decomposing vegetation resulting from the closure of Itaparica Dam on Brazil's São Francisco River led to the deaths by poisoning and gastro-enteritis of 130 people, mostly children, who drank water from the new reservoir.[46]

Table 5.4 Purposes of dams higher than 30 metres (% of dams)

	China*	India	Japan	USA
Irrigation	84	45	43	29
Electricity	44	22	45	31
Flood control	29	4	43	36
Water supply	1	9	25	40
Recreation	0	0	0	44
Navigation	1	0	0	4
No. of dams	(1,336)	(324)	(800)	(1,142)

China, India, Japan and the USA are the countries with the highest no. of large dams (excluding CIS, for which ICOLD has not published complete information). Sum of percentages >100 because of multiple counting of multipurpose dams.

* ICOLD only lists information on approximately half the dams more than 30 metres high in China.

Source: Purposes of large dams as listed in *World Register of Dams*, full edition, ICOLD, Paris 1984.

The increased clarity of the Nile due to the virtual elimination of its silt by the High Aswan Dam has caused a proliferation of algae and phytoplankton in the river. This has fouled the water supply of Cairo and other riverine cities and necessitated an increased use of chlorination, which has in turn led to an increased presence in drinking water of the carcinogenic chemicals formed when chlorine reacts with organic matter.[47]

The provision of drinking water to the drought-stricken state of Gujarat has been one of the main moral and political justifications for the Sardar Sarovar Project. Project documents claimed in 1983 that fully 28 million people would get water from the project; then in 1989 without any further explanation the authorities claimed that 32.5 million would get water; in 1992, the number to be supplied had swollen to 40 million; and then the following year the number fell back to 25 million. Official statistics for the number of villages to benefit leapt from 4,719 in the early 1980s, to 8,215 in 1991 (it was revealed in 1992 that 236 of these villages are uninhabited – but the authorities continue to claim they will get water anyway).

While these erratic claims can be ridiculed, seriously challenging their veracity is difficult as even in 1996, after four decades of planning what the authorities call the 'most studied project in India', no detailed water supply plans existed. The nearest the authorities have come to revealing the cost of laying pipes, pumping and treating water, and setting up an administrative infrastructure for an area of more than 100,000 square kilometres is that it 'would run to several' tens of billions of rupees (10 billion rupees equals around $330 million). Although drinking water is claimed as a major benefit of Sardar Sarovar, the cost of supplying it – possibly well over $1 billion – has been excluded from the project's cost–benefit analysis.[48]

SSP opponents claim that the poorest and most drought-prone areas of Gujarat will never see Narmada water, as whatever drinking water the project ever does deliver will be sucked up by the state's politically powerful and relatively wealthy major cities – where the problem is not so much an insufficient supply as a decrepit infrastructure. These fears were partly vindicated in 1995 when a World Bank report suggested that the project's financial crisis would justify diverting supplies from poor, dispersed rural areas to urban industrial and domestic users.[49]

Blocking the Passage: Dams and River Transport

> ...I think that the river
> Is a strong brown god – sullen untamed and intractable...
> Useful, untrustworthy, as a conveyor of commerce.
>
> T.S. Eliot, *Four Quartets*, 1941

Proposals for multipurpose dam projects frequently add 'navigation' on to their list of benefits. Yet, on a worldwide level, dams may well be more of a cost than a benefit to those who transport people and goods along the world's rivers. Dams can help river traffic by flooding dangerous rapids, regulating the depth of the river, and slowing down currents. However, they also block the river, requiring expensive locks which take a long time to pass through and are prone to breaking down. Many dams have been built without locks, blocking all river traffic; when locks are built these may be able to be used only by large barges and other commercial vessels – small boats and canoes used by local fishermen or other river users may have their river access either totally blocked, or only available on payment of a fee. Traditional river users can also be disadvantaged when their boats are not suitable for negotiating the wide, wind-swept waters of a reservoir, made more treacherous because of drowned tree trunks and other obstacles.

The backwater sedimentation of reservoirs can also hinder navigation in their upper reaches and require expensive dredging. Downstream, the dewatering of rivers has an obvious effect upon those who depend on boats for their livelihood: the most striking illustrations of this are the photographs of the rusting hulks of abandoned fishing boats and freighters on the desert sands which were once the bed of the Aral Sea. Farakka Barrage dries up thousands of miles of intensively used waterways in south-west Bangladesh each dry season. In China, according to the World Bank, the length of navigable waterways fell from 170,000 kilometres in 1960, to 109,000 kilometres in 1984, 'in part due to building of dams'.[50]

On some rivers, especially in North America and Europe, numerous dams have been built almost solely to improve navigation conditions. The Army Corps of Engineers built 29 'lock and dam' projects on the Upper Mississippi between 1914 and 1950, turning 800 kilometres of river into a series of slackwater navigation pools. The transformation of the Upper Mississippi into a barge superhighway cost the federal government around $12 billion in 1990 dollars. This massive subsidy has gone mainly to benefit the 20 corporations which own four-fifths of all barges in the US, and a few oil, coal and grain multinationals whose products make up the bulk of goods transported on the river. The locks and dams are now starting to deteriorate and will need expensive refurbishment at the taxpayer's expense: Locks and Dam 26 in Illinois was replaced during the early 1980s at a cost of nearly $1 billion.[51]

Many of the proposals for the major 'multipurpose' dams built in Africa have claimed navigation as a benefit, without any serious analysis as to whether any ships would ever need to make use of them. Kainji Dam, referred to in the 1960s as 'the pillar of Nigeria's economic and social development' by the country's head of state, was fitted with a huge lock served by a 6-kilometre-long access canal. The 49 metre lift lock, one of the highest in the world, can hold four 5,000 tonne barges at a time. As of 1994, almost three decades after the lock was installed, no barge had ever used it.[52] One of the claimed purposes of Manantali Dam was to regulate the Senegal River to allow barges to carry bauxite and iron ore the 900 kilometres from Kayes in Mali to the sea. However, the dredging and construction work needed to make the river navigable, even with Manantali Dam in place, would cost more than $400 million and is unlikely ever to be done.[53]

The improvement of navigation on the Yangtze, China's 'Golden Waterway', is touted as one of the main aims of Three Gorges Dam. By flooding rapids, the dam, it is claimed, will enable 10,000 tonne ships to reach the inland port of Chongqing, compared to the 3,000 tonne vessels which can make the trip now. Project opponents, however, claim that backwater sedimentation and periods of reservoir drawdown will continue to put Chongqing off-limits for the larger ships, and that navigation can be better improved by dredging. Getting 10,000 tonne vessels past the dam itself will require the installation of five of the world's largest capacity shiplocks which would have to lift ships through 113 metres, more than twice the height of any existing series of locks. Chinese experts are concerned that there will be long delays for ships waiting to pass through the locks, delays which would be much worse in the likely event that this unprecedented feat of engineering were to experience technical problems. Ships are also going to have to face inevitable and long delays passing the construction site during the twenty years or more it will take to finish the dam. Because of these concerns, there is apparently significant opposition to the project from the inland shipping industry – which is supposed to be one of the dam's main beneficiaries.[54]

The One that Got Away: Reservoir Fisheries

> Our mother [Mun River] provided us food and life. With the dam construction, husbands and wives fight, and the fish are leaving the river. We are not against a dam. We are against the disintegration of our communities.
>
> Thai village elder, at a meeting between Mun River villagers and Executive Directors of the World Bank, Bangkok, 11 October, 1991

The frequently claimed benefit of reservoir fisheries is in most project proposals nothing more than unsubstantiated public relations. Dam builders usually have next to no reliable data on existing river and estuarine fisheries or what the impact of a new dam will be upon them, and also little idea of what fish yield a new reservoir will be able to support.

Long-term fish yields from reservoirs are very difficult to predict. Data for some African and Asian reservoirs collected by fisheries biologist Robin Wellcome show that the catch per unit area of water can vary by a factor of almost 200 between different reservoirs.[55] Some reservoirs may increase the total yield of fish from a river; many, especially those which wipe out regular seasonal floods downstream and degrade estuarine ecosystems, will reduce the yield. In almost all cases, the diversity of fish species will drop. Furthermore, local people invariably have less access to fish than before as reservoir fishing requires different skills and equipment, and more capital, than river fishing. In many parts of the tropics, riverine fisheries provide one of the main sources of animal protein for rural people, and anything which affects people's access to fish can therefore have a profound affect on their lives.

US fisheries expert Peter Bayley calculates that, on average, the per unit area yield of fish from a tropical floodplain river (calculated from the maximum flooded area) is 2.5 to 4 times higher than from a reservoir. Bayley states, however, that this comparison probably understates the productivity of a floodplain river as fish yields from rivers and their associated wetlands are regularly underestimated because of the difficulty of counting catches from the widely dispersed and usually unregulated fishing activities along rivers.[56]

When vegetation and soils are flooded by a reservoir, they release huge amounts of nutrients which nourish a fish population that is suddenly able to expand into a greatly increased habitat. Fishers can therefore reap a bonanza in new reservoirs. After a number of years, however, when the flush of nutrients from rotting biomass has declined and the species which depend on the specific characteristics of river habitats start to die out, fish catches decline rapidly. In the worst cases, reservoir waters become depleted of oxygen and clogged with aquatic plants which both decrease fish productivity in the water they smother, and make it almost impossible to catch whatever fish do exist. Kainji Dam was predicted to sustain catches of around 10,000 tonnes. The initial burst of productivity yielded a maximum of 28,600 tonnes in 1970, two years after reservoir filling, but by the mid-1970s catches dropped to 4,500 tonnes and are believed to have stabilized at around this level. This catch is only slightly higher than that estimated for the stretch of river flooded by the reservoir.[57]

Even when a reservoir does create a lucrative fishery there is no guarantee that local fishers and the other people who have their livelihoods affected by the dam will be able to reap the benefits. Often it is only outside entrepreneurs and those with experience of open water fishing – which generally requires bigger boats and more expensive gear than river fishing – who have the capital and know-how to exploit a newly created reservoir fishery and get the fish to market. In this case local people lose their previously free access to the fish in the river, and then have to pay to eat fish – from a much narrower range of species – from the reservoir. Fishers living many kilometres downstream from a dam who suffer a reduction in catches may be unable to take advantage of a reservoir fishery just because it is so far away. In many Indian states local people are deliberately prevented from taking full advantage of reservoir fisheries because commercial fishing rights in reservoirs are auctioned off to contractors, to whom the local people have to sell their catches, usually at very low prices.[58]

Catches in Volta Reservoir – the world's largest reservoir by area – greatly exceeded any pre-impoundment predictions. At the end of the 1960s when the reservoir first filled, it yielded more than 60,000 tonnes of fish, and in some of the following years income from fish sales exceeded income from sales of electricity generated by Akosombo Dam. In 1979, 20,000 fishermen caught over 40,000 tonnes of fish. The 80,000 farmers who were displaced by the dam, and who have had to endure the dam's problem-plagued resettlement scheme, have, however, gained little from the fishery. Almost all the fishing is done by formerly migrant fishers who have now settled on the shores of the reservoir.[59]

A modern fishery with its associated processing and marketing infrastructure was one of the main sources of employment which Uruguay's military rulers promised would come to the country's economically depressed border region in the wake of the Salto Grande Dam. Although the dam was completed in 1980, it was not until 1988 that a processing and freezing plant was built and modern equipment provided to local fishermen with the help of German aid funds. Only six months after the processing plant opened, however, the reservoir catches began an abrupt decline, putting many of the fishermen out of work. After only a year of operation, the plant had to be shut down. The collapse of the fishery has been blamed on a number of causes, including agrochemical pollution, the poor performance of the fish ladder and the erratic fluctuations in the reservoir level. Fishers downstream have also suffered a collapse in catches.[60]

The World Bank believes that 'aquaculture and other fishery-related employment' is one of the best ways to help people displaced by dams restore their incomes.[61] Intensive fish-rearing in cages in two reservoirs on the Citarum River in West Java, Indonesia, has been promoted by the Bank as a notable success story. In 1992, according to a Bank report, around a third of the families displaced by the reservoirs were employed in the production of 10,000 tonnes of common carp. This success, however, will be difficult to replicate in most other areas. West Java, like parts of China but unlike most regions of the world, has a long tradition of freshwater cage aquaculture and a huge market for carp. The two reservoirs, Cirata and Saguling, both have water of a quality suitable for fish rearing, and the operation of the reservoirs (apart from one large drawdown which killed many of the caged fish) is favourable to the fish farmers. Aquaculture also requires capital to buy cages, stock and feed and pay wages. Most of the fish farmers on the Citarum do it as a second job, and have other more important sources of income such as trading, farming and teaching.[62]

All the Fun of the Reservoir: Dams and Recreation

> ...the bland, soft, clear, stagnant reservoir of Lake Powell. Better known as Lake Foul, or Government Sump, or the Gangrene Lagoon, or Glen Canyon National Recreation Slum...
>
> Edward Abbey, *Down the River*, 1982

Recreation is the last of the main 'add-on' benefits claimed for dams. Especially in the US, large reservoirs are regularly touted as havens for sport-fishers, boaters and other holidaymakers. Hoover Dam, a short drive from the neon fantasyland of Las Vegas – a desert oasis of overconsumption which owes its existence to the water and power from the dam – is in fact one of the most popular tourist attractions in the US. To millions of tourists, Mead and Powell Reservoirs, respectively behind Hoover and Glen Canyon Dams, are watersports playgrounds created out of arid wasteland.

The claimed recreational benefits of many dams, however, are tainted by the vested interest of their promoters. Author Fred Powledge wrote in 1982 that 'recreation has found increased favor among the [US dam] builders as a means to jack up the benefit sides of their cost–benefit ratios':

> In addition to ignoring the recreational value of a swiftly moving stream ... the builders have used questionable methodology in calculating the drawing power of their new projects. An estimated number of recreational visits per day, or year, is commonly used in figuring the recreational 'benefit' of a reservoir. But the arithmetic generally overlooks the facts that reservoirs tend to get built in places (like the Tennessee Valley) where there are many *other* reservoirs, that the *other* reservoirs were justified in part on the number of projected recreational visits, and that a recreational visit to New Reservoir A means one less recreational visit to Old Reservoir B or C.[63]

Dam proposals have also ignored the fact that reservoir water levels – especially those behind hydrodams – can fluctuate widely, which can leave jetties and boat ramps high and dry, and expose wide expanses of mud and dead vegetation between the reservoir and the holidaymaker. Creating recreation with a reservoir can also harm recreation downstream, especially where the reservoir is used to divert water. There are many cases where the erosive power of a dammed river has washed away popular beaches below the dam, and where sudden reservoir releases have caught downstream rafters and other river users unawares.

The question of whether or not a dam which floods and regulates a river is a recreational cost or benefit is often one of philosophical values rather than economic ones. Many people love wild rivers for their scenery, their wildlife, for the spiritual feelings they provoke, or for the excitement of rafting (Glen Canyon is fiercely resented by environmentalists and rafters for flooding possibly the most beautiful river canyon in the US). Others believe that a reservoir and a big dam is an improvement on a wild river. Hydraulic engineers Venkat K. Rao and Edward M. Gosschalk write in *The International Journal of Hydropower & Dams* that:

> The avoidance of change and the doctrinaire preservation of nature exactly as it happens to be at the time in question, are quite contrary to the professional training and purposes of engineers, who continually seek to improve on what has already been achieved. The achievement of aesthetic beauty, functional as a structure may also be, the enhancement of scenic beauty, and the improvement of the quality of water available for man have been, and are, fundamental objectives.[64]

Engineers certainly have a right to believe that dams and reservoirs enhance scenic beauty, but they do not have an automatic right to impose their doctrinaire aesthetics on the rest of society when this permanently deprives others of what they consider beautiful and valuable. The issue of whether or not a dam will 'improve' the beauty of a river is one for an informed and open public debate, and not one to be left to those who benefit from building dams.

In recent years, dam authorities in developing countries have started to add the promotion of 'ecotourism' to their glossy brochures. For many of these dams, the issue is much more than one of conflicting aesthetics and values: instead it is one of the right to survival of local communities and cultures, against the right of the wealthy to vacation wherever they please. The indigenous Embera-Chami people in Colombia were badly affected by Colima I Dam, first by displacement and the loss of land, and then by an influx of tourists and wealthy urbanites who took over large tracts of reservoir-side lands for holiday homes and other tourist infrastructure.[65]

Before final official approval was given for work to start on Bakun Dam, the project developer, Malaysian construction giant Ekran Berhad, had begun to build a hotel near the dam site. At an earth-breaking ceremony in September 1994, Malaysian Prime Minister Dr Mahathir Mohamad announced that 'from this resort the government's effort to promote ecotourism in Sarawak will be successful.'[66] The putative eco-tourists would jet-ski on a reservoir the size of Singapore which would have flooded tens of thousands of hectares of rainforest as well as the homes, lands and ancestral graves of nearly 10,000 indigenous people.

The great majority of dams do of course provide some benefits – especially to those who plan and build them, and who have the money and political influence to take full advantage of the services they do offer. But the full potential benefits are in many cases mutually incompatible, and are regularly exaggerated to help get the project approved. The actual realized benefits of large dam projects appear, in the majority of documented cases, to be much lower than those claimed before the project was built. Irrigation, the one major function of large dams which has not been dealt with above, is discussed in the next chapter. As will be seen, the performance of large-dam-related irrigation schemes adds further weight to the argument that dams have been justified under false pretences.

Notes

1. See, e.g., P.B. Williams, 'Sedimentation Analysis', in M. Barber and G. Ryder, *Damming the Three Gorges: What Dam Builders Don't Want You to Know*, Earthscan, London 1993, p. 142; C.F. Nordin, Jr., 'J.C. Stevens and the Silt

Problem', *International Journal of Sediment Research*, Vol. 6, No. 3, December 1991.

2. World Bank, *The World Bank and Irrigation*, OED 1995, p. 94.

3. Less than 3% of all dams in the US have hydropower as their primary purpose (D.E. Bowes, 'Dam and Hydropower Activities in the US', *Water Power & Dam Construction*, August 1993). Around 40% of the world's installed hydropower capacity is at major dams (J. Besant-Jones, *The Future Role of Hydropower in Developing Countries*, World Bank, April 1989, p. 16).

4. *Water Power & Dam Construction Handbook 1993*, WPDC, Sutton, UK, 1993, pp. 55–6; *International Water Power & Dam Construction Handbook 1994*, IWPDC, Sutton, UK, 1994, p. A-57; P.H. Gleick, 'Water and Energy', in P.H. Gleick (ed.), *Water in Crisis: A Guide to the World's Fresh Water Resources*, Oxford University Press, Oxford 1993, p. 73. Countries dependent on hydro for over 90% of their power not listed in the text are Burundi, Cameroon, Malawi, Namibia, Rwanda, Tanzania, Uganda, Zaire, Costa Rica and Fiji.

5. See, e.g., J.R. Moreira and A.D. Poole, 'Hydropower and its Constraints', in T.B. Johansson et al. (eds.), *Renewable Energy: Sources for Fuels and Electricity*, Island Press, Washington, DC, 1993, pp. 76–8.

6. J. Besant-Jones, 'A View of Multilateral Financing from a Funding Agency', in *Financing Hydro Power Projects '94*, proceedings of conference sponsored by *International Water Power & Dam Construction*, Frankfurt, 22–23 September 1994.

7. Ibid.

8. World Bank, 'Project Completion Report: Argentina Yacyretá Hydroelectric Project and Electric Power Sector Project', 14 March 1995, p. 4; P. Reynolds, 'Powering up Privately', *International Water Power & Dam Construction*, November 1994.

9. World Bank, 'Colombia: The Power Sector and the World Bank, 1970–1987. Vol. I: Overview', OED, 28 June 1990, p. 16; World Bank, 'Colombia: The Power Sector and the World Bank, 1970–1987. Vol. II: Technical Report', OED, 28 June 1990, p. 71.

10. World Bank, 'Colombia: Vol. I', p. 5.

11. 'Ambitious Senegal River Project to Start Soon', *New York Times*, 11 October 1981; T. Scudder, 'River Basin Projects in Africa', *Environment*, Vol. 31, No. 2, March 1989; T. Gopsill, 'Will Senegal Farmers Reap Barrage Benefits?', *World Water*, April 1988.

12. C.K. Annan, 'Was Ghana's Akosombo Dam the Best Option?', *World Water*, September 1989; 'Ghana to Power Up With IDA Funding', *World Bank News*, 23 February 1995; Y. Graham, 'Volta Power Grows Dim', *African Agenda*, Vol. 1, No. 1, 1995; M.J. Barnes and S. Beggs, 'Developing Hydro in Africa: Turning the Potential to Reality', *Hydro Review Worldwide*, Fall 1994.

13. R. Yearly, 'The Lights Go Out in Guatemala', *Report on Guatemala*, Oakland, CA, 1992; T. Barry, *Inside Guatemala*, IHERC, Albuquerque 1992, p. 115; J.D. Gollin, 'Trees Down, Lights Out in Honduras', *Christian Science Monitor*, 15 November 1994; 'Aún no se llena El Cajón', *Tiempo*, Tegucigalpa, 30 September 1994.

14. Besant-Jones, *The Future Role of Hydropower*, p. 14; R. Hunt and J.M. Hunt, 'How Does Hydropower Compare?', *Independent Energy*, November 1993.

15. R. Rycroft and J. Szyliowicz, 'The Technological Dimension of Decision Making: The Case of the Aswan High Dam', *World Politics: A Quarterly Journal of International Relations*, Vol. 33, No. 1, October 1980; M.T. El Safty and H.A. Younes, 'Hydro Power Generation in Egypt', in ENCOLD (ed.), *High Aswan*

Dam Vital Achievement Fully Controlled, Cairo 1993, p. 126; 'Itaipú Binacional: The Biggest Hydroelectricity Undertaking of the XXth Century' (advertisement), *New York Times*, 30 October 1992; *International Water Power & Dam Construction*, March 1995, p. 2; F.S. Tsikata (ed.), *Essays from the Ghana–Valco Renegotiations, 1982–85*, Ghana Publishing Corporation, Accra 1986.

16. 'Bakun Hydroelectric Feasibility Study', SESCO/GTZ/SAMA Consortium, 1983; 'Bakun Hydroelectric Project: Green Energy for the Future', Prime Minister's Department, Kuala Lumpur, February 1986.

17. Government of Lao PDR, 'Nam Theun 2 Hydroelectric Project: Environmental Assessment and Management Plan. Report E2. Main Report', Vientiane, April 1995.

18. S. Dharmadhikary, 'Hydropower at Sardar Sarovar: Is it Necessary, Justified and Affordable?', in W.F. Fisher (ed.), *Towards Sustainable Development? Struggling Over India's Narmada River*, M.E. Sharpe, Armonk, NY, 1995, p. 141. The pumps of California's State Water Project are the largest single consumer of electricity in the state. If the project is ever fully developed, it will include 148 pumping plants, 40 hydropower plants, 22 reservoirs and dams, and 1,000 km of aqueducts. The hydropower plants would produce over 7,000 GWh/yr, but the pumping plants would consume more than 12,400 GWh/yr (Gleick, *Water and Energy*, p. 68).

19. J.A. Veltrop, 'Water, Dams and Hydropower in the Coming Decades', *Water Power & Dam Construction*, June 1991.

20. WCED, *Our Common Future*, Oxford University Press, Oxford 1987. See also T. Russo, 'Making Hydropower Sustainable', *The International Journal of Hydropower & Dams*, November 1994.

21. See, e.g., 'Report of the 17th ICOLD Congress. Q64: Environmental Issues in Dam Projects', *Water Power & Dam Construction*, September 1991; E.T. Haws, 'How will Environmental Obligations Affect Financing?', in *Financing Hydro Power Projects '94*.

22. 'A Ten-Year Plan for Southeast Asia', *Asahi Shimbun*, 7 September 1993 (translated by Japan Tropical Forest Action Network). See also, e.g., E. Oud, 'Global Warming: A Changing Climate for Hydro', *Water Power & Dam Construction*, May 1993; T. Jackson, 'Joint Implementation and the Climate Convention', *Renewable Energy for Development*, Stockholm, Vol. 7, No. 3, November 1994.

23. J.T. Houghton et al. (eds.), *Climate Change: The IPCC Scientific Assessment*, Cambridge University Press, Cambridge 1990, pp. 20, 300; C.A. Kelly and J.W.M. Rudd, 'Fluxes of CH_4 and CO_2 to the Atmosphere from Hydroelectric Reservoirs', *CO_2/Climate Report*, Winter 1993; A.C. Kelly et al., 'Turning Attention to Reservoir Surfaces, a Neglected Area in Greenhouse Studies', *EOS*, Vol. 75, No. 29, 1994.

24. P.M. Fearnside, 'Hydroelectric Dams in the Brazilian Amazon as Sources of "Greenhouse" Gases', *Environmental Conservation*, Vol. 22, No. 1, 1995.

25. J.W.M. Rudd et al., 'Are Hydroelectric Reservoirs Significant Sources of Greenhouse Gases?', *Ambio*, Vol. 22, No. 4, June 1993.

26. Houghton et al. (eds.), *Climate Change*, p. xxi.

27. For a table ranking dams according to hydropower generated per hectare inundated, see R. Goodland, *Ethical Priorities in Environmentally Sustainable Energy Systems: The Case of Tropical Hydropower*, World Bank Environment Department, May 1994.

28. Dams could be impairing the role that oceans play in absorbing atmospheric

CO_2. Of the 26bn tonnes of CO_2 emitted each year during the 1980s due to fossil-fuel burning and land use changes, around 7bn were taken out of the atmosphere by being dissolved in the top layers of the oceans (R.T. Watson et al., 'Greenhouse Gases and Aerosols', in Houghton et al. (eds.) *Climate Change*, p. 13). The rate at which this happens may be largely dependent on the productivity of plankton, which consume carbon during photosynthesis. The productivity of plankton is in turn believed to be dependent on the nutrients in seawater – a major source of which are sediments discharged by rivers. Sediments may also play a role in speeding up the rate at which carbon sinks to the ocean depths, enabling more atmospheric CO_2 to be sequestered at the sea surface. Tiny carbon-rich particles of plankton excreta and skeletons stick to the sediments, which act as ballasts, hastening the particles' descent to the ocean floor. Some 80% of the carbon which is buried in the ocean depths each year originates around the edges of the seas in areas heavily influenced by river discharge. Dams, by trapping sediments and reducing freshwater discharge, may thus affect the oceanic uptake of atmospheric CO_2 (see, e.g., V. Ramaswamy and R. Nair, 'Measuring the Monsoon', *New Scientist*, 20 June 1992; V. Ittekkot and B. Haake, 'The Terrestrial Link in the Removal of Organic Carbon in the Sea', in V. Ittekkot et al. (eds.), *Facets of Modern Biogeochemistry*, Springer Verlag, New York 1990, p. 323). E. Oud of Lahmeyer International calculated that the construction of a 1,600 MW concrete dam in South Africa would lead to 650,000 tonnes of CO_2 emissions. According to Oud this would equal less than 8% of the CO_2 emitted in just one year by a coal-fired plant producing a comparable amount of energy (Oud, 'Global Warming'). Oud's estimate does not take into account emissions of around 250,000 tonnes of CO_2 during the manufacture of the cement used in the dam. The process of cement manufacture releases around 0.5 tonnes of CO_2 for each tonne of cement produced. Worldwide cement manufacture is responsible for around 3% of anthropogenic CO_2 (World Resources Institute, *World Resources 1994–95*, Oxford University Press, Oxford 1994, Table 23.1). For greenhouse gas emissions and land use changes see, e.g., A. Ehrlich, 'Agricultural Contributions to Global Warming', in J. Leggett (ed.), *Global Warming: The Greenpeace Report*, Oxford University Press, Oxford 1990.

29. P. Williams, 'Adapting Water Resources Management to Global Climate Change', Villach Conference on Developing Policies for Managing the Effects of Climate Change, special issue of *Climate Change*, 1989; C. Knox, 'Large Increase in Flood Magnitude in Response to Modest Changes in Climate', and V. Baker, 'Learning from the Past', both in *Nature*, Vol. 361, 4 February 1993.

30. J. Leggett, 'Insurance Industry at UN Climate Conference', Greenpeace International, 27 March 1995; Intergovernmental Panel on Climate Change, *Climate Change: The IPCC Response Strategies*, Island Press, Washington, DC, 1991, p. 181.

31. B.D. Ayres, 'Flood Revives Debate on $25 Billion in Controls', *International Herald Tribune*, 13 July 1993; J. Denning, 'When the Levee Breaks', *Civil Engineering*, January 1994, p. 3; R.S. Devine, 'The Trouble With Dams', *Atlantic Monthly*, August 1995, p. 67; Centre for Science and Environment, *The State of India's Environment – 1982: A Citizen's Report*, CSE, New Delhi 1982, p. 62.

32. See Interagency Floodplain Management Review Committee, *A Blueprint for Change. Sharing the Challenge: Floodplain Management into the 21st Century*, Report of the IFMRC to the Administration Floodplain Management Task Force, Washington, DC, June 1994; Denning, 'When the Levee Breaks'; J. Kusler and L.

Larson, 'Beyond the Ark: A New Approach to US Floodplain Management', *River Voices*, Vol. 4, No. 4, Winter 1994; P.B. Williams, 'Flood Control vs. Flood Management', *Civil Engineering*, May 1994.

33. See, e.g., J.E. Costa, 'Floods from Dam Failures', in V.R. Baker et al. (eds.), *Flood Geomorphology*, Wiley, New York 1988, p. 439.

34. A.A. Bonetto et al., 'The Increased Damming of the Paraná Basin and its Effects on the Lower Reaches', *Regulated Rivers: Research & Management*, Vol. 4, 1989, p. 341.

35. 'Salto Grande no tiene quien le escriba', *Tierra Amiga*, Montevideo, November 1993, p. 35.

36. S.A. Abbasi, *Environmental Impact of Water Resources Projects*, Discovery Publishing House, New Delhi 1991, pp. 108–9; B. Dogra, 'The Indian Experience with Large Dams', in E. Goldsmith and N. Hildyard (eds.), *The Social and Environmental Impacts of Large Dams. Vol. 2: Case Studies*, Wadebridge Ecological Centre, Cornwall 1986 (hereafter *SEELD 2*); B. Dogra, 'Dams and Floods', *Indian Express*, 21 October 1988; '"Panic" Release Might Have Worsened Indian Flood', *Water Power & Dam Construction*, November 1980.

37. B. Dogra, *The Debate on Large Dams*, New Delhi 1992, p. 38; Centre for Science and Environment, *The State of India's Environment*, p. 63.

38. 'Mismanagement Endangers California Capital', *International Dams Newsletter*, Vol. 1, No. 3, June 1986; P. Williams, 'Flood Control vs. Flood Management: The Battle over Auburn Dam', *World Rivers Review*, Vol. 7, No. 1, January/February 1992.

39. F. Powledge, *Water: The Nature, Uses, and Future of Our Most Precious and Abused Resource*, Farrar, Straus & Giroux, New York 1982, p. 292; W. Chandler, *The Myth of TVA: Conservation and Development in the Tennessee Valley 1933–1983*, Ballinger, Cambridge, MA, 1984. A 1994 TVA brochure says the Columbia Dam 'is unfinished but has not been cancelled'.

40. The mid-1995 Yangtze floods, for example, which killed 1,200 people and caused $4.4 billion in damage were mainly due to rainfall below the Three Gorges (L. O'Donnell, 'China to Pass Law to Stem Flood Havoc', *Reuter European Business Report*, 11 July 1995; M. Farley, 'In China's Floods, Blame Mankind', *San Francisco Chronicle*, 19 July 1995).

41. See P.B. Williams, 'Flood Control Analysis', in M. Barber and G. Ryder, *Damming the Three Gorges: What Dam Builders Don't Want You to Know*, second edition, Earthscan, London 1993; Z. Fang, 'The Flood Protection Function of the Three Gorges Project – Disadvantages Outweigh Advantages', in L. Shiu-Hung and J. Whitney (eds.), *Megaproject: A Case Study of China's Three Gorges Project*, M.E. Sharpe, Armonk, NY, 1993; K. Chen, 'The Limited Benefit of Flood Control. An Interview with Lu Qinkan', in Dai Qing (edited by P. Adams and J. Thibodeau), *Yangtze! Yangtze!*, Probe International, Toronto and Earthscan, London 1994.

42. Evaporation from reservoirs equals 7% of water consumed globally but 4% of water withdrawn – much water withdrawn for other uses, especially for municipal and industrial use, is returned to water bodies (see I.A. Shiklomanov, 'World Fresh Water Resources', in Gleick (ed.), *Water in Crisis*, pp. 19, 20).

43. 'Estimated Use of Water in the United States in 1990. Domestic Water Use', US Geological Survey, World Wide Web site 1995; C. Southey, 'European Cities "Wasting" Water', *Financial Times*, 13 September 1995; Gleick (ed.), *Water in Crisis*, p. 382, Table H.5.

44. See, e.g., J.M. Kalbermatten et al., *Appropriate Technology for Water Supply and Sanitation*, World Bank 1980; D.A. Okun and W.R. Ernst, *Community Piped Water Supply Systems in Developing Countries*, World Bank Technical Paper 60, 1987; J. Briscoe and D. de Ferranti, *Water for Rural Communities*, World Bank 1980.

45. M.G. Rahman, 'Reducing the Flow of the Ganges: The Consequences for Agriculture in Bangladesh', in *SEELD 2*.

46. 'Lethal Dam for the São Francisco River', *World Rivers Review*, July/August 1988.

47. G. White, 'The Environmental Effects of the High Dam at Aswan', *Environment*, Vol. 30, No. 7, 1988, p. 34.

48. R.N. Ram, *Muddy Waters: A Critical Assessment of the Benefits of the Sardar Sarovar Project*, second edition, Kalpavriksh, New Delhi, October 1993.

49. World Bank, 'Project Completion Report, India: Narmada River Development – Gujarat Sardar Sarovar Dam and Power Project', 29 March 1995, p. 52.

50. Khurshida Begum, *Tension over the Farakka Barrage: A Techno-Political Tangle in South Asia*, University Press, Dakar 1987, pp. 145–7; H.D. Frederiksen et al., *Water Resources Management in Asia. Volume I: Main Report*, World Bank Technical Paper 212, Washington, DC, 1993, p. 105.

51. Interagency Floodplain Management Review Committee, *A Blueprint for Change*, p. 39; J.C. Marlin, *Locks and Dam 26*, Coalition on American Rivers, Champaign, IL, 1977. According to Marlin, 'It is a common misconception that barges use less fuel than railroads … studies comparing the movement of similar commodities over similar routes where barges and trains actually compete show that railroads use less fuel' (ibid., p. 4).

52. Scudder, 'River Basin Projects', p. 8; J.S.O. Ayeni et al., 'The Kainji Lake Experience in Africa', in C.C. Cook (ed.), *Involuntary Resettlement in Africa: Selected Papers from Conference on Environment and Settlement Issues in Africa*, World Bank Technical Paper 227, p. 119.

53. Gopsill, 'Will Senegal Farmers Reap Barrage Benefits?', p. 21; F. Mounier, 'The Senegal River Scheme: Development for Whom?', in *SEELD 2*.

54. See essays in Dai Qing, *Yangtze! Yangtse!*, especially X. Fang and W. Li, 'Once the Golden Waterway is Severed, Can Another Yangtze River Be Dug? A Conversation with Peng De'; Y. Sun et al., 'Views and Suggestions on the Assessment Report of the Three Gorges Project'; and Dai Qing, 'An Interview with Huang Shunxing'. Also L. Sullivan, Adelphi University, personal communication.

55. R.L. Wellcome, *Fisheries Ecology of Floodplain Rivers*, Longman, London 1979, p. 251.

56. P.B. Bayley, 'The Flood Pulse Advantage and the Restoration of River-Floodplain Systems', *Regulated Rivers: Research & Management*, Vol. 6, 1991; P.B. Bayley, 'Understanding Large River-Floodplain Ecosystems', *Bioscience*, March 1995, p. 156.

57. Ayeni et al., 'The Kainji Lake Experience', p. 118.

58. See, e.g., V. Vivekanandan, 'A Damn Fine Effort', *SAMUDRA*, Madras, April 1995.

59. R.H. Lowe-McConnell, 'Summary: Reservoirs in Relation to Man – Fisheries', in W.C. Ackermann et al. (eds.), *Man-Made Lakes: Their Problems and Environmental Effects*, American Geophysical Union, Washington, DC, 1973, p. 646; Scudder, 'River Basin Projects', p. 28; R. Graham, 'Ghana's Volta Resettlement Scheme', in *SEELD 2*, p. 138; M.A. Tamakloe, 'Long-Term Impacts of Resettlement: The Akosombo Dam Experience', in Cook (ed.), *Involuntary*

Resettlement in Africa, p. 105.

60. 'Salto Grande: del festejo a la realidad', *Tierra Amiga*, Montevideo, July 1993, p. 16; 'Salto Grande no tiene quien le escriba', *Tierra Amiga*, November, 1993, p. 35.

61. World Bank, *Resettlement and Development: The Bankwide Review of Projects Involving Involuntary Resettlement 1986–1993*, 8 April, p. 4/3.

62. Ibid., p. 4/5; B.A. Costa-Pierce and O. Soemarwoto (eds.), *Reservoir Fisheries and Aquaculture Development for Resettlement in Indonesia*, PLN/IOE/ICLARM, 1990. There are many environmental problems caused by large-scale aquaculture (see, e.g., R.R. Stickney, *Principles of Aquaculture*, John Wiley & Sons, New York 1994, pp. 31–8).

63. Powledge, *Water*, p. 293.

64. V.K. Rao and E.M. Gosschalk, 'The Case for Impounding Rivers: An Engineer's Viewpoint', *The International Journal of Hydropower & Dams*, November 1994, p. 122.

65. J.-P. Fau et al., 'Accommodating Environmental, Social Issues in Project Planning', *Hydro Review Worldwide*, Spring 1995.

66. O. Tickell, 'Sarawak Set Up for the Deluge', *BBC Wildlife*, June 1995.

6

Paradise Lost: Dams And Irrigation

> He floods the desert with the mountain stream,
> And lo! it leaps transformed to paradise.
>
> Nineteenth-century Mormon hymn

More large dams are built to supply water for irrigation than for any other single purpose, and agriculture uses far more freshwater than any other sector – around two-thirds of global withdrawals. In dry areas the proportion is much higher: irrigation uses more than 80 per cent of supplied water in California; and more than 90 per cent of water in India.[1] According to the most widely cited estimates, around one-third of the total global harvest comes from the one-sixth of the world's total cropland which is irrigated. Statistics on the extent of irrigation and the yields it produces, however, need to be treated with a healthy scepticism. Worldwide, national, regional and even individual project data are often contradictory and difficult to interpret. Perhaps the biggest problem with the data is that there is no clear definition of what exactly irrigation is, and many traditional types of irrigation are left out of the statistics.[2]

The area irrigated worldwide by modern methods and the more complex traditional techniques began to increase rapidly in the early nineteenth century. Between 1800 and 1900, the extent of irrigation increased fivefold to an estimated 40 million hectares, mainly in the Indus and Ganges basins, Egypt, the Western US and Australia. Over the next 50 years the area doubled again. After 1950, the rate of expansion accelerated with the spread of large dam technology across the developing world and the availability of cheap energy and new technologies for pumping ground water. In the 1960s, the development of new 'green revolution' varieties of rice and wheat, which required high and dependable applications of water, provided a further impetus for the spread of irrigation, especially in the most fertile parts of Asia.

Since the late 1970s, however, the spread of irrigation has slowed dramatically. According to projections made for the International Commission on Irrigation and Drainage in 1981, the world's irrigated area was supposed to reach 310 million hectares in 1985 and 420 million hectares by the year 2000. Yet by 1992 irrigation covered only 249 million hectares (equivalent to a quarter of the size of Europe) and it is likely to have fallen since then.[3]

The expansion of irrigation has stagnated largely because the most fertile lands, the most accessible sources of water and the best dam sites have already been developed, substantially raising the per hectare cost of new irrigation projects. Governments can no longer afford (or are no longer willing to pay) the massive subsidies they pumped into large-scale irrigation in the past, world agricultural prices have been falling in real terms since the early 1970s, and many existing schemes are ageing and in need of expensive repairs.

Furthermore, the green revolution and its associated technologies have proven themselves inherently unsustainable. After only decades of modern perennial irrigation, soils which in many cases had supported traditional farming for hundreds or even thousands of years have become so degraded that they are now unsuitable for agriculture. Huge areas of irrigated land are now waterlogged and clogged with salts. Global statistics suggest that more irrigated land may be abandoned each year due to salinity than is being brought into production in new schemes.[4] The amount of formerly irrigated land being paved over to make way for urban expansion, especially in China and Southeast Asia, may be even greater than that lost to salt.[5] Salt and cities combined mean that total global irrigated area is now probably contracting at a significant rate.

Irrigation types and sources

Irrigation is an ancient technology which allows crops to be grown in areas with limited or no rainfall, and ensures against drought in areas where rainfall is unreliable. Where the rainy season is short, irrigation can extend the period in which crops can be grown. There are many different forms of irrigation, with no clear defining line between rainfed and irrigated farming. While it is conventionally defined by agronomists along the lines of 'the controlled application of water to crops in a timely manner' (the definition on which most of the statistics and examples used in this chapter are based), irrigation can also be used in a much wider sense to include adaptations to natural flood and rainfall patterns. These methods include flood recession agriculture – where crops are planted on floodplains at the end of the wet season to exploit the moisture left behind by retreating floods – and 'rainwater harvesting' – where rainwater is collected behind earth bunds or in small basins.[6]

Modern irrigation methods are generally divided into two types – canal and lift. The categories overlap because lift irrigation, while mainly referring to irrigation with groundwater, can include water pumped from canals and reservoirs – whereas water lifted from wells can sometimes have seeped from canals and drains.[7] Dams built for irrigation store water from the rainy season for the rest of the year, divert water into canals, and regulate the rise and fall of the river downstream to facilitate pumping schemes.

Although ICOLD lobbyists sometimes imply that irrigation is largely dependent on large dams, much of the world's irrigated land receives water from the wide variety of traditional irrigation techniques, from modern schemes using water pumped from underground, and from unregulated rivers.[8] When the UN Food and Agriculture Organization (FAO) decided in 1986 to account for traditional African irrigation methods, their estimate for the area of irrigated land in sub-Saharan Africa jumped by 37 per cent. FAO researchers concluded that almost half of the 5 million hectares in Africa they considered irrigated received water from 'small-scale and traditional systems'.[9] According to government figures, more than three-fifths of the irrigated area in India receives water from wells and the small reservoirs known as 'tanks'. A similar proportion of the irrigated area in Indonesia is serviced by small or traditional schemes. Two-thirds of the 18 million irrigated hectares in the US is watered from wells or small on-farm ponds and reservoirs.[10]

Small-scale and traditional systems not only water more land than large dam and canal schemes but also tend to be far more productive and sustainable. In India, the productivity of land watered from private wells is on average nearly twice as high as that on canal projects.[11]

Statistics of how much irrigation is dependent on large dams often conceal how much land was already irrigated before the dams were built. In some cases modern irrigation can increase yields compared to traditional systems by allowing an extra cropping season (although almost invariably at the cost of the soil's long-term fertility); in other cases, the poor operation and maintenance of modern large-scale schemes may produce less than traditional systems even in the short term.

Reservoirs and canals consume large amounts of often prime-quality farmland. In some cases the amount of cropland consumed is not appreciably less than the new land irrigated – and in a few cases it is substantially more. Bakolori Dam can irrigate at maximum 44,000 hectares but submerged 12,000 hectares of fields and wiped out cropping on a further 11,000 hectares downstream by stopping the annual flood.[12] Assad Reservoir behind Syria's Tabqua Dam on the Euphrates drowned 31,000 hectares of irrigated land (and as much again of rainfed farmland and pastures). By 1990, 17 years after the Soviet-designed and -funded dam was completed, less than 83,000 hectares could receive Assad Reservoir water – and as much as 60 per cent of this land was already irrigated by private pump schemes before the dam was built. Tens of thousands of hectares of land in the Euphrates Valley were also consumed by irrigation infrastructure linked to Tabqua Dam and ruined by unsuccessful attempts to irrigate very poor soils.[13]

According to World Bank figures for India, an area equivalent to between 5 and 13 per cent of newly irrigated land is typically lost to reservoirs and canal and drainage infrastructure.[14] However, as the area which actually receives adequate irrigation water is usually far less than estimated, and because large amounts of land often have to be taken out of production due to soil degradation, these figures are almost certain to be underestimates. One of the biggest irrigation fiascos in India is Bargi Dam on the Narmada, which submerged nearly 81,000 hectares of farmland and forest to irrigate a projected area of 440,000 hectares. Although the dam was completed in 1986, seven years later only 12,000 hectares were receiving irrigation water (3 per cent of the planned area).[15]

All but a tiny proportion of Egypt's agriculture is now dependent on the regulation of the Nile by the High Aswan Dam, one of the main purposes of which was to increase Egypt's irrigated area. Government sources claimed in 1993 that 690,000 hectares had been 'reclaimed' from the desert since the High Dam was built.[16] Yet, according to FAO statistics, the actual area of irrigated land in Egypt in 1989 – 2.6 million hectares – was virtually unchanged from the area irrigated in 1961 when construction started on the dam. There are several reasons for the statistical discrepancy. One is the tendency of Egyptian government sources to be miserly with the truth on just about every aspect of the High Dam. Others are the mining of well over 100,000 hectares of fertile topsoil by the makers of mud bricks (the loss of the annual deposit of flood-borne silt resulted in brick factories along the Nile buying up farmland to quarry) and the urbanization of more than 125,000 hectares of previously irrigated land. The degradation of formerly cultivated land due to waterlogging and the related side-effects of perennial irrigation (land which had previously withstood several millennia of traditional flood irrigation) and the appalling record of the schemes to bring water to previously uncultivated desert lands also explain Egypt's failure to expand its irrigated area. While the Egyptian government claimed that by 1982 more than 400,000 hectares of desert had been serviced with canals, roads, powerlines and pumps, geographer Gilbert White estimates that because of unsuitable soils and poor planning and management only around 15 per cent of this land was actually being farmed by 1986.[17]

Killing The Land: Irrigation and Soil Degradation

> On the one side, we carry out irrigation works and put more and more water for fresh areas, while on the other side, land goes out of cultivation due to waterlogging. This is a curious state of affairs and it is far better to stop every irrigation work than allow waterlogging. It seems to me the height of folly that while we advance on one side we retreat from another side.
>
> Indian Prime Minister Jawaharlal Nehru, 1958

All irrigation waters, whether from rivers or groundwater, contain dissolved salts washed out of rocks and soils. Evaporation from reservoirs, canals and fields increases the concentration of salts in irrigation water. When the water reaches crops, the roots absorb water but leave in the soil most of the toxic salts. Compounding irrigated agriculture's salt problem is that soils in arid and semi-arid areas tend naturally to have high salt levels.

To prevent the salinity of irrigated soils from reaching levels which would stunt plant growth, farmers apply more water to wash salts from the root zone. Flushing out the salts, however, increases the salinity of the groundwater below and, in the absence of good drainage, causes the water table to rise. Eventually, when the water table reaches to within a metre or two of the soil surface, the saline groundwater is drawn upwards by capillary action. When it reaches the surface, the water evaporates leaving behind its salt content as a crust of deadly white crystals. Thus in trying to flush out the salts, the irrigator is not only accelerating salinization, but also the waterlogging of the root zone.

A problem related to salinization and waterlogging is alkalinity (also known as 'sodicity'), which occurs when irrigation waters or soils have a high sodium content. The sodium salts are absorbed by clay particles in the soil which swell, rendering the soil impermeable to water and oxygen, and ultimately barren. Heavily alkaline soils also impede plant uptake of essential micronutrients like calcium.[18]

Irrigation-induced soil degradation is nothing new. The decline of several ancient societies, from the banks of the Indus to coastal Peru, has been ascribed, with varying degrees of persuasiveness, to falling crop yields due to the salinization of irrigated fields. An agricultural chemist appointed by the British government at the end of the nineteenth century to investigate soil degradation linked with India's growing canal system reported that thousands of square kilometres were damaged and that patches of crops appeared 'like oases in the salt-covered desert around them'.[19]

The massive expansion of poorly managed dam and canal irrigation systems in recent decades, however, has resulted in salinization and waterlogging on an unprecedented scale. A recent estimate from the

Centre for Resource and Environmental Studies (CRES) at the Australian National University indicates that around 45.4 million hectares, one-fifth of the world's irrigated land, are 'salt-affected'. According to a 1990 study quoted by the World Bank, around 2 to 3 million hectares become so badly affected by salinity each year that they have to be abandoned. This compares with an estimated annual rate at which new irrigation schemes are now built of 2 million hectares. CRES calculates that the salinization of irrigated soils worldwide is costing some $11.4 billion a year in lost income due to reduced yields. The associated salinization of water resources, CRES believes, costs a couple of billion dollars more in damages to industrial water users and water distribution systems.[20]

One of the few comprehensive studies of the farm-level effects of irrigation-induced salinity was done on the World Bank-funded Sarda Sahayak canal irrigation project in Uttar Pradesh state, northern India. The study found that wheat and rice yields were cut in half on saline and alkaline soils, and that the incomes of farmers in affected areas were slashed to as little as 3 per cent of those of farmers cultivating healthy soils. Mexican government studies of 450,000 hectares affected to some degree by salt build-up indicate that agricultural productivity on this land fell by between a third and a half during the 1980s.[21]

The salinization and waterlogging of irrigated lands not only cause problems for those whose lands are directly affected. Saline wastewater draining back into the river progressively reduces downstream water quality for other irrigators and water users, and for wildlife. The problems besetting agriculture in the Euphrates Valley in Syria, where half of the irrigated land is already affected by salinization and waterlogging, will be greatly worsened by the increased salinity – and reduced volume – of water entering the country due to the massive programme of reservoir building and irrigation expansion underway upstream in Turkey. Agriculture in Iraq, downstream of Turkey and Syria on the Euphrates, and downstream of Turkey on the Tigris, faces a 'general pattern of steadily impending crisis' according to US geographers John Kolars and William Mitchell.[22]

Down the drain

> Should government biologists produce such a deliberate misrepresentation of facts ... they would be rightly accused of perpetrating fraud upon the public, and could end up being fined or sent to prison or both.
>
> US Federal Fish and Wildlife Service comment on agribusiness study of irrigation drainage and wildlife in California's Central Valley, 1993

The key to preventing, or at least to slowing down, the onset of salinization is to provide good drainage. Although this sounds like a simple thing for irrigation engineers to do, there are several related reasons why they frequently fail to build adequate drains. First, the urge to exaggerate project benefits means that the presence of soils vulnerable to salinization are rarely recognized in project documents.[23] Second, drains have none of the high-tech, shiny-white glamour of dams and huge new canals, so alluring to politicians and development bureaucrats. 'No-one ever built a monument to themselves by installing tile drains', as John Waterbury succinctly explains in his *Hydropolitics of the Nile Valley*.[24] Governments, irrigation agencies and donors consistently show that they prefer to start new projects rather than invest in the sustainability of old ones. For related reasons, in those cases where drains are provided, they tend to be badly built and poorly maintained, and so rapidly fill with sediment and deteriorate. Third, installing drains is exorbitantly expensive, especially in areas which are already suffering from salinization.[25] A massive 'Northwest Drainage Canal' proposed by the World Bank to alleviate the drainage problems of canal irrigation schemes in northwestern India could cost a staggering $9 billion according to a 1991 estimate. Furthermore, the issue of what to do with the billions of cubic metres of saline, agrochemical-laced wastewater which would flow into the megadrain has not yet been resolved.[26]

The soils of the San Joaquin Valley, the southern part of California's great Central Valley, are naturally both highly saline and rich with selenium – an element which is biologically necessary in trace amounts but lethal in higher concentrations. Decades of irrigation from groundwater and canals have leached selenium out of the soil and concentrated it in the rising saline groundwater. In the late 1960s the Bureau of Reclamation began to build a 250 kilometre concrete drain which would ultimately discharge the San Joaquin farmers' wastewater into San Francisco Bay. Public opposition to the plan, however, stopped the San Luis Drain at Kesterson, less than halfway to its intended terminus. BuRec then persuaded the US Fish and Wildlife Service that the saline drainwater would compensate for Kesterson's freshwater, now diverted for irrigation, which had previously supported an important bird habitat.

The drainwater arrived at the newly named Kesterson National Wildlife Refuge in 1978. Five years later, government biologists – to the great fury of their bosses – revealed to the media that the birds still breeding in the 'refuge' were producing embryos and chicks with hideous deformities: 'pretzel bills, external stomachs, exposed brains, warped wings, bulging eyes, and missing legs'.[27] Fifteen thousand adult birds were dying each year at Kesterson during the mid-1980s. In early 1985, the State Water Resources Control Board designated the drainage flowing into Kesterson a 'hazardous waste', and ordered BuRec to plug the drain. Ten years later BuRec estimated the total cost of cleaning up Kesterson at $80 million.[28]

The wastewater which would have gone down the San Luis Drain is today drained into small evaporation ponds. Selenium levels in some of these 'evap ponds' have been measured at 18 times higher than the worst recorded at Kesterson. When the Kesterson story broke in the media, the Bureau insisted that selenium was a local problem; when several years later deformed birds were found in evap ponds 150 kilometres away, they insisted that the problem was limited to the Central Valley. Today, rising selenium levels have been found on irrigation projects in 17 states in the US West. Presumably, if researchers looked, high selenium levels would be found in irrigation drainage elsewhere as selenium-rich soils are widely scattered around the world. The problem, furthermore, is not just one for wildlife – high levels of selenium are as poisonous to humans as they are to birds.[29]

The stagnation of the green revolution

> There is a need to review the Green Revolution model as a whole.... If we have to produce more we need a new technological paradigm.
>
> Obaidullah Khan, Assistant Director-General, UN Food and Agriculture Organization, 1993

Canal irrigation has played a central role in the 'green revolution' in Asia, especially in northern India and Pakistan. The 'revolution', which began in the early 1960s, was based upon newly developed 'high-yielding varieties' of rice and wheat. These new hybrids, however, only perform well when they receive high inputs of fertilizers and pesticides, and dependable applications of water. Critics of the high-tech green revolution strategy therefore prefer to call these seeds 'high-response varieties'. The critics believe that agricultural policy, instead of promoting capital- and technology-intensive production for the international market, should have centred on land reform, improvements in traditional, ecologically sustainable, agricultural technologies, and the production of food for local consumption rather than for export.[30]

Whether or not the food needs of the rising numbers of people in Asia over the past few decades could have been fed without high-yielding varieties, today hundreds of millions of Asians are dependent on high-yielding variety crops – and the green revolution package is in trouble. To the great concern of the world's leading agricultural researchers, since the 1980s yields of rice on the carefully managed test plots at the Philippines International Rice Research Institute (IRRI) – where the high-yield rice varieties were first developed – have been falling. Varieties which produced 10 tons per hectare in 1966 are now yielding less than 7 tons per hectare. In Central Luzon, the Philippines, average wet-season rice yields increased from 2.5 tonnes per hectare in 1966 to 4.2 tonnes in the early 1980s. By 1990, however, yields had fallen back to 3.7 tonnes per hectare. Elsewhere in Asia rice yields have stagnated rather than fallen over the last decade or more, but only with massive increases in fertilizer use. It is very likely that the phenomenon seen on the IRRI test plots – which have been subject to green revolution practices for longer than anywhere else – will soon spread. 'The rice products of the green revolution', warns the journal *International Agricultural Development*, 'are proving to be unsustainable.'[31]

IRRI scientists are not yet sure why their rice yields are declining, but believe that the overall reason is the degradation of paddy soils due to the switch from seasonally flooded rice cultivation to perennial irrigation with two to three crops grown annually. 'Evidence is mounting', says IRRI, 'that continuously flooded ricefields may not be resilient to the pressures of intensive cropping that is currently meeting rice production needs.' Year-round flooding of fields, it is believed, is killing off essential soil microbes and so is reducing the ability of the soil to provide nutrients to the crop. The replacement of traditional manures with modern fertilizers may also be depleting essential trace elements in the soil such as zinc and sulphur.[32]

The Social Effects of Large-Scale Irrigation

> Irrigation will do more than anything else to revive the [Aral Sea basin] and regenerate it, bury the past and make the transition to socialism more certain.
>
> V.I. Lenin, 1920s

Anthropological studies of traditional irrigation systems repeatedly show an inseparable link between the economic, cultural and religious life of a community, and the management of the irrigation technology it uses. On the Indonesian island of Bali, for example, the community bodies known as *subaks* which construct and manage the island's extensive traditional rice irrigation systems (see Chapter 7) are best described, according to Balinese researchers, as 'socio-religious communities'.[33]

Large modern irrigation systems have a similarly far-reaching effect on the lives of those affected by them. As schemes relying on large dams require, by their expense, scale and technological sophistication, that they be centrally managed by government bureaucracies, so the arrival of canal water frequently means the increasing intrusion of the state in the lives of farming communities, and the consequent erosion of the ability of individuals and communities to make decisions for themselves. Frequently, the loss of decision-making power means the loss of decision-making institutions such as the *subaks*, and with this comes the loss of the communal, cultural and religious services *subak*-type bodies provide.

On large, centrally controlled schemes, irrigation bureaucrats may decide not only which farmer gets how much water and when, but also which crops (and even which varieties) they may grow, when they may plant and harvest, which pesticides and fertilizers they may apply, and whom they may sell to. Muneera Salem-Murdock of the Institute for Development Anthropology tells how the Sudanese state-owned corporation which runs the huge New Halfa irrigation scheme forces tenants on the project to grow cotton despite the fact that the crop's production costs almost invariably exceed returns to the tenants, pushing them into debt. 'All the major agricultural decisions about cotton are made,' says Salem-Murdock, 'and all inputs other than labour are provided, by the Corporation. The tenant is reduced to a provider of human energy only.'[34]

Central government diktat over the operation of irrigation schemes probably reached its apogee in the USSR. In the late 1930s, two senior party officials from Uzbekistan questioned the wisdom of turning the deserts of Central Asia into a gargantuan cotton farm (destroying the Aral Sea and local irrigated agriculture in the process) – and for their 'bourgeois nationalism' were executed.[35]

Irrigate and accumulate

> The tendency of irrigation as a regular agricultural method is to promote the accumulation of large tracts of land in the hands of single proprietors, and consequently to dispossess the smaller land-holders.
>
> George Perkins Marsh, US conservationist and diplomat, 1874

Iran's highest dam, Dez, was supposed to irrigate 80,000 hectares for the benefit of small farmers. Just as the dam neared completion in the early 1960s, however, the Shah and his advisers decided that the irrigation water would be better used by foreign agribusiness corporations producing for export. The 'farmers' who were awarded the 16,000 hectares which actually received irrigation included Mitsui, Chase Manhattan, Bank of America, Shell, John Deere & Co. and the Transworld Agricultural Development Corporation. Some 17,000 peasants were pushed off their land to make way for the dam and the corporations.[36]

The story is a familiar one, repeated from Rajasthan to California. Irrigation schemes are promoted with the promise of land to the tiller, but end up delivering it to the absentee landlord. Irrigation raises land values and yields, so while all farmers may benefit from receiving subsidized water, those with the most land gain most. Large landowners, especially corporations, are much better able to invest in the machinery, chemicals and labour needed to take advantage of the new supplies of water, more likely to have the connections and know-how to market the new crops grown, and better able to bribe and lobby officials to ensure that they get plentiful water at the right time. Small farmers, on the other hand, especially subsistence farmers in developing countries, rarely have capital or access to cheap credit, are vulnerable to having their share of water diverted to the better off, and are at risk of falling into a spiral of debt when crop prices fall, government subsidies for inputs or crops are removed, or their crops fail or go unsold. Indebted or otherwise struggling farmers are then bought out or otherwise pushed off their land.

Hundreds of thousands of landless and poor farmers were given plots of land as the first phase of the huge Indira Gandhi Canal advanced across the Rajasthan desert in the 1960s and early 1970s. The settlers needed more than just desert land and water to become successful farmers, so low-interest credit, advice from government agronomists, village amenities, clinics and schools were also to be provided. Today, only a minority of settlers have access to these services. Very few got cheap state loans, and instead most have had to borrow at interest rates of up to 50 per cent. The result is that most settlers have become deeply indebted, many becoming 'bonded labourers' – tenants on what was once their own land, but which is now owned by the moneylenders to whom they are in debt, often to levels which they will not be able to pay off in a lifetime of farming. According to government consultants, two-fifths of the Indira Gandhi settlers had lost their land by 1989.[37]

On the Sarda Sahayak canal irrigation project in Uttar Pradesh

> ...it is the general rule that the strong, the powerful, the well-connected, the local bullies dominate the use of irrigation water. They get the water first and tend to take as much of it as they please. Only after they are satisfied do they permit the mass of ordinary, unimportant, petty cultivators to have access to it.[38]

These 'irregularities', says agricultural economist Robert Repetto, 'are reported in almost all countries in which public irrigation systems are important.'[39] Women farmers may be put at a particular disadvantage when their production is made dependent on male decision-makers. In a study of Tungabhadra dam and canal irrigation scheme in south India, Priti Ramamurthy of Syracuse University in New York explains that only rich male peasants 'have the status, class characteristics, transportation, and political savvy to deal with irrigation engineers and other government officers ... women are conspicuously absent from this public domain'.[40]

The beneficiaries of the federally funded irrigation schemes of the US Bureau of Reclamation were initially supposed to be family farmers, with an upper limit on holdings to receive subsidized water set at 160 acres (65 hectares). Over the decades, however, collusion between agribusiness corporations, BuRec and politicians ensured that the limit was constantly subverted and ignored. Under the Reclamation Reform Act of 1982, the 160 acre limit was expanded sixfold, the requirement that the 'family' (often in fact a corporation) live on the irrigated land was abolished, and farmers were allowed to lease unlimited amounts of federally irrigated land beyond their new 960 acre ownership limit. One Congressman denounced the Reform Act as 'a bald-faced anti-family farm package of direct subsidies to the richest of America's agribusiness interests'.[41]

Even the generously interpreted acreage limits on federal irrigation water were too strict for agricorporations in the south of California's Central Valley. They successfully lobbied the state of California to subsidize them with its own multi-billion-dollar State Water Project, which includes the 770 kilometre California Aqueduct and two of the largest dams in the US, San Luis and Oroville. The leading beneficiaries of the project, with holdings receiving SWP water of between 6,700 and 15,300 hectares, are, in the caustic words of Donald Worster, 'a few horny-handed plowmen': Chevron USA, Tejon Ranch (part of the holdings of the *Los Angeles Times*, a staunch supporter of water development in California for 80 years), Getty Oil, Shell Oil, McCarthy Joint Venture A (a partnership including Prudential Insurance), Blackwell Land Company (owned by a consortium of foreign investors including Mitsubishi), Tenneco (a US chemicals and food conglomerate) and Southern Pacific Railroad (the largest private landowner in California).[42]

While irrigation has certainly brought wealth to these corporations, the rural communities in the Central Valley where their labourers live are some of the most depressed in California. Studies by the Macrosocial Accounting Project of the University of California show that real incomes have declined, especially among farmworkers, in areas which now receive water from the state's mammoth irrigation aqueducts. 'Every farm structure correlate of increasing surface water supplies (i.e. increasing chemical use on farms, increasing dependence on new technologies, higher levels of absentee involvement etc.) is associated with deteriorating conditions in the rural community', comments Dean MacCannell, the Accounting Project's director.[43]

Irrigation and the enclosure of the commons

The floodplains along the Senegal River provide the richest farmland in the desert nation of Mauritania and some of the best land in Senegal, as well as important spawning grounds for fisheries. In all but the very driest years, the Senegal would flood at the end of the wet season, recharging the valley aquifers, revitalizing land by depositing silt, and encouraging the growth of the riverine vegetation. As the flood receded, hundreds of thousands of farmers would follow its retreat, planting their crops to make use of the residual ground moisture. After the crops had been harvested, nomadic pastoralists would move into the valley, grazing their livestock on the remaining stubble, and providing free fertilizer for the farmers in the form of manure. Women in the valley drew water from the recharged wells to grow vegetable gardens, giving them a measure of economic independence from their husbands.[44]

Since the completion of Manantali Dam in 1987, however, this traditional floodplain economy has been under severe stress. One of the main aims of Manantali was to encourage the expansion of large irrigation schemes, supplied with water pumped from the newly regulated river, to grow rice and sugarcane for urban consumption.[45] This process was accelerated by new landownership laws in Senegal and Mauritania – strongly promoted by agencies such as the World Bank, IMF and the French Fund for Assistance and Cooperation – which enabled wealthy nationals and foreign companies to 'privatize' land in the valley on which the traditional peasant owners had no formal rights.[46]

On the north bank of the river in Mauritania, the Arab-speaking elite, the Moors or *Bidans* (literally 'whites'), have expropriated huge areas of land. The consequent increased pressure on the floodplain land remaining outside commercial control has heightened ethnic tension between black farmers, who are perceived as Senegalese, and Mauritanian herders. One border flare-up between farmers and herders in April 1989 brought the two countries to the brink of war. Looting of Mauritanian-owned shops and businesses in Senegal and anti-Senegalese riots in Mauritania resulted in around 250 deaths. At least 60,000 Moors fled or were deported from Senegal, and tens of thousand of blacks were forcibly expelled from Mauritania.

Those black farmers who have protested against the ruthless land grabbing in Mauritania have been among thousands of political prisoners subjected to brutal physical abuse. As many as 600 were executed or tortured to death. In 1994, Human Rights Watch/Africa reported that the Mauritanian side of the Senegal Valley was under an undeclared state of emergency 'characterized by a chronic and insidious pattern of violations against blacks, including indiscriminate killings, detention, rape, and beatings by the security forces'.[47]

The expropriation of land along the Senegal Valley is unusual in the horrific violence which has accompanied it: the process of enclosure of the commons, however, is commonplace when irrigation is introduced. It is not only the privatization of communally owned farmland which hurts rural communities. Land turned over to irrigation which had not previously been farmed is often thought of as having been 'wasteland', but was often in fact land which supplied grazing, fruits, fuel and other benefits, and was especially valuable to herders and the local poor and landless.[48]

Irrigation and malnutrition

> Current agricultural development policies, in particular those implemented under the green revolution, have singularly failed to address [the] primary causes of hunger. On the contrary, they have intensified and extended their grip.
>
> Declaration of the International Movement for Ecological Agriculture, 1990

Advocates of large dams commonly make the assumption that there is a direct and proportionate link between increasing crop production and reducing malnutrition. But the issue of hunger is more complicated than dam builders assume. What enables people to eat is their ability to afford food, not just food availability. Even in wealthy California, the major producer of irrigated crops in the US, 5 million people – one in six residents – suffer what University of California researchers describe as 'chronic hunger'.[49]

While hundreds of millions go hungry every day in India, Pakistan and Sri Lanka, these countries have been self-sufficient or in surplus in food grains for numerous years. In mid-1995, Indian government granaries were filled to overflowing with more than 30 million tons of unsold grain.[50] As Robert Chambers says, hunger in South Asia is not today a problem of food production, but 'is a problem of who produces the food and of who has power to obtain it'.[51] When irrigation schemes further marginalize the poor and are used to grow expensive crops for sale to the better-off in cities or abroad, they can end up increasing both crop production and hunger.

Wheat and rice were grown on two-thirds of the area newly irrigated in India between 1960 and 1983, and oilseeds, cotton and sugarcane on another fifth. Meanwhile the total amount of land under traditional cheap subsistence food crops – pulses and coarse cereals such as millets and sorghum – fell over the same period.[52] Although nutritionists believe that a traditional diet of pulses, coarse grains and dairy products is superior to a wheat-based diet, there has been little official support for traditional Indian subsistence crops, compared to the hundreds of billions of rupees spent on irrigation infrastructure and the promotion of wheat and rice growing.

Before the Indira Gandhi Canal, 135,000 hectares of land in the Thar Desert were planted to coarse grains, including the traditional grain for bread, *bajra*, and 27,000 hectares to lentils. Much of this land was watered with centuries-old, communally managed water harvesting techniques. By 1990, however, *bajra* growing had been almost eliminated and the desert, now under perennial canal irrigation, was planted with 132,000 hectares of cotton and 123,000 hectares of wheat, as well as tens of thousands of hectares of mustard and groundnut (grown for cooking oil), chickpeas, sugarcane and rice.

Seventy per cent of settlers near the Indira Gandhi Canal do not earn enough to pay off agricultural loans and meet their basic food needs. According to a government-sponsored health survey, the settlers' average per capita consumption of calories and protein is below that expected of Indians living on the poverty line. The survey also reported that malnutrition is more common among children of canal settlers than among the children of pastoralists in the poorest districts of Rajasthan not affected by the canal – children who eat a diet of dairy products and *bajra*.[53]

Almost two-thirds of modern large-scale irrigation in sub-Saharan Africa is in Sudan. The massive Gezira scheme covers some 840,000 hectares, half of the irrigated area in Sudan. Watered from the Sennar and Roseires dams on the Blue Nile, Gezira was first developed by the British in the 1920s, replacing the traditional local sorghum crop and the nomadic herding of livestock with cotton to be spun in English mills. Today, cotton for export remains the major crop grown at Gezira, as it is at the country's other large schemes. Despite the huge area under irrigation in the country, one-third of children in Sudan suffer from chronic malnutrition.[54]

By increasing the area of perenially irrigated rice, Manantali, Diama and Foum El-Gleita dams were supposedly intended to improve the diets of the inhabitants of the Senegal Valley. Yet, a 1994 US Agency for International Development-funded study found that the nutritional status of the people of the valley appears to be worse than before. While rice consumption in one village surveyed had more than doubled in the eight years since the dams started storing water, consumption of nutritionally varied traditional foods – millet, sorghum, maize (corn) and black-eyed peas (cowpeas) – had fallen by between 30 and 90 per cent. Consumption of fish, meat and dairy products also appear to have fallen among valley residents. Although reliable data on nutrition before and after the dams are not available for most of the valley, villagers interviewed for the USAID study in Mauritania and Senegal

> ...clearly state that their health has deteriorated in the past few years because of the deterioration in their diet. They are convinced that before the construction of the dams, when they produced traditional flood recession crops ... their diet was more varied and hence more healthy. They insist that it is because of their present diet, made up primarily of rice, that they are weaker and have more health problems than before.[55]

Irrigation together with inputs such as modern seed varieties and agrochemicals clearly can increase crop yields by significant amounts. Government figures indicate that average per hectare yields of rice on irrigated land in major Indian states in 1980–83 were between 27 and 369 per cent higher than in rainfed areas; yields of wheat were 7 to 391 per cent higher.[56] Critics of the green revolution, however, argue that these figures mislead as to the impact of intensive irrigation. Many irrigated areas are in fertile plains which were already more productive than other areas. As modern irrigated fields grow only a single crop, official statistics measure only the yield of this crop. In traditional peasant agriculture, however, an astonishingly wide diversity of foods and other products are obtained from fields, including fruits from trees and fish from flooded rice paddies. Traditional agroforestry systems – which combine the growing of annual crops with trees – commonly contain well over a hundred plant species per field. In addition to providing a nutritious and varied diet, traditional agro-ecosystems also produce construction materials, medicines, fuel, fodder, green manures and natural pesticides. Declining yields and degraded land in the green revolution areas also show that higher monocrop yields have been bought at the expense of long-term sustainability.[57]

The Technical and Economic Failure of Large-Scale Irrigation

> ...since 1951, 246 big surface irrigation projects have been initiated. Only 65 out of these have been completed; 181 are still under construction.... Perhaps we can safely say about [projects started after 1970] that for 16 years we have poured money out. The people have got nothing back, no irrigation, no water, no increase in production, no help in their daily life.
>
> Indian Prime Minister Rajiv Gandhi, 1986

Modern canal irrigation has a woeful record of poor design and construction, mismanagement and corruption. Water supplies to farmers are frequently erratic and unreliable – the main reason why crop yields from groundwater irrigation are far superior to those from canal irrigation. On the Bakolori project in Nigeria, yields of groundnuts were only 69 per cent of those predicted by agricultural economists; yields of rice 56 per cent; and of cotton 17 per cent.[58]

The Indian Public Accounts Committee reported in 1983 that since Independence not a single large irrigation project in the country had been completed on time and within stated cost estimates.[59] Even when projects are reported as being completed they are still likely to irrigate much less land than originally planned – well over half of the irrigation potential created on many schemes in South Asia has never received any water. In India, says Chambers, 'it may be a universal experience that the area irrigated has been less than planned in the project proposals and designs.'[60] In 1971, the Nigerian Department of Agriculture estimated that Nigeria would have 320,000 hectares under large-scale irrigation projects by 1982; yet at the end of 1980 less than 31,000 hectares were actually irrigated by modern schemes.[61]

In those areas which do receive canal water, its distribution is invariably skewed: those near the head of the canal usually receive more water than needed – often resulting in waterlogging – while those at the tail do not get enough. Chambers believes that 'between a quarter and two-fifths of the potential declared utilised in India, roughly between 6 and 10 million hectares, suffers from recognisable and damaging tailend deprivation.'[62] Studies on the Gal Oya Project in Sri Lanka showed that tailenders' rice yields were only just over half those of farmers in better locations and that the tailend families could have earned more as wage labourers than working on their own land.[63]

As soon as irrigation water begins to flow through a canal, landowners at its head start to plant profitable but water-intensive crops such as sugarcane and rice, and so establish pre-emptive rights over the water. Sugar growers in Maharashtra, India, occupy only one-tenth of the state's irrigated land, yet use half of its irrigation water.[64] The most drought-prone areas slated to get water from Sardar Sarovar – Saurashtra and Kutch – are at the tail end of the massive planned canal network; although the chronic water shortages in these areas are one of the chief justifications for building the dam, a mass of evidence indicates that they will not get the water promised to them. One sign is that despite government assurances that farmers receiving water from the scheme will not be allowed to grow sugar, 10 large sugar mills are being built near the head of the main Sardar Sarovar canal.[65]

Another reason why tailenders do not get sufficient water is that planners regularly overestimate the amount of water available to a canal system, and underestimate the system losses to leaks, evaporation and overwatering. Reservoir sedimentation also progressively reduces water supply to irrigation canals, as does the construction of dams and other irrigation projects upstream.[66]

Irrigation efficiency (measured as the percentage of water actually used for crop growth relative to the total amount of water delivered by the irrigation system) averages only around 40 per cent worldwide.[67] In India, the World Bank notes, irrigation efficiency is often assumed in project documents at 60 per cent, whereas in real life most Indian schemes probably have an efficiency of 20 to 35 per cent. The result is that half or less of the area planned to get water can actually be supplied.[68]

A 1991 World Bank internal review of irrigation in India is scathing in its criticism of the country's canal irrigation planning, construction and maintenance (much of it funded by the Bank):

> ...irrigation and drainage infrastructure is deficient and deteriorating. The principal reasons are poor initial design, poor quality of construction, and

> inadequate maintenance.... More realism concerning the availability of water and feasible efficiency of water usage is in order. Concern about ensuring an adequate benefit/cost ratio, exacerbated by political concerns to maximize planned irrigated areas, adds pressure to overextend proposed command areas and use unrealistic design assumptions.... While there are some examples of good quality construction ... inferior work is more common.... Financial factors and local pressure to take shortcuts ... are the overriding negative influences on construction ... large illicit profits can be made by using substandard materials, skimping on the thickness of linings, and labor-saving shortcuts in curing cement.[69]

By the late 1980s an estimated $250 billion of public money (in 1986 dollars) had been spent on irrigation just in developing countries, almost all of this on surface schemes. In recent decades Mexico has spent 80 per cent of its public investment in agriculture on irrigation. In Pakistan, one-tenth of total public investment is spent on irrigation. Between 1950 and 1993 the World Bank loaned some $20 billion for irrigation, 7 per cent of its total lending.[70]

Given the morass of environmental and technical problems in which surface irrigation is embroiled, it is not surprising that the returns from irrigation cannot pay back this massive investment. The 16,000 Sri Lankan families given irrigated land under the Third Mahaweli project, approved for a World Bank loan in 1981, at first paid water charges covering half of the scheme's operating and maintenance costs (there was never any hope of recovering from the farmers the $200 million spent on project construction, including the canals to bring water from the Victoria Dam). Mainly because the incomes of the settlers were only around a third of those projected, annual water fees paid plummeted, and by 1990 the fees collected were only 5 per cent of those owed. Almost all the project maintenance budget has had to be spent on staff salaries, with the result that, according to an internal World Bank evaluation, the new irrigation facilities are fast deteriorating.[71] Studies by the International Irrigation Management Institute in Indonesia, Korea, Nepal, Thailand and the Philippines show that in 1984 only in the latter country did receipts from fees paid by farmers on public irrigation systems exceed the costs of operation and management of the systems.[72]

In Mexico, only around 11 per cent of the capital, operating and maintenance costs of public irrigation are recovered from farmers. North of the Rio Grande, cost recovery on Bureau of Reclamation projects averages about 17 per cent of total costs.[73] Richard Wahl and Benjamin Simon of the University of Colorado estimate that from 1902 to 1986 BuRec irrigation projects cost taxpayers nearly $20 billion in 1986 dollars. Wahl and Simon calculate that in 1989 federal irrigation subsidies amounted to $2.2 billion.[74] In 18 BuRec irrigation projects studied in 1981, the largest 5 per cent of farmers pocketed half of the total subsidy.[75]

The 6 per cent of US farmers who benefit from cheap BuRec water have larger holdings and much higher profits than the non-irrigating farmers who are helping subsidize them. Furthermore, in the mid-1980s, 45 per cent of federally irrigated water in the US West, and 59 per cent in California, was used to grow crops that were officially in surplus and subject to expensive federal programmes to reduce production.[76]

In Africa, difficult soils, terrain and hydrology coupled with poor communications, corruption and a lack of suitable skills make surface irrigation even more difficult and expensive than in other areas. Kenya's Bura irrigation project, which relies on Tana River water regulated by the Masinga Dam, cost a staggering $55,000 for each settler family in a country where per capita income is only about $350 per year. 'At one point,' says anthropologist Thayer Scudder, '50 per cent of the Kenyan government's funds for [rural] development were wasted on Bura.'[77] Korinna Horta of the US Environment Defense Fund visited the Bura site in 1994 and found an area 'reminiscent of a ghost town' with abandoned water towers, overgrown canals and 20,000 desperate and hungry settlers.[78]

With the best sites for surface irrigation already used up, the cost of new irrigation development is soaring. In India, the cost in real terms of large canal schemes more than doubled between 1950 and 1980. Per hectare costs of developing new surface irrigation schemes are now typically between $3,000 and $5,000 in East and South Asia, nearly $6,000 in Brazil, and $10,000 in Mexico. In Africa costs are between $10,000 and $20,000 per hectare.[79] These figures do not even include most dam construction, resettlement and drainage costs; nor do they allow for the inevitable overruns. At these prices, and given current historically low crop prices, few new surface irrigation investments can be justified by even the most wildly optimistic irrigation economist.

With few exceptions the only investments in large irrigation schemes which currently make any sense in economic, environmental or social justice terms are those which attempt to improve existing systems and stop more land being ruined by bad drainage and overwatering.

Notes

1. F. van der Leeden et al., *The Water Encyclopedia,* second edition, Lewis Publishers, Chelsea, MI, 1990, Tables 5-3, 5-4, 5-9.

2. Robert Chambers writes: 'In an earlier outline for this book I set aside a chapter for sorting out irrigation definitions and statistics. Heroic patience and several lifetimes were evidently needed.... Had I not backed off, this book would never have been written. I shall use statistics throughout, but the reader is asked to take them with judiciously liberal doses of salt' (R. Chambers, *Managing Canal Irrigation: Practical Analysis from South Asia*, Cambridge University Press, Cambridge 1988, p. 17).

3. F., Ghassemi et al., *Salinisation of Land and Water Resources: Human Causes, Extent, Management and Case Studies,* CAB International, Wallingford, UK, 1995, pp. 12–13; G. Gardner, 'Irrigated Area Dips Slightly', in L. Starke (ed.), *Vital Signs 1996: The Trends that are Shaping Our Future*, W.W. Norton, New York 1996, pp. 44–5. China, India, the CIS, the US and Pakistan together account for 62% of global irrigated land.

4. D.L. Umali, *Irrigation-Induced Salinity: A Growing Problem for Development and the Environment,* World Bank Technical Paper 215, August 1993, p. 3.

5. M. Svendsen and M.W. Rosegrant, 'Irrigation Development in Southeast Asia Beyond 2000: Will the Future Be Like the Past?', *Water International*, Vol. 19, No. 1, 1994, p. 28.

6. See W.M. Adams, *Wasting the Rain: Rivers, People and Planning in Africa*, Earthscan, London 1992, p. 70.

7. Chambers comments that, 'Because of the greater convenience and control provided by groundwater, many farmers in [canal irrigated areas] dig wells or install tubewells. Often they benefit from the rising watertables resulting from canal and other seepage which provide an excellent and regularly recharged aquifer close to the surface of their land' (*Managing Canal Irrigation*, p. 215). Groundwater recharge by itself could be achieved with far smaller, cheaper and less destructive schemes than large surface storage projects (see, e.g., A. Shah, *Water for Gujarat: An Alternative. Technical Overview of the Flawed Sardar Sarovar Project and a Proposal for a Sustainable Alternative*, Jan Vikas Andolan et al., Vishakhapatnam, September 1993).

8. E.g: 'The teeming masses in the cities ... are going to be entirely dependent on new large-scale production of energy and food and these can only come from major projects, including hydroelectricity and irrigation from large dams' (E.T. Haws, 'Large Dams' Part in Flood Control', letter in *The Times*, London, 15 September 1988). See also W. Pircher, '36,000 Dams and Still More Needed', *Water Power Dam Construction*, May 1993.

9. S. Postel, *Last Oasis: Facing Water Scarcity*, W.W. Norton, New York 1992, p. 121; Adams, *Wasting the Rain*, p. 74. The FAO figures still exclude some types of traditional irrigation.

10. World Bank, 'India: Irrigation Sector Review. Volume I – Main Report', Washington, DC, 1991 p. 2; N. Sutawan et al., 'Community-Based Irrigation System in Bali, Indonesia', in W. Gooneratne and S. Hirashima (eds.), *Irrigation and Water Management in Asia*, Sterling Publishers, New Delhi 1990, p. 82; van der Leeden et al., *The Water Encyclopedia*, Table 5-73.

11. World Bank, 'India', Vol. I, p. 7.

12. Adams, *Wasting the Rain*, p. 132. This estimate also allows for the fact that irrigation should permit two crops to be grown annually by doubling the actual area irrigated.

13. J.F. Kolars and W.A. Mitchell, *The Euphrates River and the Southeast Anatolia Development Project*, Southern Illinois University Press, Carbondale 1991, pp. 144–66, 275; W. Scheumann, 'New Irrigation Schemes in Southeast Anatolia and in Northern Syria: More Competition and Conflict over the Euphrates?', *Quarterly Journal of International Agriculture*, July–September 1993. Tabqua (also known as Thawra Dam) was supposed to irrigate 640,000 hectares.

14. World Bank, 'India', Vol. I, p. 41.

15. S. Raman, 'Bargi Oustees Plough Lonely Furrow', *Economic Times*, Ahmedabad, 6 March 1993.

16. A.M. Shalaby, 'The Role of High Aswan Dam in Horizontal and Vertical Land Expansion and Yield Promotion', in Egyptian National Committee on Large Dams (ed.), *High Aswan Dam Vital Achievement Fully Controlled*, ENCOLD, Cairo 1993, p. 153.

17. G. White, 'The Environmental Effects of the High Dam at Aswan', *Environment*, Vol. 30, No. 7, 1988, pp. 11, 34; 'Irrigated Area by Region and Country', in P.H. Gleick (ed.), *Water in Crisis: A Guide to the World's Fresh Water Resources*, Oxford University Press, Oxford 1983, Table E.4; M.R.H. Ramez, 'HAD and Substitutes of Nile-Silt in Building Brick Industry', in ENCOLD (ed.), *High Aswan Dam*, p. 352.

18. Umali, *Irrigation-Induced Salinity*, p. 8. Alkalinization is a serious problem in parts of northern India, Pakistan, Armenia, Afghanistan, Iran and the West African Sahel zone (E. Goldsmith and N. Hildyard, *The Social and Environmental Impacts of Large Dams. Vol. 1*, Wadebridge Ecological Centre, Cornwall 1984, p. 136; J. Madeley, 'Will Rice Turn the Sahel to Salt?', *New Scientist*, 9 October 1993).

19. Quoted in E. Whitcombe, *Agrarian Conditions in Northern India. Volume 1: The United Provinces under British Rule, 1860–1900*, University of California Press, Berkeley 1972, p. 72.

20. Ghassemi et al., *Salinisation of Land*, pp. 13, 48; HR Wallingford, 'ODU Studies: Soil Salinization, Land Reclamation and Drainage', Project Sheet, Wallingford, UK, 1990, p. 1. According to a 1990 FAO report, 'about 20 to 30 million hectares are severely affected by salinity and an additional 60 to 80 million hectares are affected to some extent' (FAO, *An International Action Programme on Water and Sustainable Agricultural Development*, Rome 1990, p. 15).

21. Umali, *Irrigation-Induced Salinity*, pp. 13–14.

22. I. Nahal, 'Environmental and Socio-Economic Effects of Irrigation Schemes in the Arab Near East', *Desertification Bulletin*, No. 24, 1994; Kolars and Mitchell, *The Euphrates River*, p. 258.

23. See, e.g., R. Repetto, *Skimming the Water: Rent-Seeking and the Performance of Public Irrigation Systems*, WRI, Washington, DC, December 1986, pp. 21–2; B. Morse et al., *Sardar Sarovar: The Report of the Independent Review*, RFI, Ottawa 1992, pp. 305–17; Umali, *Irrigation-Induced Salinity*, p. 15.

24. J. Waterbury, *Hydropolitics of the Nile Valley*, Syracuse University Press, New York 1979, p. 153.

25. Umali, *Irrigation-Induced Salinity*, p. 43.

26. M. Goldman, '"There's a Snake on Our Chests": State and Development Crisis in India's Desert', Ph.D. thesis, University of California, Santa Cruz, December 1994, p. 213. A drain to discharge saline waters from Australia's Murray Basin to the sea would cost $1.6–$4.8bn in 1990 prices (Ghassemi et al., *Salinisation of Land*, p. xv).

27. T. Williams, 'Death in a Black Desert', *Audobon*, January–February 1994.

28. T. Harris, *Death in the Marsh*, Island Press, Washington, DC, 1991, pp. 33, 194–6; 'Farmers May Be Left Holding Kesterson Bag', *US Water News*, July 1995.

29. Harris, *Death in the Marsh*, p. 210.

30. See, e.g., V. Shiva, 'The Green Revolution in the Punjab', *The Ecologist*, Vol. 21, No. 2, March/April 1991.

31. 'Green Revolution Blues', *International Agricultural Development*, May/June 1994, p. 7; World Resources Institute, *World Resources 1994–95*, Oxford University Press, Oxford 1994, p. 108.

32. 'Green Revolution Blues'; M. Khor, 'FAO Asian Chief Calls for Move

Away from Green Revolution', Third World Network Biodiversity Convention Briefings, No. 2, Penang, Malaysia 1993; Shiva, 'The Green Revolution in the Punjab', pp. 59–60; E. Wilken, 'Assault on the Earth', *WorldWatch*, March/April 1995.

33. See Sutawan et al., 'Community-Based Irrigation System'.

34. M. Salem-Murdock, *Arabs and Nubians in New Halfa: A Study of Settlement and Irrigation*, University of Utah Press, Salt Lake City 1989, pp. 31, 47. Tenants on the New Halfa Agricultural Production Scheme include 50,000 Sudanese Nubians displaced by the High Aswan Dam. The scheme is threatened by the rapid sedimentation of the Khashm el-Girba Dam, built in the late 1950s to provide New Halfa's irrigation water.

35. F. Pearce, *The Dammed: Rivers, Dams and the Coming World Water Crisis*, Bodley Head, London 1992, p. 109; P.P. Micklin, 'Desiccation of the Aral Sea: A Water Management Disaster in the Soviet Union', *Science*, Vol. 241, 2 September 1988. Where lands receiving canal water are privately owned the irrigation bureaucrats do not have the same degree of control over the farmers' lives as is common on large tenancy schemes. Nevertheless, the arrival of canal water makes farmers increasingly dependent upon the agencies and individual engineers whose job it is to apportion water and to build, maintain and operate the canal systems (see Goldman, '"There's a Snake"', p. 145; Chambers, *Managing Canal Irrigation*, pp. 87ff.).

36. F.M. Lappé and J. Collins, *Food First*, Abacus, London 1982, pp. 217–18.

37. Goldman '"There's a Snake"', pp. 116–29, 148, 173.

38. D. and A. Thorner, 'The Weak and the Strong on the Sarda Canal', in *Land and Labour in India*, Asia Publishing House, Bombay 1962, quoted in Repetto, *Skimming the Water*, p. 24.

39. Repetto, *Skimming the Water*, p. 24. The World Bank euphemistically refers to these practices as 'rent-seeking and often disruptive political pressures' ('India', Vol. I, p. iv).

40. P. Ramamurthy, 'Rural Women and Irrigation: Patriarchy, Class and the Modernizing State in South India', *Society and Natural Resources*, Vol. 4, No. 4, 1991.

41. D. Worster, *Rivers of Empire: Water, Aridity and the Growth of the American West*, Oxford University Press, Oxford 1985, pp. 299–302.

42. Ibid., pp. 291–2; M. Reisner, *Cadillac Desert: The American West and its Disappearing Water*, Secker & Warburg, London 1986, p. 385.

43. Quoted in R. Gottlieb, *A Life of Its Own: The Politics and Power of Water*, Harcourt Brace Jovanovich, San Diego 1988, p. 89.

44. Institute for Development Anthropology, *Large Dams and Small People: Management of an African River*, Binghampton, NY, 1993, video.

45. The performance of modern irrigation in the Senegal Valley has been extremely poor. See Adams, *Wasting the Rain*, p. 203; M. Niasse, 'Village Irrigated Perimeters at Doumga Rindiaw, Senegal', *Development Anthropology Network*, Vol. 8, No. 1, Spring 1990.

46. M. Horowitz, 'Victims of Development', *Development Anthropology Network*, Vol. 7, No. 2, Fall 1989; Human Rights Watch/Africa, *Mauritania's Campaign of Terror: State-Sponsored Repression of Black Africans*, Human Rights Watch, New York 1994. See also F. Mounier, 'The Senegal River Scheme: Development for Whom?', in E. Goldsmith and N. Hildyard (eds.), *The Social and Environmental Effects of Large Dams. Vol. 2: Case Studies*, Wadebridge Ecological Centre, Cornwall 1986 (hereafter

SEELD 2); B. Ba, 'Uneven Development in Mauritania', in O. Bennett (ed.), *Greenwar: Environment and Conflict*, Panos Institute, London 1991.

47. Human Rights Watch/Africa, *Mauritania's Campaign of Terror*, p. 5.

48. See, e.g., Goldman, '"There's a Snake"', p. 200; M.B.K. Darkoh, 'The Deterioration of the Environment in Africa's Drylands and River Basins', *Deforestation Bulletin*, No. 24, 1994; Adams, *Wasting the Rain*.

49. Global statistics from FAO quoted in World Resources Institute, *World Resources 1994–95*, p. 108; Y. Wilson, 'One in Six Californians Goes Hungry, Report Says', *San Francisco Chronicle*, 7 April 1995.

50. 'How to Sit on a Useless Pile', *The Economist*, 3 June 1995.

51. Chambers, *Managing Canal Irrigation*, p. 7.

52. World Bank, 'India: Irrigation Sector Review. Volume II – Supplementary Analysis, 1991, p. 10. The tendency for canal irrigation to favour commercial and export crop production at the expense of the growing of cheap food was apparent with the huge programme of canal building in India undertaken by the British colonialists (see, e.g., Whitcombe, *Agrarian Conditions in Northern India*, p. 75). Ian Stone (*Canal Irrigation in British India: Perspectives on Technological Change in a Peasant Economy*, Cambridge University Press, Cambridge 1984) argues against Whitcombe's thesis that canal irrigation did not alleviate famines in India. For a discussion of their arguments, see Goldman, '"There's a Snake"', p. 86.

53. Goldman, '"There's a Snake"', pp. 50–54, 66, 159–60, 193, 197.

54. Adams, *Wasting the Rain*, pp. 74, 108; World Resources Institute, *World Resources 1994–95*, p. 272; T. Barnett, *The Gezira Scheme: An Illusion of Development*, Frank Cass, London 1977; N. Pollard, 'The Sudan's Gezira Scheme: A Study in Failure', in *SEELD 2*.

55. Environmental Health Project, 'Senegal River Basin Health Master Plan Study', Arlington, VA, December 1994, pp. 78–9.

56. World Bank, 'India', Vol. II, p. 6. The wide variation in increases is due largely to different climatic, topographical and soil conditions in different states, as well as to varying efficiencies of irrigation management. For statistics showing high yields from traditional farming in India (and a sustained critique of 'scientific' agriculture), see W. Pereira, *Tending the Earth: Traditional, Sustainable Agriculture in India*, Earthcare Books, Bombay 1993, p. 109.

57. M.A. Altieri, 'Traditional Farming in Latin America', *The Ecologist*, Vol. 21, No. 2, March/April 1991 (Special Issue on the UN FAO); see also Pereira, *Thending the Earth*, pp. 146–54.

58. Adams, *Wasting the Rain*, p. 170.

59. See S. Singh et al., 'Evaluating Major Irrigation Projects in India', in E.G. Thukral (ed.), *Big Dams: Displaced People, Rivers of Sorrow, Rivers of Change*, Sage Publications, New Delhi, 1992, pp. 173–4.

60. Chambers, *Managing Canal Irrigation*, p. 20.

61. Adams, *Wasting the Rain*, p. 164.

62. Chambers, *Managing Canal Irrigation*, p. 24.

63. Ibid., p. 23. See also World Bank, 'India', Vol. II, p. 15.

64. World Bank, 'India', Vol. I, p. 16.

65. R. Ram, 'Benefits of the Sardar Sarovar Project: Are the Claims Reliable?', in W.F. Fisher (ed.), *Towards Sustainable Development? Struggling Over India's Narmada River*, M.E. Sharpe, Armonk, NY 1995, pp. 124, 128. See also H. Thakker, letter to Director-General, World Bank OED et al., 13 June 1995.

66. Chambers, *Managing Canal Irrigation*, p. 112.

67. S. Postel, 'Water and Agriculture', in Gleick (ed.), *Water in Crisis*, p. 60.

68. World Bank, 'India', Vol. I, p. 16; Repetto, *Skimming the Water*, p. 17. The planners of Sardar Sarovar have – with the World Bank's stamp of approval – assumed a 60% efficiency (see Ram, 'Benefits of the Sardar Sarovar Project', p. 122).

69. World Bank, 'India', Vol. I, p. 37.

70. Repetto, *Skimming the Water*, p. 3; World Bank, 'Lending for Irrigation', OED Préçis 85.

71. World Bank, 'Sri Lanka: Mahaweli Ganga Development', OED Préçis 86.

72. Repetto, *Skimming the Water*, p. 4. In the Philippines, revenues of $17/ha were higher than operation and management costs of $14/ha but still far lower than the annualized cost of repaying the capital invested in project construction of $75/ha.

73. Ibid.

74. R.S. Devine, 'The Trouble With Dams', *Atlantic Monthly*, August 1995, p. 68.

75. Repetto, 'Skimming the Water', p. 18.

76. Ibid. In 1981 over one-third of the area irrigated with federal water was devoted to hay, alfalfa and other pasture.

77. K. Horta, 'Troubled Waters: World Bank Disasters Along Kenya's Tana River', *Multinational Monitor*, July/August 1994, p. 15.

78. Ibid., p. 14. See also Adams, *Wasting the Rain*, pp. 168, 178; 'Doubts Remain about Bura Economics', *World Water*, June 1992.

79. Postel, 'Water and Agriculture'; H.D. Frederiksen et al., *Water Resources Management in Asia. Volume I: Main Report*, World Bank Technical Paper 212, Washington, DC, 1993.

7

The Wise Use of Watersheds

I do not see the reason why
You do not use what lies to hand
Before you try to dam our land …
Your pipes cry out for renovation.
Your storage tanks corrode and leak;
The valves are loose, the washers weak.
I've seen the water gushing out
From every reservoir and spout.
Repair them it will cost far less
Than driving us to homelessness…
But that's just one of many things:
Plant trees; revive your wells and springs.
Guide from your roofs the monsoon rain
Into great tanks to use again.
Reduce your runoff and your waste
Rather than with unholy haste
Destroying beauty which, once gone,
The world will never look upon.

Vikram Seth, 'The Elephant and the Tragopan', 1991

Dam critics are often asked what are their alternatives to building large dams. The question begs an easy answer such as small dams, but this would not do justice to the arguments of dam opponents. For many critics oppose both the means *and the ends* of dam builders – they are not interested in alternative methods of providing water for huge irrigation schemes which dispossess small farmers for the benefit of agribusiness, alternative energy sources to feed the wasteful habits of cities and industries, or alternative ways of wiping out floods on which rural people and ecosystems depend.

If the question is turned from 'what are the alternatives to dams?' to 'how can we enable people to obtain adequate and equitable supplies of water and energy far into the future, reduce the destructiveness of floods, and protect our watersheds from degradation?', then it can be properly answered. This chapter describes some of the innumerable technologies, land and water management practices, and forms of social organization which can help satisfy human needs and desires for food and fibre, water and protection from dangerous floods, while also maintaining healthy rivers. Sustainable energy technologies and practices are discussed in Chapter 8.

A defining feature of most of the technologies described below is that they are small scale. Just because a technology is small, however, does not guarantee that it will not have undesired social and environmental consequences – or that it will work. Ian Smillie, former Director of the Canadian volunteer aid agency CUSO, notes that the fashion for appropriate technology among aid donors in the 1970s 'left the Third World littered with windmills that didn't turn, solar water heaters that wouldn't heat, and biogas experiments that were full of hot air before they started'.[1]

Experience shows that the socio-economic and political context in which technologies and policies are applied is the key to their success or failure, and to which sections of society end up benefiting most from them. It also shows that what works well in one community or country will not necessarily work elsewhere. If 'appropriate' technologies are to fulfil their potential to meet human needs in an equitable and non-destructive fashion, they should ideally be instigated by the people who are to benefit from them; where they are not, the supposed beneficiaries must understand what the technology is, how it works, and who stands to gain and to lose. Most important, the people in whose name the technology is being installed should willingly accept it and participate in its implementation.

Managing the Land to Manage the Water

> ...the belief that the social dilemmas created by the machine can be solved merely by inventing more machines is today a sign of half-baked thinking which verges close to quackery.
>
> Lewis Mumford, *Technics and Civilization*, 1934

Any sensible strategy of freshwater management must aim to have healthy rivers which to the greatest extent possible are unpolluted, supportive of a wide diversity of lifeforms, and able to flood according to their natural pattern. Achieving a healthy river requires a healthy watershed: the two cannot be separated. Where watersheds are degraded by deforestation, unsustainable farming practices and urbanization, then rivers will also be degraded. Maintaining or restoring watersheds with forests, wetlands and healthy soils minimizes damaging flash floods and the risk of drought, cuts down soil erosion and so the amount of sediments washed into the riverbed, increases the ability of the river system to break down and filter pollutants, and provides diverse wildlife habitats.

Often when a large dam is advocated as a means of flood control or water storage the best alternative is not a small dam or other technology, but the regeneration of watershed forests. Hydrologically, forests and the soils under them act like a sponge, soaking up rainfall and floods and then gradually releasing the water into the river or allowing it to percolate into aquifers. When the forests are cleared, the speed at which rain falling on a watershed runs into its rivers is greatly increased. In semi-arid areas, where a whole year's rain can fall in just a few intense storms, the deforestation of watersheds can greatly amplify the seasonality of rivers, leading to disastrous floods in the wet season and long droughts in the dry. The most notorious example of this is Cheerapunji in northeast India, one of the world's wettest places, with an average rainfall of more than 9 metres. Illegal logging and the expansion of farmland have denuded the once lushly forested slopes of the region, and it now suffers floods for three to four months and severe water shortages for the rest of the year.[2]

The long-term hydrological effect of deforestation depends on what type of land use follows. Some agroforestry systems can more or less replicate the hydrological role of the original forest. Heavy grazing, on the other hand, which prevents vegetation from regenerating and compacts the soil under hooves, will ensure the continuation of high rates of run-off. Urbanization, by covering the land with an impermeable layer of roads and roofs, and funnelling rainwater through sewers and drains, can drastically speed up the rate at which stormwater (polluted with oil, petrol, lead and other contaminants washed off the streets) enters a river.[3]

It is often assumed that the loss of forests not only leads to greater run-off during storms but also reduces local or regional rainfall. A hundred years of vegetation and rainfall data from India have indicated a tendency towards fewer days with rain, and less rainfall in total, as local deforestation increases.[4] There is, however, little definitive scientific evidence linking vegetation loss and decreasing rain, although this may mainly be due to the difficulty in distinguishing between the many factors which affect rainfall. A study of the watershed of the Madden Dam, which supplies water for the Panama Canal, indicated that there was little difference in the annual run-off between forested areas and those which had been cleared for farming. There was, however, a marked change in the distribution of run-off from the deforested areas, with higher flood peaks and reduced dry season flows. These hydrological changes have caused dry season water shortages in the canal.[5]

As well as worsening floods and drought, the degradation of watershed vegetation also boosts soil erosion. Farming and grazing have increased the annual sediment load of the world's rivers from an estimated 9 billion tonnes to perhaps as much as 45 billion tonnes. Apart from its consequences for the capacity of reservoirs and irrigation canals, increasing the sediments washed into rivers can worsen flooding by raising the level of the riverbed, and can also damage riverine lifeforms in a number of ways. Severe soil erosion also drastically reduces agricultural productivity.[6]

The draining and ploughing of floodplains and riverine wetlands has had a similar effect in hydrological terms to the loss of upland forests. A study by the Illinois State Water Survey found that every 1 per cent increase in watershed area covered by wetlands decreased flood peaks in streams by nearly 4 per cent.[7] Marshes and other types of wetlands help keep rivers healthy in other ways, such as by naturally filtering pollutants and excess nutrients from sewage and agricultural run-off, trapping sediments, and by providing habitat for fish and other riverine organisms. An estimated 87 million hectares of wetlands, most of them freshwater marshes, have been destroyed in the US since colonial times. Today less than 100 million hectares of US wetlands remain. Along the lower Mississippi, nearly four-fifths of the floodplain hardwood forests have been lost to agriculture. European floodplain marshes and forests have suffered even worse the depredations of river regulation and channelization, intensive agriculture and urban sprawl. Around 90 per cent of the former floodplain of the Rhine in Germany has been drained and developed.[8]

Protect and restore

Given the effects of the abuse of watershed ecosystems, part of the answer to the water problems experienced in many areas of the world lies in protecting forests and wetlands where they still exist, and regenerating watersheds which have been degraded. If this is not done then no amount of new dams or other technologies will be able to prevent droughts and floods, and the performance of existing dams will continue to worsen.

Deforestation is propelled by numerous intertwined forces, especially excessive commercial logging, ranching and other forms of agricultural expansion, and development projects like mines, dams, plantations and roads. Curtailing these forces means taking measures such as strict controls on logging, reforming land tenure laws outside forest areas so that access to land is more equitably distributed and there are fewer landless poor forced to clear the forest, and halting government subsidies and support for land clearance and destructive development projects.

As well as land reform outside the forests, the granting of secure tenure to indigenous forest peoples, and to harvesters of non-timber forest products such as the rubber-tappers of Brazil, is also vital. People who directly depend on the survival of the forest have historically shown themselves to be its best protectors: communities from the Karen ethnic minority in Thailand, for example, strictly conserve forests which they know to be a source of water for their rice paddies.[9]

Many traditional agricultural methods have been developed which help reduce the negative hydrological consequences of farming watersheds, including the terracing of steep hillsides, and agroforestry and other forms of multiple cropping which minimize the area of soil directly exposed to rainfall. Modern agricultural researchers are also finding methods, many copied from traditional techniques, of growing crops which minimize run-off and erosion. One of the key techniques of organic agriculture – building up soil organic matter by adding compost and manures – greatly increases the ability of the soil to retain moisture, with a proportionate reduction in the amount of water which runs off.[10]

The protection of floodplain wetlands depends on halting the construction of dams and other river engineering projects and overturning agricultural and urban development policies which promote wetland draining and paving. In places, protecting the rights of traditional wetland farmers, fishers, hunters and gatherers, herders and ranchers will also protect the wetlands. Education about the ecological importance of wetlands, and the recognition of their recreational value, will also help to halt their destruction.[11]

Flood Management

> Rivers [said sixth-century BC Taoist engineer Chia Jang] were like the mouths of infants – if one tried to stop them up they only yelled the louder or were suffocated.
>
> Joseph Needham, *Science and Civilization in China*, Vol. 4, 1971

Bangladesh consists largely of the huge floodplain where three of the world's largest rivers, the Meghna, Brahmaputra and Ganges, intermingle and fan out to meet the sea. The Bangladeshis' language reflects their history of living and dying with floods. Bengali distinguishes between abnormally severe floods, termed *bonna*, and the more frequent rainy season floods, or *barsha*, which Bangladeshi villagers do not consider a threat 'but rather a necessity for survival'.[12] Around the world, the failure of conventional flood control measures is creating political space for those who believe that flood damage can best be reduced by managing floods rather than trying to halt them – in essence, by adapting to *barsha* and minimizing the probability and destructiveness of *bonna*, instead of vainly trying to stop all floods.

The debate between flood 'controllers' and 'managers' is an ancient one, harkening back to arguments between Confucian 'contractionists' and Taoist 'expansionists' over whether China's unruly rivers should be constricted between high embankments, or allowed to spread out over their natural floodplains.[13] In the US, the debate dates back at least to the 1850s, when Congress was advised that large areas of the Mississippi floodplain should be used as flood storage and overflow areas. These expansionist views were passed over, however, in favour of those of the Army Corps of Engineers, who recommended embanking the Mississippi in a single channel isolated from its floodplain. This 'structural' approach was dominant for more than a century throughout the US but in recent decades has been losing scientific and public credibility.

Today, floodplain management involving non-structural methods is strongly in the ascendant. In 1993, massive flooding along the Missouri and Upper Mississippi – two of the most dammed and embanked rivers in the world – took at least 38 lives, and caused damage costing an estimated $12–$16 billion. James Durkay, the Corps of Engineers' assistant director of civil works, told the journal *Civil Engineering* in January 1994 that after the 'Great Flood of 1993', 'it's unlikely you'll see more reservoirs or more levees' on the biggest river system in the US.[14]

The principle of floodplain management is to allow some land to flood so that other land can stay dry – letting floodplain wetlands play their natural role of providing flood storage while strengthening the protection for buildings at risk from exceptional floods. Flood management requires regulations which discourage new floodplain development, financial incentives for people living in the riskiest areas to move to higher ground, improved flood warning systems, strengthened embankments around urban areas, floodproofing of farm buildings and other isolated structures by elevating them or building ring-dikes around them, and allowing the most threatened floodplain farmland to revert to wetland. Several entire small towns in the Mississippi Basin decided to move to higher ground after the 1993 flood, and hundreds more are considering moving at least some of their buildings. Thousands of hectares of the most flood-prone farmland in the basin are being bought up by conservationists and government agencies to be turned into wetland wildlife refuges.[15]

A similar change in attitudes to rivers and floods is underway in Europe. 'We've paved over too many meadows and straightened too many rivers', Josef Leinen, environment minister for the German state of Saarland, told reporters after the severe flooding on the Rhine in early 1994. A decade before, a Franco-German agreement was signed to renew wetlands along the Rhine and so help both reduce flood damage downstream and restore some of the floodplain ecosystem. The plan has moved slowly, mainly due to the cost of buying out landowners, but by 1995 two spill-over areas had been created on the German side of the Rhine.[16]

The main justification for the planned 75-metre-high Serre de la Fare Dam on France's upper Loire was that it would prevent the recurrence of floods which killed eight people in a village near the town of Le Puy in 1980. As an integral part of their campaign against Serre de la Fare, the Le Puy-based activist group SOS Loire Vivante worked with hydrologists and engineers to devise an alternative flood control strategy which would not entail the destruction of part of one of Europe's most beautiful stretches of river. SOS Loire Vivante's strategy is based on five elements: improving the flood warning system; strict enforcement of regulations against construction in areas most at risk; improved protection for the most threatened buildings; minor works to clear the riverbed and banks of obstacles to the free flow of water; and creating a committee of local residents, elected officials, NGOs and businesses to oversee the implementation of the plan. When the government confirmed in January 1994 that it would not build Serre de la Fare, SOS Loire Vivante's flood management strategy was adopted by the local authorities.[17]

Farming Drylands without Large Dams

> The desert shall rejoice and blossom as the rose.
>
> Isaiah 35:1,7

Around two-fifths of the world's land surface is defined as hyperarid, arid, semiarid or dry subhumid. Around 70 per cent of these drylands are in developing countries.[18] Dry areas are characterized not just by low rainfall, but also by its unpredictability and extreme seasonality. In a hyperarid zone, few years would ever bring enough rain to grow crops without irrigation water from outside; in arid zones, rainfed farming is marginal, successful in some years but frequently struck by years, or clusters of years, in which drought can cause almost total crop failure. In semiarid zones, rainfall is usually sufficient for farming, but droughts still occur frequently enough for crop failure to be an ever present threat.

Numerous societies have successfully adapted to the harsh and unpredictable dryland environment. It would make far more sense to encourage their traditional economies than to attempt to convert them to environmentally and economically ruinous modern irrigation schemes. Traditional herders like the Tuaregs of the Sahara and Sahel, the Maasai of East Africa and the Mongols of Central Asia survive by moving with their herds to where the rains fall. According to the Institute for Development Anthropology, the pastoral production systems of these nomads

> ...are not only environmentally sustainable, they also cost-effectively allow for the conversion of otherwise agriculturally non-productive lands into such useful products as milk, manure (for fuel and fertilizer), hides and skins, traction and meat. These systems also support ways of life that provide their people with meaning and self-respect.[19]

Strategies to increase production on drylands must therefore act to remove the forces, especially the expropriation of land and water, which are destroying pastoral economies. Colonial and post-colonial governments and development agencies, with the age-old hostility of settled peoples toward nomads, have usually considered pastoralism a primitive and inefficient technology leading to overgrazing, desertification and low livestock production. Yet efforts to 'develop' the pastoralist economy – especially through the digging of wells and the enclosure and privatization of commonly held lands – have largely achieved the opposite of their stated aims, so that rangelands are now more degraded than ever before.[20]

Harvesting the rain...

Farmers in very dry areas have developed – and are developing – numerous systems of conserving soil and water which enable them to make the most of limited and unpredictable rainfall. These systems are often highly effective, finely adapted to local ecological and social conditions, and can outperform introduced methods based on modern agronomic knowledge. Nevertheless, traditional dryland farming techniques have largely been regarded by 'experts' as unscientific and backward and have therefore largely been ignored.[21]

Numerous traditional methods of what is termed 'water harvesting' have been developed to reduce the risk of farming drylands. One of these techniques, known as 'run-off farming', which works by collecting water running off slopes and directing it onto fields below, can enable crops to be grown on all but the very driest lands. The Nabateans, a people who created a wealthy kingdom in the Negev Desert of southern Israel in the late first millennium BC, used run-off farming to support tens of thousands of people in a region where the mean winter rainfall is only 100 millimetres. Even today, 1,300 years after their original builders faded into history, the Bedouins of the Negev still use the Nabatean fields to grow fodder for their goats.[22]

Nabatean water harvesting is thought to have begun with the terracing of small, seasonal creek beds. The terrace walls slowed down the flow of the creek when the rains came, spreading the water over the small fields and trapping eroded soils. As the system developed, ridges of stone and earth were built diagonally across the hillsides above the creeks, channelling the water down to individual fields. To increase the probability of receiving adequate water, the Nabateans cleared the catchment slopes of stone and gravel and whatever sparse vegetation managed to grow. Modern experiments have shown that clearing the ground in this way can increase the run-off from the Negev catchments by as much as a fifth.[23]

Two thousand years ago in the southwest of the United States, the Anasazi ('ancient ones' in the Navajo language) developed a number of water-harvesting technologies which bear many similarities to those of the Nabateans. The Anasazi harvested rain falling on the bare, flat tops of the dramatic rock chimneys known as mesas. The water running off the mesas in seasonal creeks was impounded behind small earth dams and then channelled to fields and gardens via ditches and stone headgates.[24]

'Run-off farming' is still in use in the deserts of New Mexico and Arizona today, supplying water for both crops and livestock. Catchment treatment methods include Nabatean-style land clearing, 'soil modification' with water-repellent chemicals, and various impermeable coverings such as concrete and rubber sheeting. Gary Frazier, a researcher with the US Department of Agriculture's Southwest Rangeland Watershed Research Center, believes that the various types of run-off farming systems are 'technically sound methods of water supply for most parts of the world'.[25]

In areas with slightly higher rainfall, water-harvesting aims to reduce run-off, rather than induce it, and to use the rain as close as possible to where it falls. The Dogon people of southern Mali have a number of methods which enable them to grow crops on the thin soil of their drought-prone, rocky plateau. The most widespread is the heaping of earth and weeds into small mounds between plants. The mounds both help to reduce run-off and serve as mini-compost heaps, building up the fertility of the soil. Where there are loose stones available, the Dogon use them to build lines across their fields. Where the soil is deep enough, grids of small square basins ('microcatchments') are excavated which trap the rainfall where it falls. Another Dogon technique is to dig pits for individual plants; these collect both water and leaves blowing across the ground, the latter acting as a manure and a mulch (a moisture-conserving soil cover).[26]

...and harvesting the flood

In dry areas through which large rivers flow, traditional 'flood cropping' techniques are common. Along some rivers the crop is planted before the flood arrives and harvested either from canoes or after the flood has receded. Rice has probably been grown in this way in Africa for at least 3,000 years. So-called 'floating rice' varieties can grow at the speed of the rising flood: some Asian types can keep up with floods as deep as 4 or 5 metres. Flood-recession farming involves using the moisture, sediment and nutrients left behind after seasonal floods. It is common along Africa's great dryland rivers such as the Niger and the Senegal and also practised in other dry areas such as the semiarid northeast of Brazil.[27]

When the main flood recedes, some water is usually left behind in swamps and pools. More water can be deliberately trapped behind embankments, and in pits. The basin irrigation of Egypt, which fed the country for at least 50 centuries before the regulation of the Nile for cotton growing began in the nineteenth century, was a type of recession agriculture where the flood and its silt were retained in diked basins. A similar technique was developed in the Damodar and Ganges deltas in Bengal some 2,000 years ago.[28]

India has a wealth of different types of water harvesting systems. Long low earthen banks to impound the monsoon run-off and allow it to soak into the ground are known as *khadins* in the desert state of Rajasthan. A *khadin* system comprises two parts, a rocky catchment slope, and the cultivated area behind the embankment – which over time builds up a deep and fertile soil. Some of this silt is dug out by villagers each year and spread on their fields as fertilizer. The embankments are typically 300 to 500 metres long and 1 to 3 metres high. The upkeep of the embankments, the cultivation of the *khadin* bed, and the management of the groves of trees and pasture which often surround the *khadins* are undertaken collectively by community organizations. Although they are not included in official Indian irrigation statistics, researchers believe that around 300,000 hectares are watered by *khadins* and similar indigenous methods built to increase soil moisture and trap silt.[29]

The use of *khadins*, however, has been declining. Community organizations have been weakened and often replaced by state-appointed officials. Government-built dams and canals, especially the massive Indira Gandhi Canal, have become the favoured methods of watering the desert. In recent years, however, there has been a revival of interest in traditional water-harvesting structures in the state. An ashram set up near Jaipur in 1985 by a group of social activists began to encourage local farmers to start constructing *khadins* again. By 1994, 200 had been built and 40 villages had set up new *gram sabhas* (self-governing committees) to manage the *khadins* along with the other affairs of the community. Grain production in some areas has doubled or trebled. The local authorities, however, declared the new *khadins* illegal on the grounds that water and watercourses were government property. The *khadins*, claimed officials, were competing with a local government-built dam and were unsafe. But after the dam was washed away in a heavy downpour, and the villagers' embankments were left standing, the *khadins* were declared legal.[30]

The most widespread vernacular irrigation system in India and Sri Lanka is the tank, the term given to a small reservoir impounded by a dam across a seasonally flooded depression or gully. Unlike *khadins*, southern Indian tanks have outlets which operators use to control the flow of water into channels leading to nearby fields. Individual tanks can irrigate anything from a few hectares to several hundred. Tanks have been used for thousands of years, and incredible numbers have been built – India is estimated to have more than half a million tanks irrigating more than 3 million hectares.[31] Parts of South India are so covered in tanks that the land has been described as 'a surface of overlapping fish-scales'.[32] Over a quarter of Sri Lanka's total irrigated area was thought to be watered from tanks in the late 1970s.[33]

Although tanks have been proven by centuries of experience to be socially, economically and ecologically appropriate techniques of water and land management, over the last few decades their use has steadily declined and many are now abandoned. The main reason for the decline of the tanks appears to be the government promotion of privately owned tube-wells (deep, drilled wells), which increase private control over water, formerly a common resource. The result, says south Indian NGO worker K.A.S. Mani, is that the farms with their own wells are 'pockets of prosperity in the midst of ecological degradation and widespread poverty'.[34]

The people's dam

> Everybody, irrespective of whether he/she is rich or poor, has equal right over the water given by nature and stored by the efforts of common labour in which he/she has actively participated. Nobody should have special benefits in any way, is my firm belief and conviction.
>
> Pledge of Baliraja Smriti Dam water users' cooperative

While reviving traditional technologies and building modern structures on the principles of small size and communal ownership and maintenance would help immensely toward resolving India's chronic drought problems, it is also vital to give communities rights to their local water sources and allow them to find solutions based on how they themselves perceive their needs. The Baliraja Smriti Dam in the Indian state of Maharashtra is an excellent example of what communities can do if they have control over their water.

In the 1970s, drought, deforestation, diversions for water-intensive crops like sugarcane, and the mining of riverbed sand caused the small Yerala River in Maharashtra state to dry up for all but a few weeks at the height of the monsoon. The local water table fell and wells ran dry. Government-built dams and irrigation schemes worsened the villagers' plight by encouraging large landowners to grow more water-intensive sugarcane.

The response of two villages on the banks of the Yerala to their water crisis and the government's inability to resolve it was to build their own small dam. Work started in 1986, with voluntary contributions of labour from villagers and students, and donated technical help from an engineer. Just a few months later, however, the dam was suddenly declared illegal by the state government. 'What upset the authorities', said a March 1989 article in the *Times of India*, 'was that they found themselves superfluous to the entire process.' After more than a year of negotiations, the government finally approved the dam and agreed that the mining of riverbed sand by outside contractors be stopped, and that permits for limited mining instead be given to the villagers. Sales of sand, together with interest-free loans from supporters in nearby cities, helped to pay the 300,000 rupee ($10,000) cost of the dam, which was inaugurated in March 1989.

The Baliraja Smriti Dam is managed by a water users' cooperative comprised of all the families from the two villages. Water stored behind the dam, 4.5 metres high and 120 metres across, can irrigate 380 hectares. No families were displaced by its 600,000 cubic metre reservoir. Water entitlements depend on family size rather than the size of land-holdings, so that landless families get shares of water which they can either sell for cash or use on leased land. Water can only be used on drought-resistant crops like millet and groundnut, and at certain times of the year it is reserved for drinking. The seasonal cropping schedule for the areas to be irrigated is worked out by consultation with all the villagers. Some water is also set aside for tree nurseries with the aim of restoring the tree cover of the local watershed.

Researchers Enakshi Ganguly Thukral and Machhindra Sakate say that:

> The significance of the dam lies not so much in itself as in the concepts underlying it: that water belongs to every member of society irrespective of caste, sex or creed, and that a viable efficient system is possible only if the community is committed to it.... It is not to say that small dams like the Baliraja are always the solution. The solutions have to be location- and situation-specific. What is important is that the solution be based on people's needs and involve their participation.[35]

Going Underground

A major benefit of water harvesting – and of watershed regeneration in general – is that it encourages the recharge of groundwater. Storing water underground has several advantages over storage in surface reservoirs; in particular, it does not evaporate and it is protected from contamination by human and animal wastes. In India, drinking water is not taken directly from tanks and *khadins*, but from nearby wells which exploit the water seeping from the impoundment.

'Groundwater mining' – the pumping of groundwater at a faster rate than it is recharged – is an extremely serious problem in many parts of the world. Between 1946 and 1986, for example, the proliferation of irrigation tubewells caused the water table beneath parts of the Indian state of Karnataka to drop from 8 metres below the surface, to 48. The water table beneath Gujarat's biggest city, Ahmedabad, has fallen from 10 metres in the 1940s, to 100 metres in the 1990s.[36] Traditional dug wells cannot seriously deplete aquifers as they are limited both in the depth to which they can be dug, and by the ability of human and animal muscle to draw the water.

More sophisticated traditional methods of groundwater utilization also exist, the most famous of which are the *qanats* of Iran, tunnels dug into upland aquifers which deliver water by gravity to the plains below. Similar types of groundwater tunnels are found throughout the Middle and Near East and even as far away as Spain and northern Chile. Around 40,000 *qanats* are estimated to have been excavated in Iran over the last 3,000 years, and about half of this number were still in operation in the early 1970s. A decade before, three-quarters of Iran's total water supply was delivered through *qanats*. More recently it has become cheaper for farmers and cities to raise water with motorized pumps than to maintain the tunnels. Unlike the *qanats*, which only take water from aquifers at the rate they are replenished, the pumps have led to the mining of aquifers, and groundwater levels are falling, drying out the surviving *qanats*.

Everywhere water tables fall, wells must be deepened and greater amounts of human, animal or electrical energy expended to draw the water to the surface. Drilling wells and pumping water are expensive, so as the groundwater recedes water sinks further and further out of reach of the poor. Jayanta Bandyopadhyay of Geneva's International Academy of the Environment states that increasing water shortages in rural India are largely due to 'the artificial creation of groundwater drought' rather than to a reduction in precipitation.[37] In the state of Gujarat alone, groundwater depletion means that 12,000 villages now have no 'permanent and reliable' source of water – a fact which is used as one of the main justifications for the Sardar Sarovar Project.[38]

Sinking water tables in coastal areas can cause saline water to seep into aquifers, ultimately making them useless for either drinking water or irrigation. Nearly half the handpumps in coastal areas of Gujarat were reported in 1986 to be yielding saline water. Drinking water supplied by groundwater under a number of cities and towns along the eastern and southern coasts of the US has been contaminated by saline ingress. Aquifer depletion can also cause the land above to subside, with serious consequences for the stability of buildings: Beijing is sinking at an annual rate of around 10 centimetres and its water table dropping by up to 2 metres a year; some *barrios* in Mexico City sink by as much 30 centimetres a year. The ground under Houston, Texas, has subsided by more than 2 metres over the last four decades.[39] In areas such as rural India where most drinking water comes from hand-pumped groundwater, shrinking and salinized aquifers can force people to abandon entire villages.

Reversing groundwater mining is far from an easy task. Development projects and subsidies which promote rapid groundwater abstraction have powerful agricultural and industrial beneficiaries. The nature of groundwater – it is hidden, it is very difficult to measure, and it is not discrete but is intrinsically linked to surface water flows – makes it very hard to know what pumping rate would be sustainable. Also, the nature of the abstraction of groundwater – usually through numerous privately owned wells – means that it is difficult to control. Nevertheless, limits on groundwater pumping are a must if the world is to move towards the equitable and sustainable use of its freshwater. In the US, the state of Arizona pioneered legal controls on groundwater mining with a 1980 law which requires that groundwater basins being depleted achieve a balance between pumping and recharge by the year 2025. US environmentalists have advocated a 'groundwater depletion tax' on any abstractions which exceed natural recharge; a similar measure to this has been in effect since 1991 in the area around the Arizonan city of Phoenix.[40]

Parallel with the need to halt the overpumping of groundwater is the urgent task of recharging depleted aquifers. Most natural groundwater recharge occurs through the beds of rivers and the gravels of alluvial floodplains; protecting watersheds from urbanization and other types of development – and from flood control – thus helps maintain the level of recharge. In Rajasthan and elsewhere, 'percolation tanks' are traditionally built solely for the artificial recharge of groundwater. The Rajasthani structures, known as *rapats*, are small masonry tanks built on highly permeable sandy soils. Modern methods of artificial groundwater recharge, such as injecting water down wells or diverting rivers over alluvial gravel, are in use in a number of areas, especially California, the Netherlands and Germany.[41]

In Gujarat, a number of NGO projects are recharging groundwater through the building of water harvesting structures like small check dams and bunds, and the regeneration of watershed vegetation.[42] Ashvin Shah, a Gujarati who works for the American Society of Civil Engineers, calculates that the widespread implementation of small-scale water-harvesting schemes in Gujarat could easily collect a fifth of the rain which falls on the state, an amount 50 per cent higher than the water supposed to be delivered through the canals of the Sardar Sarovar Project. Shah believes that groundwater recharge, water harvesting and the use of water from existing reservoirs could help solve Gujarat's water crisis over a relatively short period, and, unlike SSP, could help reverse the growing gap between rich and poor farmers in the state. Shah's plan, like other suggested alternatives to SSP, also stresses the need to reduce water demand, especially by replacing crops like sugarcane with less thirsty ones, and increasing the efficiency of irrigation.[43]

Traditional Diversions

> Respect the ancient system
> And do not lightly modify it.
>
> Inscription in temple above 2,200-year-old irrigation scheme, Kuanhsien, China

Although there is no clear distinction between the different categories of indigenous irrigation, there is a general trend toward increased complexity of design and management with systems in wetter areas, where water needs to be diverted and delivered to the right fields at the right time and in the right amount, and where the control of excess water can be as important as adding to its supply. Several important features are common to most traditional irrigation systems: one is the small size of the systems and of their individual components such as dams and channels; a second is that they are largely built and managed by their users, rather than by state officials; another is that they have largely proven to be efficient, to promote the equitable distribution of water, and to be ecologically sustainable over the long term.

Traditional systems typically serve an individual village, although sometimes several or more villages are served by a single scheme. In Asia, where most of the world's irrigation is concentrated, indigenous schemes generally cover between 10 and 100 hectares, but some can provide water to several thousand hectares. The larger schemes are usually broken down into smaller sub-units for management purposes. Although most of the individual schemes are small, collectively they cover a huge area. Despite the almost total lack of official support for indigenous irrigation, it still accounts for three-quarters of irrigated land in Nepal, and about half the irrigated land in the Philippines.[44]

In some traditional systems, water is diverted directly into a channel without any obstruction being built in the river. More commonly, water is taken from behind a small wood, rock or earth dam. The Sonjo, who irrigate the slopes of Mount Kilimanjaro in Tanzania, for example, divert water with brushwood dams up to 3 metres high.[45] Small dams of this type are easily destroyed by floods, a feature which can enhance the sustainability of the overall system as the floods then wash away most of the sediments behind the dams. Because the dams are built with local materials and labour, rebuilding them is not usually a major expense. Sedimentation behind the small dams built as part of the *muang faai* systems of Thailand is minimized because silt and sand can pass through the sapling and bamboo structures.[46]

One of the few state-run irrigation schemes which has stood the test of time is the remarkable Kuanhsien system, built on the Min River in southwest China around 230 BC. Hundreds of thousands of hectares near the city of Chengdu are still irrigated with water diverted at Kuanhsien (the name means 'Irrigation City'). Although the system as a whole is huge, its individual parts are all relatively small, simple and cheap to repair. The diversion is achieved with a structure of piled stones in the middle of the riverbed known as the 'Fish Snout'. This feeds water into a 40-metre-deep rock cut known as 'Cornucopia Channel' and then eventually into thousands of distributary channels. During the dry season each year repairs are made to the Fish Snout and sediment dug out from the bottom of the channels.[47]

One of the keys to the successful management of vernacular systems is that the managers are either the farmers themselves or officials whom small groups of farmers elect, and who are directly accountable to them.[48] Larry Lohmann and Chatchewan Tongdeelert's description of *muang faai* management is widely applicable to vernacular irrigation systems in humid Asia:

> Keeping a *muang faai* system going demands cooperation and collective management, sometimes within a single village, sometimes across ... many villages. The rules or common agreements arrived at during the yearly meeting ... govern how water is to be distributed, how flow is to be controlled according to seasonal schedules, how barriers are to be maintained and channels dredged, how conflicts over water use are to be settled, and how the forest around the reservoir is to be preserved as a guarantee of a steady water supply and a source of materials to repair the system. Despite this variety of tasks, management systems are generally simple, unbureaucratic and independent (sometimes defiantly so) of government authority.[49]

The right to an equitable share of the system's available water is a common feature of indigenous irrigation, and an important distinction from the usually extremely inequitable distribution of water on government-run canal schemes. On the *zanjeras* of the northern Philippines, each member is allotted an equal amount of land divided into several plots located in different parts of the watered area. The inevitable inequity in water availability between those at the head and the tail of the system is therefore ironed out as all the farmers hold parcels of land at both ends of the network.[50] According to Lohmann and Tongdeelert, the 'fundamental principle of water rights on *muang faai* is that everyone must get enough to survive; while many patterns of distribution are possible, none can violate this basic tenet.'[51] A study of Nepalese irrigation found that only one in every eleven professionally managed government systems were able to deliver water to their 'tailenders' during the dry season; the corresponding figure for traditional farmer-managed systems was one in four. Overall agricultural productivity was found to be higher on many of the farmer-managed systems.[52]

Traditional irrigation associations often regulate the use of common resources other than water, such as community forests, pastures and land used for rainfed farming. *Zanjera* rules only allow water users to catch fish and shrimp in their canals and rivers at a few times of the year, so ensuring the sustainability of an important supplemental food source.[53] The effectiveness of these rules is shown by the fact that the areas where indigenous irrigation survives also tend to be areas where natural ecosystems are best preserved.[54] The ecological health of the areas surrounding indigenous irrigation areas are usually protected not only by rules but also by rituals and beliefs which connect the spiritual and material well-being of the community and the smooth functioning of irrigation with the integrity of features such as sacred forests, springs or mountains. The inseparability of the ritual and spiritual with the functional aspects of irrigation is illustrated by the fact that the Balinese irrigation institutions known as *subaks* spend well over half of their budget on ritual feasts, ceremonies and offerings.[55]

The ecological sophistication of *subak* management is highly impressive. Anthropologists J. Stephen Lansing and James N. Kremer of the University of Southern California describe how by regulating the rate and timing of water flowing into terraced rice paddies the *subaks* create a cycle of wet and dry phases which 'alters soil pH ... determines the activity of micro-organisms, circulates mineral nutrients, fosters the growth of nitrogen-fixing cyanobacteria, excludes weeds, stabilizes soil temperature, and ... prevents nutrients from being leached into the sub-soil'.[56]

Because the community as a whole is so closely involved in the management of indigenous irrigation, because of the ritual importance of irrigation, and because in the last resort fines and other punishments can be meted out, individual members of traditional systems are unlikely to break the rules. This contrasts sharply with state-run canal irrigation schemes where corruption and rule-breaking are usually rampant. Where rules are broken, then the efficiency of the system as a whole is reduced, and so farmers who are not prepared to bribe or steal water will be less likely to get the supplies they need, creating a vicious circle where corruption breeds inefficiency, which in turn breeds corruption. With indigenous schemes, the opposite happens: an efficient and fair system encourages the members to follow the rules, which keeps the system efficient and fair.

Although studies repeatedly show the sophistication of traditional irrigation, governments and aid agencies have usually ignored such studies and, with little understanding of the productivity or complexity of the traditional systems, have sought to 'improve' them with modern materials, agricultural inputs and professional management. Often these interventions cause yields to fall in the long run – sometimes because they are technologically unsound, but probably more often because they destroy indigenous water users' associations by turning over to the state the responsibility for system upkeep. In doing so they can have terrible consequences for the economic and cultural well-being of the community. David Groenfeldt, formerly of the Sri Lanka-based International Irrigation Management Institute, offers sound proverbial advice for experts intending to 'improve' indigenous systems: 'If it ain't broke, don't fix it.'[57]

Modern Irrigation: Back to the Future

> A sustainable agriculture is one that accepts and works carefully within the firm limits of the water cycle. It is one that exercises restraint on the demands it makes on the cycle. It is farming as close as possible to the nature of water, flowing with the current rather than obstructing it...
>
> Donald Worster, 'Thinking Like A River', 1984

Most recent projections from academics and international agencies concerned with world agriculture agree that increased irrigation development costs and growing competition for water from cities and industries mean that future increases in crop production will have to come from rainfed farming, small-scale irrigation and improving management and infrastructure on existing large schemes.[58] 'Given the dwindling sources of new water and decreasing returns to new irrigation,' said a 1995 internal evaluation of 50 years of World Bank lending for irrigation, 'the Bank should shift emphasis – from financing new irrigation to upgrading existing irrigation.' The evaluation concluded that irrigation management bodies needed to be made more financially and ecologically accountable to the irrigators; that large projects should be subdivided into small units managed by groups of water users; that the users' groups should be free from government interference and should be able to set their own punishments for rule breakers; and that the Bank should 'promote community involvement in all aspects of irrigation'.[59] The measures recommended in the evaluation are basically those developed on indigenous systems many centuries ago.

While they are certainly on the decline, it is still premature to ring the death knell for big dam and irrigation schemes. Experience shows that there is a major difference between the World Bank's policy staff issuing recommendations, and its lending staff and borrower governments actually implementing them. Furthermore, there is also a big difference between the apparent meaning of the words of development planners and what they actually mean when they are applied in projects. A vital element in the success of traditional systems is that they are based upon common property ownership – a concept which is diametrically opposed to the ideology of privatization dominant within the World Bank and many other development institutions and governments.

With indigenous systems, water – and often other resources too – is held in common and managed for the greater good of the community rather than any individuals within it. The privatization and enclosure of common resources are a major force behind environmental degradation all over the world. If the 'new thinking' on irrigation promotes the privatization of indigenous systems, it will lead to their destruction just as surely as would continuing to replace them with government-run schemes.[60]

Because irrigation uses such a large proportion of total water withdrawals, even small percentage reductions in the amount of water used by agriculture can make huge amounts of water available for drinking and other uses (as well as for rivers and wetlands). Cutting irrigation needs by one-tenth, calculates Sandra Postel of the Washington, DC, Worldwatch Institute, would free up enough water to roughly double domestic water use worldwide.[61] Huge increases in crop productivity per unit of water could potentially be gained through better management of canal irrigation: Robert Chambers calculates that increasing the reliability of water supplies to farmers could *triple* crop production from Indian canal schemes. Better management and modest infrastructure improvements in Pakistan, says Chambers, could save an amount of water equivalent to that supplied by three Tarbela Dams.[62]

Shrinking aquifers, rising costs and the reallocation of water from agriculture to cities have already spurred sizeable reductions in the water used on farms in the US, where the total irrigated area fell by 1 per cent between 1980 and 1990, and the average amount of water applied per hectare fell by nearly 7 per cent. Total use of irrigation water dropped by a tenth – 21 billion cubic metres.[63] In some areas the cuts in water use have been even more dramatic. Farmers in the High Plains of northwest Texas, who have for decades been rapidly mining the massive Ogallala Aquifer, have reduced their water use by more than 40 per cent from the peak reached in 1974. In nearby Kansas, farmers above the shrinking Ogallala who have taken up organic farming have cut their consumption of water by as much as half. Because they are more valuable than conventional crops, organic produce allow the same value of harvest to be grown on less land with less water.[64]

The most efficient method of delivering water to crops is 'drip irrigation', where water is delivered as directly as possible to the roots of each plant through perforated or porous pipes. With drip irrigation, evaporation and seepage losses are extremely low. Although drip irrigation was first commercialized by Israeli agronomists in the 1960s, indigenous drip methods have been used for many centuries. In northeastern India, farmers use bamboo pipes to drip spring water onto their fields. Another highly efficient indigenous method, described in 2,000-year-old Chinese agricultural treatises and used in a number of countries including Brazil and India, is clay-pot irrigation, which uses the water slowly seeping out of a pot buried beside the plant.[65]

Commercial 'micro-irrigation' – drip irrigation and the use of super-efficient sprinklers – has spread rapidly since the 1960s. In 1991, nearly 1.6 million hectares were watered with these methods, including 70 per cent of irrigated land in Cyprus, and half of irrigated land in Israel. The US had the largest area under micro-irrigation, 606,000 hectares, some 3 per cent of its irrigated land.[66] The main drawback to modern micro-irrigation is that it is very expensive to install and maintain, so that it is mainly suitable for farmers with access both to reasonable amounts of capital and to markets for high-value fruit and vegetables. Thus although drip irrigation is water efficient, it is an inappropriate technology for many parts of the world where the growing of affordable food should be the priority of agricultural policies.

The promotion of drip irrigation dovetails neatly with the strategy of agricultural development in poor countries favoured by the World Bank and others which promotes heavily capitalized operations producing out-of-season fruits, vegetables and cut flowers for export. In Kenya, for example, commercial irrigated farms producing for the European market have expanded rapidly in the last decade. Yet wealthy farmers and corporations taking over land to grow food and flowers for the well-fed abroad is – no matter how efficient their water use – only likely to worsen conditions for the impoverished majority of Kenyans.[67]

Somewhat confusingly, the term 'micro-irrigation' is also applied to the use of irrigation on a very small scale by gardeners growing for their own families or local markets. This form of micro-irrigation has great potential for increasing food security in poor areas. A noteworthy example is the gardens planted in the small valleys in Zimbabwe known as *dambos*. They are usually irrigated with water drawn from nearby wells in buckets. The individual gardens are usually less than half a hectare in size but collectively cover around 20,000 hectares, nearly 10 per cent of the 'official' irrigated area in Zimbabwe. During the 1986–87 drought, *dambos* were the only lands in some areas which yielded any of the staple maize (corn). The *dambos* can yield a wide variety of useful produce: one survey of a single large *dambo* plot found 23 different crops and 26 tree species, as well as bees, fish, reeds and fodder.[68]

A largely untapped source of water for irrigation and groundwater recharge is municipal wastewater. Reusing wastewater for irrigation is doubly beneficial as the nutrients in sewage are then used to feed crops rather than pollute waterways. Using reclaimed sewage from towns on farmlands was common in many industrialized countries until the early part of this century, when it fell out of favour, partly because of concerns over the transmission of disease. The reuse of water is most advanced in Israel, where 70 per cent of sewage is treated and then used on 19,000 hectares of cropland. Israeli researchers predict that by 2010 reused water will provide a fifth of the country's total water supply and a third of its irrigation.[69]

Fix the Pipe, Spare the River

> Each time the flush handle is yanked in an average urban Indian home, the entire daily consumption of an arid zone dweller in India goes down the drain.
>
> Ravi Chopra and Debashish Sen, People's Science Institute, New Delhi, 1991

Providing clean water to the more than 1 billion people who currently do not have access to it and supplying the water needs of growing populations, cities and industries is a daunting task. It is, however, one which can be solved given the political will and the abandonment of the belief that the only answer to water problems is to build more big water supply projects. A more sustainable, equitable – and invariably cheaper – approach is the building of smaller scale supply schemes combined with making current systems work better, reducing wastage by water users, and redirecting water from other uses, especially irrigation. It is also essential to reverse the depletion of groundwater and to protect all sources of freshwater from pollution.

Building new water supply projects is increasingly expensive as cities swell and have to try to capture their water from farther and farther afield: according to the World Bank, the cost of water from new projects for many cities will be two to three times the cost of current supplies.[70] In these cases, reducing water demand is likely to be cheaper than increasing supplies, even without taking into account the full social and environmental costs of new reservoirs. Less water used means less energy needed to pump it, treat it and heat it: installing efficient showerheads in 80 per cent of US bathrooms would reduce water use by nearly 3,000 million litres per day, and save an amount of electricity equal to the output of three large power plants.[71] Increasing the efficiency of water use also decreases the amount of polluted water discharged into rivers and other water bodies.

There is a huge potential to increase water deliveries by improving distribution infrastructure. Nearly one-third of Europe's water supply is lost through leaking and broken pipes. Sixty per cent of the water which enters the pipes of Manila's water utility is lost to leaks and illegal connections. The World Bank estimates it economically and technically feasible to keep water losses down to 10 to 20 per cent of water supplied. Singapore's water utility manages to deliver to its customers' taps 90 per cent of the water it supplies.[72]

Rural water supply systems suffer similar problems to their urban counterparts. Governments and aid agencies have invested more than $10 billion on rural water supply in developing countries in recent decades, yet almost all this money has been spent on building new schemes and very little on maintaining them once they have been completed. Anthony A. Churchill of the World Bank says that the result of these skewed priorities is that 'in country after country systems are going out of operation as fast as they are being built.'[73] The hundreds of village water supply schemes built in Nepal during the 1980s supposedly serve around a third of the country's rural population. Yet the majority have fallen into disuse before reaching even half of their design life of 20 years.[74]

Complementary to making supplies go further with better distribution systems is reducing demand by increasing the efficiency of water use. Environmental legislation, technological advances and increased water prices are combining to spur huge gains in the efficiency of industrial water use in many countries. Because industries rarely actually consume the water they use – but rather use it for heating, cooling or processing – they can recycle their water many times over. While US industries were using each litre of water supplied to them an average of less than twice in the mid-1950s, by the end of the 1990s they are predicted to be using each litre 17 times. Largely because of this increase in recycling, the total use of water by US industries fell by nearly two-fifths between 1950 and 1990, while total industrial output almost quadrupled.[75]

Dramatic drops in domestic water consumption have been achieved in a number of North American cities over the past two decades. The measures used to cut consumption include plugging leaks; subsidizing the distribution of water-efficient technologies like improved garden sprinklers and low-flush toilets that use only 6 litres per flush compared to the 16 litres used by conventional toilets; conservation publicity campaigns; encouraging drought-resistant landscaping; installing meters so that households pay for the amount of water they use; and increasing prices. A package of measures like this helped cut per capita water consumption in Tucson, Arizona, from 760 litres per person per day in the mid-1970s to 590 litres in 1992.[76] The Pacific Institute, a California water-research NGO, calculates that using only existing technology, average residential water use per person in the state could be almost halved between 1995 and 2020.[77]

An important reason why environmentalists won the decade-long battle to stop the Two Forks Dam, planned to supply water to Denver, Colorado, was that they were able to show that installing meters and water-saving devices in Denver households could save more water than the dam would supply, at about one-fifth of the dam's $1 billion cost. After the US Environmental Protection Agency vetoed Two Forks in 1990, the Denver Water Department actively promoted water use efficiency, helping to cut average household consumption by 9 per cent in just two years.[78]

In the drier areas of developing countries, even the most efficient flush toilets can be a highly inappropriate technology. Flush toilets can result in the relatively well-off appropriating the freshwater of surrounding regions – and then using it to wash their excreta and urine into the streams and rivers which provide drinking water for the local poor. Contrary to conventional opinion, much cheaper and more water-efficient technologies such as pit latrines, pour-flush toilets (where the used toilet is emptied by manually pouring water) and composting toilets are viable and healthy alternatives. 'Defecating into five gallons of drinking water each time, as promoted worldwide, is arguably the most serious impediment to urban sustainability today', believes World Bank environmental adviser Robert Goodland. Water-borne sewerage systems are also highly expensive. Investment costs for sewerage range from $150 to $600 per person, and are unaffordable in areas where average incomes may be only a few hundred dollars a year.[79]

Flush toilets are not the only technologies which encourage the wealthy to appropriate more than their just share of available water (as well as the other resources such as land, forests and fisheries which are lost to dams). Hotels, swimming pools and golf courses are increasingly worsening water shortages for local villagers in tourist destinations such as Thailand, Kenya and Goa – and justifying the construction of new dams.[80] High-consumption lifestyles require huge amounts of water. Manufacturing the average US car uses some 140,000 litres of water – an amount which could provide for all the domestic needs of a citizen in a typical developing country for nearly two years.[81]

Other water supply technologies

Just as people living in drylands have developed ingenious ways of providing water for their crops, so they have also invented technologies to catch and store water for their own use, and for their animals. These technologies can provide appropriate ways of supplying water which can be managed and maintained by local people and do not rely on expensive or unavailable imported spare parts and expertise. The Nabateans and their Negev Desert predecessors harvested water for themselves and their animals by directing hillside run-off into cisterns excavated in the rock and sealed with plaster. Many hundreds of these cisterns can still be seen in the Negev Desert today, and Bedouin herders continue to clean and use them.[82]

Many different traditional methods of collecting and storing drinking water exist in India. In areas which get a reasonable amount of rain but which for geological reasons have inadequate groundwater, rooftops are sometimes used as water collectors. In some drier areas, a small, round catchment area known as a *paytan* is cleared of vegetation and sealed with cement or a local material like pond silt or wood ash. Rain falling on the *paytan* runs into channels which drain into a covered tank.[83]

A high-tech method which can provide virtually unlimited supplies of freshwater is desalinization of sea or brackish water. Mariners have known for millennia that sweetwater can be produced by collecting the vapours of boiling saltwater. The high energy costs of desalinization, however, and its obvious need for proximity to plentiful saltwater, have limited its use to specialized applications such as military outposts on small islands, and to energy-rich, freshwater-poor coastal areas like the states of the Arabian Gulf. In 1994 the world's desalinization capacity was around 19 million cubic metres per day, around 60 per cent of it in the Middle East. The substantial energy needs of desalinization mean that it has a heavy environmental impact. Advances, however, in renewable energy and desalinization technology open the possibility that within the next few decades solar- or wind-powered desalinization plants may be economically feasible and environmentally sustainable for some arid regions.[84]

Notes

1. I. Smillie, *Mastering the Machine: Poverty, Aid and Technology*, Intermediate Technology, London 1991, p. 133. See also D. Burch, 'Appropriate Technology for the Third World: Why the Will is Lacking', *The Ecologist*, Vol. 12, No. 2, 1982; and W.M. Adams, *Wasting the Rain: Rivers, People and Planning in Africa*, Earthscan, London 1992, pp. 192, 194.

2. R. Rao, 'Water Scarcity Haunts World's Wettest Place', *Ambio*, Vol. 18, No. 5, 1989, p. 300; 'Deforestation Creates Drought in Wettest Spot of the World', *US Water News*, January 1995.

3. A. Goudie, *The Human Impact on the Natural Environment*, second edition, MIT Press, Cambridge, MA, 1987, pp. 158–62.

4. J. Bandyopadhyay, 'Riskful Confusion of Drought and Man-Induced Water

Scarcity', *Ambio*, Vol. 18, No. 5, 1989, p. 285.

5. P. Simons, 'Nobody Loves a Canal with No Water', *New Scientist*, 7 October 1989. For a short discussion of the debate over the link between rainfall and forests, see Goudie, *The Human Impact*, pp. 259–60. See also L.C.B. Molion, 'The Amazonian Forests and Climatic Stability', *The Ecologist*, Vol. 19, No. 6, 1989.

6. National Research Council, *Soil and Water Quality: An Agenda for Agriculture*, National Academy Press, Washington, DC, 1993, p. 337. Worldwide, erosion leads to crop production becoming impossible or uneconomic on around 20m ha every year.

7. S. Faber, 'Acquisition and Restoration of Flooded Agricultural Land', *River Voices*, Winter 1994.

8. E. Maltby, *Waterlogged Wealth: Why Waste the World's Wet Places?*, Earthscan, London 1986; J.A. Gore and F.D. Shields, Jr., 'Can Large Rivers Be Restored?, *Bioscience*, Vol. 45, No. 3, 1995; P.J. Dugan, *Wetland Conservation: A Review of Current Issues and Required Action*, IUCN, Gland, Switzerland, 1990, p. 33.

9. P. Boonkrob, 'Community Protection of a Watershed', *Watershed*, Bangkok, Vol. 1, No. 1, July 1995. See also articles in 'Save the Forests: Save the Planet. A Plan for Action', special issue of *The Ecologist*, Vol. 17, No. 4/5, 1987; and 'Amazonia: The Future in the Balance', special issue of *The Ecologist*, Vol. 19, No. 6, 1989; also see M. Colchester and L. Lohmann, *The Struggle for Land and the Fate of the Forests*, Zed Books, London 1992.

10. See, e.g., J.M. Laflen et al., 'Soil Erosion and a Sustainable Agriculture', in C.A. Edwards et al. (eds.), *Sustainable Agricultural Systems*, SWCS, Ankeny, IA, 1990, p. 353; National Research Council, *Soil and Water Quality*, p. 355.

11. The value of Canadian wetland recreation – hunting, fishing, bird watching, tourism, sailing, swimming, etc. – is estimated to have exceeded US$3.9bn in 1981 (Dugan, *Wetland Conservation*, p. 20).

12. B.K. Paul, 'Perception of and Agricultural Adjustment to Floods in Jamuna Floodplain', *Human Ecology*, Vol. 12, No. 1, 1984, p. 10, quoted in J.K. Boyce, 'Birth of a Megaproject: Political Economy of Flood Control in Bangladesh', *Environmental Management*, Vol. 14, No. 4, 1990, pp. 419–20.

13. J. Needham, *Science and Civilization in China*, Vol. 4, Part III, Cambridge University Press, Cambridge 1971, p. 235.

14. Interagency Floodplain Management Review Committee, *A Blueprint for Change. Sharing the Challenge: Floodplain Management into the 21st Century*, Report of the IFMRC to the Administration Floodplain Management Task Force, Washington, DC, June 1994; J. Denning, 'When the Levee Breaks', *Civil Engineering*, January 1994.

15. P.B. Williams, 'Flood Control vs. Flood Management', *Civil Engineering*, May 1994; Faber, 'Acquisition and Restoration'.

16. 'Germans Rethink River Management after Recent Floods', *US Water News*, March 1994; H. Simonian, 'Floods of Tears on the Rhine', *Financial Times*, 8 February 1995.

17. 'SOS Loire Vivante: Actions and Strategies', SOS Loire Vivante, Le Puy, May 1995; *SOS Loire Vivante Infos*, No. 24, March 1995.

18. F. Ghassemi et al., *Salinisation of Land and Water Resources: Human Causes, Extent, Mmanagement and Case Studies*, CAB International, Wallingford, UK, 1995, p. 11.

19. D. Brokensha et al., 'Antipastoralism, Ethnic Cleansing and Wearing the Green: An Editorial', *Development Anthropology Network*, Vol. 10, No. 2, 1992, p. 2.

20. See, e.g., R. Franke and B. Chasin, 'Peasants, Peanuts, Profits and Pastoralists', *The Ecologist*, Vol. 11, No. 4, 1981; Adams, *Wasting the Rain*, pp. 42–6; G. Monbiot, *No Man's Land: An Investigative Journey through Kenya and Tanzania*, Macmillan, London 1994; F. Pearce, 'Shepherds and Wise Men', *New Scientist*, 23/30 December 1995.

21. See, e.g., International Fund for Agricultural Development (IFAD), *Soil and Water Conservation in Sub-Saharan Africa: Towards Sustainable Production by the Rural Poor*, a report prepared for IFAD by CDCS, Free University, Amsterdam 1992, p. 23.

22. F. Pearce, *The Dammed: Rivers, Dams and the Coming World Water Crisis*, Bodley Head, London 1992, p. 52–5.

23. D.J. Hillel, *Out of the Earth: Civilization and the Life of the Soil*, Free Press, New York 1991, pp. 111–16; R. Clarke, *Water: The International Crisis*, Earthscan, London 1991, pp. 132–4.

24. Hillel, *Out of the Earth*, pp. 117–19. See also Pearce, *The Dammed*, pp. 50–52.

25. G. Frazier, 'Technical, Economic and Social Considerations of Water Harvesting and Runoff Farming', in E.E. Whitehead et al. (eds.), *Arid Lands: Today and Tomorrow*, Proceedings of an International Research and Development Conference, Tucson, Arizona, Westview Press, Boulder, CO, 1985.

26. IFAD, *Soil and Water Conservation*, pp. 81–2.

27. Adams, *Wasting the Rain*, pp. 76–89; E.R. Porto and A.S. Silva, 'Small-Scale Water Management in Farming Systems in the Brazilian Arid Zones', in Whitehead et al. (eds.), *Arid Lands*, pp. 951–2.

28. U. Shankari and E. Shah, *Water Management Traditions in India*, PPST Foundation, Madras 1993, p. 107.

29. M. Goldman, '"There's a Snake on Our Chests": State and Development Crisis in India's Desert', Ph.D. thesis, University of California, Santa Cruz, December 1994, pp. 51–2; R.T. Rosin, 'The Tradition of Groundwater Irrigation in Northwestern India', *Human Ecology*, Vol. 21, No. 1, 1993; Shankari and Shah, *Water Management Traditions*, pp. 14, 47.

30. D. Nicholson-Lord, 'Water-Harvesters of Rajasthan', *Independent on Sunday*, London, 27 March 1994.

31. W. Pereira, *Tending the Earth: Traditional Sustainable Agriculture in India*, Earthcare Books, Bombay 1993, p. 174.

32. O.H.K. Spate quoted in Goudie, *The Human Impact*, p. 150.

33. W. Gooneratne and C.M. Madduma Bandara, 'Management of Village Irrigation in the Dry Zone of Sri Lanka', in W. Gooneratne and S. Hirashima (eds.), *Irrigation and Water Management in Asia*, Sterling Publishers, New Delhi 1990, pp. 152, 153; World Bank, 'India: Irrigation Sector Review. Volume I – Main Report', Washington, DC, 1991, p. 2.

34. D.N. Reddy et al., 'Decline in Traditional Water Harvesting Systems in Drought Prone Areas of Andhra Pradesh', and K.A.S. Mani, 'Traditional Water Harvesting – Tanks Effective Drought Proofing Mechanism', both papers given at seminar on 'Traditional Water Harvesting Systems of India', organized by CSE at India International Centre, New Delhi, 9–11 October 1990.

35. E.G. Thukral and M.D. Sakate, 'Baliraja: A People's Alternative', in E.G. Thukral (ed.), *Big Dams, Displaced People: Rivers of Sorrow, Rivers of Change*, Sage Publications, New Delhi 1992, pp. 152–4.

36. A. Shah, *Water for Gujarat: An Alternative. Technical Overview of the Flawed Sardar Sarovar Project and a Proposal for a Sustainable Alternative*, Jan Vikas Andolan

et al., Vishakhapatnam, September 1993, p. 24.

37. Bandyopadhyay, 'Riskful Confusion', p. 287.

38. Shah, *Water for Gujarat*, p. 23. The depletion of aquifers by irrigators has commonly been used to justify the construction of dams and canals so that surface water can replace the overdrafted groundwater. What invariably happens in practice is that the surface water is used to increase the area under irrigation and the amount of water used on crops, and so the surface diversion ends up supplementing rather than replacing the groundwater, and the water table eventually starts to drop again.

39. S. Postel, *Last Oasis: Facing Water Scarcity*, W.W. Norton, New York 1992, pp. 31–7; Hillel, *Out of the Earth*, pp. 233–4; N. Nusser, 'As Water Crisis Worsens, Mexico City Becomes a Sinkhole', *San Francisco Chronicle*, 27 January 1996.

40. Postel, *Last Oasis*, p. 176.

41. Shankari and Shah, *Water Management Traditions*, p. 99; 'Artificial Recharge', in F. van der Leeden et al., *The Water Encyclopedia*, second edition, Lewis Publishers, Chelsea, MI, 1990, p. 294.

42. See M. Moench and M.D. Kumar (eds.), *Local Water Management Initiatives: NGO Activities in Gujarat*, VIKSAT/Pacific Institute, Collaborative Groundwater Project, Ahmedabad 1993.

43. Shah, *Water for Gujarat*. See also S. Paranjape and K.J Joy, 'The Alternative Restructuring of the Sardar Sarovar Project: Not Destructive Development but Sustainable Prosperity. A Note for Discussion', mimeo, 1994; 'Restructuring of Sardar Sarovar Project', resolution from meeting organized by the All India People's Science Network and Nehru Memorial Museum, Delhi, 19–20 August 1994.

44. D. Groenfeldt, 'Building on Tradition: Indigenous Irrigation Knowledge and Sustainable Development in Asia', *Agriculture and Human Values*, Vol. 7, Nos. 1 & 2. In practice there is no clear line between indigenous and modern systems, as many traditional ones have been extended or altered with modern materials, and now come under the control of state irrigation departments.

45. Adams, *Wasting the Rain*, p. 190.

46. 'Water Management by Local Communities', *Thai Development Newsletter*, No. 23, 1994; L. Lohmann and C. Tongdeelert, 'The *Muang Faai* Irrigation System of Northern Thailand', *The Ecologist*, Vol. 21, No. 2, 1991.

47. Needham, *Science and Civilization in China*, pp. 288–95.

48. See, e.g., E.W. Coward, Jr., 'Irrigation Management Alternatives: Themes from Indigenous Irrigation Systems', paper for workshop on *Choices in Irrigation Management*, ODI, Canterbury, UK 1976.

49. Lohmann and Tongdeleert, 'The *Muang Faai* Irrigation System', p. 103.

50. R.Y. Siy, Jr., 'Local Resource Mobilisation and Management: A Study of Indigenous Irrigation in Northern Philippines', in Gooneratne and Hirashima (eds.), *Irrigation and Water Management in Asia*, pp. 28–30.

51. Lohmann and Tongdeleert, 'The *Muang Faai* Irrigation System', p. 103.

52. 'Common Properties Managed by Users are More Sustainable and Productive, Ostrom Says in IFPRI', *International Food Policy Research Institute Report*, June 1994.

53. Siy, Jr., 'Local Resource Mobilization', p. 35.

54. Groenfeldt, 'Building on Tradition'.

55. N. Sutawan et al., 'Community-Based Irrigation System in Bali, Indonesia', in Gooneratne and Hirashima (eds.), *Irrigation and Water Management in Asia*, p. 135.

56. J.S. Lansing and J.N. Kremer, 'Emergent Properties of Balinese Water Temple Networks: Coadaptation on a Rugged Fitness Landscape', *American Anthropologist*, Vol. 95, No. 1, 1993, p. 100. The *subaks* manage land and water so that the overall stability and productivity of the system is maximized, rather than the productivity of any one farmer or *subak*. Modern interventions which seek to maximize the productivity of the individual farmer tend to reduce the overall productivity of Balinese agriculture.

57. Groenfeldt, 'Building on Tradition', p. 116. See also Adams, *Wasting the Rain*, pp. 190–96.

58. See, e.g., M. Svendsen and M.W. Rosegrant, 'Irrigation Development in Southeast Asia Beyond 2000: Will the Future Be Like the Past?', *Water International*, Vol. 19, No. 1, 1994, p. 28; I. Serageldin, 'Water Resources Management: A New Policy for a Sustainable Future', *Water International*, Vol. 20, No. 1, 1995; S. Barghouti and G. Le Moigne, 'Irrigation and the Environmental Challenge', *Finance and Development*, June 1991; 'Water Management in the Next Century', *The International Journal of Hydropower & Dams*, January 1994.

59. World Bank, 'Lending for Irrigation', Operations Evaluation Department Préçis 85, 1995.

60. See The Ecologist, *Whose Common Future?*, Earthscan, London 1992.

61. Postel, *Last Oasis*, p. 99.

62. R. Chambers, *Managing Canal Irrigation: Practical Analysis from South Asia*, Cambridge University Press, Cambridge 1988, p. 1.

63. US Geological Survey, 'Estimated Use of Water in the United States in 1990. Domestic Water Use', World Wide Web site, 1995.

64. 'While Preserving Groundwater Supply High Plains Irrigators Profit from Switch to Organic Farming', *US Water News*, April 1994.

65. Needham, *Science and Civilization in China*, p. 246; Porto and Silva, 'Small Scale Water Management'; Shankari and Shah, *Water Management Traditions*, p. 102.

66. Postel, *Last Oasis*, p. 105.

67. See Adams, *Wasting the Rain*, pp. 184–8; L.A. Thrupp, 'New Harvests, Old Problems: Feeding the Global Supermarket', *Global Pesticide Campaigner*, September 1995.

68. Postel, *Last Oasis*, pp. 122–3.

69. Ibid.; H. Watzman, 'Sewage Slakes Israel's Thirst for Water', *New Scientist*, 23/30 December 1995. Sewage is widely used on crops in developing countries, often because irrigators have no choice but to use water from contaminated rivers and drains. The use of untreated sewage on crops which are eaten raw carries considerable health risks. Wastewater contaminated with heavy metals and other industrial pollutants is also unsuitable for reuse. Water reuse is rapidly becoming more common in the Western US, particularly for groundwater recharge, crop irrigation, golf courses and urban landscaping (T. Asano, 'Reusing Urban Wastewater – An Alternative and a Reliable Water Resource', *Water International*, Vol. 19, No. 1, 1994; P.H. Gleick, 'Water and Energy', in P.H. Gleick (ed.), *Water in Crisis: A Guide to the World's Fresh Water Resources*, Oxford University Press, Oxford 1993, p. 69).

70. I. Serageldin, *Toward Sustainable Management of Water Resources*, World Bank 1995, p. 12.

71. A. Jones and J. Dyer, 'The Water Efficiency Revolution', *River Voices*, Spring 1993.

72. World Bank, 'Managing Urban Water Supply and Sanitation', OED 1995;

C. Southey, 'European Cities "Wasting" Water', *Financial Times*, 13 September 1995; E. Luce, 'Ramos Approves Plan to Sell Off Water Utility', *Financial Times*, 31 August 1995. 'Unaccounted for water' due to illegal connections or broken meters is likely to be used by the urban poor. Making people pay for this water will not increase the total amount of water available and may cause economic hardship.

73. A.A. Churchill, *Rural Water Supply and Sanitation: Time for a Change*, World Bank Discussion Paper 18, 1987, p. 3.

74. A. Dixit and J.N. Crippen, 'Issues in Maintenance Management of Community Water Supply Schemes in Nepal', *Water Nepal*, Vol. 3, No. 2–3, 1993.

75. Postel, *Last Oasis*, p. 137; R. Bhatia et al., 'Policies for Water Conservation and Reallocation "Good Practice" Cases in Improving Efficiency and Equity', a World Bank–ODI Joint Study, 1992.

76. Bhatia, 'Policies for Water Conservation', p. 5. The potential negative impact on poorer households of water metering and price rises can be mitigated by a progressive tariff structure, under which higher consumers are charged a higher unit rate, as well as by welfare support for poor households.

77. P.H. Gleick et al., *California Water 2020: A Sustainable Vision*, Pacific Institute, Oakland, CA, 1995.

78. R. Haberman, 'Water Efficiency: An Alternative to Water Supply Dams', *River Voices*, Spring 1993.

79. R. Goodland and G. Tillmann, 'Strategic Environmental Assessment', 1995 Group Environmental Assessment, Shell International, The Hague 1995. See also, e.g., J.M. Kalbermatten et al., *Appropriate Technology for Water Supply and Sanitation: A Summary of Technical and Economic Options*, World Bank 1980.

80. See, e.g., 'Public Water Sources Siphoned off by Golf Courses', *Thai Development Newsletter*, No. 24, 1994; Monbiot, *No Man's Land*; C. Alvares (ed.), *Fish Curry and Rice: A Citizens' Report on the State of the Goan Environment*, ECOFORUM, Mapusa, Goa 1994.

81. Car statistic from van der Leeden et al., *The Water Encyclopedia*, p. 357; domestic needs from Bhatia et al., 'Policies for Water Conservation'.

82. Hillel, *Out of the Earth*, p. 114; Pearce, *The Dammed*, p. 54.

83. Shankari and Shah, *Water Management Traditions*, pp. 89–95.

84. Postel, *Last Oasis*, pp. 45–7; 'Is the Cost Too High? Seawater to Freshwater', *Aqueduct 2000*, May–June 1995; Gleick, 'Water and Energy', pp. 69–70. The most efficient desalinization plants currently consume around 84,000 joules to extract salt from each litre of seawater.

8

Energy: Revolution or Catastrophe?

> Nature cares nothing for logic, our human logic: she has her own, which we do not recognize and do not acknowledge until we are crushed under its wheel.
>
> Ivan Turgenev, *Smoke*, 1867

Few, if any, societies or ecosystems have been unaffected by the massive explosion in energy consumption sparked off by the industrial revolution. This book has described hydropower's far-reaching consequences for people and nature; the unique environmental, safety and weapon proliferation problems of nuclear power are now well known. The use of fossil fuels carries appalling costs: their extraction, transport and combustion has filthied coastlines with oil spills, razed forests and farmlands to make way for stripmines, killed trees and lakes with acid rain, choked cities with smog; the urge to control their supply has sparked off wars. Most significantly, it is highly likely that the burning of fossil fuels is killing people and extinguishing species by warming the globe and causing floods, storms, droughts and fires of unprecedented frequency and severity.

Despite the obvious need for a revolution in global energy policies, industry and government bodies continue to draw up energy use forecasts which imply that the world will boldly mine, drill, dam, burn and pollute its way to ecological catastrophe during the twenty-first century. Probably the most influential projections are made by the joint industry–government association known as the World Energy Council (WEC). The WEC's 1993 assessment of future energy trends lists three main scenarios for the year 2020: a 'high economic growth case'; a 'business-as-usual' case; and an 'ecologically driven case'. The latter assumes moderate economic growth with 'dramatic' government measures to promote energy efficiency. According to the high-growth scenario, 65 per cent more oil would be burnt in 2020 than 1990, and the use of large hydro, coal and nuclear power would all at least double.

Even in the 'ecologically driven' scenario, which the WEC believes to be 'unlikely to be achievable', the use of oil, large hydro and nuclear power would all rise (by 3 per cent, 40 per cent and 75 per cent, respectively), and the use of coal would fall by less than 10 per cent. These scenarios would cause increases in energy-related carbon dioxide emissions (not counting reservoir emissions) of between 95 per cent (high growth) and 7 per cent (ecologically driven).

The UN Climate Convention signed by world leaders at the Earth Summit in Rio de Janeiro in 1992 has the 'ultimate objective' of achieving 'stabilization of greenhouse gas concentrations in the atmosphere at a level that would prevent dangerous anthropogenic interference with the climate system'. According to the UN Intergovernmental Panel on Climate Change, just to stabilize the atmospheric concentration of carbon dioxide at its 1990 level would require *cuts in CO_2 emissions from all sources of more than 60 per cent* – and there is little guarantee that stabilizing its concentration at this already high level would in fact 'prevent dangerous anthropogenic interference' with the climate.[1]

Even the WEC's 'ecologically driven' scenario with its 7 per cent rise in carbon emissions could thus lead to climate disaster. Under their 'business-as-usual' scenario, the atmospheric concentration of CO_2 would rise from 355 parts per million in 1990, to a terrifying 600 ppm in 2100. Such a rise would, according to current scientific estimates, increase world temperatures by 3 or 4 degrees centigrade, a rate of warming many times greater than any yet experienced in human history.[2]

Fortunately, the only certainty about these WEC projections is that they will be wrong. As analysts Christopher Flavin and Nicholas Lenssen of the Worldwatch Institute wrote in 1994,

> ...energy forecasters have had a track record of nearly unblemished failure during the past two decades. Reports by leading institutions in the early seventies overestimated the amount of nuclear power the world would now be using by a factor of six, while studies in 1980 said oil would cost $100 a barrel by the early nineties.

In 1996, the cost of oil was hovering around $20 a barrel.

Flavin and Lenssen convincingly argue that the world's energy sector is at the brink of a revolutionary change comparable in its scope to that seen at the beginning of the twentieth century, when electricity swept gas and candlepower from the streets and houses of North America and Europe. This transformation, say Flavin and Lenssen, will be driven by a mixture of environmental concerns, economics, regulatory changes and technological advances, and will be one to 'an energy path characterized by high levels of efficiency, extensive use of decentralized technologies, heavy reliance on natural gas and on hydrogen as an energy carrier, and a gradual shift to renewable energy sources'.[3]

While Flavin and Lenssen admit the impossibility of predicting the outcome of the 'coming energy revolution', they do draw up a scenario which shows that the energy future could be radically different from that envisaged by the WEC. Under Worldwatch's 'sustainable energy scenario', reductions in coal and oil use would enable CO_2 concentrations to level off by mid-century at around 450 ppm, and then slowly decline.[4] A 1993 study carried out for Greenpeace by the Stockholm Environment Institute shows how the metamorphosis of the global energy economy along the lines described by Flavin and Lenssen could make it possible to halve fossil-fuel use by 2050, and phase it out entirely by the end of the century, even assuming a total end to nuclear generation by 2010.[5]

The Worldwatch and Greenpeace scenarios are not meant as forecasts or recommendations, but rather as proof that, given the political will, the ecological impact of energy use could be drastically reduced even within the constraints of the current economic worldview. Both scenarios assume that there will be no major new technological breakthroughs, and that new technologies will be adopted only when they are economically viable. The scenarios also assume that global economic growth can continue indefinitely, unimpeded by other environmental, resource availability or social constraints. Greenpeace's Fossil Free Energy Scenario projects a doubled global population and a 14-fold increase in economic activity by 2100. The negative implications of such a future, Greenpeace notes, would include massively increased pressure on, and conflict over, natural resources. In a more sustainable future, with a lower population and a lower consumption lifestyle, the conversion to renewable energy sources would be much easier.[6]

More light, less power

At the heart of these two scenarios lie increasing efficiencies in the generation, distribution and use of energy, in particular electricity. Worldwatch projects that efficiency advances could reduce energy needs in 2100 to around a third of those forecasted in the WEC's 'business-as-usual' case. Under the Fossil Free Energy Scenario, energy production in 2100 would be around two-thirds that of the 'business-as-usual' case. The efficiency of electrical appliances and industrial processes has already improved by leaps and bounds since the oil shock of 1973. The 'energy productivity' of the US – the amount of goods and services produced per unit of energy used – rose by 40 per cent in the two decades after 1973; the energy productivity of Japan by 46 per cent. Electricity demand growth in industrial countries as a whole slowed from 8 per cent per year in the 1960s, to an average of 3 per cent since the 1970s. The

Table 8.1 Cost per installed kilowatt of different forms of electrical generation capacity

Technology	Cost per kW (US$)
Upgrading hydro	70–700
Adding turbines to existing dams	600–2,500
Natural gas	700
Coal	1,200
Wind	1,200
Small hydropower	1,000–5,000
Large hydropower	2,000–5,000
Fuel cells	3,000
Photovoltaic cells	4,000

Source: C. Flavin and N. Lenssen, *Power Surge: Guide to the Coming Energy Revolution*, W.W. Norton, New York 1994. Hydropower figure from data gathered by author.

WEC predicts electricity growth in North America and Western Europe of just 1 per cent a year between 1990 and 2020.[7]

One of the most effective ways of realizing the potential of energy efficiency is by changing the ways electrical utilities are regulated so that it becomes more profitable for them to meet additional demand with 'negawatts' – saved electricity – rather than more megawatts. Electricity 'demand-side management' (DSM) programmes are analogous to water utilities meeting extra demand through water-efficient showerheads and toilets, except in this case customers get subsidized energy-efficient light bulbs and appliances. US utilities – under pressure from environmental regulations and greater competition – spent an estimated $2.8 billion on efficiency measures in 1993, providing 'negawatts' at an average cost of 2.1 cents per kilowatt-hour. This is half the cost of generating megawatts from the cheapest new power plants. DSM and other programmes have helped California keep its per capita electricity generation at the same level in 1992 as it was in 1979 – while it rose by nearly a fifth in the rest of the US.[8]

In developing countries, the potential benefits of conservation programmes are huge in terms of money saved and ecological damage avoided. According to one estimate, greater efficiency could reduce electricity growth in these countries by a quarter over the next three decades, saving hundreds of billions of dollars. The Thai electricity utility launched a $189 million DSM scheme in 1991, which is projected to save 238 megawatts in peak power. Yet this is only a fraction of the

Table 8.2 Actual and projected costs of electric power generation in the US (1993 cents per kilowatt-hour)

Technology	1985	1994	2000
Natural gas	10–13	4–5	3–4
Coal	8–10	5–6	4–5
Wind	10–13	5–7	4–5
Solar thermal*	13–26	8–10	5–6
Nuclear	10–21	10–21	–†
Negawatt-producing DSM§	2		
Photovoltaic cells	150	25–40	4–6

* With natural gas as backup fuel

† No plant ordered since 1978; all orders since 1973 have subsequently been cancelled.

§ Negawatts are saved electricity attained through demand-side management efficiency programmes.

Sources: PV Cells in 2000: T.B. Johansson et al. (eds.), *Renewable Energy: Sources for Fuels and Electricity*, Island Press, Washington, DC, 1993. All others: C. Flavin and N. Lenssen, *Power Surge: Guide to the Coming Energy Revolution*, W.W. Norton, New York 1994.

potential savings from DSM in Thailand: the International Institute of Energy Conservation estimates that it could save 2,000 MW at less than half the price of building power plants to produce this amount of electricity. The highly controversial Pak Mun Dam, by comparison, provides Thailand with an additional capacity of only 136 MW. A study of the Brazilian electricity industry found that DSM measures through to 2010 could save $52 billion in avoided investment in 26,000 MW worth of new power plants. This is equal to the amount of power produced by more than two Itaipús – or well over a hundred Balbinas.[9]

Gas for now

Phasing out destructive hydro, nuclear and fossil-fuel technologies will obviously mean bringing on-line new electricity generating methods. The renewables, especially wind and solar power, have great technological and economic potential. In the next few decades while these technologies are being further developed and the infrastructure to use them put in place, natural gas is a cheap, safe and relatively environmentally benign transition fuel.

Extracting and transporting natural gas is relatively easy and non-polluting compared to other fossil fuels. Emissions from gas-fired power plants also compare favourably to those from oil, diesel or coal:

CO_2 emissions from modern gas turbines can be half those from the most advanced new coal plants, nitrogen oxide emissions 90 per cent less, and sulphur dioxide emissions 99 per cent less.[10] Constructing a gas plant currently costs around $700 per installed kilowatt – half as much as the average coal-fired power station (see Table 8.1). Falling gas prices and advances in gas-turbine efficiency more than halved the price of gas-powered electricity generation in the US between 1985 and 1994 (see Table 8.2). Gas plants can be built with surprising rapidity: a 1,875 MW combined-cycle gas plant was completed in north-east England in 1992 just two-and-a-half years after construction started.[11] A dam with a similar generating capacity would typically take a decade or more to build. Because of the site-specific nature of dams their installed capacity costs vary widely: large hydro plants currently cost somewhere between $2,000 and $5,000 per kilowatt. While the operating costs of dams are very low, the expense of dam construction means that their overall generation costs can be high, especially during periods of high interest rates (see Chapter 9, p. 270).[12]

The efficiencies of scale which have conventionally favoured huge power plants are changing with the commercialization of efficient gas turbines as small as 1 megawatt. These enable power generation to be decentralized, slashing electricity distribution losses, and allowing factories or communities to generate their own power. The huge cost overruns which invariably afflict large construction projects – especially dams – are avoided by increasing capacity incrementally with small, standardized gas plants. Such an approach also greatly reduces the risk of wasting money on excess capacity.[13]

The economic and environmental advantages of gas-fired electricity are currently fuelling a rapid expansion in its use. Global gas production outside of the Commonwealth of Independent States is growing at a rate of about 4 per cent per year, around twice the rate of growth in oil production.[13] Global reserves appear sufficient to support a worldwide natural gas boom. The ultimate constraint on gas use – as with other fossil fuels – may well not be scarce supplies but environmental concerns: when carbon-free renewable technologies are sufficiently developed, gas use should then be phased out.

The Renewables Are Coming

Renewable methods of generating electricity have until recently been regarded by most mainstream economists and energy analysts as largely a passion of eco-freaks. But this is fast changing. A 1995 survey of 'the future of energy' in the British magazine *The Economist* – hardly at the vanguard of the eco-revolution – states that:

> Little noticed, the costs of many renewables have recently been tumbling. Fossil fuels are still almost always cheaper. But a battle has begun on the fringes of the mighty $1-trillion-a-year fossil-fuel industry that could force it into retreat early in the coming century.[14]

Under Greenpeace's Fossil Free Energy Scenario, solar and windpower would together provide the bulk of the world's electricity generation by the end of the next century.

Windpower is in the short term by far the most promising of the renewables. Technological advances have caused the price of wind-generated electricity in favourable locations to plummet by more than half in the past decade. The cost of installing wind turbines fell to under $1,200 a kilowatt by 1993, and forecasts indicate that this could tumble to under $800/kW by the year 2000. In 1995, installed wind generating capacity around the world soared by 33 per cent from the previous year, to reach a total of some 4,880 MW.[16] More than 25,000 wind turbines are now producing electrical power. The bulk of the turbines are in Northern Europe and the Western US, but the industry is fast expanding from these heartlands into new areas. Hydro-Québec, one of the world's major dam builders, announced in 1994 that it planned to install 100 MW of windpower. In the same year, tax incentives and regulatory changes led to 115 MW worth of new turbines being brought on-line in India, nearly twice the country's previous installed capacity. Windpower is also spreading in Southern Europe, Argentina, Bolivia, Brazil, Chile, China, Egypt, Indonesia, Mexico and Morocco.[17]

Even when environmentally sensitive landscapes are excluded, global wind potential is roughly five times total present electricity production. According to various estimates, windpower could be producing 10–20 per cent of the world's electricity by the middle of the next century, even without significant advances in energy efficiency and conservation. The main constraint on windpower is that generation from even the best sites is intermittent, so that without efficient methods of storing electricity (see below) utilities will need some form of backup generation for calm days. Another constraint is that many of the windiest sites, such as the US Great Plains, are far from the main sources of electricity demand.[18]

If windpower is to become a major electricity producer, windfarms must be developed in such a way that they benefit the communities in which they are installed. Otherwise they are likely to be resisted just as people oppose nuclear plants and dams near their homes today. An excellent example is provided by the different reactions to the recent surge in windfarm development in Denmark and the UK. In Denmark, some 3,500 wind turbines were installed by 1994, producing around 3 per cent of Danish energy. These turbines are owned by cooperatives whose shares are typically restricted to local people. In the UK, however, where only some 400 turbines have been erected, the main economic beneficiaries of windfarms have been large landowners and corporations. Many people view the windfarms as being imposed on them by central government. This resentment has spawned a vocal anti-windpower lobby of landscape preservationists (and nuclear- and fossil-fuel lobbyists) which has succeeded in slowing down windpower development. 'If the new windmills – unlike those of earlier centuries – impose upon the landscape,' says English environmentalist Simon Fairlie, 'it is because they impose upon the community, rather than growing out of it.'[19]

Here comes the sun

There are two main techniques for directly harnessing the energy of the sun to generate electricity: 'solar thermal' systems, which use mirrors to concentrate sunlight to a temperature where it can convert water to steam, which is then used to generate electricity; and photovoltaic cells, which directly convert sunlight into electricity. There are three main configurations of solar thermal power plants: a parabolic dish that focuses light to a single point; parabolic troughs which focus light onto a liquid in a pipe; and an array of flat mirrors spread over several acres that reflect light onto a high central 'power tower'. Several solar thermal stations have been built in Southern California and elsewhere, but they have so far proved relatively expensive and unreliable. The technology is fast advancing, however, and advocates believe that its cost will be competitive with gas generation by the end of the century. Two of the biggest energy corporations in the US, Enron and Amoco, expect to bring on line a 100 MW solar thermal plant in the Nevada Desert by the end of 1996. The inherent drawbacks to solar thermal are that it is only suitable for very sunny climates, it requires another form of generation as a backup for cloudy days, and it does not have the flexibility of smallness shared by windmills and photovoltaics.[20]

Photovoltaic cells (PVs) were first developed in the 1950s but their use was constrained by low efficiencies. Recent advances, however, enable them to generate electricity even on overcast days and have brought costs down precipitously. The cost of 1 kilowatt of PV capacity plummeted from $3 million in the 1950s, to $4,000 in 1994 (in constant 1993 dollars). Researchers at the University of New South Wales believe that efficiency advances they are working on could bring PV prices down another 80 per cent within a decade, making solar electricity cheaper than coal-fuelled power.[21] Sales of PVs rose by more than 17 per cent in 1995, bringing total global installed capacity to just under 600 MW.[22] Christopher Flavin and Nicholas Lenssen believe that photovoltaics 'could become one of the world's largest industries, as well as one of its most ubiquitous power sources'.[23]

The biggest market for PVs is currently in rural areas of developing countries, where around a quarter of a million households now use solar cells for lighting, televisions and radios, and water pumps. In Kenya, 20,000 households were solar powered by 1993, and the rate at which rural households were installing solar panel systems was greater than the rate of increase of grid connections. Furthermore, PVs are not just suited to the sunny skies of the tropics: Switzerland has a programme to install at least one PV system in each of the country's villages by the year 2000; the Netherlands plans to install 250 MW of photovoltaics by 2010.[24]

A great advantage of PVs is their flexibility – they are quick to install, come in a wide range of sizes which can easily be upgraded, and can be built into rooftops or any other surface facing the sun. Even windows can now be coated with transparent solar cells. The total solar glazing potential of the UK is estimated at 68,000 MW – equivalent to half the country's 1993 power supply. Buildings with solar cells can have 'reverse meters' which enable them to use grid electricity on cloudy days, and then supply the grid with power when it is sunny.[25]

The oldest renewable: biomass

The burning of wood and crop residues is still the main form of energy used for cooking and heat by an estimated 2.5 billion people. Although theoretically renewable, in practice biomass is being used at an unsustainable rate in many areas. Making biomass consumption renewable will depend on raising the efficiency of its use, for example with improved cooking stoves, restraining population growth, and reversing the socio-economic forces which are increasing pressure on fuelwood supplies. Among the most important of these forces are the expropriation of commonlands and other traditional sources of fuel supplies for urban expansion and development projects. Measures to regenerate watershed vegetation would greatly help to increase the availability of biomass fuel for local people.

As well as being used directly for their energy content, tree and plant crops and crop residues can also be turned into commercial fuels such as ethanol, and into electricity. Some analysts envisage huge plantations supplying much of the world's commercial energy in the next century. A study carried out for the 1992 Earth Summit calls for some 4 million square kilometres of biomass energy plantations by the second quarter of the twenty-first century – equivalent to the global area of forest and woodland in 1990. These plantations would provide an amount of energy equal to around 65 per cent of present total world consumption.[26]

While there is room for biomass to be exploited for commercial energy on a limited scale, it is inconceivable that such megaplantations will ever come into being, mainly because they would be likely to cause hunger, land-grabbing and explosions of social unrest on a massive scale. Calculations of biomass potential are usually based on statistics of the millions of hectares of 'wasteland' and 'degraded land' which could be turned over to commercial energy crops: but lands defined as 'waste' by government statisticians would rarely be considered as such by local people who use them for crops, grazing, fuel, construction materials, wild foods and herbal medicines. Resentment of the expropriation of 'degraded' forest land for tree plantations in Thailand has led to villagers ripping out seedlings and burning nurseries in protest. These mega-plantations would also tend to be highly water-intensive – and finding the necessary water could lead to even more conflicts than finding the land to plant them on.[27]

Solving the storage problem

The major drawback for most renewable energy systems is that their output varies on a seasonal and often daily basis. The potential contribution of renewables to electricity supply would therefore be greatly enhanced were it possible to find a cheap method of storing large amounts of electricity. The most popular method at present is pumped-storage hydroelectricity, which involves water being pumped into a high reservoir at times of low demand and then released through turbines at peak times. While it does enable electricity to be generated when it is most valuable, pumped-storage is actually a net consumer of electricity as it takes more energy to pump water uphill than can be extracted from it falling back. Although pumped-storage reservoirs are relatively small compared to normal hydro reservoirs, some have provoked strong opposition. A pumped-storage scheme being built by the Chinese in Tibet is strongly opposed by Tibetan environmentalists and religious leaders because it uses a holy lake known as Yamdrok Tso as its storage reservoir, would cause extreme fluctuations in the lake level, and would sully its clarity by pumping up muddy water from a river below.[28]

Potentially viable techniques of electricity storage currently under development include mechanical flywheels, compressed air systems and hot rocks. The method with the greatest potential is to convert electricity into hydrogen, which can then be stored and transported in pipelines much like natural gas, for less than it now costs to transmit electricity. Christopher Flavin and Nicholas Lenssen foresee the emergence of a 'hydrogen economy' in the next century, with the gas being used not only to store and transmit electrical energy but also as a replacement for oil and natural gas for uses such as transportation, heating and cooking.

A device known as a fuel cell uses electric current to cleanly and virtually silently produce hydrogen from fresh or seawater via electrolysis;

the fuel cell can then work in reverse and produce heat or electricity from hydrogen with water as the main by-product. Fuel cells are relatively expensive at present but their price is expected to fall sharply as they move into mass production. They are also extremely versatile – they can be as large as a conventional power plant or small enough to power a car. Public buses powered by fuel cells are to go on trial in Chicago in 1996.[29] Fuel cells already supply heat and power to large buildings in California and Japan for around $3,000 per installed kilowatt.[30]

Bringing Hydro Down to Size

Small hydro cannot be seen as a direct 'alternative' to the power from large hydro on a worldwide scale, although in some cases a number of small-hydro schemes may be an appropriate alternative to a single large dam. Small-hydro plants have by definition a relatively low power output, and cumulatively they can never provide more than a very small proportion of global electricity supply. Small hydro, however, is well suited to rural areas of poor countries and remote settlements in industrialized countries where electricity demand is relatively low and the costs for connecting villages to national distribution systems high (and also of course where there are fast-flowing, perennial rivers and streams).

The generation of electricity from small-hydro plants dates back to the 1880s. Over the following half century, many thousands of small-hydro turbines were installed in Europe and North America. By the 1930s, however, many of these plants began to be abandoned, mainly because of the subsidized growth of electricity distribution grids fed from fossil fuel and large hydro plants, which provided a better quality of electricity, less prone to fluctuations in voltage and frequency. The long decline of small hydro began to be reversed in the 1970s with technological advances which largely solved the problems of fluctuating output, and various forms of government subsidies. Small hydro has also been boosted in many countries by regulatory changes which encourage independent power producers to sell electricity to the big power generation and distribution utilities.[31]

There is no consistent definition for what constitutes 'small' hydro. Most industry publications and organizations describe small hydro as a plant with up to 10 MW installed capacity, with sub-categories of mini-hydro (below 1MW), micro-hydro (below 100 kW) and, occasionally, pico-hydro (below 20 kW). Individual countries, however, have widely differing definitions: China defines mini-hydro as up to 500 kW, and small as up to 25 MW; small hydro in Japan is up to 50 MW; in Sweden the upper limit for small hydro is only 1.5 MW.[32] Micro-hydro plants need not produce electrical power: in many rural areas micro-hydro is still used to generate mechanical power for food processing – grinding grains, hulling rice, extracting edible oil – or for small industrial units such as saw mills and cotton gins.

Small-hydro stations come in many different forms. Those towards the upper limit of the definition tend to be scaled-down versions of large hydro plants, impounding water behind a concrete, earth or rock dam. Micro plants, however, rarely need a dam, but instead divert part of the river behind a small weir which keeps the water at the intake at a constant depth. Micro-hydro plants exploit the high 'head' (the vertical distance which water falls) available on mountain streams by diverting water into a channel which follows the contour of the hillside, then down a steeply sloping penstock pipe into a powerhouse, and then finally through a short tailrace back into the river, often a considerable distance downstream of the weir. In flatter areas where the lack of head is compensated by greater flows, the diverted water flows almost straight from the weir into the powerhouse, then back into the river.

Canadian government researchers calculate that in 1992 the worldwide installed capacity of small hydro (unless otherwise stated the term is used here to mean less than 10 MW) was 19,500 MW – 3 per cent of total installed hydro capacity. Nearly two-fifths of small-hydro capacity is in Western Europe and just over one-fifth in North America (see Table 8.3). The Canadian researchers give an 'optimistic' projection that, with modest government support for small hydro, worldwide installed capacity could almost quadruple by the year 2020.[33] Realistically, however, objections to the larger small-hydro plants on environmental and social grounds mean that the worldwide growth of small hydro will probably be much smaller.

A major advantage of micro- and mini-hydro for less industrialized countries is that most, and often all, of its components can be built with local or regional expertise, materials and capital. Nepal, Peru, India, Costa Rica, Chile, Brazil and especially China each have numerous indigenous companies producing mini-hydro turbines. The low cost and decentralized nature of mini-hydro plants mean that they can be community owned, even in very poor regions, with any profits being divided among local people, rather than going to outside state agencies or companies.[34]

Unfortunately there are many cases where the potential benefits of building small-hydro plants with local materials and know-how have been lost because the plants were built by highly paid foreign hydro engineers as smaller versions of large hydrodams, with unnecessarily complex and expensive designs and construction materials. Small dams and weirs made of rubble and wood may appear unacceptable to engineers accustomed to building in concrete and steel, but their temporary nature can be a benefit – when they are washed away so are

Table 8.3 Estimates of realizable regional small-hydro potential, 1990–2020 (capacity in megawatts)

Region (plant factor)	1990 A	1990 B	2000 A	2000 B	2020 A	2020 B
North America (52%)	4,300	4,300	4,860	6,830	6,150	12,900
Latin America (47%)	1,110	1,110	2,000	2,125	5,750	6,560
Western Europe (48%)	7,230	7,230	8,825	11,480	12,590	21,700
Eastern Europe and CIS (47%)	2,300	2,300	2,800	3,645	4,000	6,900
Middle East and North Africa (30%)	45	45	80	85	230	270
Sub-Saharan Africa (30%)	180	180	325	345	930	1,070
Pacific (46%)	100	100	125	160	180	300
China (45%)	3,890	3,890	6,970	7,430	20,100	22,900
Asia (45%)	345	345	615	655	1,770	2,000
Total (48%)	19,500	19,500	26,600	32,755	51,700	74,600

A = growth in small hydropower capacity assuming current economic and regulatory constraints.

B = growth assuming economic, regulatory and technological changes favourable to small hydropower.

Note: Average annual generation in megawatt-hours (MWh) can be obtained for any year by multiplying the capacity in megawatts by the capacity factor and the hours in a year (8,760).

Source: T.P. Tung et al., 'Small Hydro Development: Opportunities, Constraints and Technology Outlook', paper presented at the International Conference on Hydropower, Energy and the Environment, Stockholm, 1993.

the sediments behind them. Small hydro with temporary dams, weir diversions or reservoirs which are so small that it is practicable to clean out their accumulated sediments are, unlike most larger hydro plants, truly renewable technologies.[35]

China has almost 20 per cent of the world's small-hydro capacity – a larger share than any other single nation. Since the communist revolution, small hydro has been promoted as an inexpensive means of providing electricity for industry, agriculture and homes in rural China. Most plants have been built by local communes with little outside assistance. In 1980, there were 88,500 plants under 25 MW capacity accounting for about 40 per cent of China's total hydropower capacity.

Since then, although the small-hydro capacity has more than doubled, the actual number of plants has fallen by more than 37,000. The rise in installed capacity is due to modern small-hydro plants tending to be much bigger than earlier ones; the huge drop in the number of stations is mainly because many of the older plants were shoddily built (most were installed during the hysteria of rural industrialization which accompanied the Great Leap Forward and Cultural Revolution) and have been washed away or abandoned. Small hydro is still central to China's plans of electrifying its remote rural areas. Villages which get power from modern small-hydro plants reportedly have a more reliable power supply than areas served by the state-run grid, which suffer frequent cuts due to a nationwide power shortage.[36]

The successful campaign in the early 1990s against the $1 billion, 201 MW Arun III Dam in Nepal was started by Nepali small-hydro engineers who feared that Arun III would wipe out the country's growing small-hydro industry. Arun III would have been built almost exclusively by foreign contractors, and would have consumed virtually all the investment in the Nepali power sector for the next decade and more. The dam's opponents argued that small- and medium-sized dams could provide equivalent new generating capacity cheaper and quicker than Arun III: mini- and micro-schemes in Nepal commonly cost from $1,200 to $2,000 per installed kilowatt, far less than the projected cost of $5,000 per kW for Arun III. Small-hydro plants can be completed in two to three years – Arun III would have taken more than a decade to build. The announcement in August 1995 that the World Bank would not fund the scheme, and would help to find alternative power sources, marked a significant victory for the proponents of small hydro in Nepal and elsewhere.[37]

While a single small-hydro project will have less environmental and social impacts than a large project in the same location, this does not mean that small hydro cannot be harmful. Small dams can have as serious an impact upon the flow patterns, chemistry and temperature of streams and small rivers as large dams can have upon large rivers. Small dams can significantly reduce numbers of migratory fish, especially when several are built on the same river. Weir and diversion micro-hydro projects can also harm aquatic species by dewatering the river between the canal intake and the tailrace.[38]

Huge numbers of small-hydro plants can also cause the resettlement of huge numbers of people: according to government statistics, 70 per cent of the 10 million people displaced by Chinese reservoirs lost their land due to 'small projects'. (No definition of 'small project' is given with these statistics. They presumably include many non-hydro reservoirs.) While these data are difficult to interpret and of dubious reliability, they do give an idea of the potential scale of the problem.[39]

There are, however, a number of ways of increasing small-hydro capacity which avoid most environmental and resettlement problems. One is to install turbines in irrigation channels and municipal water supply and wastewater systems. The retrofitting of non-hydro small dams with turbines and the rehabilitation and upgrading of old small-hydro plants can in some cases increase generating capacity at little extra economic or environmental cost. Rehabilitation and upgrading (replacing old turbines and generators with more efficient modern equipment) now accounts for most of the current small-hydro development in Europe and North America. Adding capacity by upgrading small-hydro plants in the US is estimated to cost $200–$700 per kW, and adding turbines at an existing non-hydro dam $600–$2,500 per kW.[40] A variant of small hydro which could be commercialized within the next decade is the 'free-flow' turbine – the underwater equivalent of a wind turbine. Groups of these turbines would be tethered to riverbeds or hung from barges and would not require dams or diversions.[41]

The modernizing and retrofitting of large dams could also greatly increase hydropower production. During the 1980s and early 1990s, the Bureau of Reclamation added 1,600 MW of capacity to its dams, mainly by adding new turbines and refurbishing old ones. The new capacity, according to BuRec, cost only $69 per kW.[42] The capacity of Grand Coulee, the most powerful dam in the US (even before its refit), was increased from 4,500 MW to 6,500 MW in the 1980s by adding three new turbines and refurbishing its existing ones.[43] Much hydro upgrading can be done with little or no extra environmental impact; some upgrades, however, such as those which involve heightening dams and enlarging reservoirs, and those which would lead to significant changes in downstream flow patterns, could cause a great deal of damage.

The US Department of Energy calculates that there are some 2,600 disused hydrodams and flood control, water supply and navigation dams in the US which could be fitted with new generating equipment. These dams could support well over 10,000 MW of new capacity.[44] Again, however, there are environmental problems with the altered flow patterns and fisheries impact of generating power at these dams, so the actual capacity which is likely to be permitted is much smaller than the theoretical potential.[45]

While the above figures indicate that hydropower output in the US and elsewhere could rise substantially even without building new dams, there are also reasons to believe that output will fall over the long term. Sedimentation is reducing the storage capacity of most dams; environmentalists are likely to force hydrodam operators to spill more water for the benefit of fisheries and riverine ecosystems; many of the old dams which will reach the end of their economic lives over the next few decades may well be torn down in order to help restore rivers, rather than be rehabilitated; and global warming may well reduce streamflows in many regions.[46]

Tidal power is a form of hydro technology which some believe holds promise as an environmentally friendly power source. Tidal plants are comprised of lines of turbines mounted in barrages built across the mouths of bays or estuaries which can generate electricity from both ebb and flow tides. A 240 MW tidal station was built at La Rance in northern France in the 1960s and is still producing power. Some sites could potentially generate huge amounts of electricity: plans have been proposed for a 8,640 MW barrage across the Severn Estuary in Britain, and a 20,000 MW plant across Penzhina Bay in far eastern Siberia. But poor economics and ecological concerns mean that there is little chance of these or other tidal megaschemes being built in the near future.

The permanent inundation behind tidal barrages of extensive areas of estuarine mudflats – the crucial habitats for many waterfowl – is in particular likely to cause opposition to large tidal power plants. A less destructive possibility for harnessing tidal energy is the use of 'free-flow' turbine technology, but this does not yet appear economically viable.[47]

Storming the Palace Gates

Even in the face of hostility from the fossil-fuel industry and, at best, lukewarm support from governments, the renewables are fast gaining ground. Without stronger support, however, massive and potentially irreversible damage will be caused by the continued use of current energy technologies. One of the most important measures which governments could take would be to redirect the massive subsidies that they now lavish upon the fossil, hydro and nuclear industries to research and development in energy efficiency and renewables. According to the World Bank, direct subsidies for fossil fuels total some $220 billion a year. The Intergovernmental Panel on Climate Change believes that 'global emission reductions of 4 to 18 per cent together with increases in real incomes are possible from phasing out fuel subsidies.'[48]

Carbon and other pollution taxes should be levied and used to fund clean energies (and to compensate the poorer sections of society for their increased fuel costs). Governments can also help with energy efficiency programmes, such as subsidized loans or grants for home insulation or energy-efficient appliances. Much will also hinge on new systems of regulating the electricity industry which encourage utilities to invest in energy efficiency, and assist small, decentralized power suppliers to sell their electricity into the grid.

The World Bank itself provides huge subsidies to the fossil fuel and large hydro industries in terms of cheap loans and technical advice. The vast majority of the $3–$4 billion it lends to the power sector each year is spent on dams and fossil fuel extraction and combustion. Less than 1 per cent of the $67 billion lent by all the development banks in the 1980s went to improving end-use efficiency. Since then the banks have issued seemingly more progressive energy policies, and they pay increased lip service to the importance of energy efficiency and reducing the environmental damage of power generation, but there has been little tangible evidence of a new approach when it comes to actual loans.[49]

The predictions of both mainstream and environmental energy analysts may well be proved wrong by the passage of time. New renewable technologies may be developed which have not yet even been guessed at, and some technologies which now look promising may turn out to have unexpected ecological or social impacts. What is certain, however, is that if the use of coal, oil and large hydro continues to expand through the coming decades, it will not be because of unstoppable demand for hydro- or fossil-electricity, but because it is in the interest of a small number of governments and corporations to prevent change from happening.

Notes

1. J.T. Houghton et al. (eds.), *Climate Change: The IPCC Scientific Assessment*, Cambridge University Press, Cambridge 1990.
2. See H. Ager-Hanssen, 'The Energy Situation in Developing Countries: Constraints and Solutions', in *Proceedings of Conference on Hydropower and Environment: Differences in Policies and Priorities*, Norad, Oslo 1994. For at least 160,000 years before the industrial revolution, the atmospheric concentration of CO_2 never exceeded 300 ppm.
3. C. Flavin and N. Lenssen, *Power Surge: Guide to the Coming Energy Revolution*, W.W. Norton, New York 1994, p. 279.
4. Ibid., p. 278.
5. M. Lazarus et al., *Towards a Fossil Free Energy Future: The Next Energy Transition*, Stockholm Environment Institute, Boston 1993. Both Worldwatch and Greenpeace scenarios ignore the contributions of dams to global warming, and envisage a 50% increase in the output of large hydro by 2020–30.
6. Greenpeace International, *Fossil Fuels in a Changing Climate: How to Protect the World's Climate by Ending the Use of Coal, Oil and Gas*, Amsterdam 1993, p. 21.
7. Flavin and Lenssen, *Power Surge*, p. 77; 'Asia Delivers an Electric Shock', *The Economist*, 28 October 1995.
8. Flavin and Lenssen, *Power Surge*, p. 255.
9. See, e.g., EDF and NRDC, *Power Failure: A Review of the World Bank's Implementation of its New Energy Policy*, Washington, DC, 1994. Electricity utilities in developing countries could greatly increase available supply by reducing distribution losses. While losses of electricity in transmission and distribution in the US average only 8%, those in Thailand average 14%; in India 29%; and in Bangladesh 39% (M.T. Burr, 'Institutional Restructuring', *Independent Energy*, July/August 1995).
10. C. Flavin, 'Natural Gas Production Edges Up', in L. Starke (ed.), *Vital Signs 1996: The Trends That Are Shaping Our Future*, W.W. Norton, New York, 1996, p. 50.

11. In a combined cycle plant the excess heat from a gas turbine (an adaptation of a jet engine) is then used to power a steam turbine. Commercial combined cycle plants reached efficiencies of 50% in 1993, compared with efficiencies of coal and oil plants of 30–35% (Flavin and Lenssen, *Power Surge*, p. 99, 243). Turbines in development can reach 60% efficiency ('Breaking the Barrier', *Independent Energy*, July/August 1995, p. 89).

12. Hydro installed capacity figures based on a review of data for recently built and planned dams. Cost comparisons of different generating technologies are complicated because they have widely varying plant factors, and different mixes of up-front and running costs. Fossil-fuel plants, for example, have relatively low capital costs but high (and difficult to predict) fuel costs; hydro, solar and wind have zero fuel costs but relatively high capital costs.

13. Flavin and Lenssen, *Power Surge*, pp. 91–114; P. Lloyd Williams, 'The Small Turbine Revolution', *Independent Energy*, July/August 1995.

14. Flavin and Lenssen, *Power Surge*, pp. 99, 243.

15. 'The Battle for World Power', *The Economist*, 7 October 1995, p. 23.

16. C. Flavin, 'Wind Power Growth Accelerates', in Starke (ed.), *Vital Signs 1996*, p. 56.

17. Flavin and Lenssen, *Power Surge*, p. 123; C. Collette, 'Wind Thrift', *Northwest Energy News*, Summer 1995; W. Hoagland, 'Solar Energy', *Scientific American*, September 1995.

18. Flavin and Lenssen, *Power Surge*, pp. 115–31.

19. S. Fairlie, 'White Satanic Mills?', *The Ecologist*, Vol. 24, No. 3, 1994, p. 86.

20. Flavin and Lenssen, *Power Surge*, pp. 132–51; 'A New Chance for Solar Energy', *Scientific American*, September 1995.

21. V. Houlder, 'A Place in the Sun', *Financial Times*, 10 July 1995.

22. O. Tunali, 'Solar Cell Shipments Jump', in Starke (ed.), *Vital Signs 1996*, p. 58.

23. Flavin and Lenssen, *Power Surge*, p. 173.

24. R. van der Plas, 'Solar Energy Answer to Rural Power in Africa', *FDP Note* 6, World Bank, April 1994; J. Webb, 'By the Light of the Sun', *New Scientist*, 7 October 1995.

25. Flavin and Lenssen, *Power Surge*, pp. 152–73.

26. T.B. Johansson et al., 'Renewable Fuels and Electricity for a Growing World Economy', in T.B. Johansson et al. (eds.), *Renewable Energy Sources for Fuels and Electricity*, Island Press, Washington, DC, 1993.

27. See, e.g., L. Lohmann, 'Commercial Tree Plantations in Thailand: Deforestation by Any Other Name', *The Ecologist*, Vol. 20, No. 1, 1990; and various articles in *The Ecologist*, Vol. 17, No. 4/5, 1987.

28. Tibet Support Group UK, 'Death of a Sacred Lake: The Yamdrok Tso Hydro-Electric Generation Project of Tibet', London, March 1996.

29. C. Cookson, 'Fuel Cells in Power Clean-up', *Financial Times*, 4–5 November 1995.

30. Flavin and Lenssen, *Power Surge*, pp. 287–96.

31. P. Fraenkel et al., *Micro-Hydro Power: A Guide for Development Workers*, Intermediate Technology Publications, London 1991.

32. See 'World Atlas of Hydropower & Dams', *The International Journal of Hydropower & Dams*, January 1995.

33. T.P. Tung et al., 'Small Hydro Development: Opportunities, Constraints and Technology Outlook', paper presented at the International Conference on Hydropower, Energy and the Environment, Stockholm, 14–16 June 1993.

34. See, e.g., 'Introducing a New Forum for the Mini Hydro Debate', *The International Journal of Hydropower & Dams*, March 1994; B. Pandey, 'Micro Hydro

Development in Nepal Based on Local Manufacture', *The International Journal of Hydropower & Dams*, March 1994. For discussions on the local socio-economic impact of micro-hydro development, see East Consult, 'Socio-Economic Evaluation of the Impact of Micro-Hydro Schemes on Rural Communities of Nepal', Kathmandu 1990; J.S. Gore, 'When is Small Beautiful? Approaches to Decentralized Hydropower Projects in Nepal', Master's Project, University of California at Berkeley, May 1994.

35. A.R. Inversin, 'Micro-Hydropower in Developing Countries', *Alternative Sources of Energy*, June/July 1986. Inflatable rubber weirs are a high-tech answer to sedimentation: when flows are high the weir can be deflated and removed, allowing sediments to wash away (see, e.g., Tung et al., 'Small Hydro Development', p. 10).

36. R.P. Taylor, *Rural Energy Development in China*, Resources for the Future, Washington, DC, 1981; X. Cheng, 'Recent Trends in Small Hydro Power in China', *International Water Power & Dam Construction*, September 1994.

37. See, e.g., J. Bell, 'Hydrodollars in the Himalaya', *The Ecologist*, Vol. 24, No. 3, 1994; 'Victory! Arun III Cancelled: Alternatives to be Considered', *World Rivers Review*, August 1995. The 5 MW Andhi Kola scheme was completed in 1991 at a cost of only $700 per kW (Pandey, 'Micro Hydro Development in Nepal'). By 1993 Nepalese developers had installed 924 locally built turbines at small hydro sites (W. Byers, 'Small Hydro: What Will Trigger the Development Explosion?', *Hydro Review*, February 1995).

38. See, e.g., F.W. Olson et al. (eds.), *Proceedings of the Symposium on Small Hydropower and Fisheries*, American Fisheries Society, Bethesda, MD, 1985; M. Brower, *Cool Energy: Renewable Solutions to Environmental Problems*, MIT Press, Cambridge, MA, 1993, p. 116.

39. 'Resettlement Associated with Hydro Projects in China', *Water Power & Dam Construction*, February 1993.

40. Tung et al., 'Small Hydro Development', p. 11.

41. Free-flow turbines could soon be economically viable for remote, off-grid sites (J.E. Francfort, 'Free-Flow Hydroelectric River Turbines: Preliminary Market Analysis', Idaho National Engineering Laboratory, Idaho Falls, January 1995, mimeo).

42. 'Reclamation Uprating Program Nears Completion; Adds 1,600 MW of Capacity to System', *Hydro Review*, August 1994.

43. Brower, *Cool Energy*, p. 113.

44. Hydro proponents argue the huge potential for new generating capacity at non-hydro dams by quoting the figure that only 5% of 76,000 US dams have been fitted with turbines. However, the great majority of the dams are too small or remote to make electricity generation feasible, and many have little water to spare for releases through turbines (S.F. Railsback et al., *Environmental Impacts of Increased Hydroelectric Development at Existing Dams*, Oak Ridge National Laboratory, Oak Ridge, TN, 1991, p. 4).

45. See Brower, *Cool Energy*, p. 114. The plant factor of retrofitted dams tends to be relatively low as using water for power production does not usually have priority at dams built for other purposes (see Railsback et al., *Environmental Impacts*).

46. See Brower, *Cool Energy*, pp. 117–18.

47. J.E. Cavanagh et al., 'Ocean Energy Systems', in Johansson et al. (eds.), *Renewable Energy*.

48. 'Removal of Subsidies', *ECO*, Geneva, 30 October 1995.

49. See, e.g., EDF and NRDC, *Power Failure*.

9

Industry Applies, Man Conforms: The Political Economy of Damming

Science Finds,
Industry Applies,
Man Conforms.

Motto of 1933 Chicago World's Fair

Despite the terrible social, environmental and economic record of large dams, and the many other ways of satisfying needs for energy and of managing land and water, huge dam projects continue to be proposed and built. The dam-industry juggernaut maintains its momentum because constructing dams benefits powerful political and economic interests, and because the process of planning, promoting and building dams is usually secretive and insulated from democratic dissent. Those who suffer because of dams – whether directly through the loss of their livelihoods or indirectly through government subsidies to uneconomic projects – are rarely able to hold the dam-building bureaucrats and consultants accountable for their actions. The lack of accountability is clearly at its worst under authoritarian regimes and where democracy and the structures of civil society are weak. But even in supposedly advanced democracies, dam-building agencies have for years insulated themselves from public control and avoided independent scrutiny of the assumptions used to justify their projects.

The great majority of large dams have been built by state agencies, and their poor economic performance has invariably been obscured behind a veil of public subsidies. Although some $20 billion are spent on dams every year, no comprehensive reviews of the performance of large dams have been carried out comparing their actual operational record with that projected. Aid agencies sometimes carry out internal evaluations of completed dams, but these are normally confidential and usually only assess project construction and not operation.[1] This lack of independent assessments of dam performance greatly reduces the likelihood of dam builders learning – or being forced to learn – from their mistakes. Since the early 1990s, however, the veil of subsidies has started to be lifted as governments have attempted to attract private investors to pay for their dams. Private investors need to be convinced that large dams are secure and profitable investments – and the dam industry is slowly being forced to reveal that largely they are not.

The Ideology of Dams

> Water which is allowed to enter the sea is wasted.
>
> Joseph Stalin, 1929

> Quebec is a vast hydroelectric plant in the bud ... and every day, millions of potential kilowatt-hours flow downstream and out to sea. What a waste!
>
> Robert Bourassa, *Power from the North*, 1983

> It is difficult to conceive of a scenario in which India can afford to let the waters of a major river such as the Narmada run wasted to the sea.
>
> World Bank, 1987

The gargantuan scale of large dams, and their seeming ability to bring powerful and capricious natural forces under human control, gives them a unique hold on the human imagination. Perhaps more than any other technology, massive dams symbolize the progress of humanity from a life ruled by nature and superstition to one where nature is ruled by science, and superstition vanquished by rationality. They also symbolize the might of the state that built them, making huge dams a favourite of nation-builders and autocrats. When a dam is given such a powerful symbolic role, its economic and technical rationale and potential negative impacts fade into insignificance in the decision-making process.

There are a number of recurrent ideological themes in the writings and speeches of the proponents of large dams. One is the 'taming' of 'wild' or 'turbulent' rivers, the appeal of which is rooted in the biblical exhortation to go forth and subdue nature; another is the comparison of dams to temples and other places of worship. Probably the most common refrain is that undammed rivers are 'wasted'. Politicians and developers have for most of this century expounded that a river has no value unless it is in some way *controlled* (and not just used) by humans. This belief negates the intrinsic worth of rivers – the veins of the hydrological cycle, shapers of the landscape, and providers of life to many of the earth's species; it negates their cultural, aesthetic and spiritual importance, and it negates the economic value of unregulated rivers to the hundreds of millions of people who depend on them for drinking water, food, transport, recreation and other uses. The wasted river ideologues are justifying not human use of rivers, but the expropriation of rivers from one set of users to another.

Midnight at noon: The High Aswan Dam

> 'My name is Ozymandias, king of kings:
> Look on my works, ye Mighty, and despair!'
>
> Percy Bysshe Shelley, 'Ozymandias', 1819

In July 1952 a group of army officers headed by Colonel Gamal Abdel Nasser overthrew Egypt's King Farouk. Soon after taking power, the Revolutionary Command Council became fixated by a proposal circulating Egypt's ministries for a huge dam across the Nile at Aswan. The supposed purpose of the dam was to iron out the great river's yearly cycle of floods and droughts, expand irrigation and produce electricity. Perhaps even more important, however, was the political significance to the young, revolutionary government of undertaking such an audacious endeavour. Historian John Waterbury says that:

> Politically it had the advantage of being gigantic and daring, thrusting Egypt into the vanguard of modern hydraulic engineering. Moreover, during its construction and after its completion, it would be highly visible and fittingly monumental.

The Revolutionary Command Council's determination to build the dam, and their concept of it as a monument to national pride, was passed on to the rest of the government, and to the Egyptian people. Officials who had once questioned the viability of the project changed their minds or kept quiet. An official from the Ministry of Public Works explained the atmosphere at the time by quoting from the *Rubáiyát of Omar Khayyám*: 'When the King says it is midnight at noon, the wise man says behold the moon.'[2]

The primacy of the political motivations for building the high dam at Aswan is evidenced by the paucity of investigations into the dam's likely benefits and costs. According to US political scientists Robert Rycroft and Joseph Szyliowicz, the economic justification of the dam was based on calculations 'clearly of doubtful validity' which 'were based on very rough estimates that had been gathered in the first flush of enthusiasm for the project and were never refined'. The economic analysis of High Aswan 'ignored accepted means of assessing projects, particularly in the field of water resources, for which an extensive literature was available'. Agricultural benefits, for example, were calculated without any thorough surveys of the quality of the land to be brought under irrigation, and without taking account of the cost of providing the necessary canals and other irrigation infrastructure. Similarly, add Rycroft and Szyliowicz, 'no study ever evaluated the cost of generating power through the High Dam or compared it to the construction of thermal power stations.' Although many of the downstream environmental costs of the dam were anticipated, none was included in its economic analysis.[3]

In late 1955, spurred by reports that the Soviet Union was also keen to help Nasser build the dam and so strengthen its influence in Africa, the World Bank and the American and British governments put together a funding package for the project. The Western proposal came with a number of conditions, including one requiring that the Egyptian government avoid 'imprudent' financial decisions – in part a reference to arms purchases from the Soviet bloc. Furious at the conditions, Nasser rejected the offer. Seven months of fruitless negotiations followed, at the end of which the Western powers withdrew their proposal. Soon after, Nasser used what he saw as the West's insulting colonialist behaviour as a justification for seizing the Suez Canal, setting off the brief 1956 war with Israel, Britain and France.

The Suez crisis and the dispute over financing Aswan firmly established Egypt in the Soviet camp, and the dam was finally built with technical assistance and money from the USSR. It also enshrined the dam as a nationalist icon. According to Waterbury, 'Nasser and his associates could no longer regard the dam as simply a big engineering project, but rather came to hold it up as the symbol of Egypt's will to resist imperialist endeavours to destroy the revolution.' The pro-dam fervour was such that crowds gathered outside the Egyptian parliament and chanted: 'Nasser, Nasser, we come to salute you; after the Dam our land will be paradise.'[4]

A dam for all ideologies

A similar mixture of Cold War rivalries and post-colonial dreams combined to push the construction of Akosombo Dam. In 1955, just two years before the British colony Gold Coast became Ghana, the first independent state in sub-Saharan Africa, a British civil servant produced a plan for a huge dam at Akosombo. The dam would provide electricity to turn local bauxite into aluminium and so provide the Empire with its own major source of the strategically important metal. It would also power the factories which would spearhead the industrialization of the colony and enable the conversion of hundreds of thousands of hectares from dryland peasant farming to modern intensive irrigated agriculture, and it would catalyse a bustling inland shipping industry on a reservoir the size of Lebanon.

Some leading figures in the Ghanaian independence movement were suspicious of such grandiose visions and favoured smaller dams. Kwame Nkrumah, the country's charismatic first president, however, was inspired by the mammoth dams he had seen on a trip to the USSR and the role

role they had played in Stalin's programme of rapid rural electrification and industrialization. Nkrumah envisioned that Akosombo would provide the electricity to convert Ghana into a 'modern' nation-state and also become a symbol of the determination of his country and himself to play a leading role in a rapidly industrializing, post-colonial Africa. Once Nkrumah began to preach to the Ghanaian people how their young country would build an engineering marvel which would create the world's largest man-made lake and impel them toward industrial development, opposition to Akosombo became futile.

Despite his pro-Soviet sympathies, Nkrumah's compulsion to build Akosombo led him to seek funding from the World Bank and the US and British governments. The Americans also had a strong commercial interest in the project: part of the funding deal was that the US multinational Kaiser Corporation would own the aluminium smelter which would consume the bulk of the dam's power. As funding negotiations progressed it become clear that Ghana would benefit less and less from the project, but Nkrumah was not prepared to lose the dam. Kaiser insisted on a 30-year contract ensuring electricity for the smelter at a small fraction of its cost to other users; it demanded the right to use imported ore, rather than bauxite mined in Ghana; and it demanded that the dam be built and operated to maximize power generation and the irrigation plans be dropped. The original justification for the dam was thus torn to shreds. Far from bringing Ghana riches and prestige, Akosombo left the country deep in hock and swept by a wave of corruption fed by the money which flowed in to build the dam. Nkrumah inaugurated the dam in January 1966, and was overthrown in a coup just one month later.[5]

Of course it is not just in Africa that dams have become nationalistic and ideological icons. At the 1932 inauguration ceremony for Dneprostroi, the world's first major dam, the deputy chief engineer told a crowd of 60,000 workers and dignitaries that the dam was

> ...the mighty foundation of socialist construction. Only the October Revolution made possible the construction of such a giant. The proletariat of the USSR through Dneprostroevtski has shown what the Bolsheviks can do![6]

Today, large dams continue to exert a powerful attraction as political symbols. At the February 1995 dedication ceremony for the Three Gorges Dam, Chinese Premier Li Peng (a Soviet-trained hydraulic engineer) pledged that 'no difficulty will beat us ... By 2009 a magnificent Three Gorges project will stand rock solid in the great land of China.'[7] According to a report by the US-based group Human Rights Watch, 'Li Peng seems intent ... on forcing [Three Gorges] through as a means of symbolizing China's fast-emerging "superpower" status and as a vehicle for personal glorification.'[8]

Dams and Domination

> What we call Man's power over Nature turns out to be a power exercised by some men over other men with Nature as its instrument.
>
> C.S. Lewis, *The Abolition of Man*, 1943

A number of writers, most notably Karl Wittfogel and Max Horkheimer of the so-called Frankfurt School of philosophers, have argued that 'the domination of nature leads inescapably to the domination of some people by others', as environmental historian Donald Worster elegantly summarizes their arguments.[9] The domination of rivers is one of the clearest illustrations of the link between the control of nature and the control of people. Large dams are not built and operated by all of society but by an elite with bureaucratic, political or economic power. The dams give this elite the ability to direct water for their own benefit, depriving the previous users of some or all of their access to riverine resources.

Thayer Scudder of the California Institute of Technology, a consultant on a number of dam schemes around the world, wrote in 1990 that

> ...what is becoming distressingly clear is the systematic way governing elites may use river basin development projects not just to transfer resources to themselves and their supporters but also to pursue self-serving political goals at the expense of riverine populations, and of ethnic and religious minorities and opposition groups at regional and national levels.[10]

One of the clearest examples of this process at work is Sri Lanka's Mahaweli Programme. Plans written in the 1970s stated that the 60,000 hectares to be irrigated in the Mahaweli basin would be allocated to settlers from Sri Lanka's three main ethnic groups – Buddhist Sinhalese, Hindu Tamils and Muslims – according to their proportion in the national population. The local population and those displaced by the project's five dams and other infrastructure would be given priority in receiving land.

The actual land allotment pattern has been very different. In 1983 a cabal of senior officials in charge of the project began to enact a plan to settle as many Sinhalese farmers as possible in the project area, effectively driving a wedge of Sinhalese settlers between the Tamil-dominated areas to the north and south. One of the Mahaweli officials wrote at the time that the location of the project area 'gives the government a clear and extremely effective way to destroy the very foundation' of the breakaway state sought by the Tamil minority.[11] The government also sought to reduce the influence of Tamils in the Mahaweli area by intimidating them into leaving. Hundreds of Tamil youths were rounded up by security forces in 1985 and detained for two years. Tamil militants retaliated by massacring hundreds of Sinhalese settlers.[12] Throughout these political machinations and atrocities the project's foreign donors – in particular the World Bank and the governments of the US, Britain, Sweden and West Germany – turned a blind eye and continued to pump funds into the Mahaweli scheme.

Turkey's Southeast Anatolia Project, or GAP (from its Turkish acronym), envisaged eventually to include 22 dams at a cost of some $32 billion, has both domestic and international political purposes. Internally, the irrigation and hydropower megaproject is strengthening the presence of the Turkish state in a poverty-stricken, remote area of 75,000 square kilometres – nearly a tenth of the country's landmass – which is populated mainly by Kurds and is a stronghold of the militant separatist Kurdistan Workers Party (PKK). Sixty thousand Kurds were displaced by the Atatürk Dam, the centrepiece of the project, on which are emblazoned the words of modern Turkey's founder, 'Ne Mutlu Turkum Diyene' ('Lucky is the one who is a Turk'). Externally, GAP gives Turkey the ability to regulate the headwaters of the Euphrates and Tigris and so control much of the water supply for Syria and Iraq downstream, countries which already suffer chronic water shortages. 'We can stop the flow of water into Syria and Iraq for up to eight months without the same water overflowing our dams, in order to regulate their political behaviour', the site manager of the Atatürk Dam told an American journalist in 1993.[13]

Dams and Pork

The practice among members of the US Congress of jostling for federal funds for big-money schemes in their home districts is referred to as 'pork-barrel politics'. (The phrase 'pork barrel' derives from the frenzy of the hungry slaves on Southern plantations when their owners marked a special occasion by rolling out a barrel of salted pork.) For decades, water projects were, and to a lesser extent remain, the pork *par excellence* for US politicians: easy to justify (flood control, irrigation, hydropower, recreation, navigation); built by powerful federal agencies which could shield project information from the public and defeat most opposition; and hugely expensive. 'Water projects', says author Marc Reisner, 'were the oil can that lubricated the nation's legislative machinery. Important legislation – an education bill, a foreign aid bill, a conservation bill – was imprisoned until the President agreed to let a powerful committee chairman tack on a rider authorizing his pet dam.'[14]

From the late 1970s onwards, however, it became increasingly harder for US politicians to find good dam pork due to budgetary restraints, environmental opposition and growing public awareness that most water projects were economic boondoggles. By the time that President Bill Clinton appointed Daniel Beard – a staunch opponent of more big dams – as Commissioner of the Bureau of Reclamation, the corrupt system appeared to be all but dead. But, zombie-like, it reappeared from the grave in 1995 when John Doolittle, a powerful Republican Congressman from Sacramento, California – described by the *San Francisco Chronicle* as a 'legislative handmaiden for a small group of wealthy agricultural interests' – introduced a proposal into Congress to build a $2 billion multipurpose dam near Sacramento which had already been rejected several times over the previous two decades. An October 1995 editorial in the *San Francisco Chronicle* scorned Doolittle's 233-metre-high Auburn Dam as a 'concrete monstrosity that oinks'.[15] Auburn was voted down yet again by a key congressional committee in June 1996; Doolittle and the Sacramanto Chamber of Commerce, however, have vowed to continue lobbying for federal funds for the dam.

Various forms of pork-barrel politics are seen elsewhere. Philip Fearnside of the National Institute for Research in Amazonia believes that Balbina Dam was essentially an election bribe from the office of the Brazilian president to the state of Amazonas. Before the 1982 elections, the military political party was in power both in Amazonas and at the national level. Balbina was presented to the public of Amazonas, says Fearnside, 'as an example of the state governor's ability to extract benefits from Brasília'. The technical viability of the dam was irrelevant. Fearnside describes how projects like Balbina are known in Brazil as 'pharaonic works'.

> Like the pyramids of ancient Egypt, these massive public works demand the effort of an entire society to complete but bring virtually no economic returns. Even if the structures are simply built and abandoned, they serve the short-term interests of all concerned – from firms that receive construction contracts to politicians wanting the employment and commerce the projects provide to their districts during the construction phase.[16]

In 1995, a Brazilian senate commission found nearly 4,000 infrastructure projects, many of the largest ones dams, which had been abandoned during construction due to a lack of funds.[17]

Technocrats without a Cause: Dam-Building Bureaucracies

> Once it is fully established, bureaucracy is among those social structures which are the hardest to destroy.
>
> Max Weber, 'Bureaucracy', 1910

> This is the most autocratic and irresponsible department of our Government ... with personal accountability to no one.
>
> Senator Francis Tracy of New Mexico on the Bureau of Reclamation, 1912

> No more lawless or irresponsible Federal group than the Corps of Army Engineers has ever attempted to operate in the United States, either outside of or within the law.
>
> Harold Ickes, ex-US Secretary of the Interior, 1951

There are two main types of dam-building bureaucracies: national agencies such as Moscow's Hydroproject Institute and Pakistan's Water and Power Development Authority, in most cases established to build dams for specific purposes such as hydropower or irrigation; and river basin development agencies like the James Bay Development Corporation and the Organization for the Development of the Senegal River Valley (OMVS), whose mandate is more localized but more far-reaching, their influence often extending to almost every sector of the local or regional economy.

As dam-building agencies grow in size and power they increasingly lose sight of their original aims and come to confuse means with ends – a process which social theorists such as Max Weber and Ivan Illich have argued is typical with bureaucracies. Without new projects the agencies would have their budgets slashed and their prestige diminished. Their prime purpose therefore tends to become the securing of funds for building more dams – often in alliance with pork-hungry politicians – in order to ensure their own perpetuation, rather than to improve social welfare.

The overriding need to find projects to build encourages increasingly desperate and dishonest tactics. The corrupt methods that the Army Corps of Engineers used to win approval for their projects were explained to a Los Angeles audience in 1974 by the then Governor of Georgia, Jimmy Carter:

> In many of the Corps of Engineers' dam projects around the nation, the benefit/cost ratios have been grossly distorted. Data and premises on which project approvals are sought are erroneous and outdated. False justifications are attempted....
>
> A recent [General Accounting Office] analysis of the Sprewell Bluff dam project on the Flint River in Georgia indicated vividly the fallacies in existing Corps of Engineers analysis procedures. Construction costs were underestimated, extremely low interest rates were assumed, nearby lakes were ignored, population projections were exaggerated, environmental damage was concealed, power production estimates were based on overloaded generator ratings, no archaeological losses were included, and major recreational benefits were claimed in spite of official opposition from state and federal recreation agencies.[18]

The extent to which the original aims of the two main dam-building agencies in the US – the Corps and the Bureau of Reclamation – became lost to the instinct of bureaucratic self-perpetuation is shown by the intense rivalry which developed between them. Marc Reisner explains how, as suitable dam sites became harder to find, the agencies urged Congress to shell out funding for dams which they knew were unnecessary, but which one agency feared the other might build if they did not do it first.[19]

The original model for the second type of dam bureaucracy is the Tennessee Valley Authority, established during the Great Depression by President Franklin D. Roosevelt. The mainly agricultural areas along the Tennessee River, a tributary of the Mississippi, were some of the poorest in the US. Farm productivity was low and soil erosion and deforestation high. The TVA was meant to change this by taking control of the valley away from the corrupting influence of local elected officials, and placing it under the guidance of a federally funded bureaucracy staffed with highly educated technocrats and run by three directors appointed by the US President.

The 1933 bill which created the TVA charged the authority 'with the broadest duty of planning for the proper use, conservation, and development of the natural resources of the Tennessee River drainage basin'. Dams, to provide power, control floods and improve navigation, were a central part of this vision of centrally planned development. Just months after its establishment, the TVA began work on Norris Dam. By the time the last TVA dams were completed in 1979, the system included 38 large dams.[20]

The TVA's international influence was immense. Thousands of foreign planners, engineers and politicians visited the Tennessee Valley at the expense of the US government and returned home to spread the gospel that one or more multipurpose dams built by a centralized authority could quickly transform any regional economy from subsistence agriculture to agribusiness and industry. 'For a number of years after World War II,' wrote economist Albert Hirschman in 1967, 'any river valley development scheme, whether it concerned the Sao Francisco River in Brazil, the Papaloapan River in Mexico, the Cauca in Columbia, the Dez in Iran, or the Damodar in eastern India, was presented to a reassured public as a true copy ... of the Tennessee Valley Authority.'[21]

The TVA took on this totemic role without anyone knowing much about what it had actually achieved – or considering whether a model applicable to the US South could be transplanted with the same results to other parts of the world. The TVA was supposed to be the epitome of 'integrated development planning' but in fact quickly became chiefly an electricity utility, spending only a few per cent of its budget on non-power programmes such as agricultural training and reforestation. The TVA was seen as synonymous with dams, but it built few large dams after 1945: in 1955 the TVA's coal-burning capacity overtook its hydro capacity; and in 1967 it started work on the world's largest nuclear power plant. In 1993 only a seventh of the TVA's power was generated at its dams.

Until the 1980s, few studies of the impacts of the TVA had been done by anyone outside the Authority. Independent analyses carried out since then do little to vindicate the TVA's glowing international reputation. Studies show that the TVA gave little long-term assistance to the more than 50,000 people who lost land and livelihood to their reservoirs. Sociologist Nancy Grant's description of the impacts of TVA displacement echoes the failure of modern resettlement plans in developing countries:

> ...the large-scale displacement of farm units and the subsequent relocation of families caused severe economic problems for the families and the overpopulated area in which they were forced to resetttle. The tenant and poor landowner bore the brunt of readjustment ... 69 per cent of the farmers in the Wheeler Dam area were relocated to inferior land ... TVA compensated only those individuals who could show a direct, measurable loss; it ignored those who did not have written or formal access to the lands and refused to acknowledge the local custom of informal use of nontitled land as a means for supplementing income. Land speculators and swindlers descended on the Tennessee Valley, involving families in phoney or unprofitable investments ...

A disproportionate number of the poorest families displaced were black: according to Grant, the racial prejudice of both the local people and the planners meant that these families experienced particular difficulty in relocation.[22]

An analysis of the overall economic record of the TVA's first 50 years, prepared for the Washington DC-based Environmental Policy Institute, concluded that despite the spending of billions of dollars in federal money, 'evidence does not support the widely held belief that TVA contributed substantially to the economic growth of the Tennessee Valley region.'[23]

The TVA was forced to slow down the pace of its dam-building programme in the 1950s as it increasingly ran out of viable sites. The agency, however, was determined to continue building dams. TVA historians William Wheeler and Michael McDonald write that:

> TVA came to believe that projects meant progress, that dams – even on the tributaries – would bring prosperity. If citizen participation was needed, TVA would create it; if detailed justifications (in the form of cost–benefit analyses) were required, TVA would create them too.[24]

The 39-metre-high Tellico Dam, sited on a minor tributary of the Tennessee, was completed in November 1979 after 40 years of planning, lobbying and creative accounting. The TVA steamrolled over the protests of local landowners and politicians, environmentalists and Native Americans angry at the flooding of burial grounds and of the sacred Cherokee capital, Chota. In January 1979, a Congressional committee unanimously concluded that even though Tellico was 95 per cent complete, its benefits would still be less than the cost of finishing it. Despite this, two Congressional supporters of Tellico, in what Wheeler and McDonald describe as 'a blatant piece of political chicanery', managed to sneak an amendment onto a large public works bill mandating the completion of the project.

Wheeler and McDonald believe that Tellico was a largely Phyrric victory for the TVA. Their deceitful tactics made so many enemies that they would never be allowed to build another dam, and there would be little political support for measures to relieve the agency of any of its crippling debt to the federal government – $26 billion by 1995 – accumulated mainly by its disastrous nuclear power programme.[25]

The lesson of the TVA, the Corps and the Bureau is that although dam-building agencies will go to great lengths to continue building projects for the sole purpose of maintaining their power and prestige, eventually they will overreach themselves, lose public support, and – assuming some degree of democratic control – be forced to scale down their activities to managing the infrastructure they have already built. BuRec has steadily whittled down its workforce from 17,000 in the glamour days of the early 1960s, to under 6,500 in 1995. Commissioner Daniel Beard told the engineers gathered at the 1994 Congress of the International Commission on Large Dams in Durban, South Africa, that

> ...our traditional approach for solving problems – the construction of dams and associated facilities – is no longer publicly acceptable. We are going to have to get out of the dam-building business. Our future lies with improving water resource management and environmental restoration activities, not water project construction.[26]

A Vibrant Corps? Dam-Building Companies

> We want to be a vibrant corps of dam engineers who assist in uplifting the people and freeing them from the bondage of poverty.
>
> Theo P.C. van Robbroek, President of ICOLD, 1994

Dam building is a business currently worth some $20 billion each year.[27] A large proportion of this sum goes to a relatively limited number of multinational engineering, equipment manufacture and construction corporations (see Table 9.1). The huge amount of money at stake has encouraged these companies and their national and international industry groups such as ICOLD and the US National Hydropower Association to constitute an active pro-dam lobby. Some of their work is public relations: pro-dam articles in engineering journals, letters to newspaper editors, brochures, 'educational' materials, and the smart visitor centres built at many larger dams. The industry also does conventional political lobbying: in late 1995, for example, a group of US firms including turbine

Table 9.1 Major corporations in the international dam industry

Company	Country	Prominent dam projects with company involvement
Acres Consulting Services Ltd/ Acres International Ltd (ec)	Canada	Warsak, Akosombo, Karnali (Chisapani), Kpong, Lesotho Highlands, Mahaweli, Mekong 'Run-of-River' Dams, Nam Theun 2, Owen Falls, Tarbela, Three Gorges, Warsak, Xiaolangdi
Asea Brown Boveri (ABB) (c/eq)	Switzer-land/ Sweden	Atatürk, Bakun, Batang Ai, Cabora Bassa, Chicoasén, Guavio, Itaipú, Kemano, Karakaya, Macagua II, Magat, Muela (Lesotho Highlands), Nam Theun-Hinboun, Pangani, Pangue, Rantembe (Mahaweli), Sardar Sarovar, Tarbela, Tucuruí, Uri, Xeset, Xingó, Zimapán
Balfour Beatty & Co. (ec/c)	UK	Kainji, Kindaruma, Muela (Lesotho Highlands), Pergau, Samanalawewa, Victoria (Mahaweli)
Bechtel Corp. (ec/c)	USA	Bekhme, Churchill Falls, Hoover, James Bay, Karnali (Chisapani), Kemano, Nam Ngum 2, Xiaolangdi
Coyne et Bellier (ec)	France	Berke, Cabora Bassa, Diama, Kariba, Katse (Lesotho Highlands), Kedung Ombo, M'bali (Boali 3), Roseires, Sir, Tarbela, Xiaolangdi
Doka (c)	Austria	Akosombo, Balbina, Guri, Itaipú, Karakaya, Três Irmãos
Dumez (c)	France	Ertan, Itaipú, Saguling, Xiaolangdi, Yacyretá, Zimapán
ECI/ATC Engineering Consultants Inc. (ec)	USA	Acaray, Bhumibol, Kremasta, Magat, Pantabangan, Sirikit
Elektrowatt Engineering Services Ltd (ec)	Switzer-land	Aguacapa (Agua Caliente), Atatürk, Batoka, Karakaya, Khao Laem, Nam Theun 1, Nangbeto, Rantembe (Mahaweli), Samanalawewa
Elin Energie-versorgung (eq)	Austria	Agus, Bhumibol, Caruachi, Chiew Larn, Cirata, Mosul, Pak Mun, Yamdrok Tso
Energoproject (c/ec)	Yugo-slavia	Bayano, Djerdap (Iron Gates), Kafue Gorge, Kiambere, Sir
General Electric Canada (eq)	Canada	Akosombo, Brisay (James Bay), Caruachi, Churchill Falls, Ertan, Geheyan, Grand Coulee, Guavio, Guri, Itumbiara, Laforge 2 (James Bay), La Grande 1 (James Bay), Pangue, Tarbela, Tucuruí
GEC Alsthom [Neyrpic] (eq)	France/ UK	Balbina, Berke, Cabora Bassa, Churchill Falls, Diama, Eastmain 1 (James Bay), Guatape, Itaipú, Laforge 1 (James Bay), La Grande 1 & 2 (James Bay), Pergau, Petit Saut, Rio Grande, Samanalawewa, Sir, Três Irmãos, Tucuruí, Turkwell

Company	Country	Prominent dam projects with company involvement
Sir Alexander Gibb & Partners (ec)	UK	Aswan, Kariba, Katse and Mohale (Lesotho Highlands), Kiri, Victoria (Mahaweli), Owen Falls, Pergau, Roseires, Samanalawewa
Harza Engineering Co. (ec)	USA	Ambuklao, Bakun, Brokopondo, Caruachi, Cerron Grande (Silencio), Corpus Christi, Ertan, Ghazi Barotha, Guri, Kalabagh, Mohale (Lesotho Highlands), Macagua II, Mangla, Tarbela, Three Gorges, Yacyretá
Hitachi (eq)	Japan	Akosombo, Guri, Macagua II, Shuikou, Sir, Srinakharin, Tarbela, Temengor
Hochtief AG (c)	Germany	Aswan, Cabora Bassa, Chixoy, Ertan, Ghazi Barotha, Katse (Lesotho Highlands), Nangbeto, Rantembe (Mahaweli), Tarbela, Xiaolangdi
Impregilo/Cogefar/ Impresit/Girola/ Lodigiani (c)*	Italy	Akosombo, Bakolori, Chivor, Chixoy, Daniel Palacios (Amaluza/Paute), Dez, El Cajón, Ertan, Fortuna, Ghazi Barotha, Guatape, Itezhitezhi, Kainji, Kariba, Katse (Lesotho Highlands), Keban, Koussou, Kpong, La Grande 2 and 4 (James Bay), Piedra del Aguila, Roseires, Tarbela, Xiaolangdi, Yacyretá, Zimapán
Knight Piésold & Partners [Watermeyer Piésold Legge Uhlmann (WPLU)] (ec)	UK	Batoka, Corpus Christi, Katse and Mohale (Lesotho Highlands), Kiambere, Masinga, Nam Theun 2, Pergau, Turkwell
Kvaerner (eq)	Norway	Aswan, Bhumibol, Caruachi, Curua-Una, Panchet Hill (Damodar Valley), Furnas, Idukki, Kafue Gorge, Kaptai (Karnafuli), Kariba, Kotmale (Mahaweli), Kpong, Lubuge, Muela (Lesotho Highlands), Nagarjunasagar, Owen Falls, Pangue, Pergau, Roseires, Uri, Victoria (Mahaweli), Xeset, Zimapán
Lahmeyer International GmbH (ec)	Germany	Agus, Arun III, Bakun, Batoka, Chico River, Corpus Christi, Chixoy, Lang Suan, Lesotho Highlands, Mohale and Muela (Lesotho Highlands), Nam Leuk, Selingué, Yacyretá
Losinger (c/ec)	Switzer-land	Manantali, El Cajón, Khao Laem, Victoria (Mahaweli)
Mitsubishi (eq)	Japan	Chicoasén, Chixoy, Guri, Macagua II, Magat, Mangla, Piedra del Aguila, Saguling, Samanalawewa, Srinakharin, Temengor, Yacyretá
Mitsui Construction Co. (c/eq)	Japan	Guavio, Nam Ngum, Samanalawewa, Temengor, Xeset
Morrison-Knudsen Corp. [Intern'l Engineering Co., (IECO)] (ec)	USA	Hoover [Chixoy, Daniel Palacios (Amaluza/ Paute), Itaipú, Kaptai (Karnafuli), Shuikou]
Motor Colombus Consulting Engineers Inc. (ec)	Switzer-land	Bakun, Chixoy, El Cajón, Mahaweli, Nam Theun 2

Company	Country	Prominent dam projects with company involvement
Nippon Koei (ec)	Japan	Asahan, Kulekhani, Mohale (Lesotho Highlands), Nam Ngum, Samanalawewa
Norconsult/ Norpower (ec)	Norway	Epupa, Ertan, Karnali (Chisapani), Lubuge, Paulo Afonso, Theun-Hinboun, Turkwell, Yantan, Xeset
Siemens (eq)	Germany	Cabora Bassa, Daniel Palacios (Amaluza/Paute), Gabcikovo, Guavio, Guri, Itaipú, Itaparica, Macagua II, Nam Ngum 2, Nova Ponte, Tarbela, Xingó
Skanska (c)	Sweden	Gitaru, Kotmale (Mahaweli), Pergau, Serra da Mesa, Uri, Urrá I
SNC-Lavalin Inc. (ec)	Canada	Dai Ninh, Idukki, Brisay (James Bay), Karnali (Chisapani), Kpong, Laforge 1 (James Bay), La Grande 1 and 2 (James Bay), Magat, Manantali, Temengor, Three Gorges, Xiaolangdi
Snowy Mountains Engineering Co. (SMEC) (ec)	Australia	Batang Ai, Kedung Ombo, Khao Laem, Lubuge, Mohale (Lesotho Highlands), Nam Theun 2, Pergau, Sardar Sarovar, Southern Okavango Project (2 dams)
Sogreah (ec)	France	Cabora Bassa, Dai Ninh, Diama, Katse (Lesotho Highlands), Khashm El Girba, Madura Oya (Mahaweli), Nam Leuk, Nangbeto, Pak Mun, Selingué, Turkwell
Spie Batignolles (c)	France	Muela (Lesotho Highlands), Saguling, Tarbela, Turkwell
Sulzer Hydro Ltd/ Sulzer-Escher Wyss (eq)	Switzerland	Atatürk, Chixoy, Guavio, Karakaya, Kemano, Macagua II, Nangbeto, Rantembe (Mahaweli), Sir, Tarbela
Sumitomo (eq)	Japan	Guavio, Piedra del Aguila, Samanalawewa, Sardar Sarovar, Sir
Toshiba (eq)	Japan	Guavio, Guri, Macagua II, Saguling, Sir, Yacyretá
Vianini (c)	Italy	Guavio, Nam Theun-Hinboun, Pak Mun, Sirikit, Srinakharin, Xeset
Vöest Alpine (eq)	Austria	Agus, Atatürk, Cerron Grande (Silencio), Chixoy, Dadin Kowa, Daniel Palacios (Amaluza/Paute), Guavio, Jari, Kainji, Kariba, Magat, Mangla, Mosul, Piedra del Aguila, Playas, Rihand, Roseires, Salvajina, Tarbela, Yamdrok Tso, Yantan
Voith (eq)	Germany	Awash, Cabora Bassa, Itaipú, Itaparica, Itumbiara, Kompienga, Mosul, Paulo Afonso IV, Xingó, Yacyretá
Ed. Züblin AG (c)	Germany	Clyde, El Cajón, Ghazi Barotha, Kamburu, Manantali, Muela (Lesotho Highlands), Rantembe (Mahaweli), Tarbela, Xiaolangdi

manufacturer Voith Hydro and consulting engineers Harza gave a closed briefing for three Congressional sub-committees to urge the US government to help them secure contracts on the Three Gorges project.

A third type of behind-the-scenes pro-dam lobby work is much harder to track, ranging from the golf games and dinner parties of the 'old-boy network' of contractors, aid bureaucrats, dam-agency officials and politicians, to straightforward bribery. The construction industry was at the centre of a stream of scandals in the early 1990s concerning illicit payments to politicians in return for contracts, most notably in Japan, Thailand, Korea, Brazil, Italy, Spain, France and Portugal.[28] Dam building is far from unique in its venality – but it is unusually susceptible to corruption just because the amount of money at stake is greater than with most other construction projects.

In Japan, the $6 billion Nagara Estuary Dam, completed in 1994 and widely seen as serving no useful purpose, has become a notorious symbol of the so-called 'Iron Triangle' formed by the bureaucrats in the Ministry of Construction, politicians and construction companies. The bureaucrats give inside information on bids to the companies, and in return are handed lucrative private-sector jobs when they retire from public service (a practice known as *amakudari* or 'descent from heaven'). The companies also give hefty kickbacks to the politicians who promote public-works projects. Japanese journalists estimate that the payments average around a tenth of the total cost of the projects.[29]

The megadams on the Paraná River are probably the most infamous examples of hydro-corruption. Brazilian journalist Paulo Schilling and Paraguayan ex-legislator Ricardo Canese have described the building of Itaipú as 'possibly the largest fraud in the history of capitalism'. Itaipú was originally projected to cost some $3.4 billion, but skim-offs by the military rulers in Paraguay and Brazil and their cronies contributed to the cost skyrocketing to around $20 billion.[30] Yacyretá (projected cost $2.7 billion, final cost $11.5 billion), built downstream of Itaipú, was

---

Notes to Table 9.1

Square brackets indicate either a company which was taken over or merged with the main listed company, or the previous name of the company.

ec = engineering/environmental consultant; eq = equipment supplier; c = construction company

* Cogefar-Impresit SpA and Impresit-Lodigiani-Girola (Impregilo) SpA merged in 1994 to form Impregilo SpA.

Sources: List compiled from various sources. List is not exhaustive: companies and dams are selected according to available data. 'Involvement' defined as having role in pre-construction consulting and/or construction work and/or equipment supply for dam and/or directly associated infrastructure. Post-construction repair and rehabilitation work not included.

famously described by Argentinean President Carlos Menem in 1990 as a 'monument to corruption'.[31]

Just as corrupt as the direct payment of bribes, and possibly even more important in pushing uneconomic and destructive projects forward, is the process through which projects are selected. The consultants who are appointed to advise a government or funder about whether or not a dam is 'feasible' are inevitably biased toward finding that it is. This bias comes partly from the ideology and professional training of the individuals who do the studies – they are mostly engineers, taught to believe in the necessity of dams and often possessing little in-depth understanding of ecological, social and economic issues. The bias also comes from the strong vested interest of consultancy companies in having dams built: contracts linked to dam construction are often given to the same company (or a parent or other associated firm) which did the initial project studies. Even if the company doing the feasibility study does not tender for later contracts on the same project, the consultants know that if they were regularly to criticize their clients' projects their supply of work would soon dry up.

Conversely, consultants have little incentive to recommend that dams should not go ahead. If a dam turns out to be an economic white elephant and environmental disaster, it is the local people who pay the price. The experts who advised its construction will long ago have received their paycheques and moved on to other projects. The secrecy which surrounds feasibility studies and the lack of post-construction appraisals also means that no one is ever likely to compare what the consultants predicted before construction with what actually happened.

In December 1985, Australia's Snowy Mountains Engineering Corporation (SMEC) was contracted by the government of Botswana to do a technical feasibility study and environmental impact assessment for the Southern Okavango Integrated Water Development Project. SMEC's feasibility study, completed in November 1987, concluded that the two-dam project could meet its goals of increasing water availability, food production and employment for local residents, while also supplying water to a major diamond mine nearby. Five months later, SMEC was given a further contract to do detailed design studies for the project.

Just as construction on the Okavango Project was about to commence in late 1990, local people and international conservation groups started to raise concerns about the impact of the project on the productivity of nearby lands and on wildlife. Much to its credit, the Botswanan government agreed to suspend the project and, in an unprecedented move, invited the International Union for the Conservation of Nature to do an independent review. The IUCN put together a 13-member interdisciplinary team of social scientists, hydrologists, economists, biologists and engineers.

After nine months of field studies the IUCN team unanimously concluded that the SMEC assessments of project benefits were 'excessively optimistic and flawed by conceptual errors' and that there was a 'striking asymmetry in accounting for project costs and benefits' in which 'all of the benefits which could conceivably be quantified were quantified; many of the costs which could have been quantified were unquantified'. The project was suspended after the release of the IUCN report.[32] If the study had not been done, it is highly likely that the project would now be well underway.

Most engineers are supposed to follow codes of ethics drawn up by national or state engineering societies. If these codes were genuinely followed, many of the corrupt practices surrounding dam building would likely disappear. In practice, it is extremely difficult for the public to hold engineers to these ethical standards because of the secrecy which surrounds consultancy work, and the close relationships between engineering companies and consultants and the bodies which are supposed to regulate them.[33]

In 1990 the Canadian environmental and human rights group Probe International filed complaints with provincial engineering regulatory bodies against five Canadian hydro consultancies which had worked on a feasibility study of the Three Gorges Project. Probe International accused the companies – BC Hydro International, Hydro-Québec International, SNC, Lavalin International and Acres International – of 'negligence, incompetence and professional misconduct'. Probe had earlier coordinated an expert group which had written a strongly critical review of the Canadian government-funded Three Gorges feasibility study. One of the members of the group, Vaclav Smil, a geography professor at the University of Manitoba and author of several books on energy and the environment in China, described the feasibility study as 'not engineering and science, merely an expert prostitution paid [for] by Canadian taxpayers'.

Each of the three bodies legislated to regulate the engineering profession – the engineers' own professional associations – turned down the Probe complaint. Quebec's engineering society responded that they only had authority to take disciplinary action against individuals, not companies; British Columbia's Association of Professional Engineers told Probe that their complaints 'tended to be opinions ... and the discipline process of the Association is not structured to arbitrate diverse opinions'. Ontario's engineering association turned down Probe's complaint on the grounds that the consultants followed 'generally accepted international engineering standards' – but failed to define what these standards were, or who sets them or enforces them.[34]

The Ties that Bind: Dependent Industries

The commercial interests which profit from the services provided by dams also help to lobby for their construction. Agribusiness interests, water supply utilities, barge owners and cities that want flood control have teamed up with construction companies to form one side of the US's own 'Iron Triangle', the other sides comprising politicians and the water bureaucracies. Probably the earliest water development lobby group in the US was set up in 1901 to lobby for Corps of Engineers projects. This National Rivers and Harbors Congress consisted of 'local business and political figures, contractors, trade and industry bodies, key members of Congress (who were honorary members of the group), and Corps officers (who were ex-officio members)'.[35]

Electricity-intensive industries, and in particular the aluminium industry, have played a major role in promoting dam building. Unlike other forms of smelting, which rely on heat, the production of aluminium requires passing a powerful electric current through alumina (processed from the ore, bauxite). Electricity is the second biggest cost factor in aluminium production after raw materials. When the small number of multinationals which largely control the aluminium industry decide on where to build smelters, a competitively priced, uninterrupted power supply is one of their key considerations. The builders of large dams, especially those in remote areas, in turn have an interest in attracting aluminium plants as they represent a guaranteed, long-term customer for their electricity.

The hydroelectric and aluminium industries have been inextricably linked since both first emerged. As dam historian Norman Smith explains:

> The first generation of hydro-electric power around 1900 was an early stimulus to the mass production of aluminium, and in turn, as the demand for aluminium's unique properties increased this acted as an important incentive for the development of more hydro-electric projects. The fact that Norway, Canada and the United States became the world's great aluminium producers was in large measure due to these countries being able to generate large quantities of cheap hydro-electric power.[36]

Aluminium smelters are the largest customers for many of the world's most powerful dams: one-fifth of the electricity output of Guri (the world's second most powerful dam) is used to produce aluminium; as is one-third of the output of Grand Coulee (the fourth most powerful); and three-quarters that of Tucuruí (the tenth most powerful). Fifteen per cent of the electricity produced by High Aswan goes to an aluminium smelter.[37]

Hydropower has appeared to be a 'cheap' source of power for aluminium corporations only because they take advantage of considerable subsidies, usually paying a far lower price for their electricity than other users. In the former Soviet Union (the world's second biggest aluminium producer) and Egypt, both dams and aluminium smelters are state-run and the price the smelters pay for power is set by the government to make their aluminium competitive rather than to reflect the cost of electricity production. Where smelters are privately owned, governments guarantee them heavily subsidized hydroelectricity for a number of reasons: because the governments want to build the dams for political reasons and consider it better to have a smelter buy the power cheaply than have it go unsold; because of the belief that a dam–smelter complex will spark off the rapid industrialization of a region – a belief with little basis in experience; and because of the strategic and military importance of aluminium, which is vital for the aeronautic and electronics industries.[38]

The best known example of the above factors at work is in Ghana, where more than half the output of Akosombo is consumed by the Volta Aluminium Company (Valco). President Nkrumah agreed to give Valco massive tax breaks and electricity at a price as little as a quarter that paid by other users – and which was supposed to remain unchanged for three decades. The price has in fact been renegotiated twice but still remains far below the market rate.[39]

Those Who Pay the Piper: Dams and 'Aid'

> Let us remember that the main purpose of aid is not to help other nations but to help ourselves.
>
> President Richard M. Nixon, 1968

The final pillar supporting the modern dam industry is formed by the international aid agencies. Most large dams in Northern countries have been built with domestic government money. In the countries of the South, domestically generated funds for dams have been supplemented with billions of dollars in low-interest loans from development banks and aid agencies. Large dams are a particularly attractive destination for aid funds. During the Cold War, they attracted funds partly because the superpowers wanted visible signs of the dependence of their client states and advertisements for the technological wonders which followed in the wake of capitalism or communism. Macroeconomics were also important: dams offered the prospect of suddenly propelling remote 'undeveloped' areas into the international economy. Today, commercial reasons are clearly dominant in driving aid agencies to support the dam industry: as large-dam building has all but ground to a halt in most Northern countries, the governments which once paid their construction and engineering companies to build dams at home are now helping to keep the companies going by funding projects overseas.

Table 9.2 Major funders of the international dam industry

	Prominent dam projects
Multilateral development banks	
World Bank (International Bank for Reconstruction and Development (IBRD), International Development Assoc. (IDA), International Finance Corp. (IFC))	Aguacapa (Agua Caliente), Aji III, Akosombo, Al Massira (Sidi Cheho), Almatti (Upper Krishna), Amli (Ver II), Arenal (Corobici), Arun III, Awash, Bang Lang (Pattani), Bayano, Berke, Bhumibol, Cerron Grande (Silencio), Chandil, Chandoli (Warna), Chico River, Chicoasén (Manuel Moreno Torres), Chiew Larn, Chivor, Chixoy (Pueblo Viejo), Cirata, Daguangba, Dai Ninh, Dez, Dhom, El Cajón, Ertan, Estreito, Fortuna, Foum El-Gleita, Furnas, Ghazi Barotha, Gitaru, Guavio, Guri, Icha, Itaparica, Itezhitezhi, Jhuj, Kadana, Kainji, Kalabagh, Kamburu, Karakaya, Kariba, Karnali (Chisapani), Katse (Lesotho Highlands), Kedung Ombo, Khao Laem, Kiambere, Kihansi, Koyna, Kpong, Kulekhani, Lam Pao, Lang Suan, Lubuge, Lupohlo, Maduru Oya (Mahaweli), Magat, Mahaweli, Maithon (Damodar), Mangla, Marsyangdi, M'bali (Boali 3), Monasavu-Wailoa, Muela (Lesotho Highlands), Nam Choan, Nam Ngum, Nam Theun 2, Nangbeto, Narayanpur (Upper Krishna), Pak Mun, Pancheswar, Panchet Hill (Damodar) Pangue, Pantabangan, Paulo Afonso I & IV, Paute (Daniel Palacio/ Amaluza), Playas, Pong (Beas), Presidente Miguel Aleman (Temaxcal), Pujal-Coy, Ravishankar, Rio Grande, Roseires, Ruzizi II, Saguling, Salvajina, San Carlos I (Punchina), Santa Rita (Guatape II), São Simão, Sardar Sarovar, Sennar, Shuikou, Sidi Salem, Sipu, Sir, Sukhbhadar, Sukhi, Sobradinho, Srinakharin (Ban Chao), Sri Rama Sagar (Pochampad), Srisailam, Tabqua (Thawra), Tarbela, Temengor, Uben, Und, Venu II, Victoria (Mahaweli), Watrak, Weija, Yacyretá, Yantan, Xiaolangdi, Zankhari, Zimapán
Inter-American Development Bank (IDB)	Acaray, Arenal, Bayano, Caruachi, Chixoy, El Cajón, El Cuchillo, Fortuna, Guavio, Itaipú, Moxotó, Paulo Afonso IV, Paute (Daniel Palacio/Amaluza), Piedro del Aguila, Playas, Porce II, Salto Grande, Salto Santiago, San Carlos I (Punchina), Sobradinho, Yacyretá
Asian Development Bank (ADB)	Agus, Batang Ai, Chiew Larn, Ghazi Barotha, Kedung Ombo, Lang Suan, Magat, Mahaweli, Nam Leuk, Nam Theun-Hinboun, Tarbela, Xeset
African Development Bank (AfDB)	Batoka, Diama, Garafiri, Kiambere, Lesotho Highlands, Manantali, M'bali (Boali 3), Nangbeto, Selingué
European Union (European Development Fund (EDF), European Investment Bank (EIB))	Diama, Karakaya, Keban, Kpong, Lesotho Highlands, Mahaweli, Manantali, Masinga, Monasavu-Wailoa, Ruzizi II
Arab Bank for Economic Development in Africa/ OPEC Special Fund	Diama, Ghazi Barotha, El Cajón, Kpong, Manantali, M'bali (Boali 3), Nangbeto
UN agencies	
UN Development Programme (UNDP)	Bakalori, [Chixoy], Diama, [Estreito], Ghazi Barotha, [Kainji], Kalabagh, Kulekhani, Lesotho Highlands,

[previously UN Special Fund]	Lubuge, Mahaweli, Manantali, Mekong 'Run-of-River' Dams, Nam Theun 2, Nangbeto, Paute (Daniel Palacio/ Amaluza), Sardar Sarovar, Upper Mazaruni, Xeset
UN Food and Agriculture Organization	Bakalori, Kadana, Mahaweli

Bilateral aid and export credit agencies

Australia (ADAB/AusAid)	Batang Ai, Lubuge, Mangla, Monasavu-Wailoa, Tarbela
Canada (CIDA, EDC)	Caruachi, Dai Ninh, Diama, El Cajón, Guavio, Guri, Idikki, Itaipú, Kainji, Kiambere, Koussou, Kpong, Lubuge, Mahaweli, Mangla, Nangbeto, Pangue, Salto Santiago, Selingué, Tarbela, Temengor, Three Gorges, Urrá I, Warsak, Yacyretá
France (CCCE, FAC)	Balbina, Diama, Keban, Kompienga, Lesotho Highlands, Manantali, M'bali (Boali 3), Nangbeto, Ruzizi II, Tarbela, Turkwell
Germany (GTZ, Hermès, KfW)	Arun III, Bakun, Ghazi Barotha, Keban, Kompienga, Lesotho Highlands, Mahaweli, Manantali, Mangla, Marsyangdi, Nam Pong, Nangbeto, Pancheswar, Sidi Salem, Tarbela, Ubolratana
Italy (SACE)	Chixoy, Dai Ninh, Kainji, Karakaya, Keban, Lesotho Highlands, Ruzizi II, Tarbela, Three Gorges
Japan (Jexim, JICA, OECF)	Akosombo, Arun III, Asahan, Batang Ai, Chiew Larn, El Cajón, Ghazi Barotha, Itaipú, Kaptai (Karnafuli), Kedung Ombo, Kulekhani, Lang Suan, Mahaweli, Mosul, Nam Choan, Nam Ngum, Samanalawewa, Saguling, Salvajina, Sardar Sarovar, Srinagarind, Srisailam, Tarbela, Temengor
Kuwait (KFD)	Chiew Larn, Diama, Kpong, Kulekhani, Lang Suan, Manantali, M'bali (Boali 3), Nangbeto
Norway (NORAD)	Caruachi, Epupa, Ertan, Kihansi, Lubuge, Nam Theun-Hinboun, Pangani, Pangue, Xeset, Yantan
Saudi Arabia (SFD)	Diama, Kompienga, Kpong, Kiambere, Mahaweli, Manantali
Sweden (BITS, SIDA)	Arun III, Caruachi, Epupa, Kamburu, Kihansi, Kotmale (Mahaweli), Lesotho Highlands, Pangani, Pangue, Uri, Urrá I, Xeset
Switzerland (BAWI, ERG)	Atatürk, Cabora Bassa, Chixoy, El Cajón, Guavio, Guri, Itaipú, Karakaya, Manantali, Mosul, Nangbeto, Sobradinho, Tarbela, Yacyretá
UK (CDC, ECGD, ODA)	Akosombo, Cirata, El Cajón, Kainji, Kariba, Lesotho Highlands, Mangla, Monasavu-Wailoa, Pergau, Samanalawewa, Sardar Sarovar, Tarbela, Temengor, Victoria (Mahaweli)
USA (USAID, Exim)	Agus, Akosombo, Ambuklao, Bhakra, Chico River, Ertan, Itaipú, Itumbiara, Kainji, Kaptai (Karnafuli), Keban, Kossou, Magat, Mahaweli, Manantali, Mangla, Marimbondo, Pong, Rihand, Salto Santiago, São Simão, Tarbela, Three Gorges
USSR	Aswan, Hoa Binh, Kapanda, Thawra (Thaqra)

List compiled from various sources. List is not exhaustive: companies and dams are selected according to available data. Projects listed in which funders have supported pre-construction consulting and/or construction work and/or equipment supply for dam and/or directly associated infrastructure. Post-construction repair and rehabilitation work not included.

The World Bank is the most important public institution in the contemporary dam-building industry. In the first half-century after its establishment in 1944 it made 527 dam-related loans which together supported the construction, expansion or rehabilitation of more than 600 dams in 93 countries, including many of the world's largest and most controversial projects (see Table 9.2). The cumulative total of its dam-related loans between 1944 and 1994 is some $58 billion (1993 prices). The Bank's first loan to a developing country, approved in 1948, helped to build three hydrodams in Chile. Its first loans to 16 other countries were specifically for dams. For scores of countries, the largest single World Bank loan they have received has been for a dam.[40]

World Bank lending for dams peaked in the late 1970s and early 1980s at a level of more than $2 billion a year (1993 dollars). Since then – mainly because of the storm of opposition World Bank dams have provoked – its funding for dams has fallen back to an annual average of around half this figure. However, World Bank dam lending continues to set records: in April 1994 the approval of a total of $670 million in financing for China's Xiaolangdi Dam marked the largest loan package the Bank had ever approved for a single project. Just over a year later the Bank approved its second $400 million loan for Ertan, another Chinese dam, and then began the process of appraising another $430 million in loans for Xiaolangdi. It is no coincidence that the Bank is now concentrating its dam financing on a country where open opposition to government projects means risking imprisonment or worse.[41]

The World Bank is governed by a board of 24 executive directors representing the governments of its member nations – which now include most of the countries of the world. Executive directors from Northern countries (who hold the majority of the voting power) are keen to approve loans for dams because of the contracts it means for their companies; those from Southern countries are keen on dam loans as they mean large sums of cheap money moving in their direction. An important reason why World Bank staff are keen on dams is that promotion within the institution has historically been based on the volume of money which an employee shifts out the door – and dams allow a lot of money to move.[42]

Unlike private bankers, World Bank staff have little incentive to ensure that their projects actually work. Bank critic Bruce Rich explains that

> …its loans and credits are backed by the direct contributions and guarantees of the taxpayers of the industrialized world, and the borrowers are governments that pay the Bank back with general revenues extracted from their people and taxpayers. Moreover, the borrowing governments always try to repay the World Bank first, since their access to private international credit depends on promptly repaying their obligations to the Bank. With such a set-up, it makes no difference whether the projects the Bank lends for are well-managed or mismanaged, or whether some or all of the money disappears.[43]

The most comprehensive and damning indictment of World Bank project appraisal and management appeared in the report of the 'Independent Review' set up in 1991 to evaluate the Bank's role in funding Sardar Sarovar. The unprecedented review was headed by Bradford Morse, a former Republican Congressman who had also been Administrator of the UN Development Programme, and was a friend of then Bank President, Barber Conable. The World Bank appointed the review team after years of lobbying from environmental and human rights groups. The groups had protested that the largely positive reports on the progress of Sardar Sarovar that the executive directors in Washington, DC, received from the Bank's India Operations Department staff bore little resemblance to what was happening in the Narmada Valley.[44]

The Independent Review report was released as a 392-page book in June 1992. Its forthright criticism stunned project backers and opponents alike. 'We have discovered fundamental failures in the implementation of the Sardar Sarovar Projects', the review team wrote in a letter to Conable's successor Lewis Preston which introduces the report. The letter continues:

> We think the Sardar Sarovar Projects as they stand are flawed, that resettlement and rehabilitation of all those displaced by the Projects is not possible under prevailing circumstances, and that the environmental impacts of the Projects have not been properly considered or adequately addressed. Moreover, we believe that the Bank shares responsibility with the borrower for the situation that has developed...
>
> Under Bank policy at [the time of loan approval in 1985] resettlement and rehabilitation and environmental impact had to be appraised at the threshold of a project. Yet there was no proper appraisal made of the Sardar Sarovar Projects; no adequate appraisals of resettlement and rehabilitation, or of environmental impact, were made prior to approval. The projects proceeded on the basis of an extremely limited understanding of both human and environmental impact, with inadequate plans in place and inadequate mitigative measures underway...
>
> We found discrepancies in basic hydrological information related to these works.... We found there is good reason to believe that the Projects will not perform as planned...
>
> Important assumptions upon which the Projects are based are now questionable or are known to be unfounded ... benefits tend to be overstated, while social and environmental costs are frequently understated. Assertions have been substituted for analysis...[45]

The Bank's response to the Morse review vindicated the team's observation of the institution's 'tendency to press forward in a manner that avoids engagement with reality'. Rather than accept the recommendation to 'step back from the Projects and consider them afresh', Bank management attempted to plough on regardless, pretending to the executive directors that the problems identified by Morse could be fixed with more of the same approach which had failed so miserably in the past. Morse and his deputy, Canadian jurist Thomas Berger, then wrote an angry letter to Lewis Preston stating that the Bank's response 'ignores or misrepresents the main findings of our Review'.

The Morse and Berger letter, together with insistent lobbying from NGOs, forced the Bank to impose a relatively strict set of 'benchmarks' on environmental studies and resettlement which the project authorities were to meet by 31 March 1993. As the end of March drew near, it was clear to all concerned that the benchmark conditions would not be met. The day before the deadline, in what is generally interpreted as a pre-negotiated face-saving move, the Indian government formally requested the Bank to cancel the outstanding $170 million of their $450 million in loans to Sardar Sarovar.[46]

Among the worrying lessons from Sardar Sarovar is that the inadequate appraisals and broken policies occurred despite the fact that the project was, in the words of two of the Word Bank staff members closest to the project, Thomas Blinkhorn and William Smith, 'the most "supervised" of any project in the history of the institution'.[47] Its problems are also clearly by no means unique among Bank-funded projects. The Independent Review concluded that 'the problems besetting the Sardar Sarovar Projects are more the rule than the exception to resettlement operations supported by the Bank in India.'

The international pork barrel

> Here is a rule of thumb that you can safely apply wherever you may wander in the Third World: if a project is funded by foreigners it will typically also be designed by foreigners and implemented by foreigners using foreign equipment procured in foreign markets.
>
> Graham Hancock, *Lords of Poverty*, 1989

The provision of work for domestic consultancy and construction companies is the main reason why many bilateral aid agencies are keen to help fund dams in developing countries. Around a quarter of the $60 billion in aid loans and grants provided by the major donor nations each year are estimated to be directly tied to the purchase of goods and services from donor countries.[48] This so-called 'tied aid' prevents borrower countries from acquiring the best value in equipment and expertise, as well as distorting aid priorities. As *The Economist* notes, 'it is easier to tie aid to a large item of capital spending, such as a dam, road or hospital, than to a small rural project that may do more good.'[49] The amount of 'aid' which comes back to businesses in the donor countries is actually far more than the tied-aid statistics suggest: some 85 per cent of the 'untied' loans which Japan makes to the poorest countries is spent in Japan.[50]

One way in which governments ensure that their companies benefit from untied aid is by making loans for sectors in which their companies are strongest: countries such as Sweden, Norway and Austria which have some of the world's leading dam construction companies and equipment suppliers are more likely to lend for hydropower projects than countries like Belgium or Denmark with little dam-building experience. The Swedish International Development Cooperation Agency (SIDA) – which in the early 1990s was funding dams in Chile, Colombia, Nicaragua, India, Lesotho, Tanzania and Laos – estimates that up to three-quarters of the money it lends for hydro projects comes back to Swedish companies.

The dam-building sections of Swedish companies like construction giant Skanska are highly dependent on aid funding. About half of the hydro-related exports of ABB Generation (part of the Swedish–Swiss multinational Asea Brown Boveri) are linked to aid money. Scandinavian engineering and environmental consultancies working on dam projects are almost totally reliant on aid funds: Lennart Lundberg, Director of Hydropower for the consultancy Swedpower, estimates that half the company's dam-related contracts are paid for by Swedish bilateral agencies SIDA and BITS, while multinationals like the World Bank and Asian Development Bank provide the rest.[51]

The importance of aid money for the dam industry and the close links between consultancies, construction companies and aid agencies inevitably lays open to corruption the system for making decisions on whether or not a dam will be viable, whether or not its social and environmental impacts will be 'acceptable', and whether or not it should be funded. The close relationships between Nordic dam companies and aid agencies have been studied by Ann Danaiya Usher, a journalist with the Swedish Society for Nature Conservation. Usher explains that in 1994 the top civil servant in the Swedish Ministry for Development Cooperation was an ex-head of the Finance Division of Swedish dam-building utility Vattenfall, which is in turn a major shareholder in the consultancy Swedpower. Meanwhile the Director General and Deputy Director General of the Norwegian Agency for Development Cooperation (NORAD) both formerly worked with Norconsult, a consortium of Norwegian consultancies which receives funds from NORAD to assess the viability of overseas dams.[52]

If it is necessary to win contracts, donor governments have shown themselves willing to pay generous bribes. Kenya's most expensive development project to date, the 106 MW Turkwell Gorge Dam, achieved notoriety in March 1986 when the *Financial Times* obtained a European Commission memorandum which accused the French government of signing an agreement with Kenya to finance the dam for more than twice the price it should have cost. According to the EC memo, the Kenyan officials involved were 'fully aware of the disadvantages of the French deal ... but they nevertheless accepted because of high personal advantages'. Kenyan and other observers of the deal believe that these 'personal advantages' included several million dollars paid to Kenyan President Daniel Arap Moi and his then Minister for Energy, Nicholas Biwott.[53]

The French agreed to the Turkwell deal while the EC delegation in Nairobi, which was itself keen to fund the dam, was in the process of engaging consultants for hydrological, sedimentation and environmental studies on the project. The $280 million contract to build the dam was given to the French construction firm Spie Batignolles and engineering consultants Sogreah without this basic project information, without any assessments of its social impacts, and without having established the final design of the dam. One result is that Turkwell, described in the Kenyan press as 'the whitest of white elephants' and a 'stinking scandal', has proved a technical fiasco: its turbines were unable to reach even half their generation capacity for at least two-and-a-half years after they began operation in February 1991. When the dam was officially commissioned by President Moi at a ceremony in October 1993, its reservoir was less than a quarter full.[54]

A similar tale of inflated costs, aid and corruption erupted in the British press in late 1993 after a report by the National Audit Office, the UK government-spending watchdog, on the funding of the Pergau Dam in Malaysia. The NAO report revealed that Britain was supporting Pergau with £234 million in subsidized loans, despite the conclusion of the government's Overseas Development Administration that the dam would be a 'bad buy' for Malaysia, which over its 35-year life would cost Malaysian consumers £100 million more in electricity charges than gas-fired generation. Three years after the loan was approved in 1991, the former head of the ODA told a Parliamentary committee that he believed Pergau was an 'abuse of the aid system', but had been overruled by the Thatcher Cabinet.[55]

The Pergau loans were the largest sum ever provided for a single project under a programme called the Aid and Trade Provision (ATP), part of the British aid budget which *The Economist* describes as 'a thinly disguised export subsidy for Britain's largest arms firms and construction companies'. Cementation and Balfour Beatty, the British companies given the two biggest contracts on Pergau – without going through the normal process of competitive tendering – are both major funders of the Conservative Party. Allegations of irregularities also surrounded the project in Malaysia, where an opposition MP claimed there were 'phenomenal rake-offs' and 'top-level corruption' in the award of contracts. The stink of sleaze surrounding Pergau worsened when it emerged that Malaysia was offered the ATP package to encourage the signing of a protocol providing for the sale of £1.3 billion worth of British arms.[56]

Incomprehension and Intimidation: The Dam Builders' Reply

> There is an unnerving fervour about dam-builders – especially when gathered en masse at meetings of the International Commission on Large Dams ... To suggest that their creations ... might be doing harm as well as good is to invite an inquisition of your motives. To question their own motives is to invite blind incomprehension.
>
> Fred Pearce, *The Dammed*, 1992

The pro-dam lobby has not been able to ignore the storm of criticism that its practices have provoked. An ICOLD 'Committee on Dams and the Environment' was set up as early as 1972 (although its voluntary members meet only once a year and have no training in environmental science).[57] Industry spokespeople admit that some dams have had negative effects and that dams should be more carefully planned in future. 'It cannot be denied that mistakes have been made, some of them serious,' the then President of ICOLD, Wolfgang Pircher, told the British Dam Society in 1992 in a lecture entitled '36,000 Large Dams – And Still More Needed'. 'It may be that environmentalists have been quicker to recognize some negative developments than engineers lacking in experience in this field,' Pircher continued, 'and that at one time their warnings went unheeded.' But Pircher does not concede that these 'negative developments' are widespread or in any way inherent to the technology and political economy of large dams.[58]

Senior ICOLD officials strongly resist the argument that there are ethical problems in the dam-building process. At the ICOLD Congress in Vienna in 1991, Ernest Razvan of the International Institute for Hydraulic and Environmental Engineering in the Netherlands suggested ICOLD produce an environmental code of conduct. 'Dam Engineers cannot take this kind of talk', says journalist Fred Pearce, who describes the reaction to Razvan's modest proposal from Ted Haws, the British chairman of ICOLD's environment committee:

> Haws was on his feet from the platform. 'I don't think it is necessary to impugn the ethics of consultants,' he said angrily. Haws refused to accept for publication in the conference proceedings a paper submitted by Razvan...[59]

This culture of denial has led ICOLD to believe that the key to improving their poor public image, especially on environmental issues, lies in better public relations, rather than any substantive changes in their ways of doing business. Indeed in some of the Commission's pronouncements, public relations and the environment seem almost synonymous. 'Dam engineers', outgoing ICOLD Secretary General J.M. Cotillion told *Hydro Review* in 1994, 'now must be as concerned about the environment and public relations as they are about the technical matters.'[60] An article the following year in *The International Journal of Hydropower & Dams* says that 'During J. Veltrop's presidency, in the light of increasing attention on environmental issues, a Public Relations Committee was established to work in this area.'[61]

ICOLD likes to see itself as a professional organization which works to improve the practice of dam engineering and which, as Jan Veltrop, an ex-President of ICOLD and ex-Senior Vice President of Harza Engineering, wrote in 1991, 'is not involved in the promotion of dams'.[62] Yet in the same year, an ICOLD Public Relations Committee was established to provide 'objective information in a language that will permit the general public to appreciate the true facts, striking a balance between the benefits of dams on the one hand, and the disadvantages and dangers on the other'.[63] It is not difficult to guess on what side of the scales ICOLD's PR committee believes the 'true facts' lie; nor does one have to be a conspiracy theorist to conclude that the essential role of an ICOLD PR committee is to promote dams.

The belief that the dam industry's current problems stem basically from poor PR is accompanied by repeated assertions that those who criticize dams or resist being evicted from their homes to make way for them are 'biased', 'irrational' and 'emotional' – as opposed to the 'balanced', 'rational' and 'objective' men (and they are nearly all men) who make their living building dams.[64] Such attempts at denigrating dam critics are relatively harmless, but this patronizing and arrogant attitude can also have a more sinister side when dam proponents attempt to intimidate their critics by labelling them 'anti-development', 'unpatriotic' or 'agents of foreign interests'.

In Indonesia, according to Human Rights Watch/Asia, 'the label "obstructor of development" has replaced "communist" as the accusation of choice for allegedly subversive activity.'[65] John Waterbury says that as support for High Aswan became synonymous with patriotism, 'therefore any criticism of it was thought of as subversive or even treasonous ... Technical criticism – at least in public – became tantamount to aiding and abetting the enemy.'[66] In 1995, Governor Tasso Jereissati of the state of Ceará in the Brazilian north-east accused critics of the planned Castanhao Dam of using 'wicked insinuations and unfounded and unpatriotic criticisms'.[67]

A number of cases have come to light where dam proponents have tried to silence their critics by challenging their professional reputations and funding. Academics at India's prestigious M.S. University of Baroda in Gujarat who tried to research some of the negative impacts of dams in their state – where the Sardar Sarovar Dam has been at the centre of political debate for several decades – were warned by senior faculty members that the government would stop funds for their positions were they to pursue their research.[68] When Dr Weiluo

Wang, a regional planner at Dortmund University in Germany, started writing papers criticizing the assumptions made in the feasibility study for Malaysia's Bakun Dam, Lahmeyer International, the German firm that produced the study, refused to engage in an open debate on the project's merits. Instead, two of Lahmeyer's directors wrote to the head of Wang's department accusing him of making statements which were 'false and without any foundation' and 'incorrect and incompetent' and which 'not only tarnished the reputation of our company, but also have given a bad name to German engineering science and to his university'.[69]

When project opponents become too vociferous and effective, the dam industry has frequently acquiesced in the use of state repression to silence critics. In many countries peaceful anti-dam protesters have been arrested on trumped up charges, and in extreme cases beaten, tortured and even murdered. In a 1992 report, the human rights group Asia Watch concluded that thousands of opponents of Sardar Sarovar had been subjected to 'arbitrary arrest, illegal detention, beatings and other forms of physical abuse' and that these abuses 'appear to be part of an increasingly repressive campaign by the state governments involved to prevent [anti-dam] groups from organizing support … and disseminating information about the environmental and social consequences of the project'.[70]

Chinese journalist and academic Dai Qing spent 10 months in solitary confinement for the 'crime' of editing a book, *Yangtze! Yangtze!*, containing articles criticizing the Three Gorges Dam. The book was published in February 1989, during a period of relative political openness in China. Four months later, however, the tanks trundled into Tiananmen Square. Dai Qing was arrested shortly after. In September, two members of the main Three Gorges planning group denounced *Yangtze! Yangtze!* for advocating 'bourgeois liberalization' and providing 'opinions for chaos and riots'. The following month the book was formally banned and the publisher ordered to recall and destroy all unsold copies.[71]

Protests from those who will be directly affected by the Three Gorges dam have drawn an even harsher response. According to a confidential police report obtained by Human Rights Watch/Asia, 179 members of the 'Democratic Youth Party', a so-called 'counter-revolutionary clique' based in one of the counties to be submerged, were arrested in 1992 for 'disrupting the smooth progress of the Three Gorges Project'. Despite an extensive search, Human Rights Watch/Asia have been unable to find any other reports on the arrests or on what has become of the group, but they believe it likely that the 'Democratic Youth Party' 'was merely an unofficial local pressure group, formed by local residents concerned about their impending forced relocation. If the group had espoused or engaged in any violent activities, the confidential

Lupohlo	Swaziland	$50m (1987$)	c.$100m	100%	[3.75]	[4.75]	27%	4
Mahaweli (5-dams)	Sri Lanka	UK£700m	(UK£2bn) [1984]	[186%]				10
Manasavu-Wailoa	Fiji	$63m (1987$)	$114m	81%	[3.9]	[4.6]	18%	4
Nagarjuna-sagar	India	Rs.910m [1954]	Rs.6.8bn [1989]	[652%]				11
Pieman River	Australia	A$135m [early '70s]	(A$530) [1983]	200%	1985	(1986–7)		12
Ruzizi II	Zaire/ Rwanda	$73m (1987$)	$95m	30%	[4.25]	[5.25]	23%	4
Sardar Sarovar	India	Rs.42bn [1983]	(Rs.342bn) [1994]	[714%]				13
Selaulim	India	Rs.96m [1972]	Rs.730m [1985]	[660%]				14
Sriramasagar	India	Rs.640m [1964]	Rs.5bn [1987]	[694%]				15
Srisailam	India	Rs.385m	(Rs.2.6bn) [1979]	[575%]				16
Tarbela	Pakistan	$800m (1989$)	$1.5bn	87%				17
Tawa	India	Rs.139m [1956]	(Rs.914m) [1972]	[557%]	1968	1975		18
Tehri	India	Rs.2bn [1969]	(Rs.60bn) [1994]	[2,900%]				19
Three Gorges	China	$10.7bn [1990]	$30–50bn	[180–370%] [1996]				20
Xeset	Laos	$40	$50.3	26%		1991		21
Xingó	Brazil	$1.6bn	$3.2bn [1995]	[100%]				22
Yacyretá	Argentina/ Paraguay	$2.3bn [1977]	($11.5bn)	17% [1995]	12	(21)	75%	23

Table 9.3 Cost and time overruns for dam projects (selected according to available data)

Project	Country	Estimated cost [year of estimate] (year of currency unit)	Actual cost (latest estimate) [year of latest estimate]	Inflation-adjusted cost overrun [non-adjusted]	Original completion estimate [estimated years to complete]	Actual completion (latest estimate) [actual years to complete]	Time overrun	Ref.
Aguacapa	Guatemala	$100m [1977]	$183m [1981]	55%	[1.15]	[2.4]	107%	1
Balbina	Brazil	$383m [1976]	$750m [1989]	[96%]				2
Bargi	India	Rs.640m [1968]	Rs.5.7bn [1991]	[784%]				3
Chixoy	Guatemala	$400m (1987$)	$944m	136%	[6]	[9]	50%	4
Clyde	New Zealand	$325m [1981]	$900m [1992]	[177%]				5
El Cajón	Honduras	$350m	$850m [1987]	[143%]				6
Estreito	Brazil				[5]	[11]	120%	4
Fortuna	Panama	$255m (1987$)	$424m	66%	[5.4]	[6.8]	26%	4
Gezhouba	China	Y1.35bn (1970)	Y5bn	270%	[5]	[19]	280%	7
Guavio	Colombia	$1bn	>$2bn	[>100%]				8
Itaipú	Brazil/ Paraguay	$3.4bn [1973]	$20bn	[480%] [1991]	[15]	[18]	20%	9
Karakaya	Turkey	$1.1bn (1987$)	$1.5bn	38%	[10.4]	[11.9]	14%	4
Kariba North	Zambia	$124m (1987$)	$366m	195%				4

police report cited above would certainly have said so.'[72] The US businessmen and engineers who lobbied Congress for US support of Three Gorges in late 1995 made no mention of the repression of dam opposition, instead praising the Chinese for their commitment to making resettlement a 'success'. John A. Scoville, Chairman of Harza, even claimed that the Chinese were 'inviting the world to see their [resettlement] efforts, to constructively criticize'.[73]

Notes to Table 9.3

1. World Bank, 'Project Performance Audit Report on Guatemala – Aguacapa Power Project and Chixoy Power Project', OED, June 1992, p. 2.
2. P.M. Fearnside, 'Brazil's Balbina Dam: Environment versus the Legacy of the Pharaohs in Amazonia', *Environmental Management*, Vol. 13, No. 4, 1989, p. 412.
3. Justice S.M. Daud, *The Indian People's Tribunal on Environment and Human Rights. First Report*, 1993.
4. E.W. Morrow and R.F. Shangraw, Jr., *Understanding the Costs and Schedules of World Bank Supported Hydroelectric Projects.* World Bank, July 1990.
5. P. Jessup, 'Clyde: Damnation or Salvation?', *NZ Herald*, 6 June 1992.
6. 'Inauguration of El Cajón Hydroelectric', *Central America Report*, 6 July 1984; S.J. Hudson, 'Natural Resource Issues and IDB Hydroelectric Projects in Central America', Working Paper, National Wildlife Federation, Washington, DC, 23 April 1987.
7. Dai Qing, 'An Interview With Li Rui', in Dai Qing, *Yangtze! Yangtze!* (edited by P. Adams and J. Thibodeau), Probe International, Toronto and Earthscan, London 1994, p. 127.
8. P. Adams, *Odious Debts*, Earthscan, London 1991.
9. P.R. Schilling and R. Canese, *Itaipú: Geopolítica e Corrupção*, CEDI, São Paulo 1991; World Bank, *Paraguay: Country Economic Memorandum*, August 1992.
10. J. Madeley, 'Dam Costly Place to be Poor', *Guardian*, London, 5 April 1984.
11. M. Singh and R.K. Samantray, 'Whatever Happened to Muddavat Chenna? The Tale of Nagarjunasagar', in E.G. Thukral (ed.), *Big Dams, Displaced People: Rivers of Sorrow, Rivers of Change*, Sage Publications, New Delhi 1992, p. 57.
12. P. Crabb, 'Hydroelectric Power in Newfoundland, Tasmania and the South Island of New Zealand', in E. Goldsmith and N. Hildyard (eds.), *The Social and Environmental Impacts of Large Dams. Vol. 2: Case Studies*, Wadebridge Ecological Centre, Cornwall 1986 (hereafter *SEELD 2*), 1986, p. 61.
13. P. McCully, 'Sardar Sarovar Project: An Overview', IRN, Berkeley, CA, 1994. Cost estimates from dam authorities and World Bank.
14. R. Billorey, 'Selaulim Dam', in C. Alvares (ed.), *Fish Curry and Rice: A Citizens' Report on the State of the Goan Environment*, ECOFORUM, Mapusa 1993.
15. S.A. Abbasi, *Environmental Impact of Water Resources Projects*, Discovery Publishing House, New Delhi 1991.
16. The Fact-Finding Committee on the Srisailam Project, 'The Srisailam Resettlement Experience: The Untold Story', in *SEELD 2*, 1986, p. 259.
17. J.A. Dixon et al., *Dams and the Environment: Considerations in World Bank Projects*, World Bank, 1989, p. 35.
18. A. Mishra, 'The Tawa Dam: An Irrigation Project that has Reduced Farm Production', in *SEELD 2*, 1986, p. 214.
19. The Ecologist, 'Indian Cabinet Approves Tehri Dam', Action Alert, *The Ecologist*, Sturminster Newton, England, 17 March 1994.
20. M. Barber and G. Ryder, *Damming the Three Gorges: What Dam Builders Don't Want You to Know*, second edn, Earthscan, London 1993, p. 33; T. Walker, 'Building China: Big Promise but Tough Terms', *Financial Times*, London, 19 March 1996.
21. 'Xeset Nears Completion in Laos', *International Water Power and Dam Construction*, March 1991.
22. 'Brazil's Xingo Power Scheme is Inaugurated', *International Water Power and Dam Construction*, February 1995.
23. World Bank, 'Project Completion Report: Argentina Yacyretá Hydroelectric Project and Electric Power Sector Project', 14 March 1995.

Nemesis: The Economics of Large Dams

> We now realize the significant construction and operating costs of large-scale water development projects cannot be repaid.
>
> Daniel P. Beard, Commissioner, US Bureau of Reclamation, 1994

The extensive construction and operational problems of dams, the increasing requirements to pay for environmental and social mitigation measures, delays due to public opposition, and the fact that most of the best sites have already been dammed, combine to have a devastating impact on the economics of large dams. Although there has never been a comprehensive post-construction cost–benefit assessment of a large dam project, it is clear that many dams would not have been built had their true costs been assessed and publicly revealed before construction began. Now that governments around the world are cutting public spending, and private-sector financing of infrastructure projects is in vogue, dam agencies are having to reveal their balance sheets to private investors, who in general do not like what they see – especially when other developers are seeking funding for much cheaper and less risky gas-fired power plants. Large water development projects, with their high risks, huge construction costs and long payback periods, will only be built in the foreseeable future if they continue to receive generous public subsidies.

Dams consistently cost more and take longer to build than projected (see Table 9.3). World Bank research carried out in 1994 found that inflation-adjusted construction cost overruns on 70 hydropower dams funded by the Bank since the 1960s averaged 30 per cent, almost three times higher than the average cost overruns on a similar number of Bank-financed thermal power stations. The study found that, in general, the larger a hydro project is, the larger its construction cost overrun in percentage terms.[74] In the Western US, as BuRec Commissioner Dan Beard told ICOLD's 1994 Congress, 'the actual total costs of a completed [water] project exceed the original estimated costs, including inflation, by at least 50 per cent.' Furthermore, Beard added, 'often, project benefits were never realized.'[75]

Cost overruns are particularly damaging for the economics of dams because, although their operating costs are very low, their construction costs are extremely high. According to John Besant-Jones, Principal Energy Economist at the World Bank, capital costs represent around 80 per cent of the total lifetime cost of hydrodams (excluding, as dam cost calculations always do, decommissioning costs). By comparison, capital costs represent around half the lifetime costs of coal-fired plants.[76] A 30 per cent construction cost overrun for a dam is thus much more expensive than an equivalent percentage cost overrun for a coal plant. High capital costs and the frequent need for foreign loans also mean that the economic viability of dam projects is extremely vulnerable to rises in interest rates and currency devaluations.

Energy analysts José Roberto Moreira and Alan Douglas Poole illustrate the sensitivity of dam economics to changes in interest, or discount, rates:

> Consider, for example, a plant with a direct investment (excluding finance charges during construction) of $1,200 per kilowatt, a construction time of six years, a 50-year lifespan and a capacity factor of 50 per cent. With a discount rate of 6 per cent, the plant's annual capital costs would be from ¢2.0 to 2.2 per kWh; at 12 per cent the costs would rise from ¢4.6 to 4.8 per kWh. By comparison the operating costs of intermediate and large hydro plants would be on the order of only ¢0.2 to 0.4 per kWh.[77]

Time overruns can also have a disastrous effect on project economics by delaying the time from which revenues from electricity sales and water supply can start to repay the heavy debt service costs which large dams entail. The World Bank notes that a one-year delay in revenue earning will reduce the difference between the projected benefits and costs of some projects by almost a third; a two-year delay, by more than half.[78] Forty-nine hydro projects reviewed by the World Bank's Industry and Energy Department in 1990 took on average five years and eight months to build, fourteen months longer than the average pre-construction estimate.[79]

As of mid-1995, the World Bank expected Yacyretá Dam to be completed in 1998, nine years behind schedule. This delay, combined with the project's huge cost overruns, means that electricity generated by the dam is calculated to cost 9.5 cents per kilowatt-hour, compared with the 4 cents per kWh which is currently paid in Argentina. Paying for Yacyretá electricity at the market rate would give a rate of return for the project of only 5.5 per cent, according to the World Bank, compared to an opportunity cost of capital of around 10 per cent (i.e. if the money spent on Yacyretá were invested elsewhere it would likely earn nearly twice as much in interest every year as it will from being invested in the dam).[80]

Large irrigation projects appear to be even more prone to long completion delays than hydrodams. Nine major irrigation projects in Asia, Africa and Latin America reviewed by the US Department of Agriculture in 1984 ran over schedule by an average of five years (and cost almost four times as much per hectare as anticipated). Another nine irrigation projects financed by the Asian Development Bank and completed by 1980 took an average of 72 per cent longer to build than estimated (and suffered an average cost overrun of 66 per cent).[81] Many large irrigation projects are in fact *never* completed: the dam is built, some progress is made in building the network of canals, water courses, field channels and drains needed to deliver water to the farmer and take away the excess, but then the political interest in the project fades, the money runs out, and the irrigation consultants and engineers move on to their next job.

Dams and debts

The final costs of major dam projects can be stunningly high and have effects which resound throughout entire economies. The final cost of Chixoy – $944 million – represented nearly 40 per cent of Guatemala's total external debt in 1988.[82] EBI, the joint Brazilian–Paraguayan state enterprise that built and operates Itaipú, borrowed almost all the cost of the project from private foreign banks, with the loans guaranteed by the Brazilian government. The debt of EBI reached $16.6 billion in 1990, with debt service eating up 80 per cent of the revenues it received from electricity sales. By comparison, Brazil's total national external debt stood at $121 billion in 1992, and that of Paraguay at $1.7 billion. The huge capital inflow for the project not only led to corruption on an unprecedented scale, but also helped stoke the hyper-inflation which has blighted Brazil since the mid-1980s. The consequences of the dam on the much smaller Paraguayan economy included an inflationary economic boom which turned to recessionary bust once the bulk of dam construction had been completed, and a marked increase in the concentration of land ownership and wealth, especially in the part of the country nearest the dam.[83]

If China manages to complete the Three Gorges Dam its final cost will certainly dwarf even that of Itaipú. 'The Three Gorges dam project is like the US nuclear program', an American executive working for a company operating power plants in China told the magazine *Institutional Investor* in 1995. 'It will take forever, it will cost all the money in China, and it won't make any power for 30 years.' The executive quoted expects the final cost of the dam to reach more than $36 billion, making it 'very uncompetitive if you charge any capital costs for the power'. *Institutional Investor* noted that this price tag is 'similar to recent upper-range Chinese government figures but well below numbers cited by project critics'. According to Three Gorges critic Dai Qing, internal government estimates of the cost of the dam had risen by late 1995 to around $75 billion.[84]

Innocent optimists?

According to the World Bank, the primary cause of cost and time overruns is poor geological conditions, followed closely by resettlement problems. Resettlement costs in World Bank hydropower projects have been on average 54 per cent higher than original estimates. Such large increases can have a significant effect upon total project costs: resettlement commonly accounts for around one-tenth of total costs (before overruns are taken into account) and can reach more than a third of the total construction cost of dams which displace a large number of people or which involve relatively high compensation payments.[85]

The Bank's Industry and Energy Department claims that 'the key problems [of overruns] appear to devolve from optimism'.[86] In reality, however, it is clear that the consistent underestimates are due less to the innocent hopefulness of Bank staff and consultants, than to the pervasive dishonesty which surrounds huge dam projects, both in terms of bribes and skim-offs and the corrupt and corrupting project planning process. The World Bank's 1991 review of its irrigation projects in India states that it is 'common practice' when bureaucrats propose water projects in India 'to ensure project acceptance by inflating benefits and underestimating costs'.[87] Cost and time overruns are in fact beneficial to many in the dam lobby: corrupt politicians have more funds to pocket and more contracts to give to cronies; contractors have more work to do; aid bureaucrats have more loans to process.

The role which dishonesty plays in the 'optimism' over dam costs is illustrated by the way in which feasibility studies frequently understate or even totally ignore the number of people to be resettled and the sizeable costs which resettlement can entail. The World Bank's 1994 resettlement review found that only half of their currently active projects displacing more than 200 people included a budget for resettlement.[88] World Bank sociologist Michael Cernea recounts how in one project in which he was involved,

> the foreign consulting firm responsible for the feasibility study … [was required by the responsible national agency] to either reduce their estimate of displacement to one third of their initial figure, or eliminate the figure entirely. The agency was concerned that if the real scale of the displacement were to become known internal political support and/or external financing of the project would be doubtful.[89]

Cernea also tells how a team of international consultants contracted by the World Bank 'skipped over the displacement of some 80,000 people' in their nine-volume (3 feet thick) feasibility study for Pakistan's Kalabagh Dam.[90] Making a judgement about the economic feasibility of a project without including the cost of resettling 80,000 oustees can only be characterized as fraud, not 'optimism'.

Cost–benefit analyses (CBAs) for dams are usually presented as objective documents with all the economic pros and cons of the project added up and compared. In reality, CBAs are filled with assumptions which reflect the bias and interests of the consultant or bureaucrat doing the analysis. Reviews of CBAs consistently show that they inflate benefits and underestimate costs.[91] Even if CBAs were always to be done with integrity and competence, however, there are still many problems with the methodology. No allowance is made, for example, for the fact that the costs tend to be borne by different sectors of society than reap the benefits, and that invariably it is the poorest and weakest who lose most, and the wealthiest and most politically powerful with most to gain. Similarly, assessing cash values for environmental or cultural damage is fraught with controversy.[92] One important factor which is excluded from dam CBAs is the potential cost of a dam failure. In an article in the journal *Science*, R.K. Mark and D.E. Stuart-Alexander of the US Geological Survey note that 'failure to include the costs of residual risk [of a dam failure] in benefit–cost analyses clearly produces an upward bias that may result in projects that are not economically justifiable.'[93]

Opportunity knocks

An important consideration which should be taken into account when decisions are made about such massive and risky investments as dams is their opportunity cost – the cost of not using the money for other investments which may be more efficient and more socially beneficial. BuRec's Dan Beard told the 1994 ICOLD Congress that 'the actual contribution made by [large-scale water] projects to the [US] economy is small in comparison to alternative uses that could have been made with these public funds.' The crowding out of public resources for other sectors of the economy is especially serious for poor countries. Martin Karcher, a former World Bank Division Chief with responsibility for Nepal, resigned from the Bank in mid-1994 because of disagreements with Bank management over their preparation of the Arun III project, and in particular the basis for their economic justification of the dam. In a letter to Bank President Lewis Preston, Karcher pointed out that the Bank's own surveys showed 'investments in sectors such as education, health, training, transport and communications generate higher economic growth than corresponding investments in power.'[94]

At its peak the Mahaweli scheme was absorbing 6 per cent of Sri Lanka's GDP, 17 per cent of total public expenditure and 44 per cent of public investment expenditure. 'In the short term', says a World Bank-commissioned report, Mahaweli 'had strongly positive effects on growth creating "boom" conditions. However, it also came to be seen as the indicator of the success or failure of the regime, crowding out other priority public investments, and reducing the government's capacity to adjust expenditures in response to external developments.' Moreover, the report continues, 'once the initial investment boom faltered, the country was faced by renewed balance of payments and debt problems without having created the conditions for sustained growth.'[95]

The dam industry's economic woes are compounded by a clear trend of increasing real costs due to the fact that the most economic dam sites tend to get used first. And while hydropower's costs are steadily increasing, those of its gas, solar and windpower competitors are tumbling. Between 1965 and 1990, according to a World Bank study, the average cost of building hydrodams rose at an inflation-adjusted rate of nearly 4 per cent per year.[96] While around three-quarters of this cost increase was due to construction costs in general rising faster than inflation, the remaining increase was thought to be due to hydropower's unique problem of 'site depletion'.[97]

A similar trend has been seen in irrigation projects. Per hectare costs of new irrigation schemes in India rose by almost 60 per cent in real terms between 1979 and 1985. Part of the reason, says the World Bank, is that the most suitable areas have already been provided with irrigation infrastructure.[98] Another sign of the effects of site depletion has been observed by the US Geological Survey. According to author Robert S. Devine, the USGS have found that 'the amount of reservoir capacity created by each cubic foot of dam plummeted from 10.4 acre feet for dams built prior to 1930 to 2.1 acre feet for those built in the 1930s and to 0.29 acre feet for those built in the 1960s.'[99]

Private pessimists

In September 1994, 150 or so men (and two women) from the dam-building industry gathered in Frankfurt for *International Water Power & Dam Construction*'s first conference on the private financing of hydropower projects. An air of gloomy resignation pervaded the meeting. Several speakers from the financing side of the industry emphasized that private investors are discouraged from backing hydrodams because of their high initial construction costs, long capital payback periods, terrible record of construction time and cost overruns, and high operating risks, especially because of their vulnerability to drought. The speakers also made clear that financiers are dissuaded from funding dams because of 'environmental risks': delays because of opposition to resettlement and anti-dam campaigns, and new environmental legislation to regulate how dams are built and operated.

Several speakers agreed that with few exceptions the only dams likely to be built on a wholly private-sector basis in the near future are small- to medium-size run-of-river hydrodams (many dams, however, are likely to be built under joint public–private schemes, with the government guaranteeing to bail out investors should project economics sour). In a review of privately financed power projects in developing countries, John Besant-Jones of the World Bank found 30 hydropower projects in various stages of preparation and implementation. All of them were relatively small run-of-river projects.[100] One speaker commented that for a 'typical developing country' the upper limit which private investors would be likely to risk putting into a hydro project, even on a very favourable site, would be between $120 million and $150 million, enough for only a 75–100 MW plant.[101] Large multipurpose projects like Sardar Sarovar or Aswan, once the pride of the dam industry, are even less appealing to investors than dams built solely for hydropower due to the problems of collecting revenues on non-power functions, and the fact that such functions can divert water from being used for power production.

Proponents of dams have long boasted of the benefits of 'cheap hydroelectricity'. Significantly, the phrase seemed to have dropped from the dam builders' vocabulary at the meeting in Frankfurt in September 1994. 'Cheap hydroelectricity' is on its way to joining the nuclear power lobby's notorious claim that it could produce electricity 'too cheap to meter' as an ironic and rather quaint expression of 1950s technological fantasy.

Notes

1. In 1995 the World Bank started an assessment of 49 of the larger dams it has funded. At the time of writing in 1996 the report had not yet been completed, but internal sources indicate that it concentrates on construction economics rather than performance or social and environmental impacts.
2. J. Waterbury, *Hydropolitics of the Nile Valley*, Syracuse University Press, New York 1979, pp. 99, 101.
3. R. Rycroft and J. Szyliowicz, 'The Technological Dimension of Decision Making: The Case of the Aswan High Dam', *World Politics*, Vol. 33, No. 1, October 1980, pp. 48–9; G. White, 'The Environmental Effects of the High Dam at Aswan', *Environment*, Vol. 30, No. 7, 1988.
4. Waterbury, *Hydropolitics of the Nile Valley*, p. 116.
5. See, e.g., F. Pearce, *The Dammed: Rivers, Dams and the Coming World Water Crisis*, Bodley Head, London 1992, pp. 123–8; K. Gyan-Apenteng, 'Happenings on the Dam', *West Africa*, July 1983, pp. 20–26; R. Graham, 'Ghana's Volta Resettlement Scheme', in E. Goldsmith and N. Hildyard (eds.), *The Social and Environmental Impacts of Large Dams. Vol. 2: Case Studies*, Wadebridge Ecological Centre, Cornwall 1986; L. Barnes, *Africa in Eclipse*, Gollancz, London 1971, pp. 76–87.
6. A.D. Rassweiler, *The Generation of Power: The History of Dneprostroi*, Oxford University Press, Oxford 1988, p. 3.
7. R. Tempest, 'Deng's Failing Health Gives Boost to Huge Dam Project', *Los Angeles Times*, 6 February 1995.
8. Human Rights Watch/Asia, 'The Three Gorges Dam in China: Forced

Resettlement, Suppression of Dissent and Labor Rights Concerns', Human Rights Watch, New York 1995, p. 3.

9. D. Worster, 'Water and the Flow of Power', *The Ecologist*, Vol. 13, No. 5, 1983, p. 169.

10. T. Scudder, 'Victims of Development Revisited: The Political Costs of River Basin Development', *Development Anthropology Network*, Vol. 8, No. 1, 1990, p. 1.

11. M.H. Gunaratne, *For a Sovereign State*, Sarvodaya Publishing, Ratmalana 1988, p. 32.

12. Scudder, 'Victims of Development Revisited'; E. Meyer, 'Renouveau démocratique au Sri Lanka', *Le Monde Diplomatique*, March 1995.

13. R. Kaplan, 'The Coming Anarchy', *Atlantic Monthly*, February 1994, p. 67; A. Braun, 'The Megaproject of Mesopotamia', *Ceres*, March/April 1994; J. Barham, 'Demirel Raises Stakes in Tense Regional Game', *Financial Times*, 10 November 1994. One of GAP's prime proponents since the 1960s has been Turkish President Süleyman Demirel, a hydraulic engineer known as the 'king of dams', who has frequently referred to the project as an affirmation of national pride.

14. M. Reisner, *Cadillac Desert: The American West and its Disappearing Water*, Secker & Warburg, London 1986, p. 174.

15. 'Unravelling the Peace in State Water Wars', *San Francisco Chronicle*, 21 July 1995; 'Doolittle's Dam: A Monument to Pork', *San Francisco Chronicle*, 17 October 1995; L. Pottinger, 'House Committee Rejects Auburn Dam', *World Rivers Review*, Vol. 11, No. 3, July 1996.

16. P.M. Fearnside, 'Brazil's Balbina Dam: Environment versus the Legacy of the Pharaohs in Amazonia', *Environmental Management*, Vol. 13, No. 4, 1989, p. 401.

17. M. Osava, 'Sigue el desorden, pese a control de inflación', Inter-Press Service Feature, 21 October 1995.

18. Quoted in T. Palmer, *Stanislaus: The Struggle for a River*, University of California Press, Berkeley 1982, p. 102.

19. Reisner, *Cadillac Desert*, p. 178.

20. *A History of the Tennessee Valley Authority*, TVA Information Office, 1986; 'Dams and Power Plants', TVA Brochure, September 1994.

21. A.O. Hirschman, *Development Projects Observed*, Brookings Institution, Washington, DC, 1967, p. 21.

22. N.L. Grant, *TVA and Black Americans: Planning for the Status Quo*, Temple University Press, Philadelphia 1990, pp. 75–83; M.J. McDonald and J. Muldowney, *TVA and the Dispossessed*, University of Tennessee Press, Knoxville 1982.

23. W. Chandler, *The Myth of TVA.*, Ballinger, Cambridge, MA, 1984, p. 7.

24. W.B. Wheeler and M.J. McDonald, *TVA and the Tellico Dam, 1936–1979: A Bureaucratic Crisis in Post-Industrial America*, University of Tennessee Press, Knoxville 1986, p. 216.

25. Ibid., pp. 214–20; D. Droitsch and D. Daigle, 'FDR's Baby Becomes a Problem Child', *Amicus Journal*, Summer, 1994; G. Graham, 'Work to Stop on Last Nuclear Power Plants', *Financial Times*, 13 December 1994.

26. D. Beard, 'Remarks before the International Commission on Large Dams', Durban, South Africa, 9 November 1994.

27. Estimate from data on contracts in dam industry publications (research by Davor Orsic). This estimate concurs with a 1995 US National Hydropower Association figure of a $500 billion market for the hydropower industry over the next 20 years ('US Hydropower Export Initiative', NHA, Washington, DC). The UNDP estimates that total global energy investment is around $200bn (S. Silveira, 'The Climate Convention and Renewable Energy', *Renewable Energy for Development*,

Stockholm Environment Institute, August 1995).

28. See, e.g., M. Nakamoto, 'Japanese Builders Fined for Collusion', *Financial Times*, 18 April 1995; '"Irregularities" Found in Dam Bidding', *The Nation*, Bangkok, 20 April 1995; 'Brazil's Odebrecht: Pimp or Prince?', *The Economist*, 29 January 1994; 'New Police Raids in Italian Aid Scandal', *Africa Analysis*, 12 November 1993; J. Hooper, 'The Drain on Spain', *Guardian*, London, 24 June 1995; J. Ridding, 'French Utility Halts Political Payments in Ethics Campaign', *Financial Times*, 11 November 1994; P. Wise, 'Portugal Tackles Corruption', *Financial Times*, 13 June 1995.

29. J. Wilkinson, 'Lords of Corruption: The Construction Industry Scandal', *AMPO Japan–Asia Quarterly Review*, Vol. 24, No. 4, 1993; 'The Nagara Estuary Dam and Kanemaru Shin', *Japan Environment Monitor*, September 1993; M. Suzuki, 'Yoshino River Symposium', *Japan Environment Monitor*, July–August 1994.

30. P.R. Schilling and R. Canese, *Itaipú: Geopolítica e Corrupção*, CEDI, São Paulo 1991, p. 8; 'Aquí están las pruebas de la estafa del presidente de Paraguay', *La República*, Montevideo, 13 February 1996.

31. S. Christian, 'Billions Flow to Dam (and Billions Down Drain?)', *New York Times*, 4 May 1990.

32. T. Scudder et al., *The IUCN Review of the Southern Okavango Integrated Water Development Project*, IUCN, Gland, Switzerland, 1993, p. 12; T. Scudder, 'Environmental Politics: Botswana's Southern Okavango Integrated Water Development Project', *Development Anthropology Network*, Vol. 10, No. 2, Fall 1992; T. Scudder, 'Social Impacts', in A.K. Biswas (ed.), *Handbook of Water Resources and Environment*, McGraw-Hill, New York forthcoming.

33. See, e.g., L. Sklar, 'Professional Ethics: The Dam Dilemma', *World Rivers Review*, May/June 1991; L. Sklar, 'The Ethical Responsibilities of Engineers and Other Professionals Involved in Large Dam Projects', in A.D. Usher (ed.), *Nordic Dam-Building in the South: Proceedings of an International Conference in Stockholm 3–4 August, 1994*, SSNC, Stockholm 1994.

34. G. Ryder and M. Barber, *Damming the Three Gorges: What Dam Builders Don't Want You to Know*, Earthscan, London 1993, Appendix B.

35. R. Gottlieb, *A Life Of Its Own: The Politics and Power of Water*, Harcourt Brace Jovanovich, San Diego 1988, p. 7.

36. N. Smith, *A History of Dams*, Peter Davies, London 1971, p. 230.

37. J. Gitlitz, 'The Relationship between Primary Aluminium Production and the Damming of World Rivers', Working Paper 2, International Rivers Network, Berkeley, CA, 1993. Efficient modern smelters consume around 13,500 kWh/t of aluminium produced.

38. See, e.g, ibid.

39. Ibid.; World Bank, 'Early Experience with Involuntary Resettlement: Impact Evaluation on Ghana – Kpong Hydroelectric Project ', OED, 30 June 1993.

40. L. Sklar and P. McCully, 'Damming the Rivers: The World Bank's Lending for Large Dams', Working Paper 5, International Rivers Network, Berkeley, CA, November 1994.

41. Ibid.

42. See, e.g., W.A. Wapenhans et al., 'Report of the Portfolio Management Task Force', World Bank, 1 July 1992.

43. B. Rich, *Mortgaging the Earth: The World Bank, Environmental Impoverishment, and the Crisis of Development*, Beacon Press, Boston 1994, p. 256.

44. See L. Udall, 'The International Narmada Campaign: A Case Study of Sustained Advocacy', in W.F. Fisher (ed.), *Towards Sustainable Development? Struggling Over India's Narmada River*, M.E. Sharpe, Armonk, NY, 1995.

45. B. Morse et al., *Sardar Sarovar: The Report of the Independent Review*, RFI, Ottawa 1992, pp. xii–xxiv. Sardar Sarovar Projects in the plural refers to the dam and associated irrigation canals.

46. See Udall, 'The International Narmarda Campaign'; P. McCully, 'Cracks in the Dam: The World Bank in India', *Multinational Monitor*, December 1992.

47. T.A. Blinkhorn and W.T. Smith, 'India's Narmada: River of Hope. A World Bank Perspective', in Fisher (ed.), *Towards Sustainable Development?*, p. 95.

48. J. Randel and T. German (eds.), *The Reality of Aid 94: An Independent Review of International Aid*, ICVA/EUROSTEP/ACTIONAID, London 1994.

49. 'The Kindness of Strangers', *The Economist*, 7 May 1994, p. 20.

50. R. Forrest, 'Japanese Aid and the Environment', *The Ecologist*, Vol. 21, No. 1, 1991.

51. A. Usher, 'Dam Building in the South: The Nordic Connection', *Sveriges Natur*, June 1994. See also 'Aid-Financed Hydropower Projects in the Developing World – A Huge Market for Swedish Companies', *Development Today*, Vol. 14, 1994.

52. Usher, 'Dam Building in the South'.

53. 'Confidential note' from A. Kaatz, Delegation of the EC in Kenya, to J.F. Boddens-Hosang, Ambassador of the Netherlands, Nairobi, 5 February 1986; J. Ozanne, 'How Moi's Right-Hand Man Made His Wealth', *Financial Times*, London, 27 November 1991; 'A Story of Wealth and Power', *Weekly Review*, Nairobi, 22 November 1991.

54. See P. McCully, 'The Dam Builders' Web: A Story of Corporations, Contracts and Corruption', *World Rivers Review*, Fourth Quarter, 1993. Thanks to George Monbiot for slipping out of the French embassy in Nairobi the documents on which this account is based and passing them on to the International Rivers Network. A civil servant in the French foreign ministry told author Pierre Péan that Spie-Batignolles is 'one of the great French dispensers of "commissions"' (E. Kleemeier, 'La France et l'argent noir au Kenya', *Politique Africaine*, No. 40, December 1990).

55. National Audit Office, *Pergau Hydro-Electric Project*, HMSO, London 1993; Randel and German, *The Reality of Aid 94*, p. 120.

56. 'The Curse of Pergau', *The Economist*, 5 March 1994; J. Vidal and N. Cumming-Bruce, 'Dam Price Jumped £81m Days After Deal', *Guardian*, London, 19 January 1994; 'Whitehall Must Not Escape Scott-Free', *Guardian*, London, 12 February 1994.

57. W. Pircher, '36,000 Large Dams and Still More Needed', paper presented at Seventh Biennial Conference of the British Dam Society, University of Stirling, 25 June 1992.

58. Ibid.

59. F. Pearce, *The Dammed*, p. 141.

60. 'ICOLD: Meeting New Challenges in Building, Maintaining Dams', *Hydro Review*, Fall 1994, p. 17.

61. 'ICOLD's Achievements in an Era of Progress and Change', *The International Journal of Hydropower & Dams*, September 1995, p. 39.

62. J. Veltrop, 'A Response to IRN's Letter to ICOLD', *World Rivers Review*, September/October 1991, p. 11.

63. 'ICOLD's New President Looks to the Future', *International Water Power and Dam Construction*, August 1991, p. 12.

64. See, e.g., E. Razvan, 'The Environmental Impact of Large Dams', *International Water Power & Dam Construction*, October 1992; Pircher, '36,000 Large Dams'; 'A Breath of Fresh Air', *International Water Power & Dam Construction*,

December 1994; C. Vansant, 'Our Friends: The Facts', *Hydro Review*, July 1995, p. 39.

65. Human Rights Watch/Asia, 'The Three Gorges Dam in China', p. 20.

66. Waterbury, *Hydropolitics of the Nile Valley*, p. 117.

67. G. Switkes, 'Governor of Ceará Accuses NGOs For Delay In Northeastern Brazil River Diversion Project', posted on Internet conference env.dams@igc.apc.org, 30 October 1995.

68. Personal communication with M.S. University of Baroda academic.

69. Letter from Dr J. Zimmerman and R. Wigand to Professor Schoof, Faculty for Spatial Planning, Department of Urban and Regional Planning, Dortmund University, 21 August 1995. Translation by Petra Yee.

70. Asia Watch, 'Before the Deluge: Human Rights Abuses at India's Narmada Dam', Asia Watch, Washington, DC, 1992, p. 1.

71. Human Rights Watch Asia, 'The Three Gorges Dam in China', p. 7.

72. Ibid., pp. 9–11.

73. 'Testimony of John A. Scoville, Harza Engineering Company, Before a Briefing of The Subcommittee on Procurement, Exports, and Business Opportunities of the House Small Business Committee, The Subcommittee on International Economic Policy and Trade of the House International Relations Committee, and The Subcommittee on Asia and the Pacific of the House International Relations Committee', 30 November 1995.

74. J. Besant-Jones, 'A View of Multilateral Financing from a Funding Agency', in *Financing Hydro Power Projects '94*, proceedings of conference sponsored by *International Water Power & Dam Construction*, Frankfurt, 22–23 September 1994; John Besant-Jones, interview with author, 23 September 1994.

75. Beard, 'Remarks'.

76. Besant-Jones, 'A View of Multilateral Financing'. Most of the remaining 50% of a coal plant's lifetime costs are for fuel.

77. J.R. Moreira and A.D. Poole, 'Hydropower and its Constraints', in T.B. Johansson et al. (eds.), *Renewable Energy: Sources for Fuels and Electricity*, Island Press, Washington, DC, 1993, p. 112. Unrealistically low discount rates have often been used in the cost–benefit analyses of US water resources projects (see, e.g., B.T. Parry and R.B. Norgaard, 'Wasting a River', *Environment*, Vol. 17, No. 1, 1978).

78. World Bank, *Resettlement and Development: The Bankwide Review of Projects Involving Involuntary Resettlement*, 8 April 1994, p. 5/22. The economic implications of delayed benefits are not normally taken into account in calculations of cost overruns.

79. E.W. Morrow and R.F. Shangraw, *Understanding the Costs and Schedules of World Bank Supported Hydroelectric Projects*, World Bank Industry and Energy Department, 1990, pp. 11, 41.

80. World Bank, 'PCR: Argentina: Yacyretá Hydroelectric Project and Electric Power Sector Project'.

81. R. Repetto, *Skimming the Water: Rent-Seeking and the Performance of Public Irrigation Systems*, WRI, Washington, DC, December 1986, p. 4.

82. Morrow and Shangraw, *Understanding the Costs and Schedules*; World Bank, *World Development Indicators*, 1990.

83. World Bank, *Paraguay: Country Economic Memorandum*, August 1992; Schilling and Canese, *Itaipú*, p. 9; A. Miranda, *Paraguay y las Obras Hidroelectricas Binacionales*, El Lector, Asunción 1988; E. Altvater, 'Brazil: The Giant's Debts', in E. Altvater et al. (eds.), *The Poverty of Nations: A Guide to the Debt Crisis from Argentina to Zaire*, Zed Books, London 1991; World Bank, *World Development Indicators*, 1994. Itaipú's

first turbine began to generate electricity in 1985. Ninety-eight per cent of the electricity generated by Itaipú is sold to Brazil. Interest charges account for 40% of the total project cost. Prominent dam-building agencies in North America have also accumulated serious debt burdens. At the end of 1994 the total debt of Hydro-Québec stood at US$26.25bn ('Hydro-Quebec on Long-Term Debt Credit Watch', *International Water Power & Dam Construction*, December 1994).

84. C. Rademan, 'Three Gorges Befuddles Financiers', *Institutional Investor*, June 1995; Letter from Lawrence R. Sullivan, Associate Professor, Adelphi University, to Kenneth Brody, President and Chairman, Import–Export Bank, 6 December 1995.

85. World Bank, *Resettlement and Development*, pp. 5/16, 5/19.

86. Morrow and Shangraw, *Understanding the Costs*, p. 21.

87. World Bank, 'India: Irrigation Sector Review', Vol. I, Washington, DC, 1991, p. 22. It is noteworthy that when Bank staff get their sums wrong it is attributed to 'optimism', yet when Indian officials commit the same mistakes the World Bank implies that dishonesty is to blame.

88. World Bank, *Resettlement and Development*, p. 5/16.

89. M.M. Cernea, 'Involuntary Resettlement in Bank-Assisted Projects: A Review of the Applications of Bank Policies and Procedures in FY79-85 Projects', World Bank, 1986, p. 14.

90. M.M. Cernea, 'Poverty Risks from Population Displacement in Water Resources Development', Harvard Institute for International Development, 1990, p. 4. Gazdar estimates that 124,000 would be displaced by Kalabagh (M.N. Gazdar, *An Assessment of the Kalabagh Dam Project on the River Indus Pakistan*, EMS, Karachi 1990).

91. For fallacious CBAs in the US, see E. Goldsmith and N. Hildyard, *The Social and Environmental Impacts of Large Dams, Vol. 1*, Wadebridge Ecological Centre, Cornwall 1984, pp. 257–76; R.L. Berkman and W.K. Viscusi, *Damming the West: Ralph Nader's Study Group Report on the Bureau of Reclamation*, Grossman, New York 1973.

92. See, e.g., J. Adams, 'Cost–Benefit Analysis: The Problem, Not the Solution', *The Ecologist*, Vol. 26, No. 1, 1996.

93. R.K. Mark and D.E. Stuart-Alexander, 'Disasters as a Necessary Part of Benefit–Cost Analyses: Water-Project Costs Should Include the Possibility of Events Such as Dam Failures', *Science*, Vol. 197, 16 September 1977, p. 1162.

94. Letter from Martin Karcher to Lewis Preston, 12 December 1994.

95. P. Athukorala and S. Jayasuriya, 'Macroeconomic Policies, Crises, and Growth in Sri Lanka 1960 to 1990', mimeo, quoted in H.D. Frederiksen et al., *Water Resources Management in Asia. Volume I: Main Report*, World Bank Technical Paper 212, Washington, DC, 1993, p. 53.

96. Morrow and Shangraw, *Understanding the Costs*, pp. 10, 22. The 56 projects cost an average of $317 million (in 1987 dollars) and had an average installed capacity of 388 MW.

97. Ibid., p. 22, C-1.

98. World Bank, 'India', Vol. I, p. 24.

99. R.S. Devine, 'The Trouble With Dams', *Atlantic Monthly*, August 1995, p. 74.

100. Besant-Jones, 'A View of Multilateral Financing'.

101. J.G. Warnock, 'A Developers Point of View: Not For the Faint Hearted!', in *Financing Hydro Power Projects '94*, p. 142.

10

We Will Not Move: The International Anti-Dam Movement

Koi nahi hatega, bandh nahi banega
(No one will move, the dam will not be built)

Doobenge par hatenge nahin
(We will drown but we will not move)

Slogans of the Narmada Bachao Andolan

The decade since the mid-1980s has seen the emergence of an international movement against current dam-building practices. The movement comprises thousands of environmental, human rights and social activist groups on all the world's inhabited continents. It coalesced from a multitude of local, regional and national anti-dam campaigns and a smaller number of support groups working at an international level. Dam builders recognize and bemoan its effectiveness. ICOLD President Wolfgang Pircher warned the British Dam Society in 1992 that the industry faced 'a serious general counter-movement that has already succeeded in reducing the prestige of dam engineering in the public eye, and it is starting to make work difficult for our profession.'[1]

The earliest successful anti-dam campaigns were mostly led by conservationists trying to preserve wilderness areas. Resistance from those directly impacted by dams was, until recently, usually defeated. Since the 1970s, however, directly affected people have gained the power to stop dams, mostly because they have built alliances with sympathetic outsiders – environmentalists, human rights and democracy activists, peasants' and indigenous peoples' organizations, fishers and recreationists. The rise of environmentalism has greatly helped the opponents of dams – and anti-dam campaigns have in many countries played an important role in the growth of national environmental movements. Other factors contributing to the emergence of the international movement have been the overthrow of authoritarian regimes and the spread of modern communications technologies.

Dam opponents are not just 'antis', but are advocates for what they see as more sustainable, equitable and efficient technologies and management practices. Political changes which would best encourage the preservation or adoption of these technologies and practices have been a central demand of many anti-dam campaigns. Struggles that have started with the aim of improving resettlement terms or of stopping an individual dam have matured into movements advocating an entirely different model of political and economic development. That decision-making be transparent and democratic is now seen by many dam opponents as being as important as the decisions themselves. The clearest illustration of the wider political importance of anti-dam movements is the crucial role that dam struggles played in the pro-democracy movements of the 1980s in Eastern Europe and South America.

The accounts below tell the story of some of the most important anti-dam struggles and explain the main threads which have been woven together to form the international anti-dam movement. They are, however, far from a comprehensive account of all instances of organized resistance to dams, many of which are scarcely, if at all, documented. Other notable anti-dam struggles, which there is no space to do justice to here, include Californian environmentalists' hard-fought but ultimately unsuccessful campaign against the 191 metre New Melones Dam throughout the 1970s; the struggle of the Cree Indians against Quebec's mammoth James Bay Project (Cree resistance forced the last two phases of the three-part project to be suspended in 1994); that against Norway's Alta Dam which took place between 1970 and 1981 (the dam was built but important concessions were won including improved environmental regulations and the first parliament for the Sami ethnic minority); the several successful campaigns in the 1970s and 1980s of Sweden's national River Savers' Association; the successful late 1980s/early 1990s campaign of SOS Loire Vivante in France; the ongoing campaign against the dams planned for Chile's spectacular Bíobío River; the Katun Dam campaign in Russia (the dam has been suspended); the violent protests by the Igorot ethnic minority in the Philippines which stopped the Chico River dams; and the struggles of local people and their supporters against dams in Indonesia and Malaysia.[2]

Aesthetics and Taxes: Dam Fights in the US

...who knows what may avail a crowbar against that Billerica dam?

Henry David Thoreau, 'A Week on the Concord and Merrimack Rivers', 1849

'Should we also flood the Sistine Chapel', asked a full-page advertisement placed by conservationists in the major US newspapers in August 1966, 'so tourists can get nearer the ceiling?' The indignant question was a response to Interior Secretary Stewart Udall's comment that two hydropower reservoirs planned for the Grand Canyon would help motorboat-borne tourists view the scenery. The campaign against the Grand Canyon dams marked the culmination of more than a decade of battles against BuRec on the Colorado Basin, battles which ended the go-go years for dam builders in the US and played a vital role in shaping the country's modern environmental movement.

Echo Park Dam, planned for the Colorado's largest tributary, the Green River, was the first in the basin to provoke serious opposition. Conservationists' feelings ran high over the 175 metre dam, not so much because of its impact upon the river, or even because of the scenic value of the land it would flood, but on a matter of principle. Echo Park would have inundated many of the canyons of Dinosaur National Monument (a national monument is protected like a national park, but while Congress designates a park, designating a monument is a presidential prerogative). Allowing the dam to be built, conservationists believed, would have led to a deluge of development projects in other protected areas.

Echo Park first came to public prominence in 1950 when a popular national magazine, the *Saturday Evening Post*, ran an angry attack on the proposed dam by well-known Western writer Bernard DeVoto. The article was reprinted in the conservative mass-circulation *Readers' Digest*. 'Soon after,' says author Russell Martin, 'millions of Americans were aware of a little monument that theretofore they had never heard of, and they were hopping mad about what this outfit called the Bureau of Reclamation was planning to build there.' Meanwhile Howard Zahniser, executive secretary of the Wilderness Society, was quickly assembling a coalition of conservation and outdoor recreation groups which would help stoke public concern and lobby Congress against the dam.

The Sierra Club in the late 1940s was a group of mostly conservative mountaineers and hikers from California who decided that Dinosaur National Monument was not worth trying to save. At the end of 1952, however, the club got a new executive director, David Brower, a relentless, stubborn campaigner for conservation who was to become probably the second most influential figure of the twentieth-century American environmental movement (the most influential, Sierra Club-founder John Muir, died in 1914, a year after losing the fight to stop a dam in California's Yosemite National Park).

Soon after he took charge of the Sierra Club, Brower began leading boat trips through Dinosaur Monument to show club members the wild beauty of the canyons the dam would flood. Film shot on these trips was shown nationwide in support of the conservationists' cause.

Giving testimony to Congress in 1954, Brower explained with simple blackboard calculations that BuRec's engineers had massively underestimated the amount of water which would evaporate from Echo Park Reservoir and overestimated evaporation from alternative reservoirs. Congress, Brower sardonically warned, 'would be making a great mistake to rely upon the figures presented by the Bureau of Reclamation when they cannot add, subtract, multiply, or divide'. Brower's next publicity coup was a book with essays edited by Wallace Stegner accompanied by striking pictures of Dinosaur Monument. The books were sent to all the members of Congress, all high-level employees of the Interior Department, and the editor of every newspaper which might have an interest in the dam.

Western politicians and newspapers were horrified at the strength of opposition to what they had long viewed as their immutable right to federal money for dams. They derided the conservationists as 'long-haired punks' and 'abominable nature lovers' spouting 'romantic tripe'. But Brower's technical arguments were difficult to rebut, and even more discomforting were the economic arguments which exploited Eastern lawmakers' resentment over the use of their money to build Western dams. Westerners gradually began to realize that if they kept fighting for Echo Park they could end up losing not only that dam but others as well. By 1956 sufficient Western members of Congress had been swayed, and Congress voted against the dam. At Echo Park, believes historian Roderick Nash, 'the American wilderness movement had its finest hour to that date'.[3]

But Echo Park was far from an unalloyed victory. Because the conservationists did not want to be depicted as radical opponents of any kind of water development, their aim was not to stop dams on the upper Colorado, but to keep dams out of protected areas. The result of this limited objective was that their alternative to Echo Park was actually worse in terms of the destruction of natural beauty.

The greatest sin

> That Glen Canyon Dam … In all of the Rocky Mountain, Inter-Mountain West, no man-made object has been hated so much, by so many, for so long, with such good reason, as the 700,000-ton plug of gray cement, blocking our river.
>
> Edward Abbey, *Down the River*, 1982

The 1956 appropriations bill from which Echo Park had been deleted authorized Glen Canyon Dam on the Colorado, and construction began the same year. Until the late 1950s only a few non-Native Americans had ever seen Glen Canyon. The canyon was not officially protected and conservationists assumed that it had no outstanding scenic value. But after work started on the dam, tourists, photographers, artists, writers and conservationists came to visit the canyon before it disappeared forever and were staggered by the wonder of what they saw. Wallace Stegner wrote that Glen Canyon was 'almost absolutely serene ... fantastically eroded by silt side canyons, alcoves, grottoes green with redbud and maiden-hair and with springs of sweet water'. Brower visited shortly before the dam gates were closed in 1963 and was grief-stricken that he had acquiesced in the destruction of such a place of wonder. He later described his failure to try to save Glen Canyon as 'the greatest sin I have ever committed'.

The same year that Powell Reservoir started slowly to drown the slickrock of Glen Canyon, the Bureau of Reclamation announced its plans for two dams in the Grand Canyon intended to generate electricity to pump water from the Colorado to the fast-sprawling desert cities of central Arizona. Although only a small part of one of the reservoirs would directly impinge on Grand Canyon National Park itself, conservationists had had enough of dams on the Colorado canyons, inside or outside officially protected areas. This time the anti-dam forces were better prepared and more determined than ever before. They knew from Echo Park that they had the power to win, and they had the motivation from the tragedy of Glen Canyon not to let such a disaster happen again.

The conservationists used many of the same tactics as before: brochures, coffee-table books, films, magazine articles, protest letters (hundreds of thousands were sent urging the government to keep its hands off the Grand Canyon) and Congressional testimony. The Sierra Club newspaper ads were a new tactic that generated sacks full of mail to Congress and helped double the club's membership. The dam opponents also employed economic arguments and challenged the engineers' hydrological and sedimentation figures. And as with Echo Park, the conservationists took a position on alternatives which many later strongly regretted – they argued that the power to be generated by the dams could be produced more cheaply by nuclear or coal plants.

The public concern aroused by the Sierra Club and others persuaded Interior Secretary Stewart Udall to kill the dams in 1967. River activist and author Tim Palmer says that 'the battle of the Grand Canyon dams was a central, symbolic event which played a major role in awakening environmental awareness in America.'[4]

For US dam builders, and in particular for the Bureau of Reclamation, the defeat at the Grand Canyon was a major blow. The Corps of Engineers also learnt that it would have to scale back its dam-building ambitions or face repeated defeats when, in the same year he knocked out the Grand Canyon dams, Stewart Udall used economic and conservation reasons to recommend against building the massive Rampart Dam in Alaska.

The end of big dam foolishness

> The People are Getting Fed Up With Big Dam Foolishness
>
> Title of article in *Public Service Magazine*, 1953

The numerous dam fights of the 1970s were mostly fought at the local and state level, with no projects grabbing the national imagination as the Colorado dams had in the 1950s and 1960s. To provide support to the disparate groups of dam fighters across the nation and to lobby Congress on their behalf, rafters and conservationists set up the American Rivers Conservation Council (ARCC) in 1973 with an office in Washington, DC. The previous year, a doctor of philosophy named Brent Blackwelder had helped to found the Environmental Policy Center (later renamed the Environmental Policy Institute) and had become the nation's first full-time lobbyist against water projects. Between 1972 and 1983, Blackwelder helped stop some 140 dams, canals and channelization projects. In 1976, the ARCC and EPC sponsored the first national 'Dam Fighters' Conference', a meeting which was to become a popular annual event for river activists.[5]

Blackwelder and his colleagues warmly welcomed the inauguration of Jimmy Carter as President in 1977. Carter was a keen canoer and rafter and wanted to stop dams not just for economic reasons but also to save rivers. One of the first major acts of his presidency was to release a 'hit list' of 19 federal water projects, including the country's most controversial proposed dams, which he recommended should be scrapped for economic, environmental or safety reasons. But Carter had underestimated the power of the pork barrel, and in the end the water lobby forced him to approve funds for most of the 'hit list' projects. Although he ultimately caved in, Carter at least helped raise public awareness of the murky wheeling and dealing behind US dam building.[6]

It is ironic that the president who did the most to smash the water project pork barrel was not the river lover Jimmy Carter, but the butt of environmentalist scorn and dread, Ronald Reagan. His administration took office in 1981 promising both more water projects and less government spending – two aims that were clearly in conflict. It was on dams that Reagan broke his promise. In 1981 Reagan signed the first bill ever to deauthorize a group of water projects, terminating funding for seven dams which would have cost more than $2 billion. Legislative changes during Reagan's term required states and communities to pay an increased share of the costs of water projects in order to cut federal government spending. These changes greatly lessened the attractiveness of pork-barrel projects and sealed the fate of many dams.

By the time Bill Clinton came to power in 1991, budget cuts and improved environmental laws had combined to all but kill dam building in the US. Instead of concentrating solely on fighting proposed projects, dam opponents were now able to devote most of their time and energy to campaigning for smaller dams to be decommissioned and for the operating regimes of the larger ones to be redesigned to minimize their environmental damage. 'The dam building era in the United States is now over', declared BuRec Commissioner Dan Beard in 1994. 'The opportunity for any future projects is extremely remote, if not non-existent.'[7]

Arrests and Restoration in the Tasmanian Wilderness

GET OUT GREENIES AND TAKE YOUR DISEASES WITH YOU
Banner at Tasmanian pro-dam demonstration, 1983

The modern Australian environmental movement dates back to the campaign to save a relatively small lake in a national park in the mountainous southwest of the island of Tasmania. What made Lake Pedder special was a stunning kilometre-wide beach of dazzling pink quartz and the reflection in its clear waters of the surrounding jagged peaks. In 1967 the Tasmanian Hydro-Electric Commission (HEC) announced plans to dam the river draining Pedder and create a reservoir more than 34 times the size of the original 7 square kilometre lake. Conservationists campaigned hard to stop the dam but even with tacit support from the federal government in Canberra were unable to defeat the HEC, a powerful and secretive state utility.

Australian broadcaster Peter Thompson writes that although the Pedder campaign was lost, 'a strong conservation movement had been born'. In fighting to save Lake Pedder, conservationists had learnt 'how to campaign, publicise, take opinion polls, stand for election, use radio and television effectively and develop the techniques which would be so vital for success in the next battle'.

The next battle was over a dam proposed downstream in the same basin. The 180 MW Gordon-under-Franklin Dam, so called because of its location on the Gordon River below its junction with the Franklin, would have flooded part of one of the last great temperate wildernesses of the Southern Hemisphere. It would have inundated rare temperate rainforest, one of Australia's most spectacular gorges and archaeologically important caves with evidence of occupation 20,000 years before.

The HEC released its plans for the dam in 1979. The governing Tasmanian Labor party had a conservation-minded element based in the more urbanized east of the island, but also a strong pro-dam faction made up of the trade unions and of supporters in the economically depressed towns of southwest Tasmania who had been persuaded by the Commission that mass sackings would result if the dam was not built. The opposition Liberal Party and the state's powerful business community were fully behind the HEC. Coordinating the anti-dam lobby was the Tasmanian Wilderness Society (TWS) headed by Bob Brown, a medical doctor turned campaigner. The Society, says Peter Thompson, was 'the sharpest public interest movement in Australian history'.

Because the pro-dam lobby in Tasmania was so strong, the conservationists knew that defeating Gordon-under-Franklin Dam would ultimately be dependent on building up support on the mainland. Intensive lobbying succeeded in persuading the federal Labor Party, then in opposition in Canberra, to adopt a 'no dams' policy in July 1982. Soon after, the campaign got another huge boost when UNESCO accepted an Australian government recommendation to list southwest Tasmania as a World Heritage Site.

In mid-December 1982, as the HEC got ready to move its bulldozers into the rainforest, the TWS moved into position to stop it. Thousands of 'greenies' from all over Australia joined a carefully planned, peaceful blockade at the dam site. During the three-month-long action a total of 1,300 protesters were arrested and hundreds imprisoned. Bob Brown was detained on 16 December and held for over three weeks. While he sat in jail a national newspaper named him 'Australian of the Year'. The day after his release he was elected to the Tasmanian parliament. The biggest PR coup came in mid-January when British botanist and television celebrity Dr David Bellamy joined the blockade. Film of Bellamy's arrival and subsequent arrest was shown in 32 countries.

The blockade inspired tens of thousands to join anti-dam marches in cities across Australia. Although Tasmanian politicians depicted the 'greenies' as outside 'professional troublemakers' imported by the TWS, 20,000 people – one in five of the island's population – demonstrated in the state capital Hobart in support of the blockaders.

On 3 March, two days before a general election which would decide the fate of the campaign, the blockade was called off. Conservationists urged their supporters to 'vote for the Franklin' by backing Labor – and helped the party win by a landslide. Within a month the new government banned HEC activities in the World Heritage area. However, the Tasmanian government – whose Premier had once described the Franklin as a 'brown, leech-ridden ditch' – dismissed Canberra's decision as unconstitutional. The stage was set for a showdown in the High Court. On 1 July 1983, in what is recognized as one of Australia's most important constitutional cases, the court ruled in favour of the federal government. The Gordon-under-Franklin Dam was dead.[8]

In 1994, Bob Brown and David Bellamy met up again in Tasmania to launch Pedder 2000, a campaign to restore Lake Pedder by draining the reservoir which drowned it. The unprecedented restoration would, campaigners believe, 'bring hope to a new generation in the last hour of a destructive millennium' and be 'a catalyst for environmental repair around the globe'. According to studies commissioned by the campaign, the unique quartz beach and other remarkable features of the lake have been covered by only a few millimetres of sediments and could rapidly be restored to their original condition.

The mood in Tasmania is very different from two decades ago. The government and the HEC oppose draining Pedder but with much less vehemence than they supported damming it. The HEC recognizes its dam-building days are over for the foreseeable future (in Tasmania at least – in 1994 a subsidiary started feasibility studies for dams in Laos). Unplugging Pedder would reduce the capacity of the Tasmanian power system by only 60 MW, while the state already has a surplus capacity of 130 MW. As the 'greenies' had pointed out at the time, the power from the Franklin River only appeared to be needed because the HEC and other business interests chose to make it look so.[9]

Eastern Europe: Fight the Dams, Fight the System

> For us the energy and water lobbies represent the Stalinist structure. Water projects here are paramilitary, centralized, undemocratic and monolithic.
>
> Janos Vargha, Hungarian environmentalist, 1989

In the first major public demonstration since the brutally crushed uprising a generation before, 40,000 Hungarians took to the streets of Budapest on 12 September 1988. This time the demonstrators' demand was an end, not to communist rule, but to the damming of the Danube at a place called Nagymaros. Yet one result of the anti-Nagymaros Dam campaign was that it helped the Hungarian people gain confidence to speak out against, and ultimately to overthrow, their communist rulers. A similar story lies behind the fall of the authoritarian regimes in several other Central and Eastern European states, with environmental protests – and opposition to dams in particular – acting as a lightning rod for public mobilization against the deeply unpopular regimes.

Work on Nagymaros and another associated dam, 129 kilometres up-river at Gabcikovo, first began in 1978. While both banks of the river lie within Hungarian territory at Nagymaros, at Gabcikovo the north bank is in what was then the Slovak part of the federal republic of Czechoslovakia. The Czechoslovaks forged ahead with work on their part of the Gabcikovo project through the early 1980s. In Hungary, however, economic crisis during 1981 forced a halt to construction at Nagymaros and on the south bank at Gabcikovo.

As the Hungarian machinery lay idle, upstream in Austria a fight began against another planned dam. Outside the town of Hainburg is one of the largest and most ecologically diverse riverine forests left in

Europe. When the Austrian government gave permission in December 1984 to start clearing forest to make way for the Hainburg Dam, 40,000 people marched through nearby Vienna in protest. Environmentalists occupied the forest and engaged the police in a violent confrontation. Shortly after, the High Court ruled the government's logging authorization illegal.

With their own hydro plans frustrated, the Austrian government turned its attention to its more repressive neighbours, offering them capital to build Gabcikovo-Nagymaros if they would guarantee Austria a large share of the hydropower from the dams. The Austrian offer encouraged Hungary's Politburo to recommit itself publicly to Nagymaros in 1985.

Support for the Danube dams, however, was far from unanimous within the Hungarian establishment. The dams were strongly backed by the country's water management bureaucracy – and by the Soviet Union since the project would increase the distance their gunships could penetrate up the Danube. The Hungarian fossil-fuel lobby, on the other hand, opposed the project, as did other elements in the government who saw the dams as being more for the benefit of Czechoslovakia and Austria than Hungary. This official ambivalence had opened up political space in the early 1980s for hydrologists and biologists to question the potential environmental impacts of the dams. These unaccustomed challenges to Party wisdom eventually provoked a backlash, and in May 1984 the Hungarian authorities banned all public speaking on environmental issues and all media coverage of the dams.

But a small group of dam opponents, headed by biologist and journalist Janos Vargha, were not to be intimidated into silence. Three months after the crackdown, they illegally set up Duna Kor – Danube Circle – one of the very few independent citizens' groups in the Eastern bloc. The environmentalists were motivated by the belief that the dams would lead to the desiccation of the beautiful Szigetkoz (literally 'island region'), where the Danube meets the Hungarian plain and branches out to create a wildlife haven of countless streams, marshes, backwater lagoons and forested islands. They also feared that the water in Central Europe's largest aquifer, which underlies the Szigetkoz, would be contaminated by wastes from nearby cities if the purifying percolation through the wetlands were lost.

The initial aim of Duna Kor was to break the secrecy surrounding Gabcikovo-Nagymaros. Their first campaign activity was to circulate a petition asking for the Hungarian parliament to debate the project. The petitions had to be covertly passed between friends, many were confiscated by the secret police, and people were understandably reluctant to state their opposition on paper. Despite these difficulties, more than 6,000 signatures were collected.

In the face of official threats, censorship and the revoking of their passports, activists in Duna Kor continued their work, holding secret meetings, gathering more signatures, publishing *samizdat* newsletters and making links with environmentalists abroad. In 1985, they published the first environmental impact study of Nagymaros. The next year, they held an unprecedented open press conference in Budapest which was addressed by greens from Hungary, Austria and West Germany. A few weeks after the press conference, Vargha and others were summoned to a police station and threatened with 'certain consequences' when they announced plans for a march. The protest still went ahead, with some 200 marchers being met by tear-gas and clubs. Also in 1986, Vargha's political activities lost him his job. Nevertheless, he continued the campaign.

The persistence and courage of the members of Duna Kor attracted other dissenters to join. Andras Biro, a journalist who fled Hungary after the 1956 uprising, came back in 1987. 'I returned home because I could see things were changing', he told British journalist Fred Pearce in 1989. Duna Kor was the visible sign of that change. 'It was an extraordinary thing for Janos [Vargha] to do. [Duna Kor] defied the government. They diminished the fear of the people.'

Shortly before the large demonstration in Budapest on 30 October 1988, the Hungarian parliament debated Gabcikovo-Nagymaros for the first time. A new petition calling for a referendum on Nagymaros was circulated openly and attracted 150,000 signatures. In November, Miklos Nemeth, a prominent reformist, became Prime Minister. To gain popular support in their fight against the conservatives in the Communist Party, the reformists expressed support with the aims of Duna Kor – and the environmentalists used the reformists as allies in breaking down the monolithic power of the state.

In May 1989, the government suspended work at Nagymaros. Two months later, work was stopped on the Hungarian part of Gabcikovo. A parliamentary resolution abandoning Nagymaros was passed in late October. The first free elections in Hungary took place early the following spring. 'The breakthrough to political change', says Andras Biro, 'occurred when the government suspended work on the dam.'[10]

When the rabbit topples the bear

> Where the bear dominates, the rabbit drowns.
>
> From letter in a Latvian journal on Soviet-planned Daugavpils Dam, 1986

Activists from the Bulgarian citizens' group Ecoglasnost were gathering signatures outside an international conference in Sofia in October 1989 when, in full view of conference delegates and the international press, they were punched, kicked and bundled into waiting vehicles by security agents. Several days later, Ecoglasnost organized a march of 5,000 people to protest against the arrests and to deliver their petition against hydroelectric projects on the Stuma and Mesta rivers to the National Assembly. The march was the largest unofficial rally in Bulgaria since the Second World War. One dissident told a journalist, 'It will be impossible to keep the lid on alternative opinion in Bulgaria any longer. We have crossed a watershed.' Within days, Todor Zhivkov, President of Bulgaria for almost two decades, was ousted from power. The new administration agreed to suspend the hydro projects.[11]

In Latvia, the start of organized dissent against Soviet rule was a campaign against a hydrodam on the Daugava River. Two young Latvian journalists, Dainis Ivans and Arturs Snips, wrote an article in a literary journal in 1986 harshly criticizing the Daugavpils Dam. They claimed it would flood a valley which was 'one of the most beautiful and as yet untouched natural places in Latvia' and was strewn with the remains of ancient burial grounds and forts. Significantly – and provocatively – Ivans and Snips appealed to Latvian nationalism, stressing 'the Daugava's symbolic significance in our nation's history and spiritual life'.

The article sparked an unprecedented debate in the columns of the journal. Readers were urged to write to the authorities and circulate petitions calling for an open discussion on the dam in the spirit of the new policy of *glasnost.* Responding to the public concern, the Soviet authorities initiated a review of the project which found that it 'was not justifiable from an economic standpoint' and 'would incur irrecoverable ecological losses'. After reportedly receiving 30,000 protest letters, in November 1987 the Soviet Council of Ministers abandoned the project. According to the Latvian Environmental Protection Club, 'it was this grassroots victory over the forces of bureaucratic centralism that ignited Latvia's democratic independence movement, propelling upstart journalist Ivans into the presidency of the 200,000 member Popular Front and then into the vice-presidency of Latvia's new parliament.' Ivans himself has called the Daugavpils campaign 'a dress rehearsal for the Popular Front'.[12]

In the ex-Soviet republic of Georgia, the campaign against the 200 metre Khudoni Dam was 'one of the major events in the freedom movement', according to Londa Khasaya, a leading Georgian green activist. Five major demonstrations, road blockades, and an eight-day hunger strike by activists forced the Soviet authorities to halt construction on the almost-completed dam in 1989.[13]

Warriors and Workers Fight Back: Brazil

> Whoever is against Balbina is against you!
>
> Television advertisement for Balbina Dam, 1987

The warpaint-streaked woman brought down her machete in a swift arc. The curved blade stopped just millimetres short of the shoulder blade of José Antonio Muniz Lopes, chief engineer of Brazilian electricity utility Eletronorte. Muniz remained calm as the Kayapó woman, Tuira, ritually pressed the flat of the blade against his cheek. 'You are a liar', she spat at him. 'We don't need electricity. Electricity won't give us food. We need the rivers to flow freely: our future depends on it. We need our forests to hunt and gather in. We don't want your dam.'

Tuira's dramatic gesture, made in a community hall in the boomtown of Altamira in northeast Amazonia, was broadcast around the world. Watching her in the hall were hundreds of Indians in full ceremonial battle dress, journalists, environmental and indigenous rights activists, and an assortment of international rock stars, media personalities and politicians. Some 1,000 leaders from 20 different Indian tribes attended the five-day meeting, held in February 1989 – almost certainly the largest gathering of Amazonian Indians in modern times. For the organizers, led by American anthropologist Darrel Posey and Kayapó chief Paulinho Paiakan, it was a brilliant success.

The planned Xingu River Basin Hydroelectric Project, a massive six-dam scheme, would flood thousands of square kilometres of Indian land, much of it belonging to the Kayapó. Strengthening the Kayapó's determination to stop the project were the experiences of Amazonian Indians who had lost land to other dams. A chief from the Gaviãos came to Altamira to tell the story of the suffering his people endured because of Tucuruí Dam. 'They said they would compensate us', the chief told the Kayapó, 'but Eletronorte blocked our claim in court. You can't trust them. They say they are only conducting studies. They told us that. But with each study, they sealed our fate. Little by little, they moved in. Then the dam was built.'

Posey and Paiakan, together with another Kayapó chief, Kube-i, had come to the attention of the international environmental community a year before during a visit to the US. With the help of environmentalists in Washington, DC, the three had met with officials from the US government and the World Bank, which was considering helping fund the dams. Infuriated by the delegation's lobbying, the Brazilian government charged them with violating a law against foreigners interfering in Brazilian politics. But the charges against the Indians backfired badly, provoking a public outcry inside the country. One television commentator asked caustically, 'If they're foreigners, what are we?' Outside Brazil, the charges helped to raise opposition to the Xingu project and the World Bank's prospective involvement. In Europe, environmentalists and indigenous rights groups demonstrated outside banks and Brazilian embassies, wrote letters to the World Bank, and invited Paiakan on more speaking and lobbying tours.

Eletronorte reacted to the outcry by announcing that they were 'reconsidering' Babaquara, the largest dam in the scheme, an 11,000 MW giant which would cover some 7,200 square kilometres of rainforest with the world's second largest reservoir. The Kayapó and their supporters, however, were doubtful that Babaquara would actually be shelved, and kept up the pressure on the World Bank and Brazilian government. Early in 1989 the Brazilian authorities dropped the charges against Paiakan, Kube-i and Posey. In March, just a month after the Altamira meeting, the World Bank confirmed that it had withdrawn its proposed half-billion-dollar loan which would have helped build the Xingu dams.[14]

Atingidos versus *barrageiros*

Land Yes, Dams No

Title of publication from the 'First National Meeting of Workers Affected by Dams', 1989

When Brazil's huge programme of hydropower development got underway in the late 1960s, the military regime prevented the tens of thousands of displaced people from organizing effectively to improve resettlement or to stop the dams. People harmed by major projects such as Sobradinho, Itaipú, Itaparica and Tucuruí fought for better compensation through marches, dam-site occupations and other forms of civil disobedience, but failed to win significant concessions.

At the end of the 1970s, however, the political *abertura* – the Brazilian version of *glasnost* – made it easier for people affected by dams to organize, to obtain project information, and to make alliances with other groups struggling for democracy and social justice. Maria Stela Moraes, a researcher with the Brazilian Institute for Social and Economic Analysis (IBASE), says that Brazil's anti-dam movement 'played an outstanding role in the social struggle of the 1980s'. Moraes believes that dam protests boosted other movements against exploitation in rural Brazil and stalled the implementation of the cornerstone of government energy policy – the rapid expansion of electricity generation and electricity-intensive industries through the building of hydro mega-projects.[15]

Effective opposition to dams in Brazil first arose in the south after utility Eletrosul revealed plans in 1977 to build 22 dams on the Uruguay River and its tributaries. Over the next few years, priests, trade unionists, land reform activists and small farmers started to organize resistance to the first two dams slated for construction, Machadinho and Itá. In 1981, the organizers created the Comissão Regional de Atingidos por Barragens (CRAB), the Regional Commission of People Affected by Dams.[16]

The initial goals of CRAB were to force Eletrosul to reveal how many people would lose land or livelihood and then to fight for just compensation. Through the political acumen of its leadership and the forging of successful alliances with other social movements, CRAB forced Eletrosul to the negotiating table. The group's demands were backed by street demonstrations and non-violent direct action: surveyors and other company representatives were detained and thrown off private land, survey stakes torn up, construction sites blocked, and offices occupied.

CRAB rejected Eletrosul's policy of giving cash compensation and then only to those holding formal land titles. Instead, it demanded the utility buy up holdings from large ranchers, install the necessary infrastructure for new settlements, and then grant land to displaced farmers and previously landless labourers. Eletrosul was also forced to set up land purchase committees that included representatives of the displaced people, and to rule out the practice – used at Itaipú – of granting evicted farmers land on colonization schemes in the Amazon forest. The land allotted on these schemes was usually productive for only a few growing seasons once the forest had been cleared and huge tracts had been abandoned. CRAB also successfully insisted that the normal practice of the power company negotiating resettlement with individual farmers be replaced by collective bargaining with committees of community representatives, and that construction timetables be linked to progress on resolving social issues.

The improved compensation measures won by CRAB resulted in spiralling costs for Eletrosul, which forced it to postpone indefinitely the 1,200 MW Machadinho project in 1988. The 1,620 MW Itá Dam was originally scheduled to start producing electricity in 1992, but by 1995 only preliminary construction work had been done and only a few hundred out of 4,000 families had been resettled.[17]

CRAB's successes on the Uruguay River motivated the group to organize nationally. With assistance from the national workers' union and land reform and indigenous rights groups, CRAB helped people harmed by dams throughout Brazil to start their own committees. In 1989, the groups held the 'First National Meeting of Workers Affected by Dams', which ended with a call to halt any new dams until solutions were found to the problems caused by existing hydro projects.

The next year, the Committee of the People Affected by Dams in the Amazon (CABA) was formed to coordinate rural workers and indigenous groups fighting proposed dams such as those on the Xingu, as well as people needing compensation for damage caused by the Balbina and Tucuruí projects. These latter dams had not only displaced people but had also caused a multitude of other problems around the new reservoirs and downstream – including mosquito swarms, seriously contaminated water, and declining fish catches and crop yields. These experiences prompted CABA to take an outright stand against any new dams in the Amazon. In early 1991, a National Movement of People Affected by Dams (MAB) was established at a national meeting in Brasilia. MAB's stated goals were to ensure justice for affected people and to secure 'profound changes in current energy and irrigation policies'.[18]

The Brazilian anti-dams movement has combined with the country's economic woes to slow down drastically the country's ambitious dam-building plans. Many large dams have been cancelled or postponed since the late 1980s – although scores of major projects still remain on the books with the dam builders, the *barrageiros,* waiting for economic conditions to improve so that they can push ahead. MAB will ensure that they will face organized and determined opposition.

Struggle Over the River Kwai: Thailand

> What right do they have not to want [Pa Mong Dam]? It does not matter if they want it or not, as long as the government wants it.... If we listened to the people chaos would reign.
>
> Official from Thailand's Royal Irrigation Department, 1990

The breakneck rate of economic growth that Thailand has sustained over the past couple of decades has brought prosperity to many of its citizens. But the boom has been bought at the expense of the country's natural wealth and its poorer inhabitants, especially the peasant farmers and fisherpeople whose livelihoods depend directly on the well-being of forests, farmland and rivers.

The strategy of rapid industrialization and resource extraction has not gone unopposed. The environmental movement is at the forefront of this opposition, and the event which marked the coming of age of the movement – the Thai equivalent of the Grand Canyon and Franklin victories – was the indefinite postponement of Nam Choan Dam in 1988. 'The Nam Choan campaign', states geographer Philip Hirsch, an expert on Southeast Asia at the University of Sydney, 'was the benchmark of a new set of forces in Thai environmental politics.'

The Japanese-financed feasibility study for the 187-metre-high Nam Choan Dam on the upper Khwae (the River Kwai of cinematic fame) was completed in 1982. The World Bank and Japanese government pledged the funds to build what would be the country's highest dam. Thai electricity utility EGAT stated that the dam would have a capacity to produce 580 MW of electricity, while also storing water for irrigation and attracting tourists. EGAT also insisted that although the 75-kilometre-long reservoir would cut through the Thung Yai Wildlife Sanctuary, only a small percentage of the sanctuary's total area would be flooded, and it claimed the affected forest was in any case already degraded and would soon be destroyed by illegal farming and logging.

The 2,000 people from the Karen ethnic minority who would be displaced were, according to EGAT, destroying the forest and should not have been living in the sanctuary.

Opposing the dam was an *ad hoc* network of urban environmentalists and student groups together with some academics and a small number of civil servants. They countered that Thung Yai formed the core of the largest contiguous expanse of natural forest remaining in Southeast Asia. The reservoir would split the sanctuary into three, blocking migration routes for large mammals such as elephants and wild oxen. The riverine forest that would be flooded forms the most diverse and rarest of the habitats in the sanctuary. Furthermore, roads built to the dam site would attract illegal loggers, poachers and settlers. Karen farmers, dam opponents pointed out, had been in the area for centuries without destroying a significant amount of forest. Displacing the Karen, however, would force them to clear new forest land for replacement farms. The anti-dam lobby also charged that the reservoir could trigger earthquakes on two active fault lines nearby.

Critics accused EGAT of deliberately exaggerating local rainfall and thus power production. For the same investment, opponents argued, an equivalent amount of energy could be generated by upgrading existing power plants. As with other 'multipurpose' dams controlled by EGAT, Nam Choan would likely be operated to maximize power production with water kept back during the dry season when farmers needed it most. Nam Choan would thus yield few if any irrigation benefits, the critics claimed.

The outcry over the project, reported in full in Thailand's press, forced the government to suspend Nam Choan pending its reconsideration by a review committee. Nothing was ever heard from the committee and the furore died down.

In 1986, however, the Nam Choan controversy flared up again with the news that funds had been allocated for a new feasibility study. But during the intervening four years, concern had mounted over the environmental costs of Thailand's development policies and this time the opposition was better organized and broader than before. One important difference from the previous campaign was that by 1986 there was strong local opposition stemming from fears that Nam Choan would repeat the problems such as accelerated forest clearance and low downstream flows caused by nearby dams like Srinakharin and Khao Laem.

A vital element in the eventual success of the campaign was that the anti-dam groups worked not just on the local and national levels, but also built up strong links with the international environmental movement. International awareness helped discourage the World Bank and other foreign donors from pledging funds for the dam. Even foreign royalty got involved in the debate: Prince Philip of Britain in his capacity as president of the World Wildlife Fund, his son Prince Charles and Prince Bernhardt of the Netherlands all made representations emphasizing the need to preserve Thung Yai sanctuary.

Nam Choan also had powerful backers. Along with EGAT technocrats, industrialists and senior politicians and civil servants, the powerful Thai military also played a major role in pushing for the dam due to a desire to tighten control over the Thung Yai area, which in the 1970s had been a stronghold of communist guerrillas. Pro-dam tactics included anonymous leaflets and radio broadcasts variously attacking dam opponents as arms-runners, communists and hunters wanting the run of the sanctuary for themselves.

Despite government dirty tricks, the anti-dam movement continued to grow in strength through 1987. Protest rallies, marches and concerts were held all over the province of Kanchanaburi where Nam Choan would be built. Religious leaders, popular entertainers and a growing number of politicians joined the ranks of the opposition. In March 1988, political pressures persuaded a new review committee set up by the government to vote unanimously against the project and it was subsequently shelved. Soon after, Thung Yai and the adjacent Huai Kha Khaeng Wildlife Sanctuaries were granted World Heritage Site status.[19]

The lessons learned and alliances forged in the Nam Choan campaign propelled Thai environmentalists to other successes, most notably the nationwide ban on logging imposed in 1989. Student groups and NGOs such as the Bangkok-based Project for Ecological Recovery (PER) helped local people force the cancellation or postponement of three large dams in the three years after the Nam Choan decision.[20]

Pak Mun Dam, which provoked the most bitter struggle since Nam Choan, did get built. But the affected people's six-year fight for what they considered to be adequate compensation, combined with the negative national and international publicity for EGAT generated by the controversy, helped bring an end to the utility's dam-building days.[21] In early 1995, the Prime Minister's Office declared that 'for the sake of environmental protection,' Thailand would 'no longer build dams for power production'.[22] Several large flood control and water diversion projects, however, are still being pushed forward.

An unintended consequence of the anti-dam movement in Thailand is that EGAT now intends to buy hydropower from beyond its borders, effectively exporting the environmental and social problems of dam building while importing the electricity. Neighbouring Laos, Burma, Cambodia and the Chinese province of Yunnun are ideal candidates for the exchange: all have huge untapped hydro potentials and authoritarian political systems.[23] Those who opposed dams within Thailand, however, are also shifting their attention across frontiers. The Project for Ecological Recovery has helped establish Toward Ecological Recovery and Regional

Alliance (TERRA), a group which is building links between environmentally concerned activists, politicians, academics and civil servants in Thailand, Burma, Laos, Cambodia and Vietnam. As Thailand's neighbours become more democratic and non-governmental groups begin to take root in these countries, their governments are certain to face increasing opposition to proposed large dams. In the short term, however, unfavourable economics and unsavoury regimes – especially as that in Burma – will likely dissuade international financiers from backing most of the large dams planned for the region.

Clinging to the Land: Resistance to Dams in India

> Rarely have we seen the democratic process at work so palpably and so effectively [in India] as in the growing mobilisation of people against large dams.
>
> Priya Kurian, *Land and Water Review*, 1988

'We will cling to the land like a baby clings to its mother', Medha Patkar of the Narmada Bachao Andolan told the London *Guardian* in April 1993. 'When the waters [of the reservoir] rise we will face them as we have always vowed to. It is not suicide and we do not want to die but our commitment to face the waters has been the bedrock of our movement.'[24] The courage and determination of the Narmada Bachao Andolan (Save the Narmada Movement) in its campaign against the Sardar Sarovar Dam has earned the group international respect and the dam notoriety. In the words of the *Washington Post*, Sardar Sarovar has become a global 'symbol of environmental, political and cultural calamity'.[25] The struggle over the Narmada is, however, only one of a long list of examples of resistance to large dams in India.

Hirakud, the first huge multipurpose dam project completed in independent India, provoked opposition from local politicians and bureaucrats as well as the people to be evicted. Thirty thousand people marched against Hirakud in 1946. The protest was dispersed by a police *lathi* (long cane) charge and the organizers arrested. Later, violent clashes broke out between the people to be evicted and construction workers.[26] In 1970, some 4,000 people occupied the Pong Dam construction site to demand resettlement land. Work was stopped for more than two weeks, but the dam was completed soon after construction resumed. Fifty years later, a majority of the oustees are still to be resettled.[27]

In March 1978, 100,000 demonstrators marched to the site of Chandil Dam on the Subarnarekha River in the state of Bihar. The next month, police fired into a crowd of some 8,000 men, women and children gathered near the dam site. Three were shot dead; another bayoneted to death. Similar brutality was used against those demanding better compensation for displacement by Icha, an associated dam on the Subarnarekha. In 1982, police looted and destroyed the houses of leading Icha activists. One village leader was snatched from his home, tortured and murdered. Resistance to the project has since flared up intermittently and has caused long delays in project implementation. But it has failed to stop the project or substantially to improve resettlement conditions.[28]

Another campaign which began in the mid-1970s and was still continuing 20 years later is that against Tehri Dam in the western Himalayas. The Anti-Tehri Dam Struggle Committee initially had the support of all local political parties in its demand for the dam to be cancelled. As time passed, however, and construction on the dam slowly progressed, the opposition became fractured. The freeze on government and commercial investments in old Tehri town due to its impending submergence and the years of uncertainty eventually caused many local residents to give up their active opposition.

Others, however, inspired by elderly Gandhian activist Shri Sunderlal Bahuguna, have continued to struggle. Bahuguna went on protest fasts against the dam in 1989, 1992 and 1995. Each time the government agreed to review the project, and each time broke its word. In June 1996, the new Indian Prime Minister, H.V. Deve Gowda, gave a glass of lemon juice to the 70-year-old Bahuguna, ending a 75-day fast. The same day, Deve Gowda appointed a group of experts to review the seismic safety of the dam – its most controversial aspect.[29]

The first significant victory for the Indian anti-dam movement was the campaign against a 120 metre hydrodam in Silent Valley in the southwest Indian state of Kerala. Unlike most Indian dams, few people would have been displaced by the project. Opposition instead came mainly from environmentalists enraged at the prospective destruction of one of the country's few relatively undisturbed areas of rainforest. Local people initially favoured Silent Valley Dam, believing it would bring employment, but many were later convinced by activists that the dam and the deforestation which would follow in its wake would harm their livelihoods. The involvement of the national affiliates of the World Wildlife Fund and the International Union for the Conservation of Nature ensured international attention and pressure on the Indian government. Prime Minister Indira Gandhi ordered the project to be shelved in 1983.[30]

The Silent Valley victory boosted the morale of dam opponents elsewhere in India. The momentum gained carried through into the campaign against a series of hydrodams planned for the Godavari and Indravati rivers in central India. The Bhopalpatnam, Inchampalli and Bodghat dams would together have displaced over 110,000 *adivasis* and flooded many tens of thousands of hectares of forests, including part of an important tiger sanctuary. Environmentalists, *adivasis* and indigenous rights activists worked together to get the projects suspended.[31]

The long struggle

Whose are the forests and the land?
Ours, they are ours.
Whose the wood, the fuel?
Ours, they are ours.
Whose, the flowers and the grass?
Ours, they are ours.
Whose the cow, the cattle?
Ours, they are ours.
Whose are the bamboo groves?
Ours, they are ours.

Narmada Bachao Andolan song

Medha Patkar was a 30-year-old social activist and researcher when she first came to the Narmada Valley in 1985 to work in the villages to be submerged by the Sardar Sarovar Dam. Over the next few years, Patkar travelled by foot, bus and boat throughout the nearly 200-kilometre-long submergence zone, which includes parts of three states and people speaking five different languages. Patkar lived with the villagers to be displaced, listened to their fears for the future, and urged them to organize to force the government to respect their rights.

Patkar spent most of her time among the *adivasis* in the remote and rugged Satpura hills of Maharashtra state. Her oratorical and organizing skills helped build the trust of many local people and also attracted a committed coterie of young outside activists to come to the valley. These activists, who included engineers, social workers and journalists, were to play a vital role in the Narmada movement.[32] Early in 1986, Patkar and other activists and the Maharashtra villagers set up the Narmada Dharangrast Samiti (Committee for Narmada Dam-Affected People). The NDS villagers refused to be moved out or to cooperate with dam officials in any way until their demands for fair compensation and information about the impacts of the project were met.

The NDS also began to investigate the official claims of the benefits the project would provide. Among their findings were that crucial environmental studies had not been conducted, that the number of people to be displaced was not known, that estimates of the amount of land to get irrigation water were wildly optimistic, and that while the supply of drinking water to some 40 million people was supposed to be one of the project's main benefits, the massive sums needed to build the pipes and pumps to deliver this water had been left out of the estimated project costs. These findings led the NDS and two other oustees' groups they had helped to set up in Gujarat (the state where the dam is located) and Madhya Pradesh (the state where most of the reservoir would lie) to conclude that the claims of project benefits were fraudulent and just resettlement impossible. At six rallies held simultaneously in the three affected states on 18 August 1988 the NDS and their allies announced their total – but strictly non-violent – opposition to the dam.

National press coverage and awareness of the anti-Sardar Sarovar campaign burgeoned in the late 1980s and support for the Narmada activists mounted among environmental, human rights, religious, landless and *adivasi* organizations around the country. Within the valley, the activists built alliances across class and caste boundaries between *adivasi* and 'caste Hindu' areas, and between the reservoir oustees and people affected by the project in other ways – in particular, families losing land to the massive canal network. In 1989, this growing network of local and international groups was formally named the Save the Narmada Movement, or Narmada Bachao Andolan (NBA).

The international front

Interest in the growing Narmada controversy within the international environmental community was boosted by two trips Medha Patkar made to Washington in 1987 and 1989. Lori Udall from the Environmental Defense Fund (EDF) in Washington was inspired by Patkar to take the lead role in raising the NBA's concerns with the World Bank. Udall also helped build a network of committed and informed activists in North America, Europe, Japan and Australia who become known as the Narmada Action Committee.[33]

Medha Patkar met with some World Bank executive directors during her 1989 visit. 'When I hear what NGOs say about this project and then what the operations staff say,' one director remarked afterwards, 'it sounds like they are talking about two different projects.' Patkar also gave testimony at a congressional subcommittee hearing into the World Bank's performance on Sardar Sarovar. Congressional staff, journalists and environmentalists broke into spontaneous applause after her impassioned, hour-long presentation. A number of Congressmen later wrote to Bank President Barber Conable urging that the project be suspended.

The next foreign success for the NBA was a symposium in Tokyo in April 1990. Influencing opinion in Japan was vital for the Narmada campaign as the Japanese government was lending some $200 million for the turbines for Sardar Sarovar. NBA and international activists joined Japanese NGOs, academics and politicians at the Tokyo symposium, which received considerable national press coverage. The activists later met with Japanese government officials. Within a month of the symposium, the Japanese withdrew all further funding for the dam. This was the first time that a Japanese aid loan had been withdrawn for environmental and human rights reasons.

The long road to the Indian review

Back in India, the NBA had changed its straightforward 'no dam' position in March 1990 and, seeking a way of breaking the stalemate between pro- and anti-dam forces, proposed the project be suspended pending a comprehensive and open review. In an attempt to pressure the government into holding the review, the NBA organized the most spectacular action of its long campaign. On Christmas Day 1990, 5,000 oustees and NBA supporters, including the widely respected veteran social activist Baba Amte, set off for the dam site from the town of Rajghat in Madhya Pradesh on a Struggle March Towards People's Development – to become known as the 'Long March'. Eight days later the marchers reached the village of Ferkuwa on the border with Gujarat and found their way blocked by the police and a counter-demonstration organized by the Gujarat government. An angry month-long stand-off ensued.

At first the NBA attempted to break through by sending forward groups of volunteers, their hands tied in front of them to symbolize their commitment to non-violence. The police repeatedly forced back the volunteers. Some were beaten and around 140 detained. Patkar and six others then began a fast by the side of the road. The days passed but the government remained unresponsive. Then, on 29 January, the twenty-first day of the fast, news came from Washington DC that the World Bank would commission a review of the project. The following day, the hunger strike and march were called off. The Long March gained massive press coverage throughout India, greatly increased country-wide support for the NBA, and made Medha Patkar a national celebrity.

By 1991, full-scale construction on the dam had been under way for four years. Submergence was clearly possible during the upcoming monsoon, which hits the Narmada Valley between June and September every year. At a ceremony in Manibeli, the Maharashtra village closest to the dam, a group of oustees and activists vowed to be the first to face the waters rising behind the part-built dam. An NBA compound was set up at one of the lowest parts of Manibeli with a house where the *Samarpit Dal*, or 'Save or Drown Squad', would sit and wait to be engulfed by the new reservoir. In response, the government banned Patkar and other activists from the villages during the monsoon, and prohibited the villagers from holding anti-dam protests.

The NBA defied the bans, and hundreds of their supporters were arrested during the monsoon months. Members of the *Samarpit Dal* went into hiding to avoid detention and so be able to carry out their vow. A weak monsoon, however, meant that the water stayed several metres below Manibeli in 1991.

The following year the Narmada rose during one monsoon storm to within a metre of the lowest house behind the dam. Patkar was among

11 people in the house at the time. Also in 1992, police shot dead an *adivasi* woman while evicting her community from forest land which was to be given to resettled oustees.

The fiercely critical report of the World Bank-funded Independent Review team, headed by Bradford Morse, was released in June 1992, after nine months of research and writing (see Chapter 9, pp. 259–60). The NBA and its international supporters were delighted that the Review vindicated so many of their claims and they used it to step up pressure on the World Bank. Environmentalists wrote an open letter to World Bank President Lewis Preston which they published as a full-page advertisement in the London *Financial Times.* It warned that if the Bank refused to withdraw funding for Sardar Sarovar then NGOs would launch a campaign to cut government funding of the Bank. The letter was endorsed by 250 NGOs and coalitions from 37 countries. Full-page advertisements placed in the *Washington Post* and *New York Times* by US environmental groups made similar demands.

After the Bank

The Bank finally announced its withdrawal in March 1993. The Indian authorities' initial reaction was to step up the use of violence and intimidation. In November, police shot dead an *adivasi* boy. Street demonstrations against the killing were met with *lathi* charges and yet more arrests.

Without World Bank funds, work on the canal system soon all but ground to a halt. Available financial resources were poured into raising the dam wall – the most visible symbol of the project and the most intimidating to the people refusing resettlement. Large-scale submergence began during the 1993 monsoon with the dam wall 44 metres high. The lands of hundreds of villagers were inundated and the homes and possessions of 40 families washed away. Police arrested the occupants of the lowest houses and dragged them to higher ground to prevent them carrying out their pledge to drown. Similar scenes were repeated during the 1994 and 1995 monsoons. In 1995 some villagers braved water which rose to chest height before receding.

With the World Bank out of the way, the NBA stepped up pressure on the Indian government to commission a comprehensive review, one which would look at all aspects of Sardar Sarovar – the terms of reference for the Morse Commission had covered only resettlement and the environment. In June 1993, Medha Patkar and Devram Kanera, a farmer from Madhya Pradesh, began a fast in downtown Bombay. After 14 days the government agreed to start the review process – but once the fast was called off it reneged on its promise.

Ever more frustrated with the government's duplicity, the continuing arrests and beatings of activists, and the submergence of homes in the valley, the NBA decided once again to use the strongest weapon at its disposal – the lives of its own members. In July 1993, the NBA announced that unless the review process began by 6 August, seven activists would throw themselves into the monsoon-swollen Narmada. Less than 24 hours before the deadline, the central government announced that it would establish a five-member group of experts nominated by both the NBA and dam supporters to 'look into all aspects of SSP'. The group met within hours of the announcement and called on the NBA to halt their action, while assuring them that they were committed to an unbiased and comprehensive review of SSP. The *jal samarpan* – 'self-sacrifice by drowning' – was called off.

The review committee heard submissions from the NBA, affected people, central government ministries and the relevant state governments – except that of Gujarat, which boycotted the review. Scientists and engineers presented detailed suggestions for alternative methods of supplying water and power. The release of the report, however, was delayed indefinitely by legal action from the Gujarat government.

In May 1994, the NBA opened another front in its campaign by filing a comprehensive case against the project with the New Delhi Supreme Court. The case moved forward at a painfully slow pace with numerous postponements, delays and cancellations.

New hope for the campaign came in late 1994 when the Madhya Pradesh government announced that it had neither the land nor resources to resettle the state's huge numbers of oustees and that it wanted the planned dam height to be reduced. In an effort to pressure the upstream government to force Gujarat to halt the dam, the NBA decided to muster its resources for yet another round of fasts, this time to be held in Bhopal, the Madhya Pradesh capital. On 21 November 1994, Patkar and three men from the valley stopped eating. Twenty-six days later, the Madhya Pradesh government agreed to demand a halt to construction pending progress on resettlement. The NBA called off the fasts.

Three days before the end of the Bhopal fasts the Supreme Court ordered the government-commissioned review to be made public. The report questioned the basic data used to design the project and criticized the resettlement effort. The court asked the review team to investigate further the viability of the project.

The NBA received a significant boost in January 1995 when the central government in New Delhi forced Gujarat to suspend raising the dam wall with its lowest point 63 metres above the riverbed, just under half the planned final height. The suspension order came because the project was violating a court ruling that oustees must be resettled six months before their land is submerged.[34]

As of August 1996, the result of the in-depth study of project feasibility ordered by the Supreme Court had still not been made public and no final decision had yet been reached by the Supreme Court on the future of the project. Construction on the dam wall remained stalled.

Whatever the final outcome, the long struggle of the people of the valley and their supporters within India and around the world has left deep scars on the World Bank and the Indian and international dam industry. It is unlikely that the Bank will ever fund another river development project on such a scale in a democratic country. It is also unlikely for the foreseeable future that the Indian dam lobby will succeed in pushing through any projects involving such large-scale displacement. 'We are not going in for large dams any more', Indian power minister N.K.P. Salve told *International Water Power & Dam Construction* in late 1993. 'We want run of the river projects and to have smaller dams, if they are necessary at all, which will not cause any impediment whatsoever to the environmental needs.'[35]

The NBA sees its role as much more than challenging a single dam or even dam building in general. Patkar and other NBA leaders have travelled throughout India supporting other struggles against destructive state and corporate development projects which strip the poor of their right to livelihood. Together with other leading environmental, women's, lower-caste and Gandhian groups, the NBA has helped establish a National Alliance of People's Movements (NAPM). In March 1996, representatives from around 100 groups in 17 states drew up a 'People's Resolve', a common ideological platform for the NAPM around which it is hoped India's many thousands of diverse people's organizations can unite in a 'strong social, political force'.[36]

Dam Fighting on a Global Scale

> To persuade Third World governments to abandon plans to build water development schemes ... is very difficult. Nevertheless, every effort must be made by local environmental groups to do so. If necessary, they should resort to non-violent direct action at the dam site. We in the West can best prevent the construction of further dams by systematically lobbying donor governments, development banks, and international agencies, without whose financial help such schemes could not be built.
>
> Edward Goldsmith and Nicholas Hildyard, *The Social and Environmental Effects of Large Dams, Vol. 1*, 1984

Edward Goldsmith and Nicholas Hildyard's book *The Social and Environmental Effects of Large Dams*, published in 1984, helped launch the international anti-dam movement. It was the first book to gather together the main arguments against large dams and to insist that the problems dams caused were not peculiar to specific projects or regions but were largely inherent to the technology. While Goldsmith and Hildyard, editors of the English journal *The Ecologist*, were busy researching and writing, an English-born hydrologist living in San Francisco, Philip Williams, was independently reaching many of the same conclusions. Williams had for years been helping environmentalists trying to stop water projects in California. His research led him to look at the safety record of dams worldwide, which in turn led him to study the activities of the international dam-building industry.

Williams was a regular participant in the annual 'Dam Fighters' Conference' held in Washington, DC. In 1982 he suggested to Brent Blackwelder of the Environmental Policy Institute that they organize a seminar at the conference on international dams. One of the participants at this seminar was Bruce Rich, an attorney with the Natural Resources Defense Council, who was researching the environmental impacts of mega-projects funded by the World Bank and the other multilateral development banks (MDBs). In June 1983, Blackwelder, Rich and Barbara Bramble of the National Wildlife Federation gave the first ever testimony to Congress on the environmental destruction caused by MDB projects, many of the worst of them being large dams.

While the Washington-based groups were stepping up their lobbying of the World Bank, Philip Williams helped motivate a group of Californian environmentalists to start the bimonthly *International Dams Newsletter* in late 1985. The first issue included critiques of Three Gorges, Bakun and Narmada – projects which are still the focus of international campaigns a decade later. In mid-1987, the group's formal title became International Rivers Network and their newsletter was renamed *World Rivers Review*.

The IRN publication proved a valuable forum for the growing number of anti-dam activists around the world. Sixty of these activists met face to face in June 1988 at an IRN-organized conference in San Francisco. The participants endorsed a 'San Francisco Declaration' which demanded a moratorium on all new large dam projects failing to meet a list of conditions relating to the participation of the affected people in the planning process, access to project information, environmental impacts, resettlement, safety, health impacts and economics. They also endorsed a 'Watershed Management Declaration' recommending alternatives to large dams. The points made in the two declarations still sum up the basic demands of the international movement (see Appendix 1).

Over the past decade the group of international activists supporting the struggles of people resisting large dams has grown and become increasingly better connected and more sophisticated. Groups such as Probe International in Canada, the Association for International Water and Forest Studies (FIVAS) in Norway, Friends of the Earth in Japan, Both Ends in the Netherlands, the Berne Declaration in Switzerland,

Urgewald in Germany, AidWatch in Australia, *The Ecologist* in the UK, and IRN and EDF in the US have successfully worked with colleagues in developing countries to cut back international funding for large dams.

The campaigns against World Bank-funded dams – in particular the Xingu Dams in Brazil, Nam Choan, Kedung Ombo (Indonesia), Pak Mun, Arun III (Nepal) and Sardar Sarovar – have been the most effective non-governmental force pushing changes within the World Bank. The independent Inspection Panel established in 1993 to assess violations of Bank policies is a direct result of the institution's humiliating experience with Sardar Sarovar. Campaigns against dams have also played a leading role in forcing the adoption of various new World Bank policies, in particular those on resettlement, environmental assessment, indigenous people and information disclosure.

The extent of international opposition to large dams in the mid-1990s is illustrated best by the support for the Manibeli Declaration (see Appendix 2). This document, drawn up by IRN in coordination with colleagues in India and elsewhere, was submitted to World Bank President Lewis Preston in September 1994 during the Bank's 50th anniversary celebrations. It calls for a moratorium on World Bank funding of large dams until a number of conditions are met, including the establishment of a fund to provide reparations to people forcibly evicted without adequate compensation, improved practices on information disclosure and project appraisal, and an independent review of the performance of all dams built with World Bank support. The Manibeli Declaration was endorsed by 326 groups and coalitions in 44 countries. If the member groups of coalitions and networks are counted individually, the number of endorsements rises to more than 2,000. Although the Bank gave no detailed formal response to the Manibeli Declaration, four months after they received it the Bank's Operations Evaluation Department began its first ever review of a group of Bank-financed large dams.

Activists working at the local, national and international levels have together managed to tarnish seriously the lure of large dams as icons of progress and plenty. To many people, big dams have instead become symbols of the destruction of the natural world and of the corruption and arrogance of over-powerful and secretive corporations, bureaucracies and governments. Although hundreds of large dams are still under construction and many more are on engineers' drawing boards, aid funds and other public sector sources of financing are drying up, and public protests are provoked by just about every large dam that is now proposed in a democratic country. The international dam industry appears to be entering a recession from which it may never escape.

Notes

1. W. Pircher, '36,000 Large Dams and Still More Needed', paper presented at Seventh Biennial Conference of the British Dam Society, University of Stirling, 25 June 1992.

2. See, e.g., T. Palmer, *Stanislaus: The Struggle for a River*, University of California Press, Berkeley 1982; S. McCutcheon, *Electric Rivers: The Story of the James Bay Project*, Black Rose Books, Montreal 1991; Ø. Dalland, 'The Last Dam in Norway: Whose Victory?', in A.D. Usher (ed.), *Dams as Aid: A Political Anatomy of Nordic Development Thinking*, Routledge, London forthcoming; L. Lövgren, 'Moratorium in Sweden: A History of the Dams Debate', in Usher (ed.), *Dams as Aid*; A. Wallace, 'A River Runs Through Her', *Amicus Journal*, Winter 1994; 'SOS Loire Vivante: Actions and Strategies', SOS Loire Vivante, Le Puy, May 1995; J.P. Orrego, 'In Defense of the Biobío River', in Usher (ed.), *Dams as Aid*; 'International Opposition to Katun Dam', *World Rivers Review*, March/April 1990; C. Caufield, '"Ban the Dam" Protests Stall Siberian Project', *Emerging Markets*, 12 April 1992; C. Drucker, 'Dam the Chico: Hydro Development and Tribal Resistance in the Philippines', in E. Goldsmith and N. Hildyard (eds.), *The Social and Environmental Impacts of Large Dams. Vol. 2: Case Studies*, Wadebridge Ecological Centre, Cornwall 1986 (hereafter *SEELD 2*); G. Aditjondro and D. Kowaleski, 'Damning the Dams in Indonesia: A Test of Competing Perspectives', *Asian Survey*, Vol. XXXIV, No. 4, April 1994.

3. For accounts of the 'Dinosaur Battle', see T. Palmer, *Endangered Rivers and the Conservation Movement*, University of California Press, Berkeley 1986, pp. 68–74; M. Reisner, *Cadillac Desert: The American West and its Disappearing Water*, Secker & Warburg, London 1986, pp. 294–5; R. Martin, *A Story That Stands Like a Dam*. Henry Holt, New York 1989, p. 53; and R. Gottlieb, *Forcing the Spring: The Transformation of the American Environmental Movement*, Island Press, Washington, DC, 1993, pp. 41–6.

4. Palmer, *Endangered Rivers*, pp. 78–86.

5. Ibid., p. 132.

6. See ibid.; Reisner, *Cadillac Desert*, pp. 324–43; F. Powledge, *Water: The Nature, Uses, and Future of Our Most Precious and Abused Resource*, Farrar, Straus & Giroux, New York 1986, pp. 306–10.

7. D. Beard, 'Remarks before the International Commission on Irrigation and Drainage', Varna, Bulgaria, 18 May 1994.

8. P. Thompson, 'Saving Tasmania's Franklin and Gordon Wild Rivers', in *SEELD 2*, pp. 69–77; The Blockaders, *Franklin Blockade*, The Wilderness Society, Hobart 1983; W. Steffen, 'Furor Over the Franklin', *Sierra*, September/October 1984; G. Lambert and G. Colem, 'The Face of Things to Come', *Wilderness News*, May/June/July 1993.

9. 'Pedder Unplugged', *Wilderness News*, May/June/July 1994; B. Montgomery, 'Voices in the Wilderness Get Their Say on Pedder', *The Australian*, 22 February 1995. The HEC claimed that electricity demand in Tasmania would grow by over half between 1983 and 1995. Actual demand in 1995 was only 12% higher than in 1983 – close to environmentalists' projections (H. Gee, 'Pulling the Plug on Pedder', *Habitat Australia*, May 1994).

10. Main sources for Danube section: C. Caufield, 'The Last Tale of the Vienna Woods', *Not Man Apart*, January 1985; N.F. Thorpe, 'The Danube Dam and the Hungarian Greens', in *SEELD 2,* pp. 78–81; F. Pearce, *Green Warriors: The People and the Politics Behind the Environmental Revolution*, Bodley Head, London 1991, pp. 107–16; F. Pearce, *The Dammed: Rivers, Dams and the Coming World Water Crisis*, Bodley Head, London 1992, pp. 256–62; J. Sibl (ed.), *Damming the Danube: What*

Dam Builders Don't Want You to Know: A Critique of the Gabcikovo Dam Project, SZOPK/SRN, Bratislava 1993; interview with Janos Vargha, 26 October 1994.

11. Pearce, *Green Warriors*, pp. 117–18; P. Searle and M. Power, 'Sofia Cracks Down on Demonstrators', *Guardian*, London, 27 October 1989; 'Bulgaria Puts Hydro Schemes on Ice', *New Scientist*, 2 December 1989.

12. 'The Daugavpils HES: Environmentalism Sparks Revolution', in 'Latvia: Environmental Crisis/Environmental Activism', a brief prepared by the US chapter of the Environmental Protection Club of Latvia, 1990.

13. Interview with Londa Khasaya, 22 September 1995. As of early 1996 the Georgian electriciy authority was still claiming that Khudoni would be completed ('World Atlas of Hydropower & Dams', *The International Journal of Hydropower & Dams*, January 1996, p. 129).

14. For the Xingu Dam story, see N. Hildyard, 'Adios Amazonia? A Report from the Altamira Gathering', *The Ecologist*, Vol. 19, No. 2, 1989; Pearce, *Green Warriors*, pp. 132–9; B.J. Cummings, *Dam the Rivers, Damn the People*, Earthscan, London 1990, pp. 63–88; also articles in 1988 and 1989 issues of *World Rivers Review*.

15. M.S. Morais, 'Energy and Development: Victims of Hydroelectric Dams Say No!', in H. Acselrad, (ed.), *Environment and Democracy*, IBASE, Rio de Janeiro 1992.

16. '*Atingidos por Barragens*' literally means those 'hit' by the dams. It has variously been given in English as 'Victims of Dams', 'Harmed by Dams', 'Impacted by Dams' and 'Dam Refugees'. Brazilian activists prefer the translation 'Affected'.

17. C. Bermann, 'Self-Managed Resettlement – A Case Study: The Itá Dam in Southern Brazil', paper presented at conference 'Hydropower Into the Next Century', Barcelona, June 1995; A. Oliver-Smith, 'Fighting for a Place: The Policy Implications of Resistance to Development-Induced Resettlement', paper presented at conference 'Development Induced Displacement and Impoverishment', Oxford, January 1995; Morais, 'Energy and Development'.

18. CUT/CRAB, 'Terra Sim, Barragens Não', 1989; CABA, untitled MS, Altimira 1991; M.T.F. Serra, 'Resettlement Planning in the Brazilian Power Sector: Recent Changes in Approach', in M.M. Cernea and S.E. Guggenheim (eds.), *Anthropological Approaches To Resettlement: Policy, Practice and Theory*, Westview Press, Boulder, CO, 1993.

19. P. Hirsch, *Political Economy of Environment in Thailand*, Journal of Contemporary Asia Publishers, Manila 1993; N. Tuntawiroon and P. Samootsakorn, 'Thailand's Dam Building Programme: Past, Present and Future', in *SEELD 2*; J. Rigg, 'Thailand's Nam Choan Dam Project: A Case Study in the "greening" of South-East Asia', *Global Ecology and Biogeography Letters*, Vol. 1, 1991; *The Ecologist*, Vol. 17, No. 6, 1987.

20. A.D. Usher, 'Villagers Still Stranded From First WB Hydro Dam', *The Nation*, Bangkok, 9 October 1991.

21. See, e.g., 'Ongoing Protests over Pak Moon', *Thai Development Newsletter*, Bangkok, No. 24, 1994; G. Ryder, 'Case Study: Pak Mun Dam in Thailand', paper presented at symposium 'Both Sides of the Dam', Delft University of Technology, 22 February 1995; D. Hubbel, 'Thailand's Pak Mun Dam: A Case Study', *World Rivers Review*, Fourth Quarter, 1994; 'EGAT Set to Pay Up on Pak Mool Dam', *The Nation*, Bangkok, 24 March 1995.

22. 'Savit: Dams Will Not be Built for Power Production', *Bangkok Post*, 24 February 1995. Although environmental protection is the stated reason for the halt to dam building, economics are likely to be at least as important.

23. See 'Special Mekong Issue', *World Rivers Review*, Fourth Quarter, 1994.

24. P. McCully, 'Why I Will Drown', *Guardian*, London, 16 April 1993.

25. M. Moore, 'India's Lifeline or Man-Made Disaster?', *Washington Post*, 24 August 1993.

26. S.K. Pattanak et al., 'Hirakud Dam Project: Expectations and Realities', in A. Chaudhary and K. Singh (compilers), *People and Dams*, PRIA, New Delhi 1990, pp. 52–3; P. Viegas, 'The Hirakud Dam Oustees: Thirty Years After', in E.G. Thukral (ed.), *Big Dams, Displaced People: Rivers of Sorrow, Rivers of Change*, Sage Publications, New Delhi 1992, pp. 45–7.

27. R. Bhanot and M. Singh, 'The Oustees of Pong Dam: Their Search for a Home', in Thukral (ed.), *Big Dams, Displaced People*, p. 101.

28. M. Areeparampil, 'The Impact of Subarnarekha Multipurpose Project on the Indigenous People of Singhbhum', in Chaudhary and Singh (compilers), *People and Dams*, p. 101. Construction slowly continued on the Subarnarekha Project – with funding from the World Bank – through the 1980s. In 1988, the year the gates were closed on Chandil Dam, the World Bank suspended its loans due to the appalling resettlement situation, but two years later it recommenced disbursements. In 1993 the World Bank decided to withdraw its proposal to give new loans to complete the scheme (B. Rich, *Mortgaging the Earth: The World Bank, Environmental Impoverishment, and the Crisis of Development*, Beacon Press, Boston 1994, pp. 43–6).

29. Pearce, *The Dammed*, pp. 144–58; Tehri Action Group, 'Prime Minister Betrays Bahuguna Again on Tehri Dam Review', New Delhi, 29 August 1995; A. Brown, 'Tehri Stalled by Powerful Fast', *World Rivers Review*, Vol. 11, No. 3, July 1996.

30. Centre for Science and Environment, *The State of India's Environment – 1982: A Citizen's Report*, CSE, New Delhi 1982, p. 64; R.K. Palat, 'A Tropical Rainforest: Development or Conservation'? *Land Use Policy*, July 1985.

31. The Bodhghat Dam was suspended when the World Bank withdrew its offer of funding in 1988. It was finally cancelled by the Madhya Pradesh government in 1995 ('Bank Halts Bodhghat Funding', *World Rivers Review*, Sept./Oct. 1988; 'India Province Cancels Project', *Hydro Review Worldwide*, Summer 1995).

32. Among the many outside activists to work on the Narmada campaign, Alok Agarwal, Shripad Dharmadhikary, Arundhati Dhuru, Nandini Oza, Sanjay Sangvai and Himanshu Thakker have played a particularly important role.

33. Bruce Rich from the Environmental Defense Fund and Marcus Colchester of the UK-based Survival International both visited the Narmada Valley before Patkar's first trip to the US, and were the first to lobby actively against the World Bank support of the project.

34. Numerous newspaper accounts and other sources were used for this account. Of particular use were back issues of *World Rivers Review*; Asia Watch, 'Before the Deluge: Human Rights Abuses at India's Narmada Dam', *Asia Watch*, Vol. 4, No. 15, 1992; Lawyers Committee for Human Rights, 'Unacceptable Means: India's Sardar Sarovar Project and Violations of Human Rights. October 1992 through February 1993', LCHR, New York 1993; M. Patkar (in conversation with Smitu Kothari), 'The Struggle for Participation and Justice: An Historical Narrative', W.F. Fisher, 'Development and Resistance in the Narmada Valley', L. Udall, 'The International Narmada Campaign: A Case of Sustained Advocacy', all in W.F. Fisher (ed.), *Towards Sustainable Development? Struggling Over India's Narmada River*, M.E. Sharpe, Armonk, NY, 1995; C. Caulfield, *The Illusion of Plenty: The World Bank and the Poverty of Nations*, Henry Holt, New York 1997. See also *A Valley Rises*, a film by Ali Kazimi (1994), and *Narmada Diary*, a video by Anand Padwardhan (1995). Also personal communications with Medha Patkar, Shripad Dharmadhikary and Himanshu Thakker.

35. P. O'Neil, 'India: Eternal Snows Versus Finite Fuels', *International Water Power & Dam Construction*, January 1995.

36. National Alliance of People's Movements', NAPM, Bombay 1996, p. 2.

Afterword:
From the Dam to the Watershed

Bringing the dam industry under democratic control will remove a major threat to the integrity of riverine ecosystems and human communities. It will also help clear the way for the preservation and implementation of more sustainable and equitable technologies and methods of freshwater management. It will not, however, on its own ensure the survival of healthy rivers – many human activities other than dam building harm rivers.

The key to protecting and restoring rivers lies in treating with care and respect their entire watersheds. Thinking on the watershed level means seeing rivers as integral parts of a complex and dynamic system of land and water and biota. Disrupting any part of the system will eventually affect all other parts. Looking after rivers thus means looking after water, soils, ecosystems and the air (much of the pollution entering aquatic systems is first spewed into the atmosphere before falling back to earth).

Watershed thinking means dropping the language and accompanying concepts of 'controlling' and 'enslaving' 'wild', 'unruly' and 'wasted' rivers – one cannot 'control' a watershed. It requires recognizing and respecting the complexity of the interactions between land, water and atmosphere. It means adapting to this complexity rather than making counter-productive efforts to control and simplify it. It also means respecting the diversity of different watersheds and the natural and human communities that live within them.

Ways of living which allow human economic, cultural and spiritual needs to be satisfied while maintaining healthy watersheds must be encouraged while the forces which are destroying watersheds – that is, destroying the natural world in general – must be curbed. Over the long term, healthy societies cannot exist without healthy watersheds.

Appendix 1

A. The San Francisco Declaration of the International Rivers Network

The Position of Citizens' Organizations on Large Dams and Water Resource Management

In June 1988 IRN sponsored an international conference in San Francisco for citizens' organizations concerned with protecting rivers and water resources from their most immediate threat – construction of large dams. Sixty people from 26 countries attended and initiated a program of action that forms the basis of IRN's global campaign to protect the world's rivers. The following position statement adopted by the conference and subsequently extended by our network organizations (the last six points appearing here) forms the foundation of our campaign:

- The specific goals of the dam project must be clearly stated, providing a clear basis for measuring the future success or failure of the project.
- During project planning, all alternatives to the project goals, both structural and non-structural, must be clearly analyzed.
- Any governmental or international agency that funds big dam projects must allow free access to information on the project to citizens of both lending and recipient countries.
- A full assessment of the short and long-term environmental, social and economic effects of the project must be carried out, and an adequate opportunity provided for review and critique by independent experts.
- All people affected by the dam, both in the reservoir area and downstream, must be notified of the probable effect on their livelihood, must be consulted in the planning process, and must have effective political means for vetoing the project.
- All people who lose homes, land or livelihood to a dam project must be fully compensated by accountable agencies.
- The threat to public safety due to potential collapse of the dam must be

investigated and the analysis be made freely available to anyone living in the area potentially affected by the flood wave.

- Any irrigation project associated with a large dam must have as its primary goal the production of food crops for local consumption rather than cash crops for export.
- Any irrigation project associated with a large dam must include a fully integrated program to prevent waterlogging and salinization in order to allow the sustainable use of irrigated land.
- The dam project must be demonstrated to have no significant adverse impact (such as those caused by loss of nutrients and soil salinization) on the food supply or livelihood of people dependent on floodplain agriculture downstream.
- The dam project must be demonstrated to pose no threat to the water quality and water supplies of those living downstream.
- The project must improve public health, and must not threaten to increase the incidence of waterborne disease.
- The environmental impacts of industrial users dependent on electricity generated by the dam must be included in the project planning.
- The dam project must be demonstrated to have no significant adverse effect on downstream riverine, estuarine, or coastal fisheries.
- The dam project must not adversely affect any national park, heritage site, designated area of scientific and educational importance or any area inhabited by threatened or endangered species.
- An adequate program for reforesting or erosion control in the reservoir watershed must be fully integrated into the project design.
- The plan for the dam project must identify whether or not the project is sustainable. It should specifically address reservoir sedimentation, soil salinization and changes in reservoir inflow due to watershed degradation. If the project is not sustainable a restoration program should be included as part of the project design.
- Projected economic costs must include all the economic costs of environmental damage, and all the costs associated with construction, preparation, maintenance, and decommissioning.
- The economic analysis for a dam project must identify the range of uncertainty in the estimates of costs and benefits.
- Projected economic benefits and costs of the dam project must be based on demonstrated benefits and costs of prior projects.
- Plans for hydroelectric dams must present an analysis of the relative benefit and costs of alternative means of electricity generation and energy conservation.
- There must be an effective means to ensure that the operation and maintenance of the dam and associated facilities will actually be carried out to achieve the promised benefits.

B. Watershed Management Declaration

1. International efforts must be increased to bring back the vegetation that once acted as groundcover for the river catchment areas. The loss of this groundcover in the last century is a major reason for the depletion of groundwater, soil erosion, droughts and floods in many countries.

2. Groundwater must be considered a renewable resource and its use should not exceed its natural recharge.

3. The need for water must first be identified at the community level, and any solution devised to meet those needs must include the explicit identification of users and beneficiaries. Solutions must be appropriate to indigenous resource-use patterns.

4. Local productions systems should be strengthened by phasing out use of capital-intensive, agricultural chemicals, fossil fuel derivatives, and excessive water in favor of low-cost, ecologically safe alternatives.

5. The timetable of a water project should not be determined by donor-driven funding cycles. Appropriate development is an economic solution for the long term. Therefore, its planning and implementation must be determined by the cultural and economic aspects of the community in question.

6. Reinstitute traditional methods of water preservation and use. Rather than building reservoirs bring back methods, such as those used in India where forested buffer zones around catchment systems, ponds, water tanks, and wells helped protect water supplies.

7. Rainforest preservation of the earth's great watersheds, such as those of the Amazon and Congo regions, requires our most urgent attention. Rainforests play a crucial role of maintaining the health of the biosphere.

8. Legal and political rights to protect the environment are simply not recognized in many countries. Therefore we request that all countries
   - create and strengthen environmental regulation for water management;
   - democratize and decentralize decision making for environmental protection and natural resource management. This includes a public-hearings process for all project proposals;
   - uphold the human rights of environmentalists and water project critics.

9. Create an International Code of Water Resource Management that would provide the legal guidelines for water development and for public interest groups to challenge violations of the law.

10. A compilation of successful sustainable water programs should be prepared and published by member organizations of IRN. This can help encourage the academic community and development experts to re-examine the traditional systems and help rebuild the self-respect and self-reliance of indigenous peoples.

Appendix 2

Manibeli Declaration*

Calling for a Moratorium on World Bank Funding of Large Dams (June 1994)

WHEREAS:

1. The World Bank is the greatest single source of funds for large dam construction, having provided more than U$50 billion (1992 dollars) for construction of more than 500 large dams in 92 countries. Despite this enormous investment, no independent analysis or evidence exists to demonstrate that the financial, social and environmental costs were justified by the benefits realized;
2. Since 1948, the World Bank has financed large dam projects which have forcibly displaced in the order of ten million people from their homes and lands. The Bank's own 1994 'Resettlement and Development' review admits that the vast majority of women, men and children evicted by Bank-funded projects never regained their former incomes nor received any direct benefits from the dams for which they were forced to sacrifice their homes and lands. The Bank has consistently failed to implement and enforce its own policy on forced resettlement, first established in 1980, and despite several policy reviews the Bank has no plans to fundamentally change its approach to forced resettlement;
3. The World Bank is planning to fund over the next three years 18 large dam projects which will forcibly displace another 450,000 people, without any credible guarantee that its policy on resettlement will be enforced. Meanwhile the Bank has no plans to properly compensate and re-

* In honour of the heroic resistance by the people of the village of Manibeli and others in India's Narmada Valley to the World-Bank-funded Sardar Sarovar Dam, and of the millions of reservoir refugees around the world.

habilitate the millions displaced by past Bank-funded dam projects, including populations displaced since 1980 in violation of the Bank's policy;

4. World Bank-funded large dams have had extensive negative environmental impacts, destroying forests, wetlands, fisheries, and habitat for threatened and endangered species, and increasing the spread of waterborne diseases;

5. The environmental and social costs of World Bank-funded large dams, in terms of people forced from their homes, destruction of forests and fisheries, and spread of waterborne diseases, have fallen disproportionately on women, indigenous communities, tribal peoples and the poorest and most marginalized sectors of the population. This is in direct contradiction to the World Bank's often-stated 'overarching objective of alleviating poverty';

6. The World Bank has prioritized lending for large dams which provide electricity to transnational industry and to urban elites, and irrigation water supply for export-oriented agriculture, neglecting the most pressing needs of the rural poor and other disadvantaged groups. The Bank has provided $8.3 billion (1992 dollars) for large dams through the International Development Association (IDA), the 'soft' credit window which is supposed to aid the poorest populations in developing countries;

7. The World Bank has tolerated and thus contributed to gross violations of human rights by governments in the process of implementing Bank-funded large dams, including arbitrary arrests, beatings, rapes, and shootings of peaceful demonstrators. Many Bank-funded large dam projects cannot be implemented without gross violations of human rights because affected communities inevitably resist the imposition of projects so harmful to their interests;

8. The World Bank plans, designs, funds, and monitors the construction of large dams in a secretive and unaccountable manner, imposing projects without meaningful consultation or participation by the communities affected, often denying access to information even to local governments in the areas affected;

9. The World Bank has consistently ignored cost-effective and environmentally and socially sound alternatives to large dams, including wind, solar and biomass energy sources, energy demand management, irrigation rehabilitation, efficiency improvements and rainwater harvesting, and non-structural flood management. The Bank has even convinced governments to accept loans for large dams when more cost-effective and less destructive alternative plans existed, as may be the case again with the Arun III project in Nepal;

10. The economic analyses on which the World Bank bases its decisions to fund large dams fail to apply the lessons learned from the poor record of past Bank-funded dams, underestimating the potential for delays and cost overruns. Project appraisals are typically based on unrealistically optimistic assumptions about project performance, and fail to account for the direct and indirect costs of negative environmental and social impacts. The Bank's own 1992 portfolio review admits that project appraisals are treated as 'marketing devices' which fail to establish that projects are in the public interest;

11. The primary beneficiaries of procurement contracts for World Bank-funded large dams have been consultants, manufacturers and contractors based in the donor countries, who profit while citizens of the borrowing countries are burdened by debt and the destructive economic, environmental and social impacts of the large dams themselves. The Bank has consistently failed to build local capacity and expertise, promoting dependency instead;

12. World Bank-funded large dams have flooded cultural monuments, religious and sacred sites, and national parks and other wildlife sanctuaries;

13. In its lending for large dams the World Bank has tolerated and condoned theft of funds supplied by the Bank, often by corrupt military and undemocratic regimes, and has often made additional loans to cover cost overruns brought on by what the Bank refers to as 'rent seeking behavior.' Examples include Yacyretá Dam in Argentina and Chixoy in Guatemala;

14. The World Bank has consistently violated its policy on environmental assessment, and has allowed environmental assessments to be produced by project promoters and used to justify prior decisions to proceed with destructive large dam projects;

15. The World Bank has never addressed in policy, research, or project planning documents, the decommissioning of large dams after their useful lifetime has expired due to reservoir sedimentation and physical deterioration;

16. The World Bank has never properly assessed its record of funding large dams and has no mechanism for measuring the actual long-term costs and benefits of the large dams it funds;

17. Throughout its involvement in the Sardar Sarovar Dam in the Narmada Valley, a worldwide symbol of destructive development, the World Bank has consistently ignored its own policy guidelines regarding resettlement and environmental assessment, and attempted to cover up the conclusions of the severely critical official independent review, the

Morse Report. With the ongoing forcible evictions and flooding of tribal lands, the Bank bears direct legal and moral responsibility for the human rights abuses taking place in the Narmada Valley.

THEREFORE, the undersigned organizations:

- CONCLUDE that the World Bank has to date been unwilling and incapable of reforming its lending for large dams; and

- CALL for an immediate moratorium on all World Bank funding of large dams including all projects currently in the funding pipeline, until:

1. The World Bank establishes a fund to provide reparations to the people forcibly evicted from their homes and lands by Bank-funded large dams without adequate compensation and rehabilitation. The fund should be administered by a transparent and accountable institution completely independent of the Bank and should provide funds to communities affected by Bank-funded large dams to prepare reparations claims;

2. The World Bank strengthens its policies and operational practices to guarantee that no large dam projects which require forced resettlement will be funded in countries that do not have policies and legal frameworks in place to assure restoration of the living standards of displaced peoples. Furthermore, communities to be displaced must be involved throughout the identification, design, implementation and monitoring of the projects, and give their informed consent before the project can be implemented;

3. The World Bank commissions, reviews, and implements the recommendations of an independent comprehensive review of all Bank-funded large dam projects to establish the actual costs, including direct and indirect economic, environmental and social costs, and the actually realized benefits of each project. The review should evaluate the degree to which project appraisals erred in estimating costs and benefits, identify specific violations of Bank policies and staff responsible, and address opportunity costs of not supporting project alternatives. The review must be conducted by individuals completely independent of the Bank without any stake in the outcome of the review;

4. The World Bank cancels the debt owed for large dam projects in which the economic, environmental and social costs are found to outweigh the realized benefits;

5. The World Bank develops new project appraisal techniques to assure that estimates of the costs and benefits, and risks and impacts, of large dams under consideration are rigorously based on the actual experience with past Bank-funded large dams;

6. The World Bank requires that any large dam under consideration be a necessary part of a locally-approved comprehensive river basin manage-

ment plan, and that the project be a last resort after all less damaging and costly alternatives for flood management, transportation, water supply, irrigation and power supply are exhausted;

7. The World Bank makes all information on large dam projects, including past and current projects and projects under consideration, freely available to the public;
8. The World Bank requires independent monitoring and evaluation of preparation of large dam projects, as well as systematic monitoring and auditing of project implementation, by persons outside the Bank and with no stake in the outcome of the project;
9. A formal decision is taken by the Bank to permanently halt all funding of large dams through the International Development Association (IDA), funding which is inconsistent with the IDA-10 donor's agreement.

Endorsed by 326 groups and coalitions in 44 countries

Appendix 3

Dams Involving Forced Resettlement

Dam/Project	River	State/province	Country
Piedra del Aguila	Limay	Neuquen/Rio Negro	Argentina
Yacyretá	Paraná		Argentina/Paraguay
Salto Grande	Uruguay		Argentina/Uruguay
Kaptai (Karnafuli)	Karnafuli	Chittagong Hill Tracts	Bangladesh
Avila	Avila	Rondônia	Brazil
Balbina	Uatumã	Amazonas	Brazil
Cana Brava	Cana Brava	Minas Gerais	Brazil
Furnas	Grande	Minas Gerais	Brazil
Itaparica	São Francisco	Bahia/Pernambuco	Brazil
Itumbiara	Paranaiba	Goiás/Minas Gerais	Brazil
Moxotó	São Francisco	Alagôas/Bahia/ Pernambuco	Brazil
Nova Ponte	Araguari	Minas Gerais	Brazil
Pedra do Cavalo	Paruaguaçu	Bahia	Brazil
Salto Santiago	Iguaçu	Paraná	Brazil
Samuel	Jamari	Rondonia	Brazil
São Simão	Paranáiba	Minas Gerais/Goiás	Brazil
Segredo	Iguaçu	Paraná	Brazil
Sobradinho	São Francisco	Bahia/Pernambuco	Brazil
Taquaruçu	Paranapanema	Paraná	Brazil
Três Irmãos	Tietê	São Paulo/ Mato Grosso do Sul	Brazil
Tucuruí (Raul G. Lhano)	Tocantins	Pará	Brazil
Xingó	São Francisco	Alagôas/Sergipe	Brazil
Itaipú	Paraná	Paraná	Brazil/Paraguay
La Grande Project (4 dams)	La Grande	Quebec	Canada
M'bali (Boali 3)	M'bali		Cent. African Rep.
Danjiangkou	Hanjiang	Hubei	China
Dongjiang	Laishui	Hunan	China
Dongpinghu			China
Geheyan	Qingjiang	Hubei	China
Gezhouba	Yangtze	Hubei	China
Lubuge I	Huangni	Yunnan	China
Sanmenxia	Huang He	Henan	China
Shuikou	Minjiang	Fujian	China
Wuqiangxi	Yuanshui	Hunan	China
Xijin	Yu Jiang	Guangxi	China
Xinanjiang	Xinanjiang	Zhejiang	China
Yantan	Hongshui	Guangxi	China
Zhaxi (Zhexi)	Zi Shui	Hunan	China
Chivor (La Esmeralda)	Batá	Boyaca	Colombia
Guavio	Guavio	Cundinamarca	Colombia
Playas	Guatape	Boyaca	Colombia
Rio Grande	Rio Grande	Boyaca	Colombia
Salvajina	Cauca	Cauca	Colombia

o. displaced	Res. area (ha)	Dam height (m)	Installed cap. (MW)	Completion year	Primary purpose	Ref.
9,000	29,200	163	1,400	1991	P	1
50,400	172,000	43	3,100	1998	P	58
8,000	78,300	65	1,890	1979	P	1
100,000	65,600	46	230	1962	P	2
100		38	28	1990	P	3
1,100	314,700	33	250	1989	P	4
500		25	480	1983	P	3
8,500	144,000	127	1,216	1963	P	1
40,100	83,400	105	2,500	1988	P	5
3,700	76,000	106	2,080	1980	P	1
1,000	8,800	34	2,440	1977	P	6
5,000	44,300	142	510	1994	P	7
4,400		142	600	1985	P	3
1,500	22,500	39	2,000	1980	P	1
1,800	57,900	60	216	1989	P	3
14,000	68,000	127	2,680	1978	P	1
2,700	8,200	140	1,260	1993	P	1
72,000	412,400	41	1,050	1978	P	5
200		58	500	1985	P	3
1,600	82,000	62	1,292	1990	P	3
23,900	225,000	93	4200	1984	P	8
150	6,000	140	3,000	1996	P	3
42,400	135,000	196	12,600	1982	P	9
1,900	1,590,000		15,719	1996	P	1
700		30		1991	M	10
383,000		97	900	1974	M	11
53,000	16,000	157	500	1989	P	1
278,000				1958		11
26,700	7,200	151	1,200	1995	P	12
26,000		47	2,715	1988	P	13
5,000	400	97	450	1992	P	1
410,000		106	250	1960		12
67,200	9,300	101	1,400	1996	P	1
84,800	17,000	87	1,200	1995	P	1
89,300		41	234	1964		12
306,000		105	663	1960		11
40,000		111		1994		11
141,000		104		1961		11
1,400		237	1,000	1982	P	14
5,500	1,440	243	1,600	1990	P	1
1,400	1,000	65	200	1985	P	1
1,200	1,000		324	1993	M	1
10,000	2,200	160		1985	P	15

Dam/Project	River	State/province	Country
San Carlos			Colombia
Santa Rita (Guatape II)	Nare	Antioquia	Colombia
Arenal	San Carlos		Costa Rica
Kossou	Bandama		Côte d'Ivoire
High Aswan	Nile	Aswan	Egypt/Sudan
Cerron Grande (Silencio)	Lempa		El Salvador
Awash Project (3 dams)	Awash		Ethiopia
Akosombo	Volta		Ghana
Kpong	Volta		Ghana
Weija	Densu		Ghana
Chixoy (Pueblo Viejo)	Chixoy		Guatemala
El Cajón	Humuya		Honduras
Aji III	Aji	Gujarat	India
Amli (Ver II)	Ver	Gujarat	India
Bargi	Narmada	Madhya Pradesh	India
Bhakra	Sutlej	Punjab	India
Bhima (Ujjani)	Bhima	Maharashtra	India
Chandil (Subarnarekha Multipurpose Project)	Subarnarekha	Bihar	India
Chandoli (Warna)	Warna	Maharastra	India
Damodar Valley Project (4 dams)	Damodar	Bihar/West Bengal	India
Dhom (Dhon)	Krishna	Maharashtra	India
Gandhi Sagar	Chambal	Madhya Pradesh	India
Hirakud	Mahanadi	Orissa/Madhya Pradesh	India
Jhuj	Kaveri	Gujarat	India
Kabini	Kabini	Karnataka	India
Kadana	Mahi	Gujarat	India
Lower Manair (Pochampad Project)	Manair	Andhra Pradesh	India
Machhanala	Machhan	Gujarat	India
Nagarjunasagar	Krishna	Andhra Pradesh	India
Narayanpur (Upper Krishna Project)	Krishna	Karnataka	India
Pong	Beas	H. Pradesh/Rajasthan/ Punjab/Harayana	India
Rajghat	Betwa	Madhya Pradesh/ Uttar Pradesh	India
Ravishankar	Ravishankar		India
Rengali	Brahmani	Orissa	India
Rihand (Singrauli)	Rihand	Uttar Pradesh	India
Saravathi (Sharavathy)	Talakalale	Karnataka	India
Selaulim	Selaulim	Goa	India
Sipu	Sipu	Gujarat	India
Sri Rama Sagar (Pochampad Project)	Godavari	Andhra Pradesh	India

No. displaced	Res. area (ha)	Dam height (m)	Installed cap. (MW)	Completion year	Primary purpose	Ref.
350		75	1,550	1987	P	14
3,000		60		1978		16
2,500	8,300	70	157	1980	M	1
85,000	178,000	58	174	1972	P	1
113,000	400,000	111	2,100	1970	M	17
10,000		80		1973	P	18
20,000				1960s	M	19
84,000	848,200	134	833	1965	P	10
7,000	3,500	20	160	1982	P	1
2,000		16		1978		18
3,400	1,400	108	300	1985	P	14
4,700	9,400	234	292	1985	P	1
3,500		25		1980s	I	18
2,300		29		1984	I	18
113,600	80,900	69	105	1990	M	20
36,000	16,600	226	1,204	1963	M	15
57,000	3,400	56		1980	I	21
38,000	16,600	56		1990s	M	62
4,900		91		1990s	I	18
93,000				1959	M	15
39,000	2,500	51		1978	I	22
52,000	68,000	64	115	1960	M	23
110,000	74,300	59	270	1957	M	24
1,100	272	97		1980s	I	18
15,000	6,100	58	32	1974	M	25
45,200		65		1978		18
78,000	8,100	42		1980s	I	26
2,100		32		1982	I	18
28,000	28,500	125	810	1974	M	1
80,000	13,200	30		1990s	I	10
150,000	29,000	133	360	1974	M	27
19,000	22,400	44		1980s	I	28
8,400		39		1980s		18
80,000	41,400	69	60	1980s	M	29
60,000	46,900	93	300	1962	M	30
12,500	5,900	62	510	1964	M	30
3,200		42		1990s		31
10,400	2,900	40		1968	I	18
16,000	43,400	43	36	1983	M	18

Dam/Project	River	State/province	Country
Srisailam	Krishna	Andhra Pradesh	India
Sukhbhadar	Sukhbhadar		India
Sukhi	Sukhi	Gujarat	India
Uben	Uben	Gujarat	India
Ukai	Tapi	Gujarat	India
Und	Und	Gujarat	India
Venu II	Venu	Gujarat	India
Watrak	Watrak	Gujarat	India
Zankhari	Zankhari		India
Cirata	Citarum	Western Java	Indonesia
Kedung Ombo	Serang	Java	Indonesia
Saguling	Citarum	Western Java	Indonesia
Dez	Dez		Iran
Kiambere	Tana		Kenya
Thika			Kenya
Nam Ngum	Nam Ngum		Laos
Katse (Lesotho Highlands Water Project 1A)	Malibamatso		Lesotho
Batang Ai	Batang Ai	Sarawak	Malaysia
Temengor	Perak	Perak	Malaysia
Manantali	Bafing		Mali
Selingué	Sankarani		Mali
Foum-Gleita	Gorgol		Mauritania
Aguamilpa	Santiago	Nayarit	Mexico
Apatzingán (Chilatan)	Apatzingán	Michoacán	Mexico
Bajo Candelaria	Candelaria	Campeche	Mexico
Caracol (Carlos Ramirez Ulloa)	Balsas	Guerrero	Mexico
Cerro de Oro	Santo Domingo	Oaxaca	Mexico
Colorado (El Tapiro)	Cerro Colorado		Mexico
Culiacán	Culiacán	Sinaloa	Mexico
Gustavo Diaz Ordaz Pdte. (Bacurato)	Sinaloa	Sinaloa	Mexico
La Angostura	Grijalva	Chiapas	Mexico
Netzahualcoyotl	Grijalva	Chiapas	Mexico
Presidente M. Aleman (Temascal/Papaloapan)	Tonto	Oaxaca	Mexico
Pujal-Coy I			Mexico
Pujal-Coy II			Mexico
Zimapán	Tula/Moctezuma		Mexico
Al Massira (Sidi Cheho)	Oum Er R'bia	Settat	Morocco
Cabora Bassa	Zambesi		Mozambique
Kulekhani	Kulekhani		Nepal
Marsayangdi	Marsayangdi		Nepal
Clyde	Clutha	Otago	New Zealand
Bakolori	Sokoto	Sokoto	Nigeria

o. displaced	Res. area (ha)	Dam height (m)	Installed cap. (MW)	Completion year	Primary purpose	Ref.
100,000	60,600	143	440	1984	M	1
2,400		20		1980s	I	18
11,200	2,900	38		1980s	I	18
1,400		19		1982	I	18
80,000	60,000	81	300	1972	M	1
6,500		25		1990s	I	18
3,300		13		1990s	I	18
16,000		43		1990s	I	18
2,900		30		1980s	I	18
56,000	6,200	125	500	1987	P	1
29,000	4,600	61	29	1993	M	1
60,000	5,300	98	700	1984	P	1
17,000	6,300	203	840	1978	M	32
7,000	2,500	112	142	1988	P	10
500	500		2	1990s	M	1
3,000	37,000	40	150	1972	P	1
21,700*	3,600	185		1996	W	33
3,000	8,500	85	92	1985	P	1
1,500	15,000	115	348	1977	P	34
11,000	48,000	70	200†	1988	M	10
12,500	40,900	35	44	1980	M	35
3,000				1980s	I	10
1,000	13,000	187	960	1995	P	1
400	2,400	103	28	1995	M	14
5,800				1982		36
7,000		126		1986	P	36
18,000	17,000	56		1989	M	36
13,300	300	38		1982	I	36
25,200				1967		36
2,900	5,600	114		1982	I	14
5,500	64,400	146	1,100	1974	P	36
1,500	29,200	138	1,080	1964	P	37
21,000		76	154	1955	M	36
23,400				1982		36
10,800				1982		36
2,500	2,300	207	292	1994	P	1
5,500	13,700	83		1979	M	18
25,000	380,000	171	2,250	1974	P	1
2,500	220	114	92	1982	P	1
3,000	60	24	69	1989	P	1
280	20,000	75	430	1979	P	1
13,000	12,000	48		1978	I	38

Dam/Project	River	State/province	Country
Dadin Kowa	Gongola	Bauchi	Nigeria
Kainji	Niger	Kwara/Niger	Nigeria
Kiri	Gongola	Gongola	Nigeria
Mangla	Jhelum	Punjab	Pakistan
Tarbela	Indus	NWFP	Pakistan
Bayano	Bayano		Panama
Fortuna			Panama
Magat	Magat	Luzon	Philippines
Pantabangan	Papanga	Nueva Ecjia	Philippines
Portile de Fier I (Iron Gates)	Danube		Romania/Yugoslavia
Diama	Senegal		Senegal/Mauritania
Chung Ju	Namhan		South Korea
Riaño	Esla	León	Spain
Kotmale	Kotmale Oya		Sri Lanka
Victoria	Mahaweli		Sri Lanka
Roseires	Blue Nile		Sudan
Brokopondo	Suriname		Surinam
Lupohlo	Lusutshwana		Swaziland
Tabqua (Thawra/Assad)	Euphrates		Syria
Mtera	Great Ruaha		Tanzania
Bang Lang (Pattani)	Pattani		Thailand
Bhumibol	Ping		Thailand
Chiew Larn	Khlong Saeng		Thailand
Khao Laem	Kwae		Thailand
Lam Pao	Lam Pao		Thailand
Lang Suan			Thailand
Nam Pong	Nam Pong		Thailand
Pak Mun	Mun	Ratchathani	Thailand
Srinakharin (Srinagarind/Ban Chao Nen)	Kwae Yai	Kanchanaburi	Thailand
Ubolratana	Nam Pong		Thailand
Nangbeto	Mono		Togo/Benin
Sidi Salem	Medjerda		Tunisia
Atatürk	Euphrates		Turkey
Karakaya	Euphrates		Turkey
Keban	Euphrates		Turkey
Sir	Ceyhan		Turkey
Big Bend	Missouri	S. Dakota	USA
Conemaugh	Conemaugh	Pennsylvania	USA
Fort Randall	Missouri	S. Dakota	USA
Garrison	Missouri	N. Dakota	USA
Kinzua	Allegheny	Pennsylvania	USA
Navajo	San Juan	New Mexico	USA
Norris	Clinch/Powell	Tennessee	USA

No. displaced	Res. area (ha)	Dam height (m)	Installed cap. (MW)	Completion year	Primary purpose	Ref.
26,000	53,000			1980s	I	10
44,000	125,000	66	760	1968	P	39
19,000	13,000	20		1982	I	10
110,000	25,300	138	1,000	1967	M	40
96,000	24,280	143	3,478	1976	M	41
4,500	30,000	72	300	1976	P	42
600	1,000	108	255	1982	P	14
1,500	4,500	105	360	1983	M	1
13,000	8,900	107	100	1977	M	14
23,000	5,200	60	2,100	1972	P	1
3,400		18		1986	I	43
46,500	9,700	90	460	1985	M	14
3,100	2,000	98		1987	I	44
13,000	950	87	200	1988	M	1
45,000	2,300	122	210	1984	P	1
10,000		60	130	1965	M	14
5,000	150,000	66	30	1965	P	15
300	120	45	20	1984	P	1
60,000	60,000	60	800	1976	M	10
3,000	65,000	45	280	1988	P	1
3,300	5,100	85	72	1981	M	18
20,000	30,000	154	535	1964	M	45
1,600	16,500	95	240	1987	P	46
10,800	38,800	90	300	1986	M	1
30,000	40,000	33		1970	M	47
9,800		91	135	1980s	P	48
30,000	2,000	40		1965	M	23
4,900	6,000	17	136	1994	P	1
9,400	41,900	140	720	1981	M	1
30,000	41,000	32	25	1965	M	49
12,000	18,000	44	63	1987	P	10
3,500	55,000	70	36	1984	M	14
60,000	81,700	184	2,400	1992	M	50
20,000	29,800	173	1,800	1987	P	1
30,000	67,500	207	1,330	1974	M	1
7,000	4,800	120	284	1991	P	1
445	5,900	29		1950s	M	51
2,500	12,140	52		1952	M	52
680	38,500	50		1952	M	51
1,800	149,000	64		1953	M	53
700	4,900	70		1996	F	77
1,250	3,000	123		1963	M	54
17,500	55,400	81		1937	M	55

Dam/Project	River	State/province	Country
Oahe	Missouri	S. Dakota	USA
Tuttle Creek	Big Blue	Kansas	USA
Youghiogheny	Youghiogheny	Pennsylvania	USA
Guri	Caroní	Bolivar	Venezuela
Dau Tieng	Saigon		Vietnam
Hoa Binh	Song Da		Vietnam
Thac Mo	Song Be		Vietnam
Ruzizi II	Ruzizi		Zaire/Rwanda/Buru
Kariba	Zambesi		Zambia/Zimbabwe
Under construction			
Itá	Uruguay	Rio Grande do Sul/ Santa Catarina	Brazil
Serra da Mesa	Tocantins	Goiás	Brazil
Daguangba			China
Ertan	Yalong	Sichuan	China
Three Gorges	Yangtze	Hubei	China
Tianshengqiao 1	Nanpanjiang	Guangxi	China
Xiaolangdi	Yellow	Henan	China
Urrá I	Sinú		Colombia
Mohale (Lesotho Highlands Water Project 1B)	Senqu (Orange)		Lesotho
Muela (Lesotho Highlands Water Project 1A)	Ngoe		Lesotho
Bakun	Balui	Sarawak	Malaysia
Ghazi Barotha	Indus		Pakistan
Casecnan	Cagayan	Quirino	Philippines
Lam Takhong			Thailand
Pasak	Pasak	Lop Buri	Thailand
Berke	Ceyhan		Turkey
Caruachi	Caroní	Bolivar	Venezuela
Yali Falls	Se San		Vietnam
Stalled/suspended			
Almatti (Upper Krishna Project)	Krishna	Karnataka	India
Icha (Subarnarekha Multipurpose Project)	Kharkai	Bihar/Orissa	India
Narmada Sagar	Narmada	Madhya Pradesh	India
Sardar Sarovar	Narmada	Gujarat	India
Tehri	Bhagirathi	Uttar Pradesh	India
Tillari	Tillari	Maharashtra/Goa	India
Upper Indravati	Indravati	Orissa	India
Rogun	Vakhsh		Tadjikistan

o. displaced	Res. area (ha)	Dam height (m)	Installed cap. (MW)	Completion year	Primary purpose	Ref.
900	145,300	75		1958	M	51
4,000	6,400	41		1962	M	52
300	1,150	57		1948	M	52
1,500	426,000	162	10,300	1986	P	1
500		27		1980s		18
58,000	20,000	128	1,920	1993	P	1
1,600		42	150	1995	P	56
15,000			40	1980s	P	10
57,000	510,000	128	1,266	1959	P	57
19,200	10,300	125	1,620	1999	P	29
6,800		144	1,200	1998	P	3
23,800	9,900	56	240		P	1
35,000	10,100	245	3,300	1999	P	1
1,300,000	110,000	175	18,200	2015	M	60
48,800		178	1,200	1999		12
181,600	27,200	154	1,800	2001	M	1
2,000	7,000	74	340		P	61
8,400*		145		2004	W	33
2,700*		55	72	2003	P	33
9,400	70,000	204	2,400	2002	P	64
900	2,640		1,450	2000	P	1
20,000	3,600	197	156		M	65
225	4,500		250		M	1
23,000					I	66
140	780	200	510		P	1
1,000	23,800	55	2,076		P	65
7,400		65	720		P	56
160,000		48			I	10
30,000	12,700				M	62
300,000	90,800	84			M	74
320,000#	37,600	163	1,450		M	63
105,000	4,200	261	2,000		M	10
50,000		71		UC		31
16,100	12,865	65	1,000		M	59
28,200		335	3,600		M	75

Dam/Project	River	State/province	Country
Machadinho	Uruguay	Rio Grande do Sul/ Santa Catarina	Brazil
Porta Primavera	Paraná	Minas Gerais/São Paulo	Brazil
Nam Choan	Khwae	Kanchanaburi/Tak	Thailand
Planned			
Itatí-Itacorá	Paraná		Argentina
Cachoeira Porteira	Trombetas	Pará	Brazil
Castanhão	Jaguaribe	Ceará	Brazil
Ji-Paraná	Ji-Paraná	Rondônia	Brazil
Garabi	Uruguay		Brazil/Argentina
Sambor	Mekong		Cambodia
Stung Treng	Mekong		Cambodia
Ralco	Biobio		Chile
Jiangya	Yangtze		China
Jingping 1-Y			China
Longtan	Hongshui	Guangxi	China
Garafiri			Guinea
Luang Prabang	Mekong		Laos
Nam Mang 3	Nam Mang		Laos
Nam Ngiep 1	Nam Ngiep		Laos
Nam Ngum 2	Nam Ngum		Laos
Nam Ngum 3	Nam Ngum		Laos
Nam Tha 1	Nam Tha		Laos
Nam Theun 2	Nam Theun		Laos
Pak Beng	Mekong		Laos
Pak Lay	Mekong		Laos
Sayaburi	Mekong		Laos
Ban Koum	Mekong		Laos/Thailand
Chiang Khan	Mekong		Laos/Thailand
Low Pa Mong	Mekong		Laos/Thailand
Pa Mong 'A'	Mekong		Laos/Thailand
San Juan Tetelecingo	Balsas	Guerrero	Mexico
Karnali (Chisapani)	Karnali		Nepal
Pancheswar	Mahakali		Nepal
Kalabagh (Indus)	Indus		Pakistan
Kayraktepe	Goksu		Turkey
An Khe	Ba		Vietnam
Ban Mai	Ca		Vietnam
Buon Kuop	Sre Pok		Vietnam
Dai Ninh	Dong Nai		Vietnam
Dai Thi	Lo Gam		Vietnam
Ta Bu	Song Da		Vietnam

No. displaced	Res. area (ha)	Dam height (m)	Installed cap. (MW)	Completion year	Primary purpose	Ref.
15,700	25,200		1,200		P	9
7,000		38	1,800		P	3
2,000	14,700	187	580		M	76
3,000			1,000		P	37
8,000	91,100		1,400		P	5
12,000	22,900		75		M	5
2,700			612	2002	P	3
15,000	81,000	85	1,800		P	67
5,100	88,000	63	3,300		P	1
9,200	64,000	31	980		P	1
700	3,400	155	570		P	68
12,000						69
5,800	9,500		3,200		P	1
73,000	37,000	192	4,200	2005	P	1
1,500	8,800		75		P	1
6,600	11,000	67	1,410		P	1
675	1,400		30		P	1
1,400	16,000		440		P	1
4,000	11,000		320		P	1
4,400	5,870		400		P	1
5,700	26,500		230		P	1
4,500	45,000	50	681		P	1
1,700	11,000	66	1,230		P	1
11,800	11,000	67	1,320		P	1
1,700	3,000	62	1,260		P	1
2,600	13,000	45	2,330		P	1
13,000	9,000	50	570		P	1
52,000	56,000		2,670		P	1
23,300	12,000	69	2,030		P	1
28,000	14,000		620		P	70
60,000	34,100	270	3,000		P	71
60,000	12,100	315	7,200		P	1
124,000	55,000	93	2,400		M	72
10,000	13,300	199	420		P	73
10,800			116		P	56
15,000			450		P	56
3,600			81		P	56
14,100			300		P	56
20,600					P	56
112,400		181	3,600		P	56

Notes

Table includes dams involving resettlement of >100 people (>1000 in China and India) for which data is available.

Key: M = Multipurpose; P = Power; I = Irrigation; F = Flood control

† Turbines still to be installed.
* Figure includes 'affected' people who lose land and livelihood but are not displaced.
# Figure includes oustees from canals.

Sources

1. R. Goodland, 'How to Distinguish Better Hydros from Worse', unpublished MS, December 1995.
2. A. Oliver-Smith, 'Involuntary Resettlement, Resistance and Political Empowerment', *Journal of Refugee Studies*, Vol. 4, No. 2, 1991.
3. L.A. de O. Santos and L.M.M. de Andrade (eds.), *Hydroelectric Dams on Brazil's Xingu River and Indigenous Peoples*, Cultural Survival, Cambridge, MA, 1990.
4. P.M. Fearnside, 'Brazil's Balbina Dam: Environment versus the Legacy of the Pharaohs in Amazonia', *Environmental Management*, Vol. 13, No. 4, 1989.
5. CUT/CRAB, 'Terra Sim, Barragens Não', 1989.
6. A. Vianna and L. Menezes, *O Pólo Sindical e a Luta dos Atingidos pela Barragem de Itaparica*, CEDI/KOINONIA, Rio de Janeiro 1994.
7. C. Baumgratz Viotti, 'Review of the relocation of Nova Ponte town in Brazil', *Hydropower & Dams*, November 1995.
8. CPI/SP, 'Tucurui Hydroelectric Plant: The Disaster Continues', mimeo, 1991.
9. C. Bermann, 'Self-Managed Resettlement – A Case Study: The Itá Dam in Southern Brazil', paper presented at conference 'Hydropower Into the Next Century', Barcelona, June 1995.
10. M.M. Cernea, 'African Population Resettlement in a Global Context', in C.C. Cook (ed.), *Involuntary Resettlement in Africa: Selected Papers from a Conference on Environment and Settlement Issues in Africa*, World Bank Technical Paper 227, 1994.
11. World Bank, 'China: Involuntary Resettlement', 8 June 1993.
12. X. Cheung, 'Unleashing Hydroelectric Potential in a Challenging Environment', *Hydro Review Worldwide*, Winter 1993.
13. Y. Liu, 'The Gezhouba Project in Operation', *IWPDC*, August 1994.
14. World Bank Operations Evaluation Department Large Dams Review 1995 (draft).
15. P.H. Gleick (ed.), *Water in Crisis: A Guide to the World's Fresh Water Resources*, Oxford University Press, Oxford 1993, Table G.11.
16. World Bank Press Release.
17. G. White, 'The Environmental Effects of the High Dam at Aswan', *Environment*, Vol. 30, No. 7, 1988.
18. World Bank, 'Inventory of Dams Related to World Bank Projects', 1985.
19. A. Weiderstein and H. Haberl, *Die Beteiligung Österreichischer Firmen am Kraftwerksbau in Afrika, Asien und Lateinamerika*, Ökologie Institut, Vienna 1990.
20. Justice S.M. Daud, *The Indian People's Tribunal on Environment and Human Rights, First Report*, Bombay 1993.
21. R. Chambers, *Managing Canal Irrigation: Practical Analysis from South Asia*, Cambridge University Press, Cambridge 1988.
22. World Bank, 'Early Experience with Involuntary Resettlement: Impact Evaluation on India – Maharashtra Irrigation II Project', OED, 29 June 1993.
23. T. Scudder, 'Summary: Resettlement', in Ackerman et al. (eds.), *Man-Made Lakes: Their Problems and Environmental Effects*, American Geophysical Union, Washington, DC, 1973.
24. P. Viegas, 'The Hirakud Dam Oustees: Thirty Years After', in E.G. Thukral (ed.), *Big Dams, Displaced People: Rivers of Sorrow, Rivers of Change*, Sage Publications, New Delhi 1992.
25. *India Today*, 10 September 1993.
26. C. Maloney, 'Environmental and Project Displacement of Population in India', *UFSI Field Staff Reports*, No. 14, 1990.

27. R. Bhanot and M. Singh, 'The Oustees of Pong Dam: Their Search for a Home', in Thukral (ed.), *Big Dams, Displaced People.*
28. E. Goldsmith and N. Hildyard (eds.), *The Social and Environmental Impacts of Large Dams. Vol. 1*, Wadebridge Ecological Centre, Cornwall 1984.
29. M.M. Cernea and S.E. Guggenheim (eds.), *Anthropological Approaches To Resettlement: Policy, Practice and Theory*, Westview Press, Boulder, CO, 1993.
30. Motor-Colombus/Appio & Associates, 'Lokoja Hydroelectric Project Feasibility Study Appendix C2: International Resettlement Experience', NEPA, Lagos 1979.
31. R. Billorey, 'Selaulim Dam', in C. Alvares (ed.), *Fish Curry and Rice: A Citizens' Report on the State of the Goan Environment*, ECOFORUM, Mapusa, Goa 1993.
32. F.M. Lappé and J. Collins, *Food First*, Abacus, London 1982.
33. Lesotho Highlands Development Authority, 'Key Environmental Information for the LHWP', Environment Division, LHDA, Maseru 1995.
34. 'Report of the 17th ICOLD Congress', *IWPDC*, September 1991.
35. ICOLD, *Dams and Environment: Case Studies*, ICOLD, Paris 1988.
36. S.E. Guggenheim, 'Peasants, Planners, and Participation: Resettlement in Mexico', in M.M. Cernea and S.E. Guggenheim (eds.), *Anthropological Approaches To Resettlement: Policy, Practice and Theory*, Westview Press, Boulder, CO, 1993.
37. F. Szekely, 'Impacto ambiental de las grandes presas en el trópico', *Ciencia y Desarrollo*, No. 11, November/December 1976.
38. B. Beckman, 'Bakolori: Peasants versus State and Industry in Nigeria', in E. Goldsmith and N. Hildyard (eds.), *The Social and Environmental Impacts of Large Dams. Vol. 2: Case Studies*, Wadebridge Ecological Centre, Cornwall 1986 (hereafter *SEELD 2*).
39. J.S.O. Ayeni et al., 'The Kainji Lake Experience in Africa', in Cook (ed.) *Involuntary Resettlement in Africa.*
40. Development Education Centre (South Yorkshire), 'A Study of Change and Development in Mirpur, "Azad" Jammu Kashmir and Pakistan', 1995.
41. Peter Ames, Harza Engineering, personal communication.
42. A. Wali, 'The Transformation of a Frontier: State and Regional Relationships in Panama, 1972–1990', *Human Organization*, Vol. 52, No. 2, Summer 1993.
43. F. Mounier, 'The Senegal River Scheme: Development for Whom?', in *SEELD 2.*
44. *International Dams Newsletter*, May/June 1987.
45. *The Nation*, Bangkok, 10 June 1990.
46. World Bank Press Release 81/101, 22 May 1981.
47. E. El-Hinnawi, *Environmental Refugees*, UNEP, Nairobi 1985.
48. World Bank Press Release 81/101, 22 May 1981.
49. A.K. Biswas, 'Environmental Implications of Water Development for Developing Countries', in C. Widstrand (ed.), *The Social and Ecological Effects of Water Development in Developing Countries*, Pergamon Press, Oxford 1978.
50. A. Braun, 'The Megaproject of Mesapotamia', *Ceres*, March/April 1994.
51. M.L. Lawson, *Damned Indians*, University of Oklahoma Press, Norman 1982.
52. T. Palmer, *Endangered Rivers and the Conservation Movement.* University of California Press, Berkeley, CA, 1986.
53. S.F. Bates et al., *Searching out the Headwaters*, Island Press, Washington, DC, 1993.
54. C. Wilkinson, 'Remembering Rosa', in *Arrested Rivers*, University Press of Colorado, Niwot 1994.
55. M.J. McDonald and J. Muldowney, *TVA and the Dispossessed*, University of Tennessee Press, Knoxville 1982.
56. C. Lang, 'Hydropower Projects in Vietnam', mimeo, 1995.
57. T. Scudder, 'Development-Induced Relocation and Refugee Studies: 37 Years of Change and Continuity Among Zambia's Gwembe Tonga', *Journal of Refugee Studies*, Vol. 6, No. 2, 1993.
58. World Bank, 'Project Completion Report: Argentina Yacyretá Hydroelectric Project and Electric Power Sector Project', 1995.
59. World Bank, 'Resettlement and Rehabilitation in India: A Status Update of Projects Involving Involuntary Resettlement', April 1994.
60. Dai Qing (edited by P. Adams and J. Thibodeau), *Yangtze! Yangtze!*, Probe International, Toronto and Earthscan, London, 1994.
61. Organización Nacional Indigena de Colombia, personal communication, 1995.

62. B. Rich, *Mortgaging the Earth: The World Bank, Environmental Impoverishment, and the Crisis of Development*, Beacon Press, Boston, MA, 1994.
63. Narmada Bachao Andolan, 'Supreme Court of India Writ Petition', NBA, Baroda, Gujarat, India 1994.
64. *Bakun Hydroelectric Project: Green Energy for the Future*, Economic Planning Unit, Prime Minister's Department, Kuala Lumpur, 1996.
65. FIVAS, *Power Conflicts: Norwegian Hydropower Developers in the Third World*, FIVAS, Oslo 1996.
66. N. Singkhran, 'Compensation Dispute Persists Over Pasak Dam', *Bangkok Post*, 11 September 1995.
67. CRAB, 'Usina Hidrelétrica Garabi: mais um crime contra o homem e a natureza', CRAB/CEDI 1989.
68. *Corrientes*, Santiago, August 1995.
69. World Bank, 'Monthly Operational Summary', April 1995.
70. Environmental Defense Fund, 'The San Juan Tetelcingo Hydroelectric Project', mimeo, 1991.
71. Himalayan Power Consultants, 'Karnali (Chisapani) Multipurpose Project: Feasibility Study', HMG Nepal, Ministry of Water Resources, 1989.
72. Gazdar, Muhammad Nasir, *An Assessment of the Kalabagh Dam Project on the River Indus, Pakistan*, Environmental Management Society, Karachi 1990.
73. Y. Biro, 'Economic Valuation of the Environmental Impacts of the Kayraktepe Dam/ Hydroelectric Power Plant in Turkey', M.Sc. thesis, ERG, University of California – Berkeley, 1995.
74. Himanshu Thakker (NBA), personal communication.
75. M. Burkhana, 'Ecological-Economic Problems of Constructing Large Mountain Reservoirs', mimeo, 1991.
76. P. Hirsch, *Political Economy of Environment in Thailand*, Journal of Contemporary Asia Publishers, Manila 1993.
77. P.C. Rosier, 'Dam Building and Treaty Breaking: The Kinzua Dam Controversy, 1936–1958', *The Pennsylvania Magazine of History and Biography*, Vol. CXIX, No. 4, October 1995.

Contact Addresses

International Rivers Network
1847 Berkeley Way
Berkeley
CA 94703
USA
Fax +1 510 848 1008
irn@irn.org
http://www.irn.org

The Ecologist
Agriculture House
Bath Road
Sturminster Newton
Dorset DT10 1DU
UK
Fax +44 (0)1258 473748
ecologist@gn.apc.org

International Commission on Large Dams (ICOLD)
151 boulevard Haussmann
75008 Paris
France
Tel. +33 1 40 42 67 33
Fax +33 1 40 42 60 71

World Bank
1818 H Street, NW
Washington, DC, 20433
USA
Tel. +1 202 477 1234
Fax +1 202 676 0483

International Finance Corporation
1850 I Street, NW
Washington, DC, 20433
USA
Tel. +1 202 477 1234
Fax +1 202 477 6391

Inter-American Development Bank
1300 New York Avenue, NW
Washington, DC, 20577
USA
Tel. +1 202 623 1000
Fax +1 202 623 3096

Asian Development Bank
PO Box 789
1099 Manila
Philippines
Tel. +63 2 711 3851
Fax +63 2 741 7961

African Development Bank
01 BP No. 1387
Abidjan 01
Côte d'Ivoire
Tel. +225 20 41 99
Fax +225 20 49 07

United Nations Development Programme
1 UN Plaza
New York NY 10017
USA
Tel. +1 212 906 5000
Fax +1 212 826 2057

Bilateral Funders

Canadian International Development Agency (CIDA)
200 Promenade du Portage
Hull
Quebec K1A 0G4
Canada

Caisse Française de Developpement
Cité du Retiro
35/37 rue Boissy d'Anglas
Paris Cedex 08
France

Deutsche Gezelschaft für Technische Zusammenarbeit (GTZ)
Postfach 5180
65726 Eschborn
Germany

Kreditanstalt für Wiederaufbau (KfW)
Charlottenstrasse 33/33a
10117 Berlin
Germany

Overseas Economic Coperation Fund (OECF)
1-4-1 Ohtemachi Chiyoda-ku
Tokyo 100
Japan

Norwegian Agency for Development Cooperation (NORAD)
PO Box 8034
Oslo
Norway

Swedish International Development Authority (SIDA)
Birger Jarlsgatan 61
10525 Stockholm
Sweden

Swiss Development Cooperation (SDC)
Eigerstrasse 73
Bern
Switzerland

Overseas Development Administration (ODA)
94 Victoria Street
London SW1E 5JL
UK

Export–Import Bank
811 Vermont Avenue, NW
Washington, DC, 20571
USA

Index